The Encyclopedia of
DNA & GENETICS

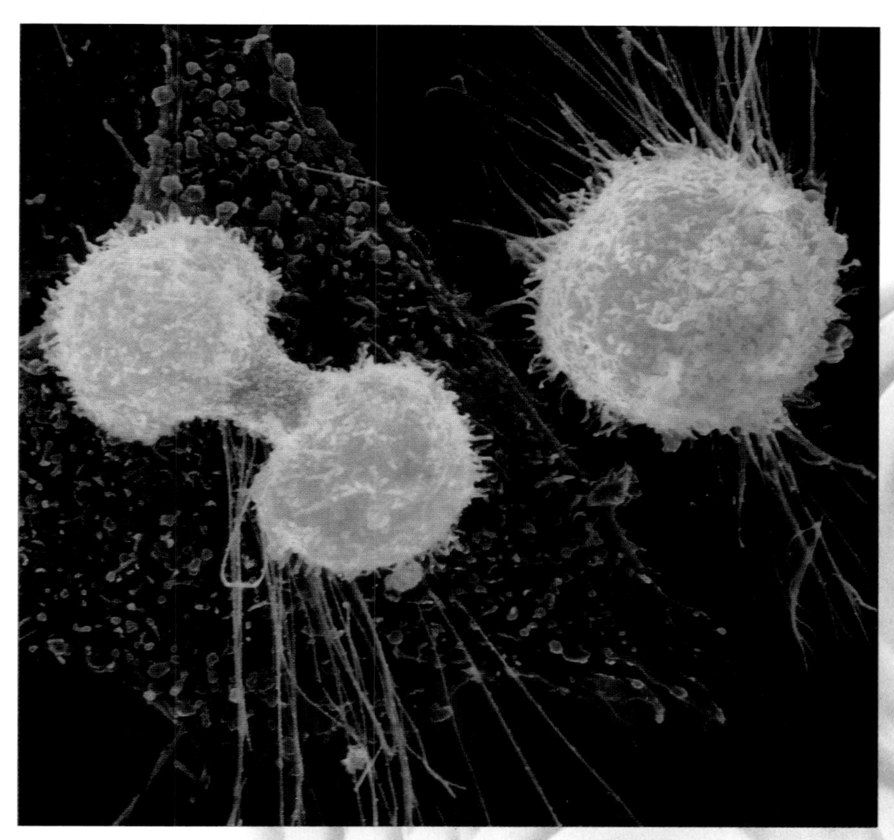

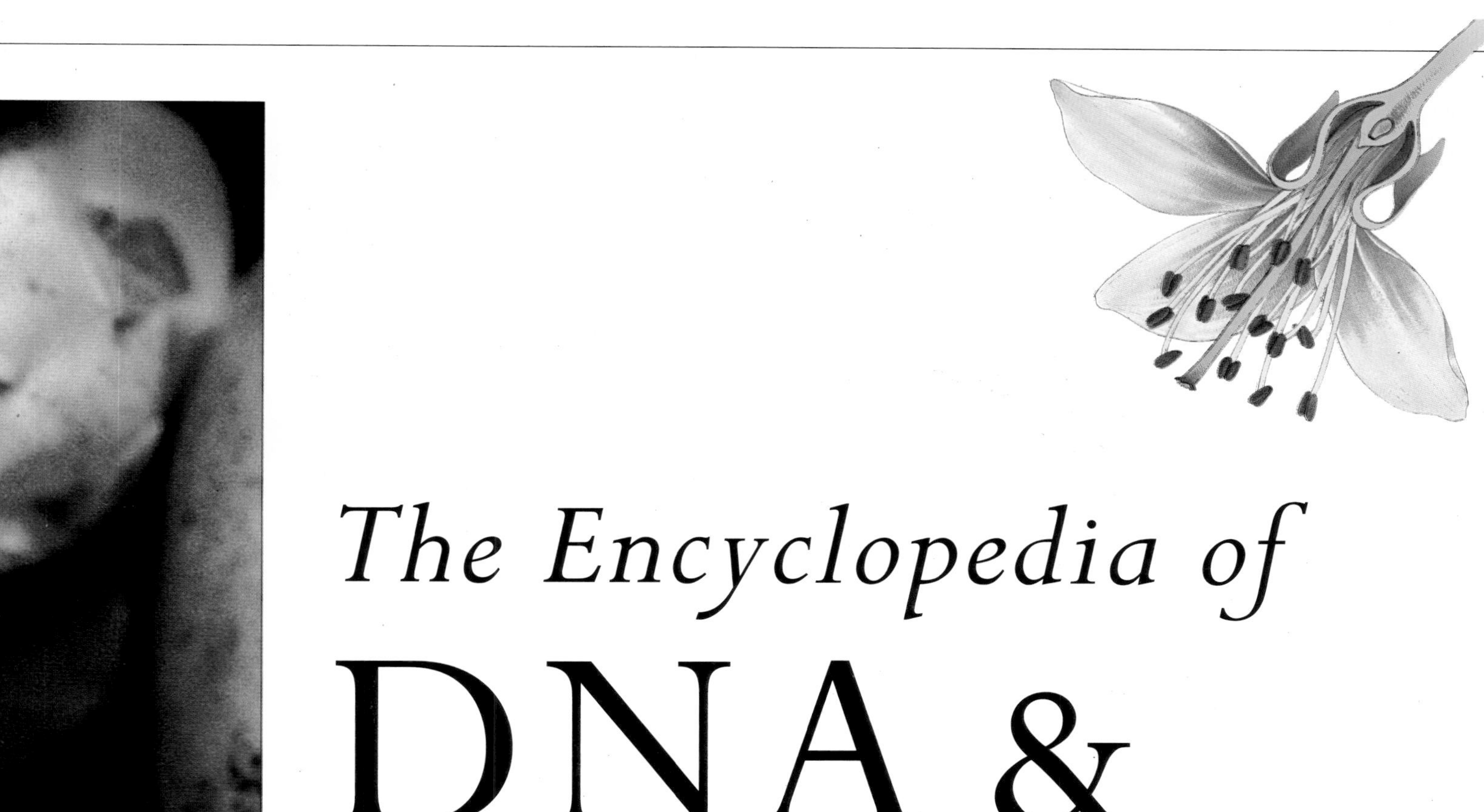

The Encyclopedia of DNA & GENETICS

JILL BAILEY

ANDROMEDA OXFORD

CONTENTS

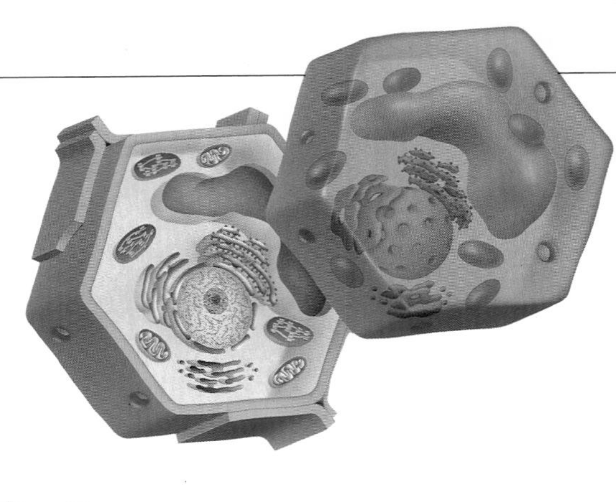

Project editor Peter Furtado
Editors Lauren Bourque, John Clark
Editorial assistant Marian Dreier

Art editor Ayala Kingsley
Visualization and artwork Ted McCausland/ Siena Artworks
Senior designer Martin Anderson
Designer Roger Hutchins

Picture manager Jo Rapley
Picture research Alison Floyd
Production Clive Sparling

Produced and published by
Andromeda Oxford Ltd
9-15 The Vineyard
Abingdon
Oxfordshire OX14 3PX

ISBN 1 871869 55 2

Printed in Spain by Graficromo SA, Cordoba

INTRODUCTION

IN THE 1960S, the popular notion of the "mad scientist" was typically a nuclear physicist, pursuing schemes of harnessing the power of the atom and totally indifferent to the concerns of other people. Today, the lay person's fear of science has been transferred to the researcher into genetics and biotechnology. In the minds of the public, the molecular biologist is interfering with the processes of life itself, and possibly creating a Frankenstein's monster that will destroy the human race, if not the whole planet.

Less often remembered are the ways in which genetic research has already delivered some great benefits, at least for those wealthy enough to enjoy them, and the even greater prospects for alleviating disease and hunger in the future.

It was less than 50 years ago that the fundamental discovery – that of the structure of DNA, the molecule of inheritance – was made, a discovery that made possible the modern fields of genetics and molecular biology. Since that time, scientists have rapidly found novel ways to apply this knowledge, and are continuously pushing back the frontiers of medicine, archeology, botany and agriculture, and other disciplines. They have learned to identify and isolate specific genes, and to trace through the ways in which they are expressed in living bodies. They have learned a great deal about viruses and infections; they have found new ways of identifying individuals, and their probable family relations, by analysis of their DNA; they have learned to identify genetic disorders in babies long before they are born; and they have developed important new strains of food crops, which may in future reduce reliance on chemical fertilizers and pesticides. They have also learned to transfer genes from one organism to another, making it possible to "build" an organism with chosen characteristics. A vast and powerful new industry has emerged, and companies have taken out patents on genes that they have isolated from humans or other organisms, just as if they were newly invented machines.

In such ways genetic researchers have impressed themselves on the public consciousness as undermining cherished assumptions about what life is. The ability to sequence the human genome not only helps scientists to explain the way we are today and to explore our evolutionary past; it also offers the opportunity to rewrite the blueprint and alter our future – for better or for worse. It is vital that people understand what DNA is and how it works; and what can be achieved by scientists working in this field. Only by such an understanding can we hope for informed discussion of the ethical issues that are raised by some of the current research.

This book begins by discussing the building blocks of life – cells and their components, especially DNA; then looks at the ways in which information is carried on the DNA molecule, and how it is translated into making the proteins and larger structures that make up a living body. Next, it examines the processes by which variations occur between individuals, from the ways in which genes are mixed during reproduction, to (on a larger scale) the way they are mixed through natural selection. This leads to a discussion of the variety of life, the millions of species that exist today, and the many more millions that are now extinct. From this point, the text explores modern genetic research: the techniques of isolating particular genes, splicing them into the DNA of other organisms, and cloning them to make thousands of identical copies. These techniques make possible biotechnology: making drugs or protein for food by "growing" them in bacteria or other living organisms, rather than by chemical processes. The study of human genetics is particularly important in medicine, forensics and history. Finally, the text looks at the ethical issues involved.

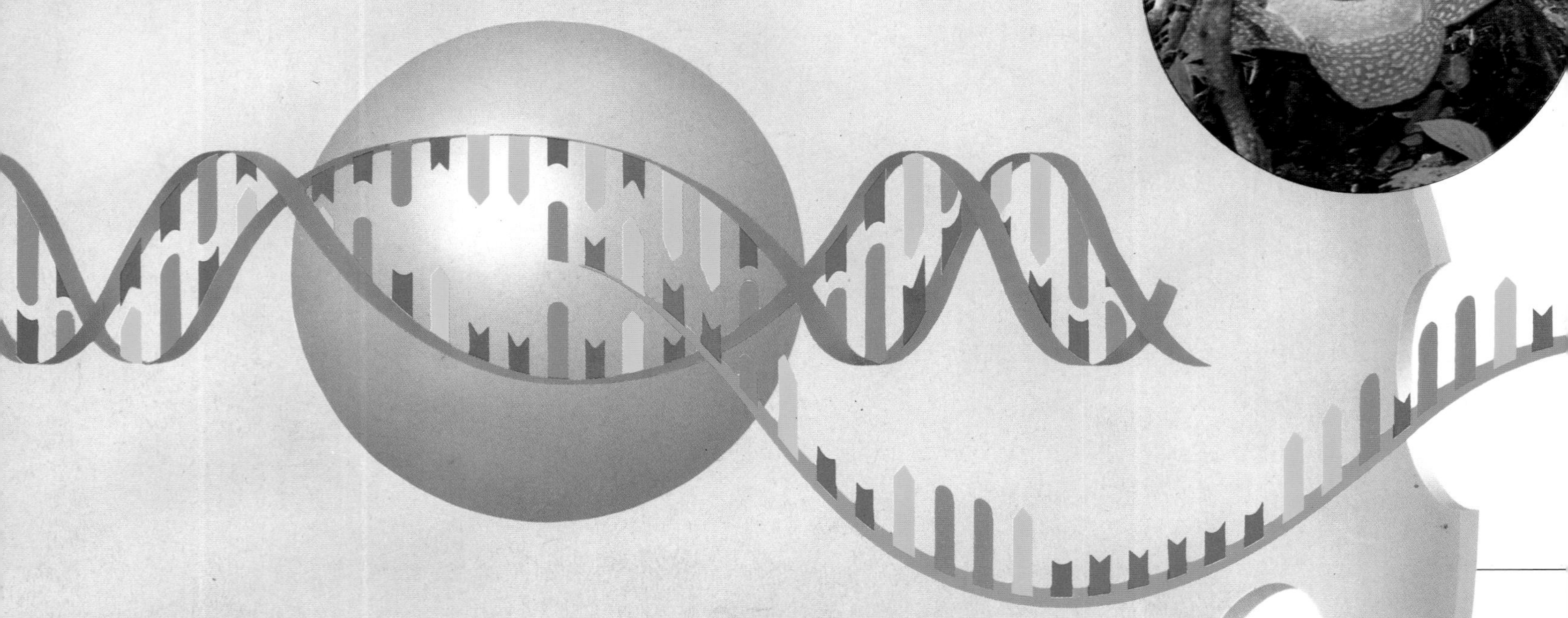

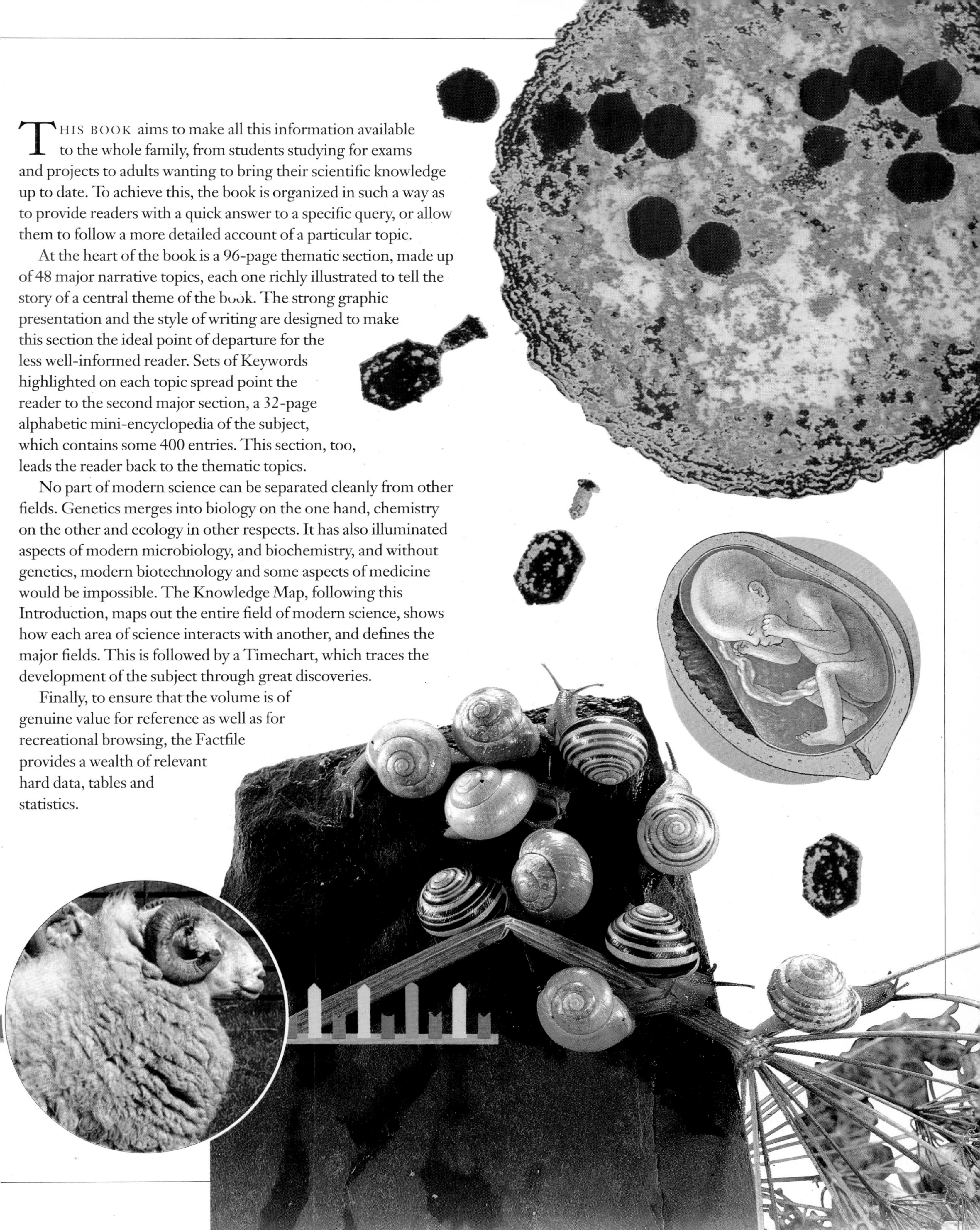

THIS BOOK aims to make all this information available to the whole family, from students studying for exams and projects to adults wanting to bring their scientific knowledge up to date. To achieve this, the book is organized in such a way as to provide readers with a quick answer to a specific query, or allow them to follow a more detailed account of a particular topic.

At the heart of the book is a 96-page thematic section, made up of 48 major narrative topics, each one richly illustrated to tell the story of a central theme of the book. The strong graphic presentation and the style of writing are designed to make this section the ideal point of departure for the less well-informed reader. Sets of Keywords highlighted on each topic spread point the reader to the second major section, a 32-page alphabetic mini-encyclopedia of the subject, which contains some 400 entries. This section, too, leads the reader back to the thematic topics.

No part of modern science can be separated cleanly from other fields. Genetics merges into biology on the one hand, chemistry on the other and ecology in other respects. It has also illuminated aspects of modern microbiology, and biochemistry, and without genetics, modern biotechnology and some aspects of medicine would be impossible. The Knowledge Map, following this Introduction, maps out the entire field of modern science, shows how each area of science interacts with another, and defines the major fields. This is followed by a Timechart, which traces the development of the subject through great discoveries.

Finally, to ensure that the volume is of genuine value for reference as well as for recreational browsing, the Factfile provides a wealth of relevant hard data, tables and statistics.

Knowledge Map

Key Fields of Modern Science

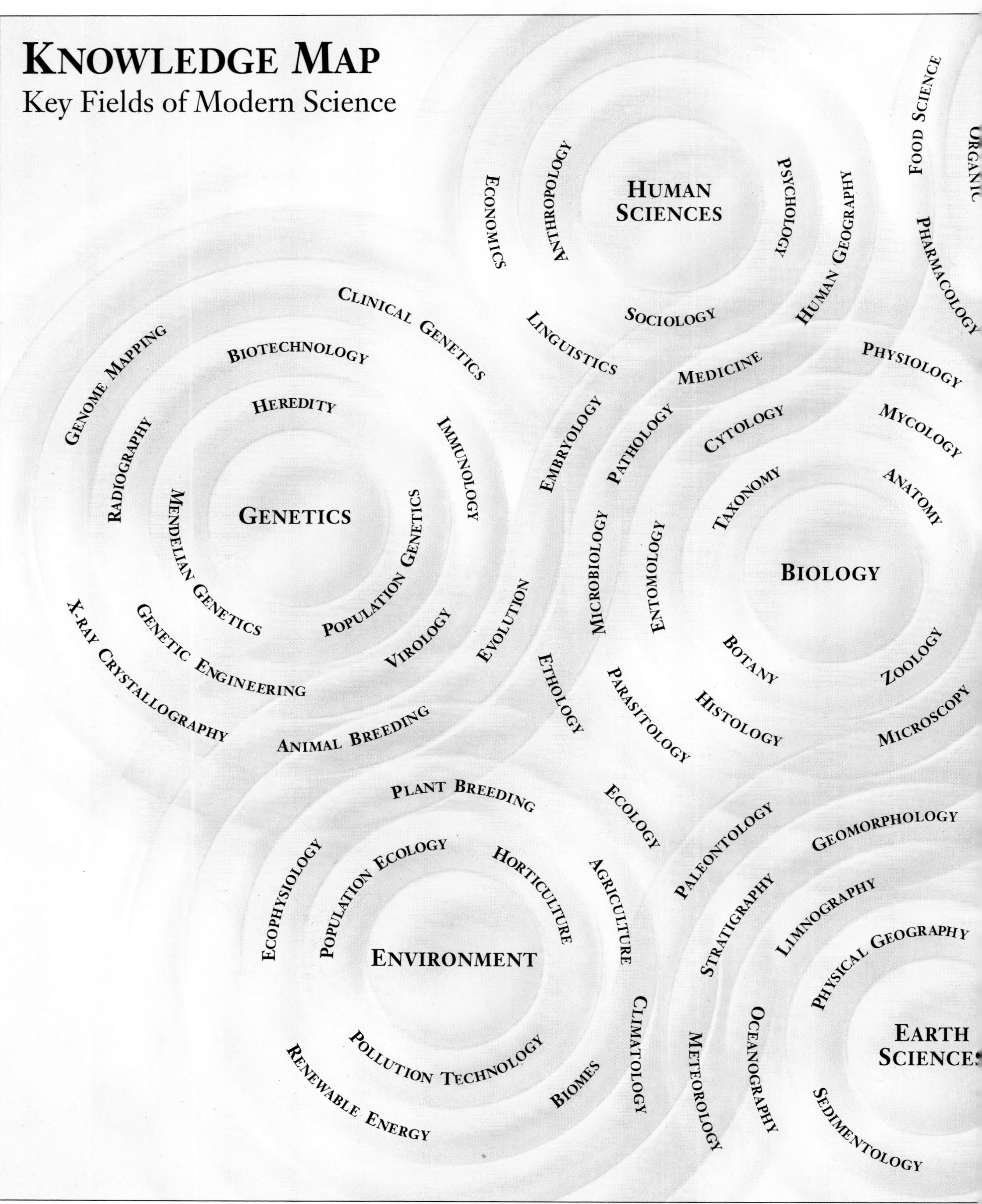

Human Sciences
Economics
Anthropology
Psychology
Human Geography
Sociology
Linguistics
Food Science
Organic
Pharmacology
Genetics
Clinical Genetics
Biotechnology
Genome Mapping
Heredity
Radiography
Immunology
Mendelian Genetics
Population Genetics
Genetic Engineering
X-ray Crystallography
Virology
Evolution
Animal Breeding
Biology
Medicine
Physiology
Cytology
Mycology
Pathology
Embryology
Taxonomy
Anatomy
Microbiology
Entomology
Botany
Zoology
Ethology
Parasitology
Histology
Microscopy
Environment
Plant Breeding
Ecology
Ecophysiology
Population Ecology
Horticulture
Agriculture
Pollution Technology
Renewable Energy
Biomes
Climatology
Earth Sciences
Paleontology
Geomorphology
Stratigraphy
Limnography
Physical Geography
Meteorology
Oceanography
Sedimentology

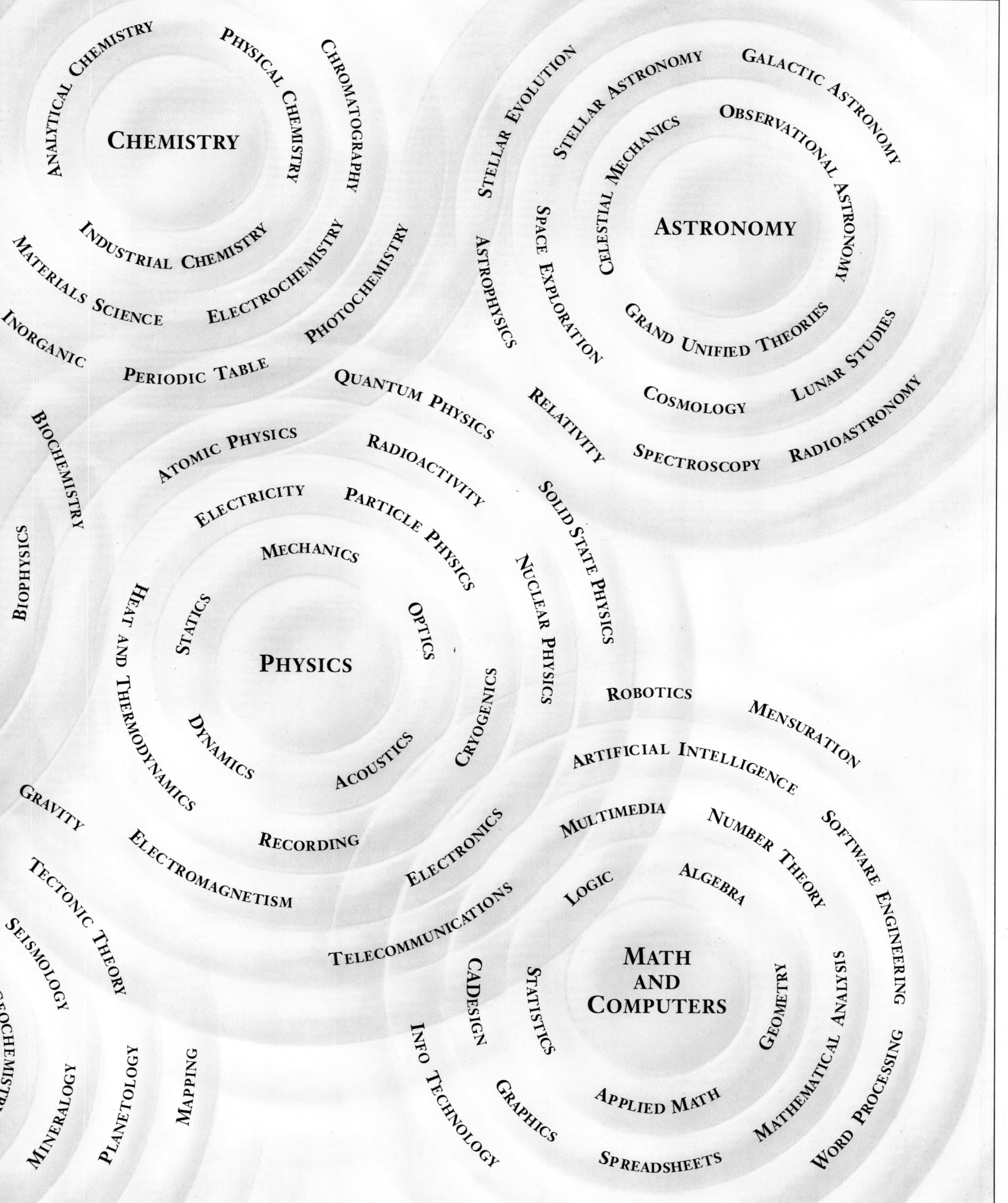
Chemistry
Analytical Chemistry
Physical Chemistry
Chromatography
Industrial Chemistry
Electrochemistry
Photochemistry
Materials Science
Inorganic
Periodic Table
Biochemistry
Biophysics
Astronomy
Stellar Evolution
Stellar Astronomy
Galactic Astronomy
Celestial Mechanics
Observational Astronomy
Space Exploration
Astrophysics
Grand Unified Theories
Cosmology
Lunar Studies
Relativity
Spectroscopy
Radioastronomy
Quantum Physics
Physics
Atomic Physics
Radioactivity
Electricity
Particle Physics
Mechanics
Solid State Physics
Nuclear Physics
Statics
Optics
Heat and Thermodynamics
Dynamics
Acoustics
Cryogenics
Recording
Electromagnetism
Electronics
Gravity
Tectonic Theory
Seismology
Geochemistry
Mineralogy
Planetology
Mapping
Telecommunications
Math and Computers
Robotics
Mensuration
Artificial Intelligence
Multimedia
Number Theory
Software Engineering
Logic
Algebra
CADesign
Statistics
Geometry
Mathematical Analysis
Info Technology
Graphics
Applied Math
Spreadsheets
Word Processing

Knowledge Map

Modern Genetics

Genetic Engineering

Altering the DNA of organisms, often by incorporating DNA from other species. Recombinant DNA technology uses enzymes to splice together DNA from different organisms, or to incorporate synthetic DNA. Altered DNA may be inserted directly into cells.

Clinical Genetics

The application of genetics to study and treat human disease. The pattern of inheritance of genetic defects can be determined. Some defects can now be corrected at the molecular level. DNA mapping may permit the design of drugs to block gene action.

Evolutionary Biology

The study of how living organisms change over generations, adapting better to their environment, or adapting to a changing environment, through accumulated genetic changes. Evolutionary biology includes the study of past and present evolutionary changes, and of the underlying genetic processes.

Animal Breeding

Breeding selected animals to produce offspring with certain characteristics. Modern domestic breeds of livestock and pets have been produced this way. Artificial insemination is often used. Genetic engineering offers a faster method of altering the genetic material of livestock, and of introducing DNA from other species.

Biotechnology

The applied science of biology. It commonly refers to the production of living organisms for industrial, medical or other uses, as in genetically-engineered plants or bacteria. It also refers to techniques to provide long-term solutions to environmental problems based on knowledge of ecosystems – for example, renewable energy.

X-Ray Crystallography

The study of crystal structure by analysis of the diffraction patterns produced by X-rays passing through the crystalline solid. The diffraction pattern can be recorded on photographic film or by special detectors linked to computers for analysis. The technique is valuable in the study of proteins and other complex biological molecules, and was a key procedure in determining the structure of DNA.

Immunology

The study of immunity, immune responses and their causes. Immunology is concerned with responses of the body to disease-producing organisms and foreign substances, and with the recognition of cells by other cells of the same organism. A knowledge of immunology is vital for predicting responses to organ transplants and blood transfusions, devising programmes to control and eliminate diseases, and understanding communications between body cells.

Genome Mapping

Determining the sequence of nucleotide bases of DNA. It involves using enzymes to cleave the DNA at particular base sequences, then separating the fragments and plotting their distribution. The Human Genome Project aims to map the entire human genome of 3 million nucleotides.

Virology

The study of viruses: structure, physiology, ecology and distribution and their effect on living organisms.Virology can shed light on many diseases – human, plant and animal. In biotechnology, viruses are used to transfer genetic material between organisms.

EUGENICS

The application of genetics to improving human characteristics. It involves balancing moral and ethical considerations against potential "benefits" of genetically engineering the human genome, and of less direct actions such as the selective abortion of fetuses that are thought to carry genetic defects (or even such characteristics as not being of the desired sex).

GENETICS

The science of inheritance – the way in which characters are passed on; and how the information contained in cells, in the form of nucleic acids, controls the development and activities of the organism. Genetics includes the study of evolution and adaptation.

EMBRYOLOGY

The study of the formation and development of embryos, including the interaction of the embryo with its physical and chemical environment, and the the genes controlling different stages of development.

MENDELIAN GENETICS

The study of the rules of characters determined by single genes. Genes exist in more than one form, producing different versions of a character. Mendelian laws predict the result of mating organisms with contrasting characteristics.

BIOCHEMISTRY

The study of chemical compounds and processes in living organisms. It involves extracting and analyzing compounds involved in cell structure and metabolism, and the study of metabolic reactions, to help understand processes such as converting food to energy, building of body structures and the expression of hereditary information.

MICROBIOLOGY

The study of microorganisms, such as bacteria, viruses, protozoa and microscopic fungi and algae; their physiology, biochemistry, reproduction and genetics, and interactions with their environment and with other organisms. Clinical aspects include the study of microbial diseases and parasites. Many microorganisms are grown on a commercial scale to produce organic compounds (such as penicillin).

CYTOLOGY

The study of cells, including the physical and chemical processes inside cells, interactions between cells, and their detailed microscopic structure. Growing cells artificially allows research and offers potential cures for hereditary diseases.

PATHOLOGY

The study of the causes and nature of diseases, and their effects on living organisms. The organisms studied range from large multicellular parasites to microscopic protozoans, bacteria and viruses, and parasitic fungi. Pathology studies their lifecycles, the means by which they exert effects on the body, and the ways in which the body defends itself against them.

PALEONTOLOGY

The study of fossils: their appearance, structure, classification, distribution, evolution and ecology. It is used to date and correlate layers of rock, by analyzing "index" fossils which lived in specific habitats for relatively short periods of geological time. It is also used to determine evolutionary relationships.

PHOTOCHEMISTRY

The study of the chemical changes that are produced in living and non-living objects by radiant energy, especially by visible and ultraviolet wavelengths of light, and the chemical processes that result in the emission of such energy. The biological applications of photochemistry include the study of photosynthesis in plants and the study of fluorescence (the emission of light) in animals as well as plants.

TIMECHART

Organisms change over time: the species of animals and plants that currently populate the planet have not been here for its whole history. But how did they develop? The ancient Greek philosophers applied themselves to the question of the origin of life. Empedocles developed an ingenious but eccentric version of evolution. Aristotle, however, was convinced that species were fixed. For the next 2000 years there were few developments. This was partly because of Aristotle's lasting influence, and partly because of the dominance of biblical ideas.

Xenophanes of Colophon discovers FOSSIL FISH in Sicily (500 BC)
Greek philosopher EMPEDOCLES proposes that animals and plants arose by the chance joining together of separate organs, for example, heads, eyes, and limbs (450 BC)
Greek physician Hippocrates proposes a theory of INHERITANCE, in which "seed material" is transported from all parts of the body to the reproductive organs (420 BC)
JAMES USSHER, Archbishop of Armagh, Ireland, uses biblical evidence to calculate the origin of the Earth as occurring in 4004 BC (1650)
German philosopher GOTTFRIED LEIBNIZ proposes a law of continuity, in which nature is seen as changing slowly and continuously, rather than suddenly (1712)
French naturalist George Louis Leclerc, COMTE DE BUFFON, publishes the first part of his monumental Histoire Naturelle. Buffon supports fixity of species and rejects the possibility that humans and apes could have a common ancestor (1749)
The Comte de Buffon calculates the AGE OF THE EARTH as 168,000 years, a great increase on previous estimates (1778)
English economist and cleric THOMAS MALTHUS publishes his Essay on the Principles of Population, which argues that famine, disease and war act as necessary checks on explosive population increases. Charles Darwin later reads this essay, which he finds suggestive of similar selective processes in nature (1798)
PALEONTOLOGY
EVOLUTION OF LIFE
GENETICS AND HEREDITY
MOLECULAR BIOLOGY
GENETIC ENGINEERING
AD1
1700
ARISTOTLE rejects Empedocles' evolutionary theories and states that man and other animals can neither arise nor become extinct. Instead he claims that species are eternal (350 BC)
ARISTOTLE speculates that semen and menstrual blood interact to bestow inherited sex (350 BC)
The Holy Roman Emperor Frederick II writes The Art of Falconry, describing in detail the life and BIOLOGY OF BIRDS. His interest in accurate observation is a rare example of early scientific method (1220)
ANDREAS VESALIUS, Belgian anatomist, uses dissection and strict observation describe human anatomy. This early example of scientific method allows the subsequent development of comparative anatomy and paleontology (1543)
ERASMUS DARWIN, grandfather of Charles Darwin, writes Zoonomia, a whimsical but unscientific synthesis of evolutionary ideas (1754)
Swedish botanist CARL VON LINNÉ (LINNAEUS) produces new hybrids of plants, cross-pollinating by hand. He describes the hybrids as "new species" and enters them in his authoritative classification system (1753)
Scottish geologist JAMES HUTTON proposes that the Earth is indefinitely old, and shaped by the slow action of immensely strong forces, rather than by sudden catastrophe such as flood. This concept of gradual change becomes an important aspect of Darwinism (1788)

Modern science began to develop during the 16th and 17th centuries. The break with Aristotelian thought, and the emphasis on experiment and observation, allowed a burst of new analytical thinking. The Belgian anatomist Andreas Vesalius (1514-64) was among its earliest exponents. He pursued knowledge about the human body, though his method – dissection, now routinely practiced by medical students – was condemned by many as un-Christian. The Swedish botanist Carl von Linné (Linnaeus, 1707-78) laid the foundation for genetic engineering by cross-

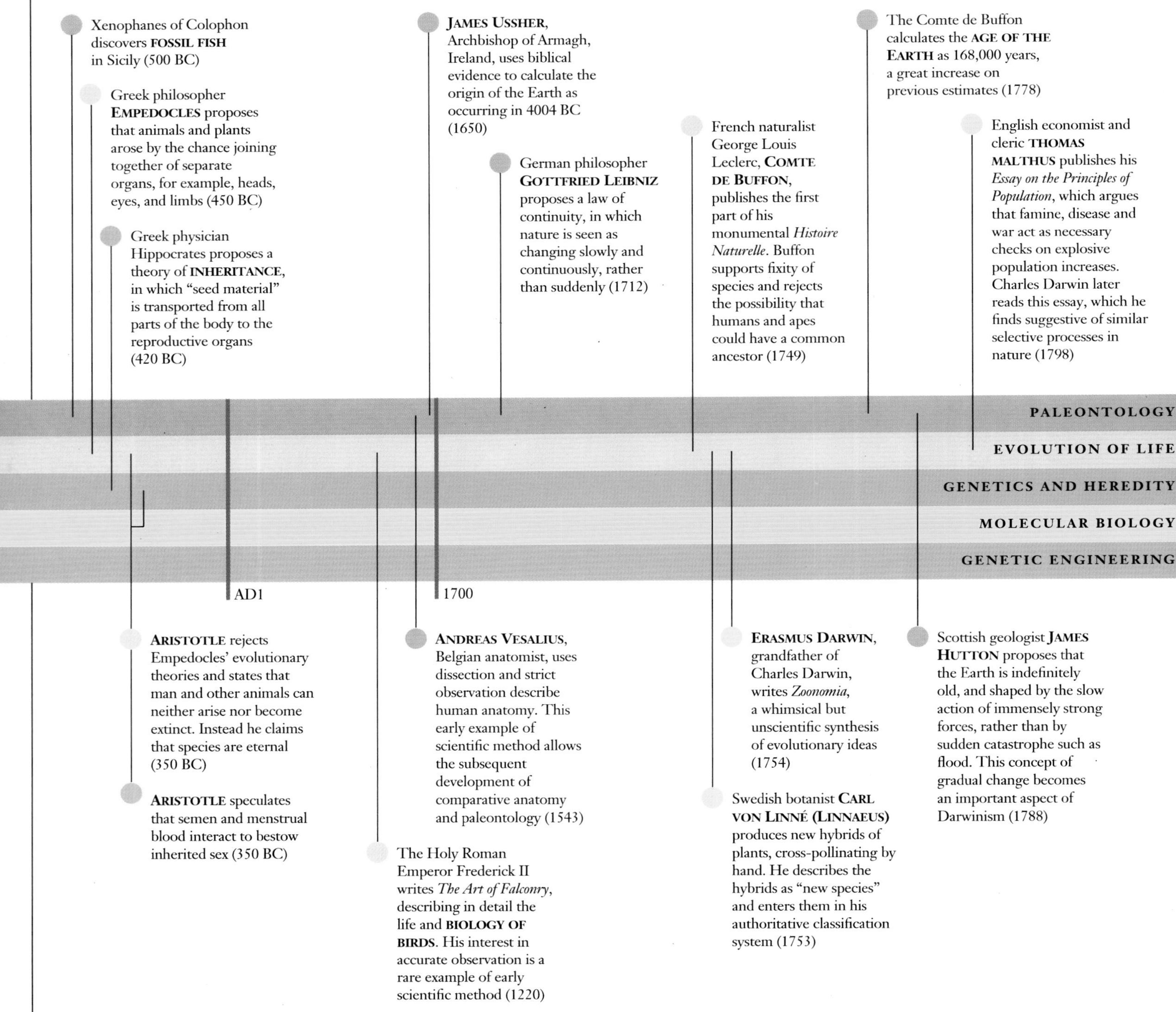

pollinating plants to produce hybrid species. Several new thinkers proposed that the Earth was much older than anyone had previously believed, and that changes to the environment had occurred gradually, rather than suddenly and as a result of catastrophic phenomena. Fossil discoveries in the 18th and 19th centuries suggested that some species had become extinct, while others had arisen quite recently.

During the 19th century, with the zoos and museums of the United States and Europe filling with specimens, the similarities between humans and apes began to appear more evident. The idea that they shared a common ancestor dated back to at least the mid-18th century, although it was widely ridiculed and dismissed. In the early 19th century it was taken up again by the French biologist Jean Baptiste de Lamarck (1744-1829).

French naturalist **GEORGE CUVIER** dies in the Paris cholera epidemic. His realization that fossils in deep geological strata are older than those in more superficial layers establishes him as the founder of paleontology (1812)
Scottish geologist **CHARLES LYELL** publishes his *Principles of Geology*, a work asserting that the common – and slow – geological processes of the present day can be used to explain satisfactorily the Earth's rock formations (1830)
CHARLES DARWIN, suffering from a mysterious disease, retires to the country and devotes himself to studying evolution (1842)
Swiss-American biologist **LOUIS AGASSIZ** argues the human races are distinct species, ranked on a scale of evolution (1850)
Archaeopteryx, a fossil resembling both bird and reptile, is brought to London. It becomes known as "the first bird" (1863)
The Austrian monk **GREGOR MENDEL** publishes his theory of inheritance. Although the paper is sent to 200 leading scientists, his insights are ignored for another 32 years (1866)
CESARE LOMBROSO publishes *L'uomo delinquente* (The Criminal Man), asserting that criminality is caused by regression to an evolutionary past (1876)
American paleontologist **O. C. MARSH** estimates the length of the newly-discovered dinosaur *Brontosaurus* as 25m (70–80ft) (1879)
1850
JEAN BAPTISTE DE LAMARCK, French biologist, proposes the first complete theory of evolution, claiming that new species originate by natural processes and that man has an ape ancestry. Lamarck's suggestion that the use or disuse of organs inexorably leads to inherited changes becomes a major influence on evolutionary thinking over the next 125 years (1809)
German chemist **FRIEDRICH WOHLER** synthesises urea, thus refuting the idea that organic molecules can only be made by living things (1828)
CHARLES DARWIN, British naturalist aboard the surveying ship *HMS Beagle*, visits the Galapagos Islands (1835)
English anatomist Richard Owen suggests the term **"DINOSAUR"** for a range of recently discovered fossil reptiles (1841)
The Origin of Species, Charles Darwin's description of his theory of evolution by natural selection, is published (1859)
Scottish engineer **FLEMING JENKINS** attacks Darwin for his inadequate theory of inheritance (1867)
CHROMOSOMES are observed inside the cell (1870)
Swiss scientist **FRIEDRICH MIESCHER** finds a non-protein material in the cell nucleus. He names it "nuclein" (1871)
German biologist **AUGUST WEISMANN** asserts that all genetic material is contained within the nucleus. He argues that heredity is brought about by the transmission of such material from generation to generation (1883)
German biologist Theodor Bovari proves that **CHROMOSOMES** are essential to life, and asserts that they exist through the cell cycle, not just at division. He also suggests that half of a cell's chromosomes come from each parent (1891)

But it was the English naturalist Charles Darwin (1809-82) who made evolution respectable. His chief work *On the Origin of Species by Means of Natural Selection*, published in 1859, summarized the enormous amount of information then known about

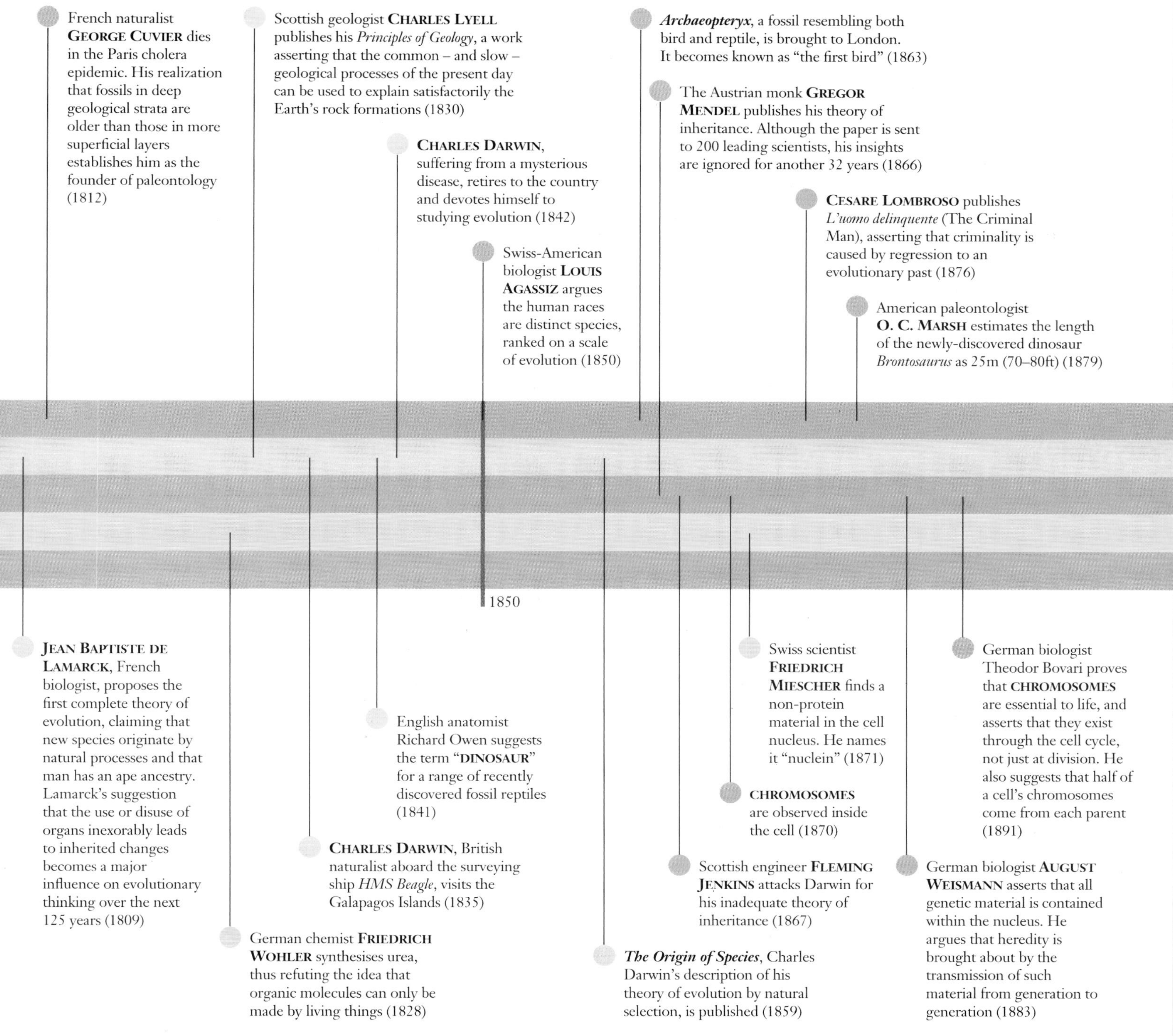

the mutability of species, and proposed a theory that explained how evolutionary changes could take place. This is what sets Darwin apart. He not only knew that evolution had taken place, but also proposed an explanation that became the basis of modern biology. Darwin's mechanism of change depended on two crucial facts. The first is that the environment itself changes with time. The second is that no two individuals within a species are the same, and this variation is inherited. Darwin put these facts together: organisms change over time, forming new species, because the environment favors individuals with particular characteristics, the ones which were by chance adapted to the changed conditions.

Darwin changed the way we look at evolution. Yet, as he himself constantly pointed out, he relied heavily on the work of others. Three of Darwin's particular influences – Lamarck, Thomas Malthus and Charles Lyell – published important work in the 60 years preceding *The Origin of Species*, but it was the 19th century that saw the birth of scientific evolutionary studies.

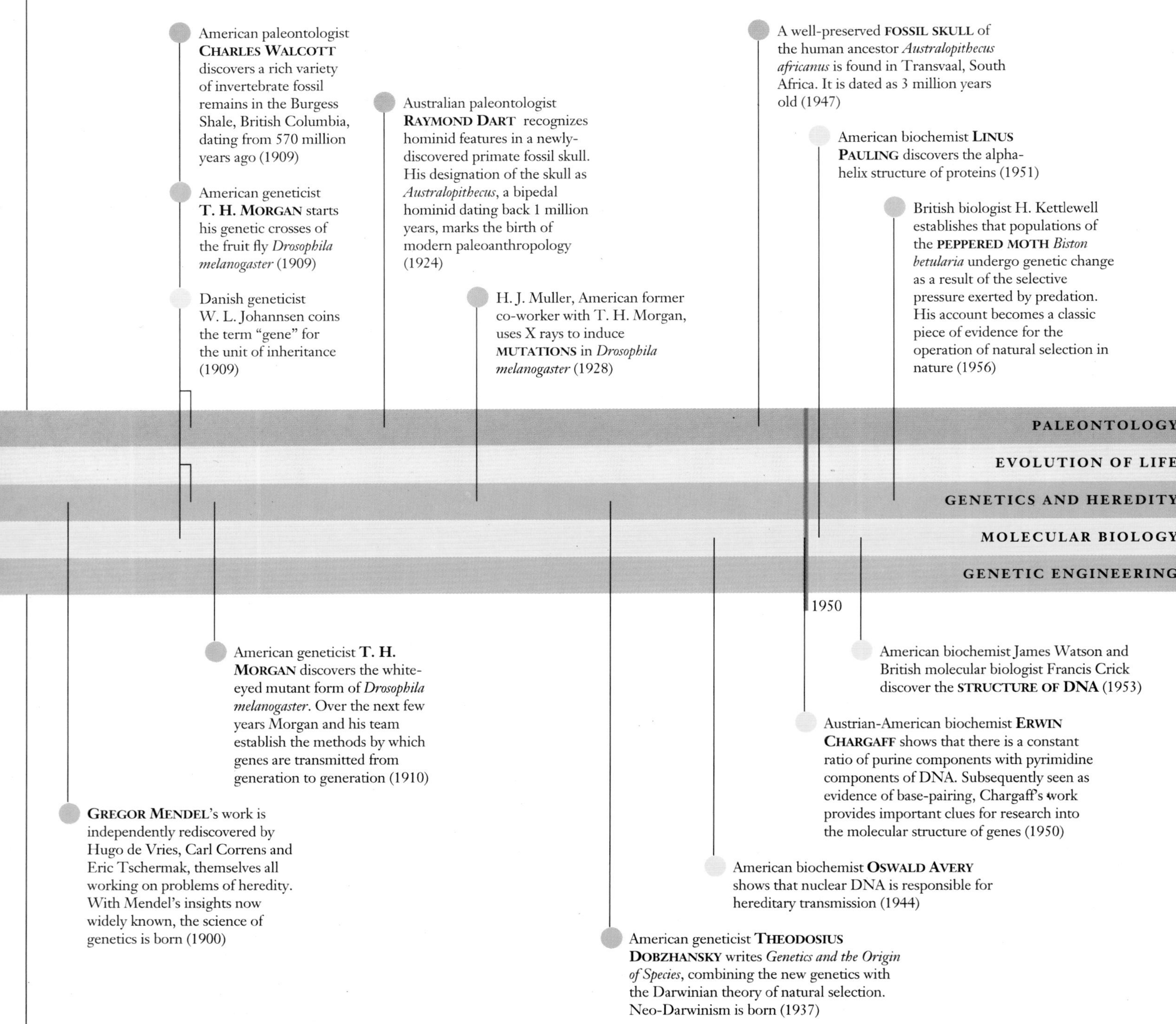

American paleontologist **CHARLES WALCOTT** discovers a rich variety of invertebrate fossil remains in the Burgess Shale, British Columbia, dating from 570 million years ago (1909)
American geneticist **T. H. MORGAN** starts his genetic crosses of the fruit fly *Drosophila melanogaster* (1909)
Danish geneticist W. L. Johannsen coins the term "gene" for the unit of inheritance (1909)
Australian paleontologist **RAYMOND DART** recognizes hominid features in a newly-discovered primate fossil skull. His designation of the skull as *Australopithecus*, a bipedal hominid dating back 1 million years, marks the birth of modern paleoanthropology (1924)
H. J. Muller, American former co-worker with T. H. Morgan, uses X rays to induce **MUTATIONS** in *Drosophila melanogaster* (1928)
A well-preserved **FOSSIL SKULL** of the human ancestor *Australopithecus africanus* is found in Transvaal, South Africa. It is dated as 3 million years old (1947)
American biochemist **LINUS PAULING** discovers the alpha-helix structure of proteins (1951)
British biologist H. Kettlewell establishes that populations of the **PEPPERED MOTH** *Biston betularia* undergo genetic change as a result of the selective pressure exerted by predation. His account becomes a classic piece of evidence for the operation of natural selection in nature (1956)
PALEONTOLOGY
EVOLUTION OF LIFE
GENETICS AND HEREDITY
MOLECULAR BIOLOGY
GENETIC ENGINEERING
1950
American geneticist **T. H. MORGAN** discovers the white-eyed mutant form of *Drosophila melanogaster*. Over the next few years Morgan and his team establish the methods by which genes are transmitted from generation to generation (1910)
GREGOR MENDEL's work is independently rediscovered by Hugo de Vries, Carl Correns and Eric Tschermak, themselves all working on problems of heredity. With Mendel's insights now widely known, the science of genetics is born (1900)
American biochemist James Watson and British molecular biologist Francis Crick discover the **STRUCTURE OF DNA** (1953)
Austrian-American biochemist **ERWIN CHARGAFF** shows that there is a constant ratio of purine components with pyrimidine components of DNA. Subsequently seen as evidence of base-pairing, Chargaff's work provides important clues for research into the molecular structure of genes (1950)
American biochemist **OSWALD AVERY** shows that nuclear DNA is responsible for hereditary transmission (1944)
American geneticist **THEODOSIUS DOBZHANSKY** writes *Genetics and the Origin of Species*, combining the new genetics with the Darwinian theory of natural selection. Neo-Darwinism is born (1937)

Between 1900 and 1930 Darwinism was revised, using new knowledge about chromosomes and inheritance. It introduced the idea that the variation Darwin observed was carried by genes. The study of genes has become one of the most important research fields in 20th-century biology. Genes, we now know, are made of DNA. They carry a genetic code, which is not only central to the individual's development but is transmitted over generations.

As the 20th century draws to a close, the fields of evolution and genetics have taken on a new responsibility. It is possible to map the position of genes on chromosomes and to determine their function. This, in particular, is the role of the Human Genome Project, the biggest science initiative since the Apollo moonshots. Defective genes, such as those causing the disease cystic fibrosis, have already been tracked down. Meanwhile, the techniques for manipulating and altering genes become ever more refined. This new technology, called genetic engineering, ensures that the fields of evolution and genetics will continue to be as controversial and challenging as ever.

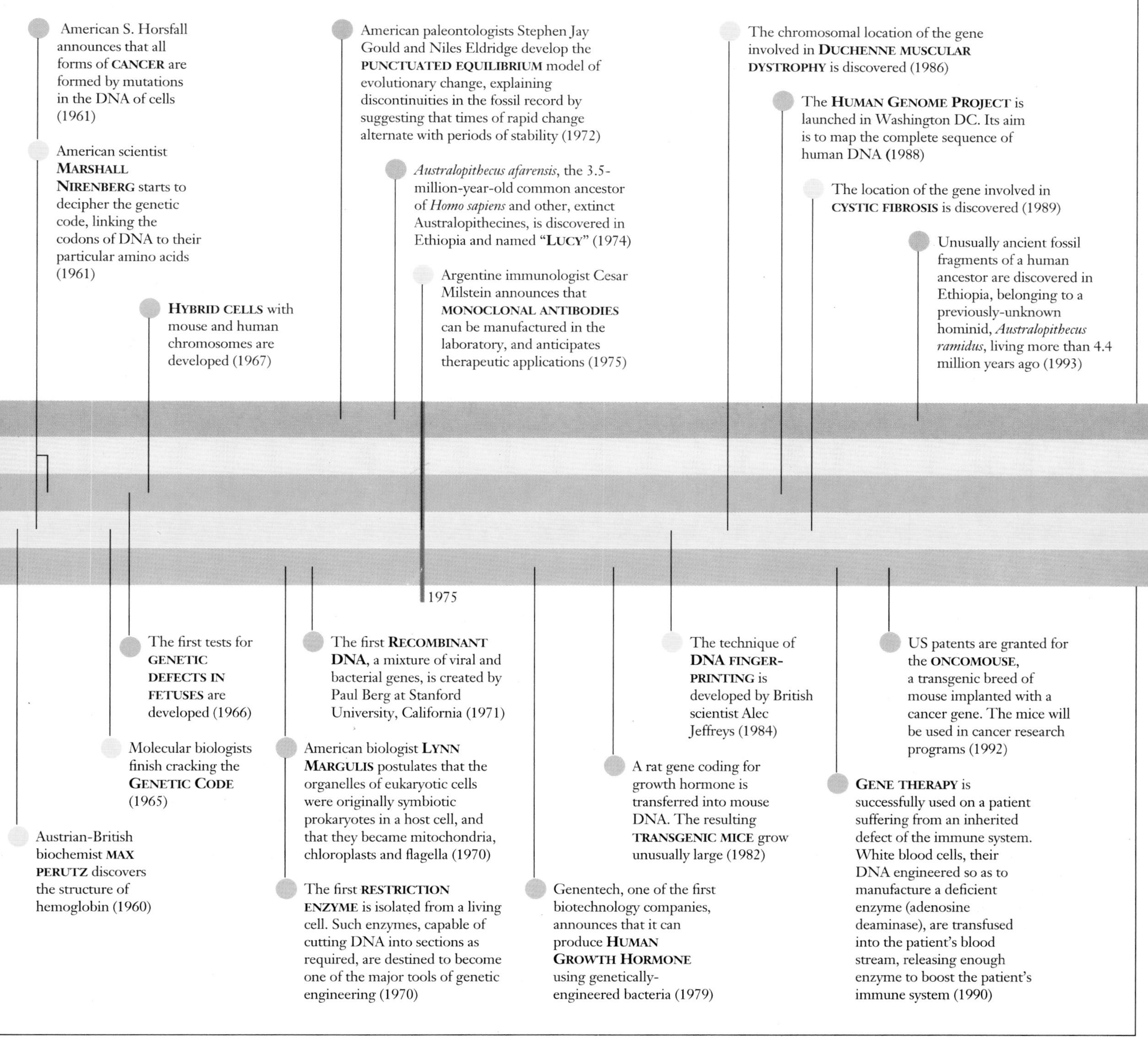

Austrian-British biochemist **MAX PERUTZ** discovers the structure of hemoglobin (1960)
American S. Horsfall announces that all forms of **CANCER** are formed by mutations in the DNA of cells (1961)
American scientist **MARSHALL NIRENBERG** starts to decipher the genetic code, linking the codons of DNA to their particular amino acids (1961)
Molecular biologists finish cracking the **GENETIC CODE** (1965)
The first tests for **GENETIC DEFECTS IN FETUSES** are developed (1966)
HYBRID CELLS with mouse and human chromosomes are developed (1967)
The first **RESTRICTION ENZYME** is isolated from a living cell. Such enzymes, capable of cutting DNA into sections as required, are destined to become one of the major tools of genetic engineering (1970)
American biologist **LYNN MARGULIS** postulates that the organelles of eukaryotic cells were originally symbiotic prokaryotes in a host cell, and that they became mitochondria, chloroplasts and flagella (1970)
The first **RECOMBINANT DNA**, a mixture of viral and bacterial genes, is created by Paul Berg at Stanford University, California (1971)
American paleontologists Stephen Jay Gould and Niles Eldridge develop the **PUNCTUATED EQUILIBRIUM** model of evolutionary change, explaining discontinuities in the fossil record by suggesting that times of rapid change alternate with periods of stability (1972)
Australopithecus afarensis, the 3.5-million-year-old common ancestor of *Homo sapiens* and other, extinct Australopithecines, is discovered in Ethiopia and named **"LUCY"** (1974)
Argentine immunologist Cesar Milstein announces that **MONOCLONAL ANTIBODIES** can be manufactured in the laboratory, and anticipates therapeutic applications (1975)
1975
Genentech, one of the first biotechnology companies, announces that it can produce **HUMAN GROWTH HORMONE** using genetically-engineered bacteria (1979)
A rat gene coding for growth hormone is transferred into mouse DNA. The resulting **TRANSGENIC MICE** grow unusually large (1982)
The technique of **DNA FINGER-PRINTING** is developed by British scientist Alec Jeffreys (1984)
The chromosomal location of the gene involved in **DUCHENNE MUSCULAR DYSTROPHY** is discovered (1986)
The **HUMAN GENOME PROJECT** is launched in Washington DC. Its aim is to map the complete sequence of human DNA (1988)
The location of the gene involved in **CYSTIC FIBROSIS** is discovered (1989)
GENE THERAPY is successfully used on a patient suffering from an inherited defect of the immune system. White blood cells, their DNA engineered so as to manufacture a deficient enzyme (adenosine deaminase), are transfused into the patient's blood stream, releasing enough enzyme to boost the patient's immune system (1990)
US patents are granted for the **ONCOMOUSE**, a transgenic breed of mouse implanted with a cancer gene. The mice will be used in cancer research programs (1992)
Unusually ancient fossil fragments of a human ancestor are discovered in Ethiopia, belonging to a previously-unknown hominid, *Australopithecus ramidus*, living more than 4.4 million years ago (1993)

Genetics KEYWORDS

acquired characteristic
A feature of the body that develops during the lifetime of an individual, brought about by the effect of environment on body tissues. These characteristics are confined to the **somatic cells**, and are not passed on to the next generation. In **Lamarckism** the term is used to describe features that are acquired during the lifetime as a result of repeated use or disuse of body parts. *See* **inheritance of acquired characteristics**.

CONNECTIONS

EVOLUTION AND VARIATION **86**
EVOLUTION BY NATURAL SELECTION **88**

activator
A substance that binds to a particular segment of **DNA** and stimulates the **transcription** of a particular **gene** or genes. Activators are important agents in the control of metabolism. For example, in the metabolic pathways of digestion, a particular food substance may act as an activator of the gene(s) coding for **enzymes** that catalyze its breakdown.

active site
Specific region on an **enzyme**'s surface that allows it to bind to a particular molecule or molecules, the substrate or substrates, to form an enzyme-substrate complex. The enzyme and substrate are said to fit together like a "lock and key".

adaptation
Any change in the structure or function of an organism that allows it to survive and reproduce more effectively in its environment.

CONNECTIONS

EVOLUTION BY NATURAL SELECTION **88**
RELATED OR ADAPTED **94**
STRATEGIES FOR SURVIVAL **102**

adaptive radiation
The **evolution** of a related group of organisms along a number of different lines involving **adaptation** to a variety of environments. These may be subdivisions of the original ancestral environment or new environments which are being invaded. Adaptive radiation is a result of **divergent evolution**.

adenine
A **purine base** that occurs in both **DNA** and **RNA**. Adenine molecules pair with **thymine** in DNA, and with **uracil** in RNA.

AIDS
Acquired immune deficiency syndrome; a disease caused by the human immunodeficiency **virus** (HIV), a **retrovirus**. HIV is transmitted in body fluids, mainly blood and sexual secretions. The virus has a short life outside the body, which makes transmission of the infection by methods other than sexual contact, blood transfusion and shared needles extremely unlikely. Infection with HIV is not synonymous with having AIDS; many people who have the virus in their blood are not ill. The effect of the virus on those who become ill is to devastate the immune system, leaving the victim susceptible to a range of diseases that would not otherwise develop.

allele
Common shortening of "allelomorph": any of one or more alternative forms of a specific **gene**, occupying identical positions (loci) on **homologous chromosomes**.

CONNECTIONS

THE GENETIC CODE **66**
MENDEL'S BREAKTHROUGH **80**
CROSSOVER AND LINKAGE **82**

allopatric speciation
The **evolution** of new species as a result of certain populations becoming geographically isolated from the parent stock. If the geographical barriers are subsequently removed, allopatric species may still be capable of interbreeding.

allopolyploid
A **polyploid** (an individual possessing three or more sets of chromosomes) in which the **chromosome** sets are from different **species**. The rate of occurrence of allopolyploidy can be increased by **colchicine** or shortwave radiation. Allopolyploidy is

ALTERNATION OF GENERATIONS

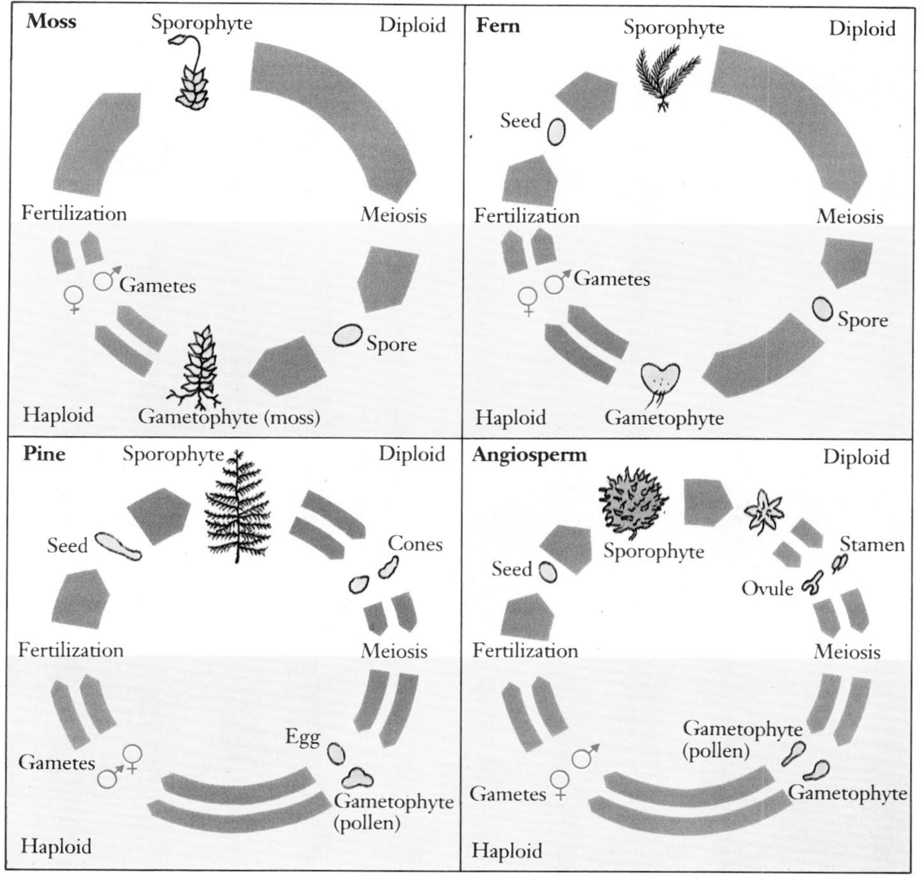

widely utilized in plant breeding, particularly in the production of new cereals. *See* **autopolyploid**.

allosteric control

A mechanism of **enzyme** regulation in which the catalytic activity of the enzyme is influenced by the binding of a certain molecule at a site other than the active (catalytic) site. Enzymes regulated in this way are called allosteric enzymes. The binding of the regulator molecule often results in the distortion of the active site or alteration of the distribution of electrical charges on its surface. *See* **end-product inhibition** and **operon**.

alternation of generations

A reproductive process occurring in all plants and some fungi in which diploid (having two sets of chromosomes) and haploid (having one set of chromosomes) forms occur alternately. The diploid generation produces haploid spores by **meiosis**, and is called the sporophyte; the haploid generation produces gametes, and is called the gametophyte. The gametes fuse to form a diploid **zygote** which develops into a new sporophyte; thus the sporophyte and gametophyte alternate.

altruism

Unselfish behavior by one member of a **species** which benefits other members. It may diminish reproductive success, and even lead to self-destruction. Examples are worker bees which rear the offspring of their queen, and communal care of the young in mammals such as hunting dogs, in which only the dominant pair reproduces.

amino acid

Any of a group of water-soluble organic molecules, mainly composed of carbon, oxygen, hydrogen and nitrogen, containing both a basic amino group ($-NH_2$) and an acidic carboxyl group ($-COOH$). The building blocks of proteins are 20 amino acids. Two or more joined together are called peptides. **Proteins** are made up of interacting **polypeptides** (peptide chains consisting of more than three amino acids), which are folded or twisted into characteristic shapes.

CONNECTIONS
MAKING THE MESSAGE 56
PROTEINS AND AMINO ACIDS 64
THE GENETIC CODE 66

amniocentesis

The technique used for sampling the amniotic fluid surrounding a fetus in the uterus in order to detect genetic abnormalities such as Down's syndrome and spina bifida before birth. This fluid, containing shed fetal cells, can be cultured to provide a chromosomal profile (fetal **karyotype**).

amniotic egg

An egg characterized by the presence of an amnion during embryonic development. The amnion is the innermost of the fetal membranes and encloses a fluid-filled amniotic cavity in which the fetus develops. The amnion helps to cushion the embryo against injury. A typical amniotic egg contains two more membrane sacs: the yolk sac, containing a nutritive fluid, and the allantois, into which the embryo's liquid wastes are discharged. Amniotic eggs are typical of mammals, birds and reptiles.

analogous structures

Features of organisms that are superficially similar but that have evolved in different ways. For example, the wings of butterflies and birds are analogous organs, and so are the tendrils of plants, which may be derived from leaves, branches or flowers.

CONNECTIONS
HIDDEN CLUES TO THE PAST 92
RELATED OR ADAPTED 94

anaphase

The stage of nuclear division in **mitosis** and **meiosis** in which the chromosomes move from the **spindle** equator to the spindle poles. The start of anaphase is the separation of **sister chromatids** as the **centromeres** divide; it ends with the poleward movement of the chromosomes. *See also* **metaphase, prophase** and **telophase**.

aneuploid

Differing from the normal chromosome number characteristic of a **species** by one or more complete **chromosomes**; for example, $2n + 1$ (trisomy) or $2n - 1$ (monosomy), where n is the number of chromosomes. *See also* **diploid, haploid** and **polyploid**.

annealing

The pairing of two single-stranded **nucleic acid** molecules (polynucleotides) to form a double-stranded molecule. It may take place between two complementary **DNA** chains, two complementary **RNA** chains, or a DNA chain and a complementary RNA chain (to form a DNA–RNA hybrid).

ANTIBODY

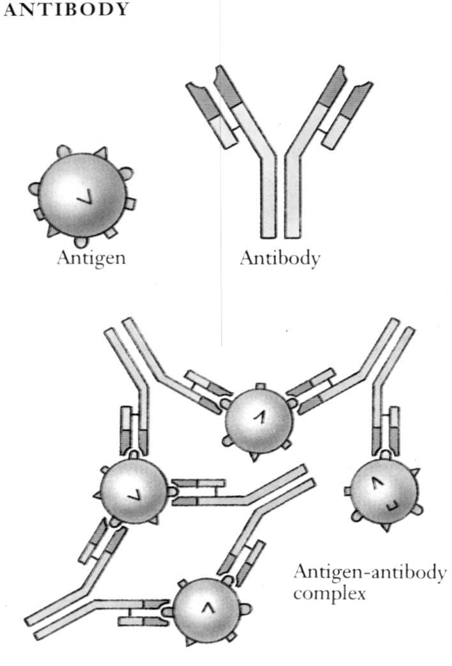

antibody
A defensive **protein** molecule (also called an immunoglobulin) produced in the blood by lymphocytes (white blood cells) in response to the presence of foreign or invading substances (**antigens**). Antibodies bind to specific antigens, tagging them for destruction by phagocytes (white blood cells that engulf and destroy invading bodies) or activating a chemical system that renders them harmless. Each antibody is specific to a particular antigen. Large quantities of identical, very specific antibodies (monoclonal antibodies) can now be produced in the laboratory and are widely used in molecular biology.

anticoding (noncoding) strand
The strand of a double-stranded **DNA** molecule that does not act as a template for **messenger RNA** synthesis during **transcription**. *See* **coding strand**.

anticodon
The group of three **nucleotides** in **transfer RNA** that pairs with three complementary nucleotides (a codon) in **messenger RNA** during **protein synthesis**. *See* **genetic code**.

antigen
Any substance that causes the production of antibodies. Common antigens include the **proteins** carried on the surface of bacteria, viruses and pollen grains. The proteins of incompatible blood groups or tissues also act as antigens. *See* **antibody**.

artificial selection
See **selective breeding**.

asexual reproduction
Any form of reproduction that does not involve the production and fusion of gametes (sex cells) from two parents. Only one parent is involved, and the offspring therefore inherit the **genes** of that parent only. Asexual reproduction has the advantage that there is no need to search for a mate or to develop complex pollinating mechanisms. The disadvantage is that only identical individuals (*see* **clone**) are produced, so there is no **variation** and no potential for **adaptation** to changing circumstances.

CONNECTIONS

THE REASONS FOR SEX **98**
REPRODUCTION WITHOUT SEX **100**

assortative mating
The preferential selection of a mate with a particular **genotype** (and hence **phenotype**). If sufficiently consistent, it can result in a distinct breeding subgroup within a **population**, which may eventually evolve into a new **species** without **geographical isolation**. *See* **allopatric speciation**.

autopolyploid
A polyploid (an individual with three or more chromosome sets) in which all of the sets are of the same species. *See* **polyploidy**.

ANTICODING STRAND

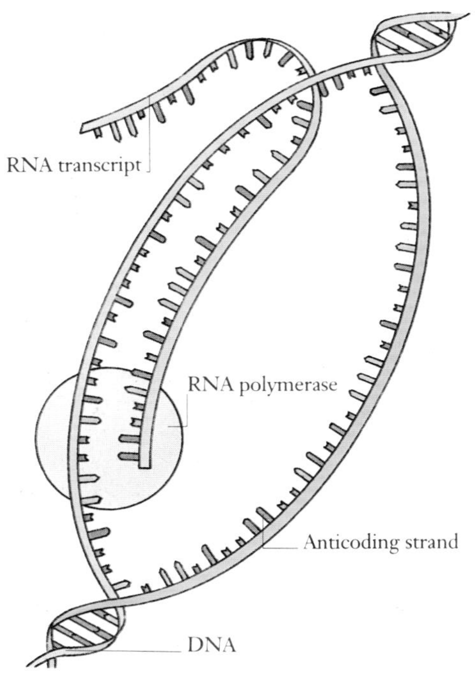

autosome
Any chromosome in the cell other than a sex chromosome. Autosomes are of the same number and kind in both males and females of a species.

B cell
A lymphocyte (white blood cell) produced in the bone marrow. Each B cell produces one **antibody** to a particular **antigen** (a foreign substance that provokes an immune response). When a B cell binds to its antigen, it responds to stimulation from other lymphocytes and starts dividing rapidly, producing multiple copies of the antibody, which are secreted into the body fluid. Some B cells act as memory cells, which are primed to respond rapidly if the antigen appears again. *See also* **immunity**.

backcross
The crossing of an F_1 hybrid (the first generation offspring of a cross between two parents) with an individual that is identical to one of its parents. It can be used to determine the genetic makeup (genotypes) of the original parents. In the most common backcross, a heterozygous (possessing two different **alleles** for the same **gene**) individual is backcrossed to a homozygous recessive (individual with two recessive alleles for the same gene) – backcrossing will reveal any recessive characteristics present in the original organism. *See also* **testcross**.

bacteriophage
A **virus** that attacks bacteria (also known as a phage). Virulent phages always destroy the host cell, whereas temperate phages can establish a stable relationship with the host. Many hundred different phages are known. They are widely used to transfer genetic material in **genetic engineering**.

bacterium
Any of a diverse group of microscopic single-celled organisms whose genetic material is not enclosed in a membrane-bounded **nucleus** (*see* **prokaryote**). Bacteria have a single **chromosome** – a circular **DNA** molecule. Many bacteria also have **plasmids**, separate circlets of genetic material. Most bacteria have a cell wall. Some bacteria are photosynthetic. Others obtain their energy from inorganic chemicals, or by decomposing organic materials. Bacteria usually reproduce by binary fission, and because this may occur approximately every 20 minutes, a single bacterium is potentially capable of producing 16 million copies of itself in a day. Bacteria are the most important group of organisms in the Kingdom Monera (the prokaryotes).

BASE PAIRS

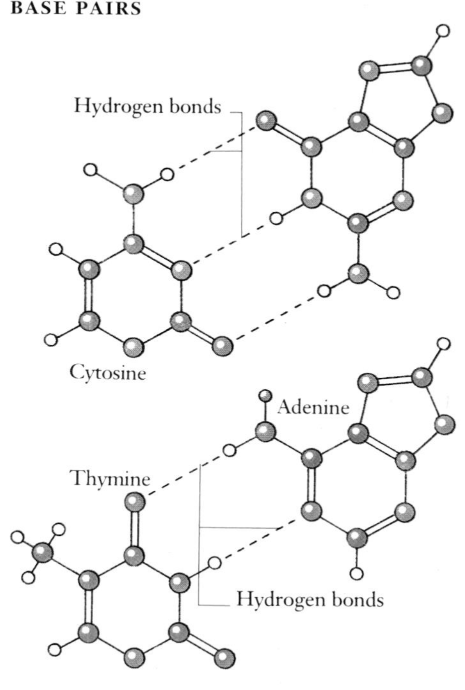

base
Any chemical substance that accepts protons or donates electrons. Bases can contain negative ions such as the hydroxide ion (OH^-) or be molecules such as ammonia (NH_3). Many organic compounds that contain nitrogen are bases. **Nucleic acids** contain the **nucleotide** bases **adenine**, **cytosine**, **guanine**, **thymine** and **uracil**.

base pairs
A pair of **nucleotide bases** that are joined to each other by hydrogen bonds. Classical base pairs always contain one **pyrimidine** (**thymine**, **cytosine** or **uracil**) and one **purine** (**adenine** or **guanine**) – the bases are said to be complementary to each other. Base pairing holds together the strands of double-stranded **DNA,** and in the case of some viruses, double-stranded **RNA**. The pairing of purine with pyrimidine maintains the constant diameter of the double helix. Pairing is a key process in the replication of DNA and in the synthesis (**transcription**) of **messenger RNA** using complementary DNA as a template during **protein synthesis**. The specificity of base pairing provides the basis for the **genetic code**.

CONNECTIONS

TRACKING DOWN THE MOLECULES **54**
MAKING THE MESSAGE **56**
PASSING ON THE MESSAGE **58**
TRANSLATING THE CODE **68**

binary fission
A form of **asexual reproduction** whereby a single-celled organism, such as an ameba, divides into two smaller, identical "daughter" cells. It can also occur in a few simple multicellular organisms, such as sea anemones.

biotechnology
The use of living organisms in the industrial and commercial manufacture of food, drugs or other products. The brewing and baking industries have long relied on yeast for fermentation, while dairies employ a range of bacteria and fungi to convert milk into cheese and yogurt. Various microorganisms are cultured to produce antibiotics. The techniques of **genetic engineering** are used to modify the DNA of single-celled organisms to enable cells to manufacture insulin and other drugs. Enzymes, whether extracted from cells or synthesized, are central to most biotechnological applications.

CONNECTIONS

FINDING THE GENES **128**
LIVING FACTORIES **130**
THE NEW FARMING REVOLUTION **132**

blastoderm
1 A flat disk of cells formed following cleavage of a heavily yolked egg (*see* **amniotic egg**). **2** A layer of cells formed inside the blastula (the early form of an animal embryo consisting of a sphere of cells around a central fluid-filled cavity).

blending inheritance
The now-discarded idea that parental characteristics become blended together in the offspring, and are inherited in blended form – in other words, that **alleles** do not remain discrete from one generation to the next. The logical conclusion of this theory is that the pool of inherited variability tends to be reduced with each successive generation, resulting in increasing uniformity.

bottleneck
The sudden reduction in the genetic variation within a population due to a significant decrease in population size. The survivors may have a different **gene frequency** from the ancestral population and from other populations of the species. Subsequent evolution may cause further genetic divergence.

breakage and reunion
A model of **recombination** (crossing over) that involves **chromatid** breakage, exchange of the broken fragments of chromatid and rejoining of the exchanged fragments to form complete recombinant chromatids during the prophase stage of **meiosis**.

breeding system
The combination of genetic and other **incompatibility** mechanisms that determine which animals or plants of a particular **species** or group of species mate with each other, hence controlling the **gene flow** in the **population**. A breeding system might be described by the XY/XX system of sex determination together with monogamy (having only one mate) or polygamy (having more than one mate); or the pattern of relatedness of animals in a breeding group (in lion prides, for example, the females are usually sisters, while the males are unrelated); or the system of chemical incompatibility that prevents pollen of a certain genotype from germinating on the stigma of a plant of the same or a similar genotype. *See* **inbreeding, outbreeding, heterostyly**.

callus
1 Undifferentiated tissue that forms at a damaged plant surface. Its grows over and around the wound, eventually covering the exposed area. **2** The mass of colorless, undifferentiated plant cells produced in the early stages of plant **tissue culture**. **3** Tissue that forms between the ends of a broken bone as it heals.

Cambrian explosion
The rapid increase in both numbers and diversity of **fossils** during the early Cambrian period. It was a period of diversification in fundamental body patterns rather than simple **speciation**: all but one of the major phyla, including the chordates (which include the vertebrates), were present by the end of the Cambrian period.

capsid
The protein coat or shell that surrounds the nucleic acid or nucleoprotein core of a **virus** particle. *See* **virus**.

carrier
An individual carrying a recessive **allele** for a disease or defect.

cDNA
See **complementary DNA**.

cell cycle
The cycle of events that constitutes vegetative growth and division in cells. The cell increases in mass, and roughly doubles its number of **organelles** and other cytoplasmic components, the **DNA** then replicates, and finally nuclear and cellular (cytoplasmic) division occurs. The events in the cell cycle al-

ways occur in the same order, and are regulated by factors both inside and outside the cell. In a typical **eukaryotic cell**, the cell cycle consists of the S phase (DNA replication), the G_2 phase (the period between the end of the DNA replication and the start of **mitosis**, the M phase (mitosis and cell division) and the G_1 phase (the period between cell division and the beginning of DNA replication). Resting (noncycling) cells are sometimes said to be in the G_0 phase.

CONNECTIONS
THE LIVING CELL **50**
PASSING ON THE MESSAGE **58**

cell division
The formation of two daughter cells from a single mother cell. The nucleus divides, followed by the formation of a **cell membrane** between daughter cell nuclei and (in plant, algal and bacterial cells) a new cell wall. In **meiosis**, associated with sexual reproduction, the daughter nuclei contain half the number of chromosomes of the mother cell. In **mitosis** (associated with growth, cell replacement or repair, or asexual reproduction), the daughter nuclei are identical to the original nucleus.

cell hybrid
A cell produced by fusing cells from individuals of different species *in vitro*. Hybrid cells from humans and mice are widely used in genetic and cancer research.

cell membrane
A selectively permeable membrane that surrounds the **cytoplasm** in **prokaryotic** and **eukaryotic cells**. The main components of the cell membrane are lipids (fatty substances) and **proteins**. It is thought that the lipid molecules form a double layer (bilayer) in which the protein molecules are wholly or partly embedded. The polar groups of the lipids form the hydrophilic (water-loving) outer surfaces of the membrane and their hydrocarbon groups form the hydrophobic (water-repelling) interior of the membrane. One of the main functions of the cell membrane is to regulate the composition of the cytoplasm by controlling the transport of ions and molecules in and out of the cell. The cell membrane is a fluid, dynamic, constantly changing structure continually adapting to the needs of the cell and to stimuli from its surroundings.

central dogma
The basic principle of genetics that genetic information flows from **DNA** to **RNA** to **protein**, and not vice versa. The central dogma rules out the **inheritance of acquired characteristics**, which would require flow in the opposite direction.

centriole
A structure that acts as a focus for the **polymerization** (joining together) of **microtubules** to form specialized structures such as the mitotic and meiotic **spindles** (formed during nuclear division), the flagella of sperm and the flagella and cilia of various microorganisms. Each centriole consists of triplets of microtubules arranged in a hollow cylinder near the **nucleus**. Centrioles associated with spindle formation occur in pairs at right angles to each other in most animal cells, and in some plant and algal cells. They are not present in flowering plants. During the **cell cycle**, the centrioles replicate at the same time as the **DNA**. At the start of nuclear division the replicated centrioles migrate so that there is a pair at each pole of the developing spindle. *See* **meiosis** and **mitosis**.

centromere
A specialized, complex region of a **chromosome** with few or no **genes**. Under the microscope, it appears as a constriction in the chromosome. The centromere links together **sister chromatids**, and also contains a structure (the kinetochore) to which the spindle fibers are attached during **mitosis** and **meiosis**. The centromere therefore assists in the movement of chromosomes toward the poles.

CENTROMERE

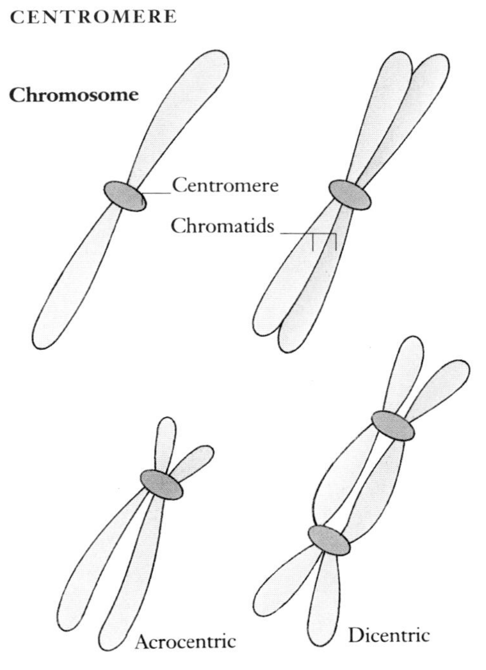

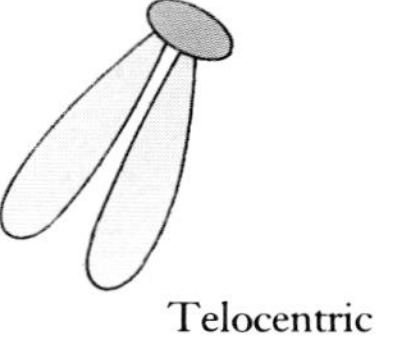

centrosome
A self-replicating body found in an area of clear **cytoplasm** near the **nucleus**. The centrosome, which consists of two centrioles and surrounding matrix material, organizes the microtubules of the spundle during nuclear division. Centrosomes are present in animal cells, and in the cells of some lower plants and algae.

characteristic
Any well-marked phenotypic feature that helps to distinguish one species from another. In genetics it is any readily defined feature that is transmitted from the parent to the offspring. *See* **phenotype**.

chiasma
The visible connection or crossover of two nonsister **chromatids** of **homologous chromosomes** (paired chromosomes) that is observed during prophase I in **meiosis**. Chiasmata result in genetic **recombination**.

chimera
An organism that contains two or more types of genetically different tissue. Chimeras may arise naturally, or they may be created in the laboratory. *See also* **genetic engineering, mosaic** and **transgenic**..

chloroplast
The structure (**organelle**) within a plant or algal cell which contains the green pigment chlorophyll. Chloroplasts are the site of **photosynthesis**. Their structure is typically flattened and disk-like, with a double unit membrane enclosing the stroma, a gel-like matrix. Within the stroma are stacks of membrane vesicles (thylakoids), which bear the chlorophyll. These are the site of the light-absorbing (photochemical) reactions of photosynthesis. The fixation of carbon from carbon dioxide and other synthesis reactions take place in the stroma, which contains the **enzymes** and storage products of photosynthesis.

chloroplast DNA (ctDNA)
DNA found in a **chloroplast** that normally exists in the form of circular molecules that lack **histone**. Each chloroplast contains multiple ctDNA molecules. *See also* **extranuclear gene** and **histone**.

CHLOROPLAST

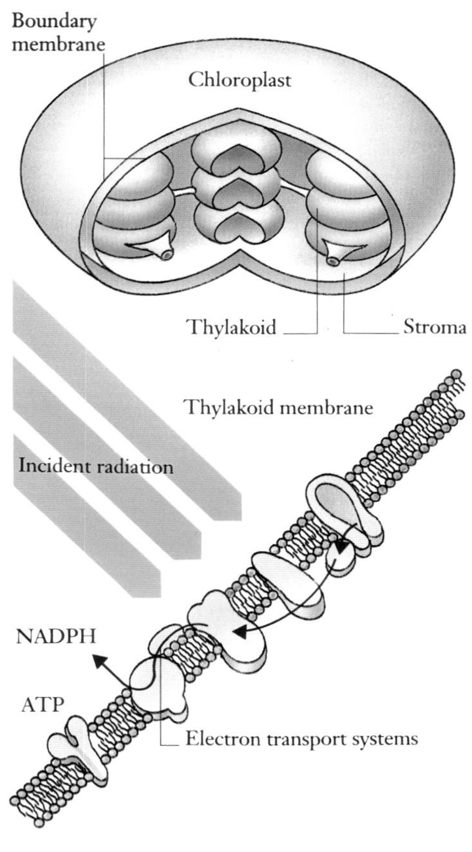

chorionic villus sampling
Removing fetal cells from the chorionic villi of the placenta in the 6th to 10th week of pregnancy to test for genetic abnormalities.

chromatid
One of the two halves of a duplicated eukaryotic (*see* **eukaryote**) **chromosome** that is joined to a **sister chromatid** by a common **centromere**. When the centromere divides in the anaphase of **mitosis** or the second stage of **meiosis**, the sister chromatids become separate chromosomes. Each chromatid consists of a single double-stranded **DNA** molecule associated with **proteins**.

chromatin
The DNA-protein complex (nucleoprotein) that makes up **chromosomes**. Two types of chromatin can be distinguished in the interphase (nondividing) nucleus: heterochromatin, in which the nucleoprotein fibers are very densely packed, and euchromatin, in which the fibers are less densely packed.

chromomeres
Small, bead-like stainable thickenings, visible during the **prophase** of **mitosis**, that are arranged linearly along a **chromosome**.

chromosomal aberration
An abnormality in the structure or number of **chromosomes** in a cell. A chromosome may have lost a section (deletion); a segment may have moved to another site on the same chromosome or a different chromosome (translocation); a segment may take up a reverse orientation at the same site (inversion) or it may be duplicated (duplication).

chromosome
A thread-like structure in the **eukaryotic cell** nucleus that carries the genetic information (**genes**). Each chromosome consists of a long, much-folded and coiled molecule of **DNA** associated with a highly structured complex of **proteins** (*see* **histones**). The circular DNA molecule of a **prokaryote cell** is sometimes called the bacterial chromosome. Only a few proteins are associated with it. The point on a chromosome where a particular gene occurs is known as its locus. The cells (excluding the sex cells or **gametes**) of most higher organisms contain two copies of each chromosome (diploid) but the sex cells (gametes) contain only one copy (haploid).

CONNECTIONS
INSIDE THE NUCLEUS 52
TRACKING DOWN THE MOLECULES 54
PASSING ON THE MESSAGE 58
SEXUAL REPRODUCTION 78
SICKNESS IN THE GENES 136

chromosome map
A diagrammatic representation of a **chromosome** showing the relative positions of the various known **genes** and other DNA markers located on that particular chromosome. Also known as a linkage map.

cistron
A section of **DNA** that codes for one **polypeptide**.

cladistics
A method of biological classification that assigns organisms to taxonomic groups by assessing the extent to which they share characteristics. Taxonomic groups (species, genus, family) are termed clades. Cladograms are diagrammatic representations of the relationship between clades. Cladistics was first formulated by the German biologist W. Hennig in 1950 and is based on the general principles of genealogy and the application of phylogenetic systematics. However, it does not necessarily express evolutionary (phylogenetic) relationships: different relationships are obtained according to the number and choice of characteristics.

cladogram
A branching diagram that shows the relationships between organisms based on which characteristics they do or do not share. In general, members of a group share a more recent common ancestor with each other than with members of other groups, but the system is not infallible. For a truly phylogenetic classification, a very large number of characters would need to be assessed. *See* **cladism** and **phylogeny**.

class
A category of classification that consists of similar or closely related orders. Similar classes are grouped into a phylum in animals and a division (or phylum) in plants.

classification
The organization of all known organisms into a hierarchy of groups on the basis of their similarities in biochemical, anatomical, physiological, genetic or other characteristics (*see* **comparative biology**). The basic grouping is a species, several of which may constitute a genus, which in turn are grouped into families, and so on up through orders, classes, and phyla (formerly called divisions in plants) to kingdoms. The number of similarities between members of the group decreases with each higher level of the hierarchy. Classification is thought to mirror the evolutionary relationships between organisms. The science of classification is known as taxonomy.

CONNECTIONS
HOW SPECIES ARISE 104
SPECIES AND OTHER KIN 30

cleavage
1 The breaking of DNA at specific sites by using a method such as **restriction endonuclease** enzymes. **2** The process by which the **cytoplasm** of a cell is divided by an infurrowing of the cell membrane during **cell division**. **3** The process by which a **zygote** divides to give rise to the cells of the early embryo (*see* **sexual reproduction**). In "determinate" cleavage, the cell division follows a set pattern that allows the cell lineages to be traced. *See also* **fate map**.

cline
The gradient of variation in the genetic makeup or phenotypic characters (*see* **phenotype**) of a given **species** across a specified geographical area. An example is the variation in genetically programmed height and form of a plant species across the zone from a coast uphill to a mountain top.

clone
1 Any one of a group of cells or organisms that are derived from a single ancestral cell or individual by asexual cell division (**mitosis**) and are often genetically identical. **2** A set of recombinant DNA molecules containing the same inserted sequence.

coding strand
The strand of a double-stranded **DNA** molecule that acts as a template for **messenger RNA** synthesis (that is, the strand complementary to messenger RNA). *See* **anticoding strand**.

codominant allele
An allele controlling a particular characteristic that fails to show the recessive–dominant relationship. Instead, aspects of both may show in the phenotype of **heterozygotes**. The snapdragon (*Antirrhinum*) shows codominance in respect to color: if two contrasting alleles of the gene for petal color, one for red petals and the other for white, occur in the same plant, the petals are pink.

codon
A sequence of three consecutive **bases** on a **DNA** or **mRNA** molecule that specify a particular **amino acid** to be inserted into the **protein** coded for by that section of the **nucleic acid**. Conventionally, the mRNA bases are referred to as codons. Each codon is specific to a particular amino acid. Some amino acids are coded by more than one codon. A few codons are nonsense codons, with no known function. A few serve as start or stop signals during the transcription and translation stages of **protein synthesis**.

coevolution
The **evolution** of two or more interacting **species** in which evolutionary changes in one species alter the **selection pressures** acting on the other species, causing it also to evolve, usually in ways that reinforce the relationship between the species. An example is the evolution of complex flower structures together with their highly specialized insect pollinators.

community
An assemblage of interacting plants, animals and other organisms living within a circumscribed area. Communities are usually named by reference to a dominant feature such as characteristic plant species (a beechwood community) or a prominent physical feature (a freshwater pond community).

comparative biology
The branch of biology dealing with the differences and similarities between organisms. It looks for fundamentally similar structures which may indicate a common ancestor. Such structures are described as homologous. Comparative biology plays an important part in evolutionary theories, initially through the study of comparative anatomy and more recently through the use of molecular biology and immunology techniques.

competition
The interaction between two or more organisms, or groups of organisms, that use a common resource that is in short supply. Competition invariably results in a reduction in the numbers of one or both competitors, and in **evolution** contributes both to the decline of certain species and to the evolution of **adaptations**.

CONNECTIONS

EVOLUTION BY NATURAL SELECTION **88**
THE GENETICS OF POPULATIONS **108**

complementary DNA (cDNA)
DNA produced by the reverse transcription (using the RNA molecule as template) of an **RNA** molecule, usually **messenger RNA**, using a **reverse transcriptase** enzyme. Some RNA-containing viruses naturally synthesize DNA from RNA after they invade living cells. cDNAs are commonly used to clone **genes** (*see* **clone**); segments of mRNA containing the desired gene are converted to cDNA by reverse transcriptase.

CONVERGENT EVOLUTION

Dolphin

Shark

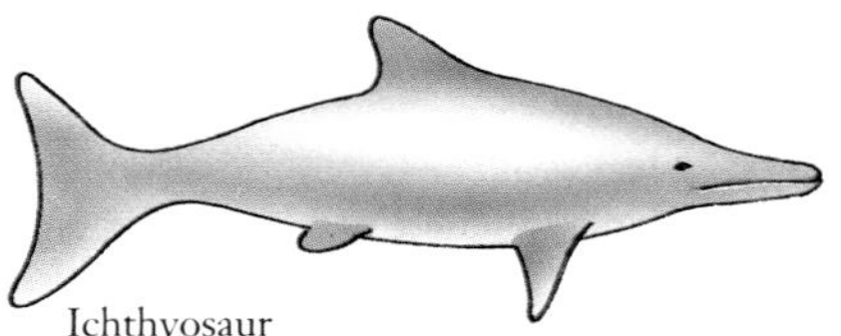
Ichthyosaur

congenital
Present at birth. The term is commonly used in the context of congenital diseases, which are not necessarily genetic in origin; a baby may contract congenital herpes as it passes through its mother's birth canal, and deformities may be due to the effect of drugs such as thalidomide on the developing embryo.

conjugation
1 The bacterial equivalent of **sexual reproduction**. A fragment of **DNA** from one bacterium is passed along a thin tube, the pilus, into the cell of another bacterium. **2** A form of sexual reproduction found in some fungi and algae, in which non-motile cells fuse together.

convergent evolution
Evolution in which groups of organisms that are only distantly related tend to evolve similar structures as **adaptations** to a similar **habitat** or way of life. The groups show no evidence of a common ancestry, so the similarities are said to be analogous rather than homologous. Sharks (fish), dolphins (mammals) and icthyosaurs (extinct reptiles that resembled dolphins) provide a good example of convergent evolution.

creationism
A theory that claims, as stated in the Bible, that the world was created by a supernatural being not more than 6000 years ago, and that **species** have separate origins and are unchanging. Developed in response to Darwin's theory of **evolution**, it is not recognized by most scientists as factual.

crossing over
A recombination process that occurs during **meiosis** or **mitosis**. While the **chromosomes** are lying alongside each other in pairs, each partner may twist around the other and exchange corresponding segments of **chromatids**. **Chiasmata** (temporary joins) are evidence of crossing over. It is an important source of genetic **variation**. *See* **recombination**.

CONNECTIONS

SEXUAL REPRODUCTION **78**
CROSSOVER AND LINKAGE **82**

cross-pollination
In gymnosperms (cone-bearing plants) and angiosperms (flowering plants), the transfer of pollen from the male reproductive organs to the receptive part of the female reproductive organ on a different plant of the same species. *See* **self-pollination**.

cyclic AMP
Adenosine 3',5'-cyclic monophosphate. Cyclic AMP plays an important role in the activation of **genes** and cellular processes in response to hormone signals.

cytokinesis
The events that occur as the **cytoplasm** (as opposed to the **nucleus**) divides during cell division. These events include the distribution of **organelles** and cytoplasm between newly forming daughter cells, and sometimes also the synthesis of new cell wall material for the daughter cells. In animal cells, the **cell membrane** develops a more or less circular furrow which gradually constricts the cell into two (cleavage). In plant and algal cells, there is no such furrow: new membrane and cell wall deposits form and coalesce along the plane of cleavage.

cytoplasm
The material making up all of the cell apart from the **nucleus** or **nucleoid**. It includes all the **organelles**, such as the **mitochondria** and **chloroplasts**, but often cytoplasm is used to refer to the jellylike matter in which the organelles are embedded (correctly termed the cytosol). In many cells, the cytoplasm is made up of two parts: the ectoplasm (or plasmagel), a dense gelatinous outer layer concerned with cell movement, and the endoplasm (or plasmasol), a more fluid inner part where most of the organelles are found.

cytoplasmic inheritance
Inheritance which is governed or influenced by **genes** located in the **mitochondria** or **chloroplasts** within the **cytoplasm** rather than in the **nucleus**. They are not governed by Mendelian laws of segregation and assortment. This type of inheritance is also known as extrachromosomal inheritance and non-Mendelian inheritance.

cytosine
A **pyrimidine** base in **DNA** and **RNA** that pairs with **guanine**. *See* **base** and **base pairs**.

cytoskeleton
The matrix of **protein** filaments and tubules in the **cytoplasm** of **eukaryotic cells**. It gives the cell definite shape and is involved in cell movement, organizing of new membrane and cell wall material, and the formation of the **spindle** during nuclear division.

Darwinism
A theory of **evolution** proposed by the English natural scientist Charles Robert Darwin (1809–82). His main argument, now known as the theory of **natural selection**, concerned the variation existing between members of a sexually reproducing population. According to Darwin, those members with variations better fitted to the environment would be more likely to survive and breed (*see* **survival of the fittest**), subsequently passing on these favorable characteristics to their offspring. Over time the genetic make-up of the population would change accordingly and, given enough time, a new **species** would form. Thus existing species would have originated by evolution from other species. *See* **neo-Darwinism**.

CONNECTIONS

EVOLUTION AND VARIATION **86**
EVOLUTION BY NATURAL SELECTION **88**
THE GENETICS OF POPULATIONS **108**

degeneracy
The term applied to a **genetic code** in which a particular **amino acid** is coded for by two or more **codons** (triplets of bases on DNA or RNA).

deletion
A **chromosome aberration** in which part of a **chromosome** has been lost, or a **point mutation** in which a single **base pair** has been lost from a DNA molecule.

deme
A local population of interbreeding organisms. Different demes of the same **species** are not necessarily separated by any physical barriers.

denaturation (DNA)
The breakdown of double-stranded **DNA** into randomly folded single-stranded DNA molecules as a result of high temperatures (around 80°C). This happens because the bonds between the **bases** of the double helix are weakened, producing complete unravelling of the molecule.

denaturation (protein)
Irreversible changes to the structure of the **polypeptide** chains of proteins, usually caused by changes in pH or temperature, by radiation or by chemical treatments. Heat will destroy the complex structure of **enzymes**, so that the usual interactions between enzyme and substrate can no longer occur. *See* **active site**.

deoxyribonucleic acid
See **DNA**.

derived traits
In **cladistics**, traits that distinguish one group of organisms from other groups descended from the same ancestor. The traits appeared after the groups diverged.

diakinesis
The later part of prophase 1 in **meiosis**, when the **chromosomes** are highly condensed and well separated from each other. *See* **condensation**.

dicentric chromosome
See **centromere**.

differentiation
The changes that are undergone by developing cells, tissues and organs as they become specialized for particular functions. Differentiation occurs during embryonic growth and development, during regeneration and repair of damaged tissues, and during the secondary growth of higher plants.

dioecious
Describing an organism in which the male and female reproductive structures appear in different individuals, as in most animals. *See also* **monoecious**.

diploid
Having two sets of **chromosomes** in each cell. In sexually reproducing species, one set of chromosomes is derived from each parent. The gametes, or sex cells, of each parent are haploid (have only one set of chromosomes), so the **zygote** formed by **fertilization** is diploid. Most organisms with **eukaryotic cells** are diploid. Exceptions include some lower plants and algae, and certain castes of social insects.

CONNECTIONS

SEXUAL REPRODUCTION **78**
MENDEL'S RBEAKTHROUGH **80**

directional evolution
An outmoded theory of **evolution** that proposes that evolution occurs along a predetermined path. The idea was particularly attractive to the creationists who followed the idea of a divine plan. *See* **creationism** and **Darwinism**.

directional selection
Selection that causes a change in the **gene** (**allele**) frequencies in a **population** in a steady, consistent direction, so that for a particular trait **phenotypes** at one end of the range of **variation** become commoner than the intermediate forms. An example is selection which leads to an increase in body size. Directional selection is used in **artificial selection**. *See* **selective breeding**.

DISRUPTIVE SELECTION

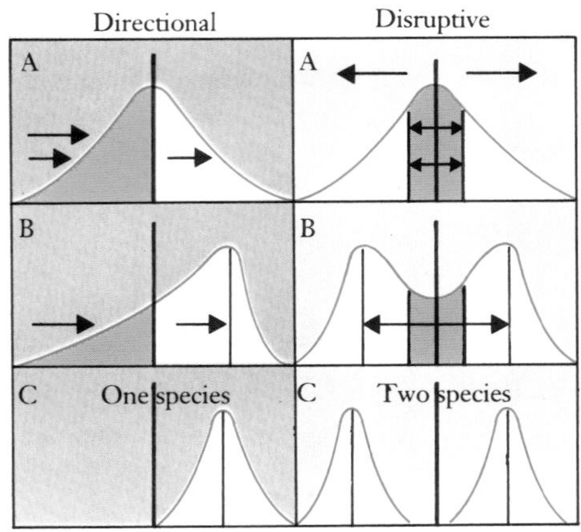

disjunction
The separation of **chromosomes** during **anaphase** of **mitosis** or **meiosis** and their movement toward the poles of the **spindle**. *See* **nondisjunction**.

disruptive selection
A form of **natural selection** that increases the number of individuals displaying two extremes of a trait, but acts against individuals showing intermediate forms. This gives rise to two distinct groups in the population, showing different phenotypes, and may lead to **speciation** if selection acts on such traits as breeding season. *See also* **directional selection** and **sexual selection**.

divergent evolution
1 The increasing differences in **allele** frequencies that occur over time between two reproductively isolated **populations** of a **species. 2** The **evolution** of closely related species in different directions, often as a result of diverging life-styles, ultimately producing two very distinct species. *See* **reproductive isolation, convergent evolution**.

DNA (deoxyribose nucleic acid)
A large complex molecule that contains, in chemically coded form, all the information needed by a living organism. It is a double-stranded **nucleic acid** that forms the basis of genetic inheritance in virtually all living organisms. In organisms other than bacteria it is organized into **chromosomes** and contained in the cell **nucleus**. DNA is made up of two chains of **nucleotide** subunits, each made up of deoxyribose sugar attached to a phosphate group and an organic base, which may be a **purine** (adenine or guanine) or **pyrimidine** (cytosine or thymine). Alternating sugars and phosphates form the backbone; the bases link up with each other (adenine with thymine, and cytosine with guanine) by hydrogen bonds to form base pairs that connect the two strands of the DNA molecule like the rungs of a twisted ladder. The sequence of these bases forms the **genetic code** that programs the development and activities of cells and organisms.

CONNECTIONS

TRACKING DOWN THE MOLECULES **54**
MAKING THE MESSAGE **56**
THE GENETIC CODE **66**
SWITCHING GENES ON AND OFF **70**

DNAase/DNase/deoxyribonuclease
An enzyme that hydrolyzes (breaks down) DNA. *See* **hydrolysis**.

DNA hybrid
A double-stranded **DNA** molecule synthesized in the laboratory, in which the two strands come from different sources. This process is used to find out the degree of similarity between the DNA from two different organisms – only complementary segments of DNA will pair up.

DNA library
A collection of cloned **DNA** fragments produced by cutting up DNA by means of **restriction endonucleases** (enzymes) and incorporating them into **plasmids, bacteriophages** or other structures for storage.

DNA polymerase
Any of a system of **enzymes** that catalyzes the synthesis of **DNA** from phosphorylated **nucleotide** units using a single strand of DNA as template (as occurs during DNA replication). Energy for the reaction comes from the breaking of the high-energy phosphate bonds as phosphate is eliminated. DNA polymerase ensures that the correct bases are paired; it is also used to correct mismatched base pairs. *See* **base pairs**.

DNA replicase system
The entire complex of 30 or more **enzymes** and specialized **proteins** required for biological **DNA replication**. Also known as the replisome.

domain
1 A geographical region containing plants or animals or having specific characteristics. **2** A segment of a **protein** that is responsible for a particular structure or function. The term is especially used for distinct regions of immunoglobulins (**antibodies**).

dominance hierarchy
1 A system of behavior and interactions in a group of animals in which certain individuals dominate or are dominated by other individuals. **2** The hierarchy of dominance of **alleles** for a particular characteristic which is determined by more than two alleles for the same gene locus (*see* **chromosome**). **B**lood groups in humans are an example, in which A and B are codominant (*see* **codominance**), but both are dominant to O.

ENDOCYTOSIS

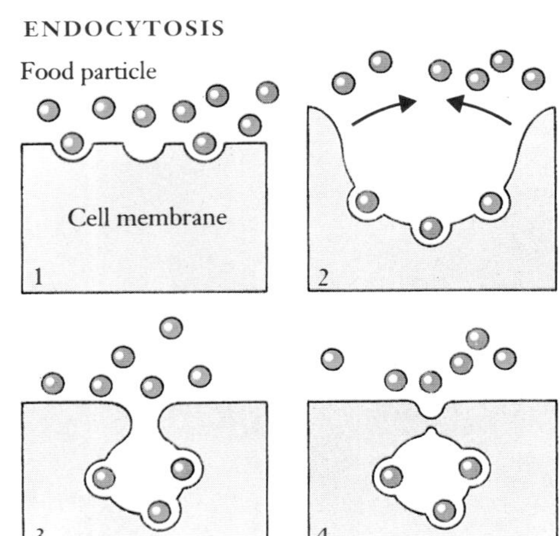

dominant
Describing one of a pair of **alleles** that is expressed over the other (the recessive allele), completely (complete dominance) or in part (incomplete dominance). *See* **codominant**.

CONNECTIONS

MENDEL'S BREAKTHROUGH **80**
CROSSOVER AND LINKAGE **82**

duplication
A **chromosome aberration** in which part of a chromosome has been repeated (*see* **chromosome aberration**), or a **point mutation** in which a single **base pair** is repeated in the **DNA** molecule.

electrophoresis
The movement of charged particles in an electric field through a fluid or gel. The technique is used to separate mixtures of charged particles, such as those produced during the quantitative and qualitative analysis of **proteins** and **nucleic acids**.

embryo
The early developmental stage of an animal, plant or multicellular alga following **fertilization** of an ovum (egg cell) or activation of an ovum by **parthenogenesis** (where an unfertilized egg develops). In animals the embryo exists either within an egg (where

it is nourished by food contained in the yolk) or, in most mammals, in the uterus (womb) of the mother. An egg may be laid at an early stage of development or may be retained inside the mother until hatching. In some invertebrates, such as water fleas and copepods, embryos may develop in a special pouch in or on the mother's body. In seed-bearing plants the embryo is in the seed.

endemic
1 Describing a **species**, **family** or other group of organisms found only in a specific geographical region and thought to have originated there. **2** Describing a disease permanently established in a particular area.

endocytosis
The intake of material into a cell by invagination of the **cell membrane**, which forms a vacuole (membrane-bounded, fluid-filled sac) around it. The material may enter the cell in the fluid enclosed by the vacuole or attached to its membrane. There are two common forms: in phagocytosis, foreign or food particles are engulfed and broken down as the vacuole fuses with a lysosome (a membrane sac containing enzymes); in pinocytosis, the cell engulfs a small droplet of liquid.

endoplasmic reticulum
A complex double-unit membrane network of tubes, channels and flattened sacs that form compartments within **eukaryotic cells** and is continuous with the **nuclear membrane**. It stores, modifies and transports proteins in cells and also carries various **enzymes** needed for the synthesis of fats. **Ribosomes** carrying out **protein synthesis** are attached to parts of the endoplasmic reticulum. *See* **rough endoplasmic reticulum** and **smooth endoplasmic reticulum**.

ELECTROPHORESIS

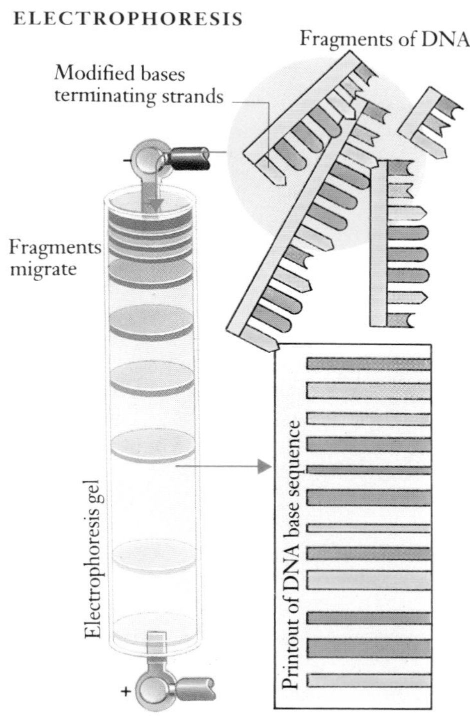

end-product inhibition
The inhibition of an early stage in a series of metabolic reactions by the end product of the sequence. The end product may bind to an allosteric enzyme (*see* **allosteric control**) or it may affect the switching on or off of a **gene** controlling enzyme production, for instance by binding with its **promoter**.

enzyme
A large, complex **protein** molecule produced by cells that acts as a catalyst for the chemical reactions necessary for life (metabolic reactions). During these reactions one or more substances (substrates) are converted into one or more different substances (products). Each chemical reaction requires its own enzyme. The substrate fits into a slot of complementary shape and charge distribution in the enzyme molecule (the active site), forming an enzyme-substrate complex that lasts until the substrate is altered or split, after which the enzyme can fall away. The activity and efficiency of enzymes are influenced by temperature, pH and other factors.

CONNECTIONS

PROTEINS AND AMINO ACIDS 64
TRANSLATING THE CODE 68
SWITCHING GENES ON AND OFF 70

episome
A **plasmid** that can exist independently in host cells or integrate into the host cell chromosome.

epistasis
A phenomenon that occurs when an **allele** of one *gene* suppresses the **phenotype** caused by an allele of a different gene. If alleles *b* and *a* (of genes *B* and *A*) produce different phenotypes from each other, but *ab* heterozygotes show only the phenotype of *b*, then *b* is said to be epistatic to *a*. Epistasis often indicates that genes *A* and *B* interact in a regulatory genetic pathway.

estrus cycle
The cycle of **hormone** production that occurs in female mammals of reproductive age, preparing the body for pregnancy mainly through the control of the hormones estrogen and progesterone. At the beginning of the cycle, a Graafian (egg) follicle develops in the ovary and the inner wall of the uterus forms a spongy lining. The egg is released from the ovary and the lining of the uterus becomes filled with blood vessels in preparation for implantation of the embryo. If **fertilization** does not occur, the corpus luteum (remains of the Graafian follicle) degenerates, and the lining breaks down and is shed.

EVE HYPOTHESIS

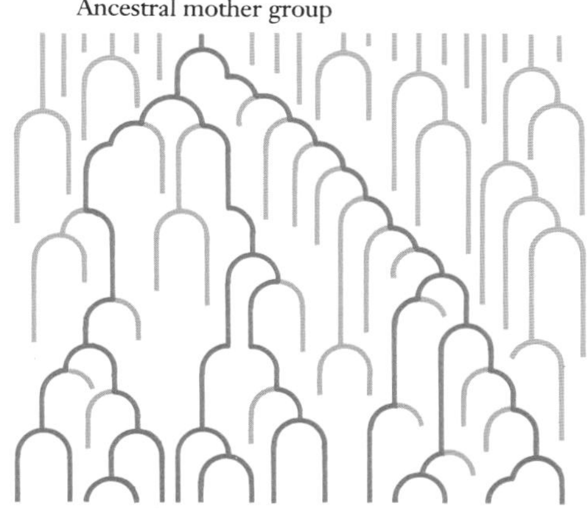

Eubacteria
A kingdom of **prokaryotes** that includes all bacteria not classified as Archaebacteria. Members of the two kingdoms are differentiated mainly on the basis of their **ribosomal RNA** and lipids. Cyanobacteria, mycoplasmas, enterobacteria, **chloroplasts** and most Gram-positive bacteria are Eubacteria.

euchromatin
The regions of **chromosome** material that are not condensed during **interphase** (when the cell **nucleus** is not dividing), but condensed during nuclear division, reaching maximum condensation during interphase. They contain the bulk of the genes.

eukaryote
An organism whose cells possess a clearly defined **nucleus** bounded by a membrane, within which **DNA** is arranged in distinct **chromosomes**. Eukaryotic cells may also contain **mitochondria**, **chloroplasts** and other membrane-bounded structures (organelles) that are lacking in the cells of other organisms (**prokaryotes**). Eukaryotes include all organisms except bacteria and cyanobacteria, which are prokaryotes.

Eve hypothesis
The hypothesis that modern humans are all descended from a single origin in Africa about 150,000–200,000 years ago. It is based on studies of **mitochondrial DNA** (mtDNA), which is passed on only from mother to offspring (sperm do not con-

tribute any cytoplasm to the **zygote**). mtDNA accumulates **mutations** about 10 times faster than nuclear DNA, so it is particularly useful for tracing evolutionary relationships. The term "Eve hypothesis" is derived from the mistaken popular idea that all humans descended from a single ancestral female, nicknamed "mitochondrial Eve". In fact, "Eve" is more likely to have been a small population of about 10,000 individuals.

evolution

The process of biological change by which organisms come to differ from their ancestors. The idea of gradual evolution (as opposed to **creationism**) gained acceptance in the 19th century but remained controversial well into the 20th because it contradicted many traditional religious beliefs. The English naturalist Charles Darwin (1809–1882) assigned the major role in evolutionary change to **natural selection** (that is, environmental pressures acting through competition for resources) acting on randomly occurring **variations** (*see* **Darwinism**). The current theory of evolution (*see* **neo-Darwinism**) combines Darwin's theory with the genetic theories of Austrian biologist Gregor Mendel (*see* **Mendelian inheritance**) and Hugo de Vries's discovery of genetic **mutation**. **Sexual selection** (selection based on mating preference and success) and chance, producing **genetic drift**, may play a large part in deciding which **genes** become characteristic of a population. Evolutionary change can have long periods of relative stability interspersed with periods of rapid change (**punctuated equilibrium**).

EVOLUTIONARY TREE

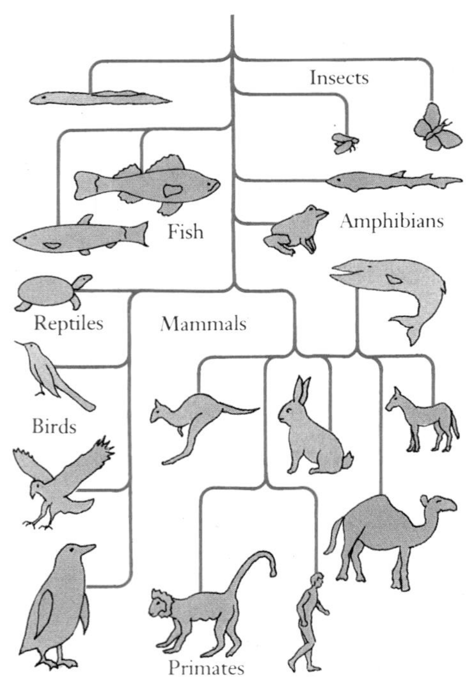

CONNECTIONS

evolutionary tree

A diagram representing the **evolution** of a group of related **species**, in which the length of a branch represents the degree to which different species or groups are related. In **molecular evolution** and in trees derived from analysis of **DNA**, the branch length can represent the number of **mutations** by which the different species differ in respect of a given **protein** or DNA segment.

excision-repair systems

A process for the repair of damage to only one strand of a double-stranded **DNA** molecule (for example, a missing **base**). The damaged region is removed and the gap is filled by the appropriate bases, by means of a **DNA polymerase** using the "good" strand as a template. The damaged section is then sealed using the enzyme **DNA ligase**.

exocytosis

The way in which material is discharged from a cell by the fusion of internal vesicles with the **cell membrane**. *See* **endocytosis**.

exon

A segment of **DNA** that is transcribed and translated into a **protein**. Exons code for particular **polypeptide** chains or their **messenger RNA** transcript (essential for **protein synthesis). Introns** may be transcribed to mRNA, but are excised before the mRNA leaves the **nucleus**.

extinction

The complete disappearance of a **species** or other group of organisms, which occurs when its reproduction rate falls below its mortality rate. In the past, most extinctions occurred because species were unable to adapt quickly enough to a naturally changing environment. Today, most environmental change is due to human activity. Mass extinctions are episodes during which whole groups of species have become extinct, the best known being the extinction of the dinosaurs, other large reptiles and various marine invertebrates about 65 million years ago. Another mass extinction occurred about 10,000 years ago when many giant species of mammal died out. This is known as the Pleistocene overkill because their disappearance was probably hastened by the hunting activities of prehistoric humans.

extranuclear genes

Genes that are not located on the bacterial chromosome or in the nucleus of a **eukaryotic cell**. In **prokaryotes** such genes are carried on **plasmids**, whereas in eukaryotes the genes are located in the **chloroplasts** and **mitochondria**. Also known as cytoplasmic genes and extrachromosomal genes.

F_1 generation

The first generation produced from a given genetic cross between two parental lines (which are referred to as the P generation).

F_2 generation

The second generation produced from interbreeding ("selfing") F_1 individuals.

family

A category used in the classification of organisms, consisting of one or more similar or closely related genera (*see* **genus**). Similar families are grouped into orders. In botany, families are sometimes called natural orders.

fate map

A spatial plan of the unspecialized cells in an embryo which shows their ultimate destinations in specific tissues. *See* **differentiation**.

F_1 F_2 GENERATION

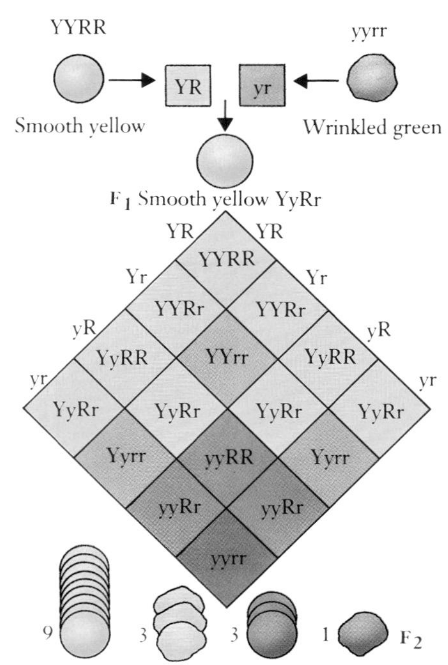

F factor (fertility factor)
A **plasmid** (segment of double-stranded **DNA** that may be independent of or incorporated into the bacterial chromosome) that determines how a bacterial cell will behave during **conjugation** (sexual reproduction). An F factor must be present for the cell to act as a donor (F^+) of **DNA** during conjugation. Cells lacking an F factor act as recipients (F^-) of DNA.

fertilization
The fusion of two **gametes** (haploid sex cells) of different sex or mating type to form a diploid **zygote**. *See* **sexual reproduction**.

fingerprinting (DNA)
A technique used to distinguish the **DNA** of different individuals from the same species. At various sites on the **genome** there are sets of similar repeated sequences. The number of repeats at each site (and often the exact sequence of the repeats) varies widely among different individuals, but a probe can be prepared that will hybridize with a common "core sequence" of each repeat. The DNA is cut into fragments by a **restriction enzyme** and subjected to gel **electrophoresis**; then the probe is applied to the gel. The pattern of bands that results is characteristic of only one particular individual – hence the likeness to fingerprinting. The technique is sensitive enough to distinguish close relatives in the same population, and has been applied to forensic work and paternity testing, and to studying the breeding behavior and genetic variation of populations of wild animals.

CONNECTIONS

THE GENETIC CODE **66**
TRANSLATING THE CODE **68**

fitness
1 The degree to which an organism is adapted to the environment and is therefore successful in the struggle for survival. **2** In Darwin's theory of **evolution**, the extent to which an individual passes on its **genes** (a function of how long it survives after reaching breeding age, how successfully it breeds and how well its offspring survive). **3** A measure of the success with which a genetically determined character can spread in future generations. The normal character is assigned a fitness of one and variants (determined by other **alleles**) are assigned fitness values relative to this. Those with fitness greater than one will spread more rapidly and will ultimately replace the normal allele; those with fitness less than one will gradually die out. *See* **adaptation** and **Darwinism**.

fossil
The remains or traces of an animal, plant or other organism preserved in rocks.

fossil record
The evidence for the increase in diversity and **speciation** of life on Earth supplied from the study of **fossils**.

founder effect
The establishment of a new colony of a **species** from a small number of migrants. The founders represent only a small sample of the **gene pool** to which they belong, and **natural selection** acting on this restricted genetic **variation** produces a gene frequency that differs from that of the ancestral population. *See* **bottleneck**.

frameshift mutation
A deletion or addition of one or two **bases** (or any number not divisible by three) of **DNA** which causes part of the coded information to be read in the wrong frame, thus changing all the subsequent **codons**.

G_1
Gap phase 1, the period between cell division and the start of **DNA replication** in a typical **eukaryotic cell** cycle. G_2, or gap phase 2, is the period between the end of DNA replication and the start of **mitosis** in a **eukaryotic cell** cycle. *See* **cell cycle**.

gamete
A **haploid** sex cell of either the male (*see* **sperm**) or the female (*see* **ovum**) which fuses with its opposite number (that is, sperm with ovum) during **fertilization** to produce the **zygote**, which is **diploid**. *See also* **sexual reproduction**.

gametophyte
The phase in the life cycle of a plant or alga that reproduces sexually, producing **gametes**. It is usually **haploid**. *See* **alternation of generations**.

gene
The basic unit of inheritance that controls a characteristic of an organism. It can be considered a length of **DNA** organized in a very specific manner. The term, coined in 1909 by the Danish geneticist Wilhelm Johannsen (1857–1927), refers to the inherited factor that affects a characteristic (for example, eye color). It occurs at a particular point or locus on a particular **chromosome** and may have several variants (**alleles**), each specifying a particular form of that character (alleles for blue or brown eyes). In the 1940s, it was established that a gene could be identified with a particular length of DNA, which coded for a complete protein molecule, leading to the one-gene-one-enzyme principle. Later it was realized that proteins can be made up of several **polypeptide** chains, each with a separate gene, so this principle was modified to one-gene-one-polypeptide. The fundamental idea remains the same: genes produce their visible effects by coding for proteins; they control the structure of proteins via the **genetic code**, as well as the amounts produced and the timing. Some genes encode functional RNA molecules, for example ribosomal RNA and transfer RNA. Genes undergo **mutation** and **recombination** to produce the **variation** on which natural selection operates.

CONNECTIONS

PASSING ON THE MESSAGE **58**
THE GENETIC CODE **66**
TRANSLATING THE CODE **68**
SWITCHING GENES ON AND OFF **70**
LIFE'S BLUEPRINT UNFOLDS **72**

gene cluster
A cluster of functionally related genes. Each gene codes for a separate protein.

gene conversion
The conversion of one **allele** of a gene into another by a mistake during **DNA** replication or repair, so that a wrong **base** is incorporated into the DNA. This gives rise to an unexpected ratio of alleles when they segregate during **meiosis**. *See* **recombination** and **segregation**.

gene flow
The movement of genes between adjacent **populations** through meetings between migrants and residents, and the distribution of genes throughout each interbreeding population. Disruption of the gene flow through isolation may lead to the evolution of new species. *See* **isolating mechanism**.

gene frequency/allele frequency
The relative abundance of different **alleles** in a given **population.** It is usually calculated by dividing the number of loci at which the gene occurs by the number of loci at which it could occur and is expressed as a number between 0 and 1. *See* **locus** and **gene flow**.

gene library
A collection of cloned **DNA** fragments maintained in appropriate cells (usually in **plasmids** or incorporated into the DNA of the cells of microorganisms such as bacteria or yeasts). If it represents the entire **genome** of an organism, it is called a genomic library.

gene pool
All the **alleles** (gene variants) of the members of a given breeding **population** or **species** alive at a particular time within a clearly defined geographical area. Between the individuals there are variations in the **phenotype** and associated variations in the **genotype**. If the environment is stable, the gene pool is stable. However, if the environment changes, some phenotypes will be at an advantage (they will be selected) and some will be at a disadvantage (not selected). In this situation the gene pool will change; some alleles will become more frequent and others less frequent or even lost altogether.

gene therapy
The medical replacement of defective **genes** or the insertion of normal genes into living cells to compensate for a genetic defect (for example, where a defective gene fails to produce a necessary protein). The correct segment of **DNA** may be injected directly into the tissues in the hope that some cells will take it up and incorporate it; or the patient's cells can be removed from the body, cultured in the laboratory and the techniques of **genetic engineering** used to correct the genetic material. Cells can then be injected back into the original tissue in the hope that they will survive and reproduce. Gene therapy is most suitable for genetic blood diseases, because blood cells are easy to remove, grow well in tissue culture and will repopulate the bone marrow successfully when injected. While gene therapy may cure the patient, it cannot prevent the defect being passed on to offspring.

genetic code
The information for building proteins (the basic structural molecules of living matter), written in the genetic material (*see* **DNA**). A protein's uniqueness is determined by the linear sequence of **amino acids** which make up its component **polypeptides**. The four **nucleotides** that make up the **DNA** are arranged in groups of three along the length of the DNA strand. Each group (*see* **codon**) specifies a particular amino acid. This relationship between the sequence of bases and the sequence of amino acids is the basis of heredity. The genetic code is the same in almost all organisms, except for a few minor differences recently discovered in some protozoa and in **mitochondrial DNA**. *See* **protein synthesis**.

CONNECTIONS

PASSING ON THE MESSAGE **58**
THE GENETIC CODE **66**

genetic counseling
Guidance given to individuals at risk of producing genetically abnormal offspring. A genetic counselor may look at the family history of a couple who are considering having a baby and advise them of any genetic risk. Genetic counseling also employs various techniques (*see* **chorionic villus sampling** and **amniocentesis**) to identify genetic abnormalities before birth.

genetic drift
The changes in the frequency with which different **alleles** occur in a given **population**. Genetic drift is the result of random **mutations** and random mating within the population. Genetic drift may be an important evolutionary mechanism in small or isolated populations. *See* **founder principle, bottleneck, evolution** and **speciation**.

genetic engineering
The manipulation of genetic material by biochemical techniques such as introducing new **DNA**, usually by means of a virus or **plasmid** (*see* **vector**). The purpose can be research into cell function and reproduction or to breed specific plants, animals or microorganisms. Organisms that include an added foreign gene are said to be transgenic. Practical applications include the production of growth hormone, insulin and other hormones, hepatitis-B vaccine and interferon by transgenic animals or genetically engineered microorganisms. Basic techniques include cutting and recombining DNA in the laboratory, producing new combinations of **genes**, incorporating or deleting segments of genetic material, and forming hybrid cells in which the DNA may be derived from two individuals of the same or different species.

CONNECTIONS

FINDING THE GENES **128**
LIVING FACTORIES **130**
THE NEW FARMING REVOLUTION **132**

genetic isolation
An isolating mechanism that results from genetic differences in organisms even though mating may be possible. Gametes may be prevented from fusing or, if **fertilization** does occur, the zygotes may fail to develop.

genetic load
The genetic burden (caused by mutations and other aberrations) that reduces the **fitness** of a **population**. Many disadvantageous **alleles** are present as recessive forms in **heterozygotes**, but may be expressed in subsequent generations.

genetic marker
An **allele** whose presence is detectable from its phenotypic expression or by molecular techniques and is used to identify chromosomes, cells or individuals with that allele.

genetics
The study of inheritance and its units (genes). It was founded by the Austrian monk Gregor Mendel (1822–1884), whose experiments with plants showed that inheritance takes place by means of discrete particles, later called genes. Before Mendel, the characteristics of the parents had been assumed to blend during inheritance. Mendel showed that genes remain intact, though their combinations change. Genetics has advanced greatly, first through breeding experiments and light-microscope observations (classical genetics), later by means of biochemical and electron-microscope studies (molecular genetics). The discovery of the structure of DNA and the cracking of the genetic code brought the possibility of manipulating genes (*see* **genetic engineering**).

genetic variation
The difference in the frequency of **alleles** among individuals of a **population**. Environmental influences and genetic variation produce the variation in **phenotype** seen in individuals of that population.

genome
The total information carried by the genetic code of an organism. The term is also used specifically (rather than the term chromosome) for the DNA of bacteria and viruses.

genotype
The genetic constitution of a cell or an individual. It may refer to all the **alleles** of the individual, or simply to the alleles of a particular **gene** or genes. *See* **phenotype**.

GENOTYPE

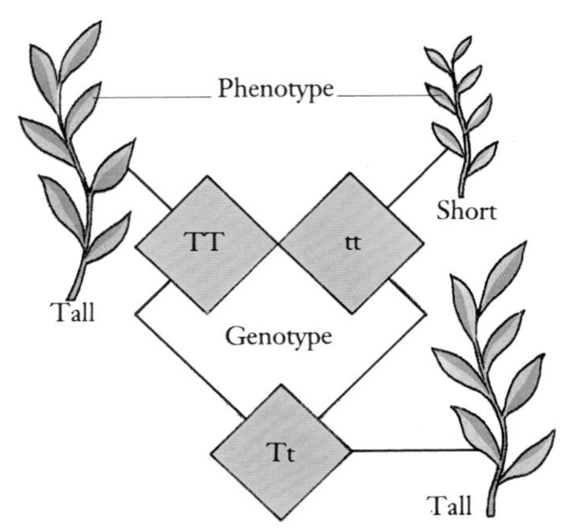

genus
A category used in the classification of organisms that consists of a number of similar or closely related **species**. Similar genera are grouped into families. *See* **classification**.

geographical isolation
The separation of an interbreeding **population** from the ancestral population by environmental barriers that prevent further interbreeding, such as water, forests, mountain ranges or continental drift. This is a common cause of **speciation**.

germ cell
A gamete (sperm or ova) of an animal, or one of the cells that give rise to it. *See* **somatic cell**.

germ plasm
The contents of the reproductive cells that are passed on unchanged to progeny and are thus unaffected by any changes undergone by the rest of the body. The theory of the continuation of germ plasm, published by August Weissmann (1834–1914) in 1886, rules out the possibility of inheriting acquired characteristics and has become an important principle of neo-Darwinism.

Golgi apparatus
A series of vesicles and folded membranous cavities (cisternae) in the **cytoplasm** of most **eukaryotic cells**. Its functions include forming **lysosomes**, modifying proteins to form glycoproteins, and forming secretory vesicles with which various macromolecules can be transported to the cell surface. It also plays a role in the formation of the cell wall.

gradualist theory
The theory of long-term gradual evolutionary change as envisaged by Darwin and supported by the **fossil record**. *See* **punctuated equilibrium**.

group selection
A form of **natural selection** that explains altruistic behavior that favors a family, population or species, rather than an individual.

guanine
A **purine base** that occurs in both **DNA** and **RNA**. Guanine molecules pair with **cytosine**. *See* **base pair**.

haploid
A eukaryotic (*see* **eukaryote**) individual or cell with only one copy of each **chromosome**. Examples are the gametes produced in **sexual reproduction** and the gametophyte stage of many plants. *See* **alternation of generations, diploid** and **meiosis**.

haplodiploidy (haploid-diploid mechanism)
A system of sex determination whereby females develop from fertilized eggs and are **diploid**, while males develop from unfertilized cells and are **haploid**, as in honeybees.

Hardy–Weinberg equilibrium
The theoretical relationship between **allele** frequencies and genotype frequencies within a population of a species, when there is no migration, immigration, mutation or selection. For alleles *A* and *a* at the same locus, the frequencies of the genotypes AA, Aa and aa is p^2, $2pq$ and q^2, where p is the frequency of A and q is the frequency of a.

hemophilia
Any of several inherited diseases in which normal blood clotting is impaired, prolonged bleeding results from even small wounds, and painful internal bleeding occurs without apparent cause. Hemophilias are nearly always sex-linked (*see* **sex linkage**). Males affected by the most common form are unable to synthesize Factor VIII, a protein involved in the clotting of blood.

heredity
The transmission of the genetic factors that determine the characteristics of individuals from one generation to another.

CONNECTIONS

MENDEL'S BREAKTHROUGH **80**
CROSSOVER AND LINKAGE **82**
PATTERNS TO ORDER **84**

heritability
The extent to which a particular characteristic is determined by inheritance. Heritability can be expressed numerically as the ratio of the genotypic variation to the observed phenotypic variation.

hermaphrodite
1 An organism with both male and female reproductive organs – a common condition in plants and in some invertebrates, such as earthworms and snails. **2** A flowering plant which has both male and female reproductive organs present in the same flower. *See* **dioecious** and **monoecious**.

heterochromatin
In **eukaryote** cells, chromatin in which the nucleoprotein strands are densely packed (coiled). It includes the **centromere** and other parts of **chromosomes** where the DNA is not actively transcribed. *See* **transcription, chromatin** and **euchromatin**.

HETEROSTYLY

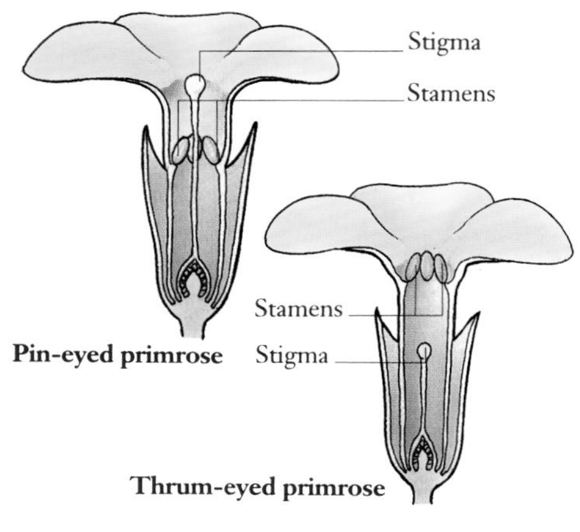

heterogametic sex
The sex having two or more different types of **sex chromosome**, producing **gametes** with different sex chromosomes. In humans, the male produces both X and Y sperms.

heterogamy
1 Reproduction by the fusion of two different **gametes**. **2** In an animal, the alternation between asexual and sexual reproduction in successive generations. For example, some aphids reproduce alternately by **parthenogenesis** and the fusion of gametes.

heterogeneity
Describes the situation in which different genotypes produce the same phenotype.

heterokaryon/heterokaryote
1 A cell or organism containing genetically different **nuclei** in a common **cytoplasm**. Fungi are an example. **2** A **somatic cell hybrid** containing separate nuclei from more than one species.

heterosis
The superiority of hybrid offspring over their parents for a given trait. *See* **hybrid vigor**.

heterostyly
The condition in which the flowers of different plants of the same species have styles and anthers of different relative lengths, preventing self-pollination and encouraging cross-pollination. *See* **cross-pollination**.

heterozygous
An organism having two different **alleles** for a trait. In homozygous organisms, by contrast, both chromosomes carry the same allele. In an **outbreeding** population an individual organism is generally heterozygous for some **genes** but homozygous for others.

heterozygote
An individual whose **chromosomes** contain different **alleles** for a given **gene** locus. Heterozygotes produce more than one kind of **gamete** for a particular **locus**. *See also* **homozygote**.

histone
Any of a group of basic **proteins**, low in molecular weight, rich in the **amino acids** arginine and/or lysine, that form a complex with **DNA**. They are the major component of **chromosomes** in cells of **eukaryotes,** and are involved in condensing and coiling of chromosomes during cell division.

homeobox
A characteristic type of DNA sequence, found in a group of homeotic genes that regulate the assignment of spatial identity by groups of cells and tissues during development. The homeobox encodes the homeodomain region of the protein product. Homeobox sequences are not all identical but share many features, even between widely differing animal species. *See* **homeotic gene** and **homeodomain protein**.

homeodomain protein
A protein encoded by a gene containing a **homeobox**. The homeodomain is a 60-amino-acid region that is involved in the DNA-binding function of the homeodomain protein, thus mediating the protein's ability to regulate expression of other genes.

homeotic gene
A **gene** that controls other genes involved in the organization of body tissues during development. A **mutation** in a homeotic gene results in dramatic disruptions. For example, the *antennipedia* mutant in the fruitfly *Drosophila* causes the head to have legs instead of antennae.

homogametic sex
The sex that has two identical **sex chromosomes** and thus produces gametes that are all alike with regard to the sex chromosomes. In humans, for example, the female (XX) produces only X ova.

homokaryon
1 A cell or organism that contains more than one genetically identical nucleus in a common cytoplasm. **2** A **somatic cell hybrid** which contains separate nuclei from the same species.

homologous
1 Describing structures in different species that, while serving different functions in the adult, are fundamentally similar, suggesting descent from a common ancestor. The forearms of humans and the wings of birds are examples. *See* **analogous**. **2** Having identical gene loci.

homologous chromosome/homolog
One of a pair of **chromosomes** (in a diploid eukaryote) that are morphologically alike and bear the same gene loci. Each chromosome of such a pair is the homolog of the other and pairs with it at **meiosis**. The X and Y **sex chromosomes** have different loci but behave like homologous chromosomes at meiosis. *See* **diploid** and **eukaryote**.

homozygote
An individual whose **chromosomes** contain identical **alleles** for a given **gene** locus. Homozygotes produce one kind of gamete for a particular locus. *See* **heterozygote**.

homozygous
An organism having two identical **alleles** for a given trait. Individuals homozygous for a trait always breed true for that trait: they produce offspring that resemble them in appearance (phenotype) when bred with another individual homozygous for the trait. Inbred (*see* **inbreeding**) varieties or species are homozygous for most traits. **Recessive alleles** are expressed only in the homozygous condition. *See also* **heterozygous**.

hormone
A chemical substance secreted in one part of the body, usually in small amounts, and transported to another part, where it produces a response.

hotspot
1 A region of **DNA** that is particularly susceptible to attack from **mutagens** or to **transposition**. **2** A geographical region with a very high diversity of **species.**

housekeeping genes
Genes that regulate the basal cell function.

hybrid
The offspring of a cross between individuals of different genotypes. Hybrids may be intraspecific (parents from the same species) or interspecific (parents from different speci). In most cases, hybrids between different species are infertile. In some hybrid plants, however, doubling the chromosome number (*see* **polyploid**) can restore fertility.

CONNECTIONS

CROSSOVER AND LINKAGE **82**
PATTERNS TO ORDER **84**

hybrid DNA
Double-stranded **DNA** containing single strands from different sources. *See* **hybridization**.

hybridization
1 The formation of double-stranded nucleic acid by base pairing between single-stranded nucleic acids usually obtained from different sources. See base pairs. **2** The formation of a new organism by the sexual reproduction or protoplast fusion between two different populations or species.

hybridoma
The product of cell fusion between a tumor cell and a nontumor cell. The *in vitro* production of hybridomas is carried out to provide continuously replicating ("hybrid") cells which exhibit some or all of the characteristics of the nontumor cell and so can be used in cancer research.

hybrid vigor
The improved phenotypic effects seen in **hybrid** organisms when compared with the parental species or varieties (that is, the cross breed or hybrid is more fit than its parents). Hybrid vigor improves such features as growth rate, reproductive capacity and general viability when compared with the parent plants. It is often attributed to the increase in heterozygosity in the hybrid compared with the more inbred, more **homozygous** parents. *See* **heterozygote** and **heterosis**.

hybrid zone
A geographical region in which the range of significantly different forms or closely related forms of the same **species** overlap, and where **hybridization** takes place.

hydrolysis/hydrolytic reaction
The cleavage of a molecule into two or more smaller molecules by reaction with water. In biological systems, enzyme-catalyzed hydrolysis is often used to break down larger polymers into their component subunits; for example, proteins are hydrolyzed to peptides and amino acids, and polysaccharides to simple sugars.

idiogram
See **karyogram**.

immunity
1 An organism's ability to distinguish "self" from "non-self" at cellular level, giving resistance to a number of diseases – either naturally, by the body's normal production of **antibodies** and other defenses, or by artificially introduced antibodies or by vaccination. **2** In bacteria, immunity can also refer

to resistance to certain antibiotics or heavy metals. Such resistance is genetically based, and may be acquired through infection by various phages (*see* **bacteriophage**) and **plasmids** containing specific resistance **genes**.

immunoglobulin
One of a family of **proteins** that act as **antibodies**. An immunoglobulin consists of **polypeptide** chains linked together to form a Y-shaped molecule. The amino acid sequences of the ends of the arms (variable regions) are highly variable, providing a variety of **antigen**-binding sites. This variability arises because each of the polypeptide chains is coded for by a number of **genes**, each of which exists as several different **alleles**.

imprinting
The behavior of many young animals in which they tend to follow, or imprint on, their parents. This is based on responses to stimuli (such as the appearance or sound of the parent) which they experience very early in life. This is advantageous for survival during the early stages of an animal's life when parental protection is important.

inbreeding
Continual breeding over several generations within a group of closely related (hence genetically similar) individuals. A population of inbreeding individuals generally shows less genetic **variation** than an **outbreeding** population, with many **alleles** present in the **homozygous** state. Continual inbreeding leads to inbreeding depression (the opposite of **hybrid vigor**) and increased incidence of harmful characteristics. *See* **outbreeding**.

inclusive fitness
The success with which an individual's **genes** (or a particular **allele**) are passed on to the next generation both through their own offspring and through the additional number of shared genes passed on as a result of their contribution toward the breeding of their close relatives (for example, by helping to care for relatives' young). The concept was formulated as a way of explaining the evolution of **altruism** in terms of natural selection. *See also* **fitness** and **kin selection**.

incompatibility
Any mechanism of genetic incompatibility. For example, in flowering plants, there is a genetically based chemical mechanism by which pollen from one individual is unable to fertilize a flower of the same or a genetically similar plant. This prevents self-pollination and promotes **outbreeding**. *See* **cross-pollination** and *see* **heterostyly**.

independent assortment
The principle that during **meiosis** alleles at a given gene locus tend to be distributed into **gametes** independently of the alleles at other gene loci located on nonhomologous chromosomes. *See* **homologous chromosomes** and **Mendelian inheritance**.

induced mutations
Mutations produced by specific agents (such as ultraviolet light, X-rays or chemicals) as opposed to spontaneous mutations.

inducer
A molecule that is capable of inducing the synthesis of a given **enzyme**. The inducer is often the substrate of the enzyme itself. An inducer may act by combining with a repressor molecule, thereby preventing repression and thus activating the gene responsible for synthesizing the enzyme. *See* **repressor protein, operator** and **operon**.

induction of enzyme synthesis
The triggering of **enzyme** synthesis by a specific chemical substance, which may be the substrate of the enzyme or may be a **hormone**. The inducing chemical acts by combining with a repressor of gene activity to lift the repression or directly with an **operator** (a short sequence of DNA **bases** near the start of a **gene**, which is involved in regulation of the activity of that gene).

inheritance of acquired characteristics
A central concept of Lamarckian evolution (*see* **Lamarckian inheritance**), the theory that beneficial characteristics acquired during an individual's lifetime can be handed on to any offspring. This would imply, for example that a weight-lifter who had developed large arm muscles would produce children born with large arm muscles. Modern evolutionary theory does not recognize the inheritance of acquired characteristics because there is no reliable evidence that it occurs and because no mechanism is known whereby bodily change can influence the genes (*see* **central dogma**).

CONNECTIONS
EVOLUTION AND VARIATION 86
EVOLUTION BY NATURAL SELECTION 88

insertion
A **chromosome aberration** in which extra material has been inserted into a **chromosome**, or a **point mutation** in which a **base pair** has been inserted into a **DNA** molecule. Insertions may occur as a result of mistakes during DNA replication or **meiosis**, but can also occur as a result of the insertion of a transposable element (*see* **transposon**) or a **prophage**. *See* **frameshift mutation**.

integration
The incorporation of one **DNA** sequence into another; especially, the integration of **prophage** nucleic acid into the DNA of the bacterial host cell.

interphase
The period in the **cell cycle** when the **nucleus** is not dividing. During this time the cell undergoes an increase in mass, accompanied by a doubling of its organelles and the replication of its **DNA**.

intron
An intervening non-protein-coding sequence between two protein-coding segments (exons) of a gene. Introns are transcribed into RNA, but are excised by splicing before the RNA leaves the nucleus. *See* **exon** and **protein synthesis**.

CONNECTIONS
TRANSLATING THE CODE 68
SWITCHING GENES ON AND OFF 70

inversion
A reversal in the order of a block of **genes** within a particular **chromosome** or of a sequence of bases within the DNA molecule.

***in vitro* fertilization**
The fusion of a sperm and an egg in the test tube to form a **zygote**.

isogamy
The fusion of **gametes** of similar **phenotype** in **sexual reproduction**. Gametes with no visible differences may differ chemically.

isolating mechanism
Any mechanism that prevents **gene flow** in a breeding **population**. Geographical isolation occurs when a physical barrier divides a population into two parts. Ecological isolation occurs when two populations inhabit the same region but have different habitats. Seasonal isolation occurs when two populations mate or flower at different times of year. Behavioral isolation occurs when courtship behavior differs so that mating does not take place. Mechanical isolation occurs where differences in the reproductive organs prevent successful copulation. Genetic isolation plays an important role in the development of new variants and **species**, as separated populations evolve in different directions. *See* **speciation**.

karyogram
A cut-and-paste photographic representation of all the chromosomes of a specific **eukaryotic cell** as seen at **metaphase** of **mitosis**, arranged in a specific sequence to show the relative lengths of the various pairs of **homologous chromosomes**, the positions of their centromeres and sometimes also banding patterns that are revealed by certain stains.

karyotype
The full complement of chromosomes for a **eukaryotic cell**, usually defined in terms of the number, size and morphology (form and structure) of the chromosomes. It is characteristic of the whole species (for example, the human karyotype). *See* **karyogram**.

CONNECTIONS
INSIDE THE NUCLEUS **52**
SICKNESS IN THE GENES **136**

kinetochore
A specialized group of proteins associated with the **centromere** of a **metaphase** chromosome, to which **spindle** microtubules attach during mitosis or meiosis. Each **chromatid** has its own kinetochore.

kingdom
The highest category into which organisms are classified. The kingdoms include Animalia (all multicellular animals); Plantae (all plants, including seaweeds and other algae); Fungi (all fungi, including the unicellular yeasts, but not slime molds); Protoctista (protozoa, diatoms, dinoflagellates, slime molds and various other lower organisms with eukaryotic cells); and Monera (all prokaryotes). *See* **classification**.

KARYOGRAM

1 2 3 4 5
6 7 8 9 10 11 12
13 14 15 16 17 18
19 20 21 22 23
Human female XX

kin selection
A controversial theory of **evolution** that attempts to explain altruistic behavior by proposing that particular **genes** are selected because their carrier behaves in such a way that it reduces its own chance of reproducing, while increasing the chances of successful reproduction of a related individual or individuals. Alarm calling in response to predators is an example of a behavior that may have evolved through kin selection: relatives that are warned of danger can escape and continue to breed, even if the alarm caller is caught. *See* **altruism, inclusive fitness** and **natural selection**.

Lamarckian inheritance/Lamarckism
The theory of the inheritance of acquired characteristics proposed by the French naturalist Jean Baptiste Lamarck (1744–1829) in the early 19th century. He argued that use of an organ or limb strengthens it, and that this improvement can be passed on to succeeding generations by reproduction. *See* **inheritance of acquired characteristics**.

larva
The juvenile stage between hatching and adulthood in species such as tadpoles and caterpillars in which the young have a different appearance and way of life from the adults. Larvae are typical of invertebrates, some of which (for example, shrimps) have two or more distinct larval stages. Among vertebrates, only the amphibians and some fish have a larval stage. *See* **metamorphosis**.

leader
The region of an **RNA** molecule between the (**promoter**) end and the sequence of the first **structural gene**. It is generally a noncoding sequence, though it may occasionally encode a small regulatory (leader) **peptide**.

lethal allele
An **allele**, either dominant, incompletely dominant or recessive (*see* **Mendelian inheritance**), whose expression results in the death of the carrier. Lethal alleles may exert their effect at any time from the **fertilization** of the egg to advanced age.

leukocyte
A white blood cell. Leukocytes are part of the body's defenses and give immunity against disease. There are several different types. Some (phagocytes and macrophages) engulf invading microorganisms; others kill infected cells. Lymphocytes (**B cells** and **T cells**) produce specific immune responses.

lineage
A line of direct descent from an ancestor.

linkage
The association between two or more **genes** that tend to be inherited together because they are located on the same **chromosome**. *See also* **linkage group** and **linkage map**.

linkage group
A group of linked genes on the same chromosome or all the genes located on a given chromosome. *See* **linkage.**

linkage map
A **chromosome map** in which genes and other genetic markers are ordered by calculating their degree of **linkage** – that is, the extent to which they tend to be inherited together. The genes on a chromosome are mapped in terms of their crossover value: the likelihood that, during **crossing over in meiosis**, the genes of the two parental chromosomes will cross over. A low crossover value suggests that the genes are located close together on the chromosome. The map unit, or centiMorgan, is the unit used to map genes on a chromosome. One centiMorgan is the distance that yields a crossover value of 1 percent.

Linnaean classification
The classification of organisms using a two-part latinized name developed by the Swedish botanist Carl von Linné (Linnaeus) (1707–1778) and first published in 1735 in his *Systema Naturae*. It is also known as the binomial system of classification. The first

LINKAGE MAP

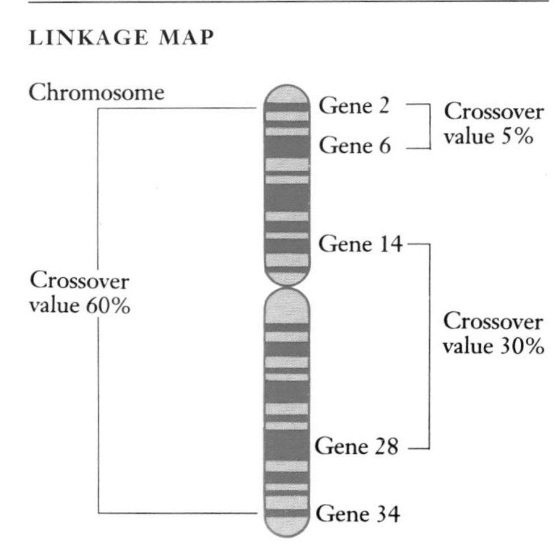

part of the name is the genus name and the second is the species name. The Latin name is usually printed in italics. Modern classification is based on the Linnaean system; higher taxonomic groups such as families and orders are printed in Roman lettering.

living fossil
A living organism that is almost identical to long-extinct species or group and is known only from the fossil record. For example, the fossil record of the coelacanth terminates about 70 million years ago, yet one was caught off the coast of South Africa in 1938 and a number of others have been caught subsequently. In fact, in such cases, evolution has occurred – very slowly – and "living fossils" are not identical to their fossil group.

locus
The specific location occupied by a particular **gene** on a **chromosome**, **plasmid** or other genetic molecule. Each locus can be occupied by only one gene; if that gene can take several forms (*see* **allele**), then only one of these is present at a given locus.

lymphocyte
A type of white blood cell with a large nucleus, produced in the bone marrow. Most occur in the lymph and blood, and around sites of infection, where they produce specific immune responses. B lymphocytes or **B cells** are responsible for producing antibodies. T lymphocytes or **T cells** have several roles in the mechanism of immunity.

lysis
The destruction of a living cell by rupturing its wall and releasing its contents. **Bacteriophage** infection leads to the lysis of bacteria with the release of virions (the smallest units of mature viruses). See also **virus**.

CONNECTIONS

BACTERIA AND VIRUSES **60**
FINDING THE GENES **128**

lysogeny
The phenomenon by which a **temperate phage** can exist in nonlytic form (*see* **lysis**) in a host bacterial cell without producing progeny **virions**. The host cell continues to grow and the phage **genome** (prophage) replicates together with the bacterial genome, so that the phage is inherited by both daughter cells. A prophage normally retains the ability to cause cell lysis, but the lytic functions are repressed by synthesis of a phage-directed **repressor protein**. Inactivation of the repressor results in induction of the lytic cycle.

lysosome
A membrane-enclosed **organelle**, principally found in **eukaryotic cells**, that develops in the **Golgi apparatus**. Lysosomes contain a wide range of **enzymes** that can break down **proteins** and other biological substances. They play an important role in intercellular digestion, and in the white blood cells known as phagocytes the lysosome enzymes attack ingested bacteria. *See* **endocytosis**.

macroevolution
The largescale trends in **evolution** that occur above the species level, leading to the emergence of new body plans. The evolution of the vertebrates is an example. *See* **microevolution**.

marker (genetic)
1 A **gene** that is associated with a specific, readily detectable phenotypic characteristic (*see* **phenotype**), such as a bacterial gene for antibiotic resistance, and which is used to identify a particular class of individual, **chromosome** or specific gene which is known to be linked to the marker gene (*see* **linkage**). **2** A segment of **DNA**, produced by treatment with **restriction endonuclease** enzymes, which is used to identify an individual or chromosomes carrying a particular gene.

maternal inheritance
A mechanism of inheritance in which certain characteristics of the offspring are determined by the **cytoplasm** of the egg. (This happens because usually the egg contributes far more cytoplasm to the zygote than does the male sex cell.) A typical example is that of shell coiling in the wandering snail (*Limnaea pereger*) in which the **genotype** of the mother's cytoplasm (through **mitochondrial DNA**) determines the **phenotype** (left- or right-handed coiling) of the offspring. *See* **extranuclear genes**.

meiosis
Also known as reduction division, a process of nuclear division in which the number of chromosomes in the cell is halved. It occurs only in **eukaryotic cells** and is part of a life cycle that involves **sexual reproduction**; it allows the **genes** of both parents to be combined without the total number of chromosomes increasing. Meiosis occurs in two stages; in the first stage, pairs of **homologous chromosomes** align themselves on either side of the equator of the **spindle**, then travel to opposite poles; the second stage resembles **mitosis**, as the chromatids of each chromosome separate into daughter cells. The end result is four **haploid** cells. In sexually reproducing **diploid** animals, meiosis occurs during the formation of **gametes**, so that the gametes are **haploid**. When the gametes unite during **fertilization**, the diploid condition is restored. In plants meiosis occurs just before spore formation, so the spores are haploid; in lower plants such as mosses they develop into the gametophyte generation (*see* **alternation of generations**), which eventually produces the gametes. Meiosis is the stage of the life cycle in which genetic **variation** arises; every gamete is slightly different, resulting in non-identical offspring. This variation arises because during meiosis, in the process of **crossing-over**, **sister chromatids** exchange segments of chromosomes, so the resulting daughter chromosomes contain different combinations of genes from those of the parent cells.

CONNECTIONS

SEXUAL REPRODUCTION **78**
CROSSOVER AND LINKAGE **82**

Mendelian inheritance
The theory of heredity proposed by the Austrian biologist Gregor Johann Mendel (1822–1884) in 1866 that forms the basis of classical **genetics**. Mendel suggested that, in sexually reproducing **species**, all characteristics are inherited through indivisible factors (now identified with genes) contributed by each parent to its offspring. The outcome of crosses can be understood in terms of the behavior of chromosomes during **meiosis**. Deviations from classical Mendelian inheritance occur in cases of incomplete dominance (*see* **codominant alleles**), characteristics controlled by multiple **alleles**, characteristics controlled by multiple **genes** and characteristics controlled by two or more pairs of alleles interacting.

CONNECTIONS

PATTERNS OF INHERITANCE **76**
MENDEL'S BREAKTHROUGH **80**

Mendel's first law
Also known as the law of segregation, this states that each hereditary characteristic is controlled by two factors (now called **alleles**) that segregate and pass into reproductive cells (**germ cells** or **gametes**).

Mendel's second law
Also known as the law of independent assortment, this states that pairs of factors (now called alleles) segregate independently of each other when germ cells (gametes) are formed. *See* **independent assortment**.

messenger RNA
RNA that acts as a template for the assembly of **amino acids** on **ribosomes** during **protein synthesis**. It is transcribed (*see* **transcription**) from and complementary to the original DNA cistron (the segment of DNA that codes for one polypeptide).

metabolism
The chemical processes in the cells of living organisms which consist of constantly alternating states of building up (anabolism) and breaking down (catabolism). For example, green plants build up complex organic substances from water, carbon dioxide and mineral salts through **photosynthesis**. By digestion and **respiration**, animals partly break down complex organic substances ingested as food to synthesize other compounds, using energy derived from the breakdown of food in respiration. Plants also use respiration to break down large storage molecules synthesized by photosynthesis, so that they can be used in metabolism.

metamorphosis
The period during the life cycle of many invertebrates, most amphibians and some fish, during which the body changes through a major reconstitution of its tissues.

metaphase
The stage during the division of the **nucleus** when the **chromosomes** are situated on the equatorial plate of the **spindle** immediately before the **centromeres** divide.

metastasis
The movement of a disease from a localized site in the body to distant sites. The term is most commonly used in the context of cancer and infectious diseases such as tuberculosis. Cancer metastasis is thought to involve a reduction in the adhesion between cells, so that the cancer cells become free to migrate.

microbe/microorganism
The general term for any living organism invisible to the naked eye but visible under a microscope, including viruses and single-celled organisms such as bacteria, protozoa, yeasts and some algae. It has no taxonomic significance in biology.

microevolution
Evolution below the **species** level, primarily as a result of changes in **allele** frequencies due to **natural selection**, but also involving **mutation**, **gene flow** and **genetic drift**.

microtubules
Hollow, tubular cytoplasmic components found in all **eukaryotic cells**. Microtubules are made mainly of subunits of the protein tubulin. In addition to forming the **spindle** during nuclear division (*see* **mitosis** and **meiosis**), they help to define the shape and structure of a cell by forming scaffolding. They also aid in some types of motility by forming cilia and flagella, and by effecting changes in the rigidity of the **cytoplasm**.

mitochondrial DNA (mtDNA)
DNA found in **mitochondria**. It typically occurs in the form of circular, double-stranded molecules that differ from nuclear DNA in base composition and density. Mitochondrial genes use a **genetic code** that differs slightly from the "universal code" used by nuclear genes.

mitochondrion
One of the semi-autonomous, membrane-enclosed **organelles** within **eukaryotic cells**, containing **enzymes** responsible for energy production during aerobic **respiration**. These rodlike or spherical bodies are thought to be derived from free-living bacteria that, at a very early stage in the history of life, invaded larger cells and took up a symbiotic way of life inside the cell (*see* **coevolution**). Each mitochondrion still contains its own small loop of DNA (*see* **mitochondrial DNA**) and new mitochondria arise by division or fragmentation of existing ones.

CONNECTIONS

THE LIVING CELL 50
TRACKING DOWN THE MOLECULES 54
THE GENETIC CODE 66

mitosis
The normal process of cell division, which produces daughter cells with a genetic content identical to that of the parent cell. The genetic material of **eukaryotic cells** is carried on a number of **chromosomes**. To control their movements during cell division so that both new cells get a full complement, a system of **protein** tubules, known as the **spindle**, organizes the chromosomes into position in the middle of the cell before they replicate.

By this stage the DNA of the chromosomes has already replicated, and the chromosomes consist of two **sister chromatids** joined together at the **centromere**. The chromosomes align themselves on the equator of the spindle, attached to the spindle tubules by a special structure in the centromere, the **kinetochore**. Each chromatid has its own kinetochore so that when the centromere finally replicates, daughter chromosomes are pulled to opposite poles of the spindle, and become incorporated into different nuclei. A number of stages of mitosis are recognized (interphase, prophase, metaphase, anaphase and telophase). *See* **meiosis** and **cell division**.

MITOCHONDRION

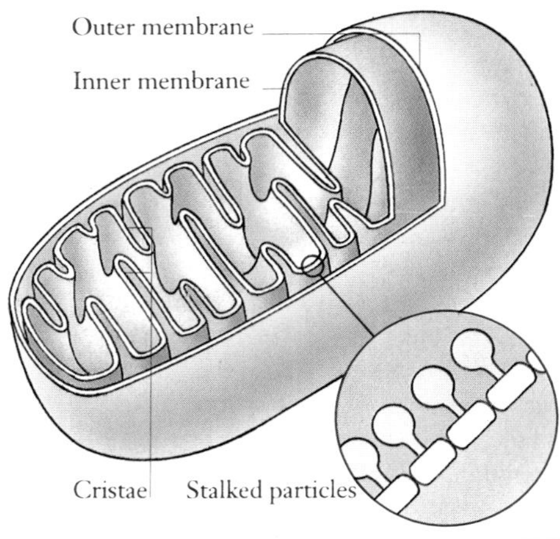

modifier
A **gene** whose activity affects the expression of another gene or genes, although it has no other known effect.

molecular clock
The use of rates of **mutation** in genetic material to calculate the length of time elapsed since two related **species** diverged from each other during **evolution**. The method depends on the assumption that mutation rates at "neutral" positions (that is, mutations that do not change regulatory sequences or encoded proteins) are the same in corresponding genes from different species .

monocistronic RNA
RNA that contains the transcript (*see* **transcription**) of a single **gene**. Also known as monogenic RNA. Monocistronic RNA codes for a single **polypeptide**. *See* **polycistronic RNA**.

monoecious
1 Describing flowering plants that have separate male and female flowers on the same plant. **2** Other plants and algae that produce male and female **gametes** on the same individual. **3** Animals that have both male and female reproductive organs on the same individual (*see* **hermaphrodite**). *See* **dioecious**.

monogamy
The practice of having only one mate.

monogony
Another name for **asexual reproduction**.

monohybrid inheritance
The pattern of inheritance seen in simple **genetics** experiments, where the inheritance of a single **gene** is being followed through several generations. Monohybrid inheritance is usually studied in genes that have only two forms or alleles, usually coding for some obvious character, such as seed color. True-breeding parent organisms, each displaying a different allele, are crossed. The offspring are monohybrids: they are hybrids for that one specific gene, having received one allele from each parent. Known as the F_1 generation, they are genotypically (in genetic makeup) and phenotypically (in appearance) identical, and usually resemble one parent, whose version of the gene (the dominant allele) masks the effect of the other version (the recessive allele). Although the characteristic for the recessive allele completely disappears in this generation, it can reappear in the next generation in individuals which have two recessive alleles. When individuals of the F_1 generation are bred together, the resulting generation, the F_2 generation, shows a ratio of 3:1 for the characteristic in question, 75 percent being like the original parent with the dominant allele, and 25 percent displaying the recessive form of the characteristic. *See* **Mendelian inheritance**.

morphogenesis
The processes by which the structure and form of an organism change as it develops from an embryo into an adult. Morphogenesis involves the organization of differentiated cells into tissues and organs. It is influenced by both genetic and environmental factors. *See* **metamorphosis.**

morphology
The study of the physical structure and form of organisms, especially their external form.

mosaic
1 An organism produced by a single **embryo** in which different parts of a tissue or organ have different phenotypes as a result of the action of different **alleles** or **genes**. In a calico cat, different alleles of the gene(s) for color are expressed in different parts of the coat. **2** An individual derived from a single **zygote** whose cells differ genetically (for example, some with 45 chromosomes and others with 47 as a result of **nondisjunction** in early embryo development).

multiple allele system
Situation where there are three or more **alleles** of the same **gene** any of which may occur at the same locus (site) on the **chromosome**.

mutagen
Any agent that brings about or increases the rate of gene **mutation** in a population. Mutagens operate either by causing changes in the **DNA** of the **genes**, thus interfering with the coding system (*see* **genetic code**), or by causing direct damage to the **chromosome** structure. Irradiation and various chemicals (for example, **colchicine**) have been identified as mutagens.

mutation
A heritable change in a **gene** of an organism, produced by an alteration in the nucleotide **base** sequence of its **nucleic acid**. Mutations result from mistakes during the replication of **DNA** molecules, from errors in **crossing over** during **meiosis**, or by the agency of certain chemicals and certain types of radiation (*see* **mutagen**).

Common mutations include deletions or insertions of bases within a particular gene. These are known as point mutations. Where the number of bases involved is not divisible by three, this constitutes a **frameshift mutation**. Larger-scale mutations include removal of a whole segment of DNA or its inversion within the DNA strand, or the insertion of a segment of DNA from another **chromosome** (*see* **chromosomal aberrations**).

Not all mutations affect the organism, because there is a certain amount of redundancy in the genetic information. If a mutation simply results in a **codon** (*see* **genetic code**) coding for the same **amino acid** as the original one, if it occurs in a non-coding part of the DNA, or if it codes for a non-functional part of a protein, it may have no detectable effect. This is known as a neutral mutation, and is of importance in **molecular clock** studies because such mutations tend to accumulate gradually as time passes and are not subject to **natural selection**. Some mutations affect genes that control protein production or the functional parts of proteins, and most of these are lethal to the organism (*see* **lethal genes**).

CONNECTIONS

VARIATIONS IN THE GENETIC CODE **96**
SICKNESS IN THE GENES **136**

mutation rate
The probability that any particular cell will undergo a specific spontaneous **mutation** during cell division. The mutation rate a is given by $a = m/d$, where m is the number of specific mutations that have occurred within the **population** and d is the number of individual division cycles within the population.

natural selection
The process whereby **gene frequencies** in a **population** change through certain individuals producing more descendants than others because they are better able to survive and reproduce in their environment. As most environments are slowly but constantly changing, natural selection continually discriminates between members of a population, enhancing the reproductive success of those organisms that possess favorable characteristics. The accumulated effect of natural selection is to produce specialized **adaptations**. The process of natural selection is slow, relying firstly on random **variation** in the **genes** of an organism being produced by **mutation** and secondly on the genetic **recombination** of **sexual reproduction**. It was recognized by English naturalists Charles Darwin (1809–1882) and Alfred Russel Wallace (1823–1913) as the main process driving evolution. *See* **Darwinism**.

CONNECTIONS

EVOLUTION AND VARIATION **86**
EVOLUTION BY NATURAL SELECTION **88**
THE GENETICS OF POPULATIONS **108**

negative control
A form of gene regulation in which the **transcription** of a particular **gene** is suppressed by the action of a protein produced by a **regulator gene**. *See* **repressor protein**.

neo-Darwinism
A modern theory of **evolution**, built up since the 1930s by integrating the 19th-century English scientist Charles Darwin's theory of evolution through **natural selection** (*see* **Darwinism**) with the theory of genetic inheritance founded on the work of the Austrian biologist Gregor Mendel (*see* **Mendelian inheritance**).

neoteny
The retention of some juvenile characteristics in a sexually mature animal. An example is the axolotl salamander, which can reproduce sexually though still in its larval form. It has been suggested that new species could arise in this way, and that our own species evolved from apelike ancestors by neoteny, on the grounds that facially a human resembles a young ape. *See also* **pedogenesis**.

neutral theory
The theory that most evolutionary changes are due to **genetic drift** (random changes in allele frequencies) rather than to **natural selection**. The theory is based on the fact that many genetic mutations are essentially

neutral and do not significantly affect the success of the carrier. They thus become fixed in the **genome** at a random rate and changes in their frequency are due more to chance than to natural selection. However, the theory does not apply to mutations that have increased or decreased adaptive value – these are subject to natural selection.

niche
The status or role of a particular organism or **species** in a specific environment or ecosystem. The niche that an organism occupies is defined by the chemical, physical and biotic (biological) factors which affect it. Two species cannot occupy the same niche and both survive.

nondisjunction
The failure of a pair of **homologous chromosomes** or sister chromatids to segregate correctly to the poles of the **spindle** during **meiosis** or **mitosis**. In meiosis it results in half of the **gametes** having two of the chromosomes and the other half having none.

nonsense codon
Any **codon** that does not specify an **amino acid** according to the **genetic code**. Some nonsense codons (also known as stop or termination codons) specify the termination of **polypeptide** synthesis.

nonsense mutation
Any **mutation** that produces a **nonsense codon** resulting in premature termination of the synthesis of a **polypeptide** chain.

nuclear membrane/nuclear envelope
The double membrane (*see* **plasma membrane**) that surrounds the cell **nucleus** and is perforated by a number of pores. The outermost membrane is continuous with the **endoplasmic reticulum** and the space between the two membranes is known as the perinuclear space.

CONNECTIONS

INSIDE THE NUCLEUS 52
TRANSLATING THE CODE 68
SWITCHING GENES ON AND OFF 70

nucleic acid
A complex organic acid made up of a long chain of **nucleotides**, present in the **nucleus** and sometimes the **cytoplasm** of the living cell. The two types, known as **DNA** (deoxyribonucleic acid) and **RNA** (ribonucleic acid), form the basis of heredity. The nucleotides are made up of a sugar (deoxyribose or ribose respectively), a phosphate group and one of four **purine** or **pyrimidine** bases. Their order along the nucleic acid strand makes up the **genetic code**.

CONNECTIONS

TRACKING DOWN THE MOLECULES 54
MAKING THE MESSAGE 56

nucleoid
A specialized region within a **prokaryote cell** which contains the DNA.

nucleolar organizer
A specific region of a **chromosome** in the **nucleolus** that contains the **genes** coding for **ribosomal RNA**. The chromosome may show a distinct constriction at this point during **metaphase**, and may have a distinctive pattern of stain uptake.

nucleolus
A distinct region found in most types of eukaryotic cell nucleus that contains the genes coding for ribosomal proteins, and in which **ribosomal RNA** is synthesized and assembled into ribosome subunits. The ribosomal RNA is transcribed (*see* **transcription**) from a **nucleolar organizer**.

nucleoside
Any compound that consists of a **purine** or **pyrimidine** base linked to a pentose sugar molecule. In ribonucleosides the sugar is ribose and in deoxyribonucleosides the sugar is 2-deoxyribose. *See* **nucleotide**.

nucleosome
The short, disk-shaped bead on a eukaryotic cell chromosome, composed of tightly coiled chromatin containing about 145 **base pairs** of **DNA** separated by less highly folded chromatin. *See also* **chromosome**.

NUCLEUS

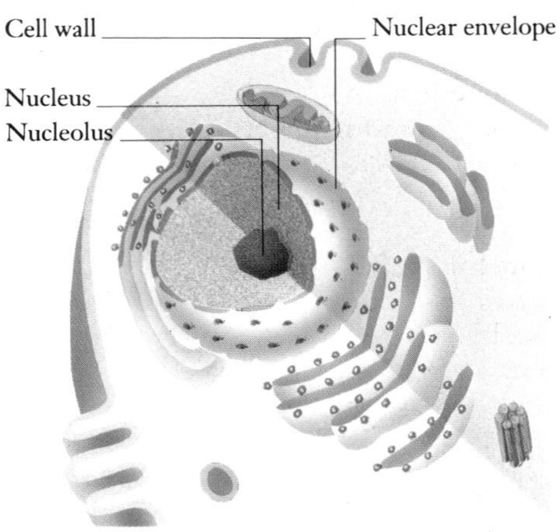

Cell wall
Nuclear envelope
Nucleus
Nucleolus

nucleotide
A **nucleoside** in which the sugar molecule is linked to one or more phosphate groups. **DNA** and **RNA** are made up of long chains of nucleotides (polynucleotides).

nucleus
In **eukaryotes**, the membrane-enclosed part of the **cell** that contains the **DNA** in the form of **chromosomes** and one or more **nucleoli**. A cell may contain more than one nucleus; ciliate protozoans typically contain two (macronucleus and micronucleus).

oncogene
A gene that can potentially induce a cell in which it occurs or to which it is introduced to divide abnormally, giving rise to a cancer. Oncogenes arise from **mutations** in **genes** found in normal cells. They are also found in viruses capable of transforming normal cells into tumor cells. These are able to insert their oncogenes into the host cell's **DNA**, causing it to divide uncontrollably. More than one oncogene may be necessary to transform a cell in this way. Most oncogenes work by counteracting the cell's natural repression of cell division or by preventing genetically programmed cell death, rather than by increasing the rate of cell division.

ontogeny
The history of the development of an individual organism. *See* **phylogeny** and **recapitulation theory**.

operator
In bacteria, a short segment of **DNA** associated with one or more **structural genes** and involved in regulating the activity of genes. It is located before the main coding section of DNA (the **cistron** or cistrons) and may bind with the protein product of a **regulator gene** to control **transcription**. *See* **operon**.

operon
A system of **cistrons**, **operator** and **promoter** sequences that are situated close together on the same **chromosome** and are switched on and off as an integrated unit. They usually produce **enzymes** that control different steps in the same biochemical pathway. Operons were discovered in bacteria. They are less commonly found in higher organisms, in which metabolism is more complex. They operate as a method of enzyme regulation by controlling the synthesis of the enzyme. *See* **end-product inhibition.**

order
A category used in the classification of organisms that consists of one or more closely related families. The horse, rhinoc-

eros and tapir families are grouped in the order Perissodactyla, the odd-toed ungulates, because they all have either one or three toes on each foot. Related orders are grouped together in a class.

organelle
In **eukaryote** cells, a discrete specialized compartment of **cytoplasm** which has a specific function. Most organelles are enclosed within membranes. Examples of organelles include **mitochondria**, **chloroplasts**, **lysosomes**, and the **nucleus**. Organelles separate sequences of metabolic reactions whose components might otherwise interact with each other, and provide specialized microenvironments that enable particular reactions to proceed at maximum efficiency. *See also* **cell cycle**.

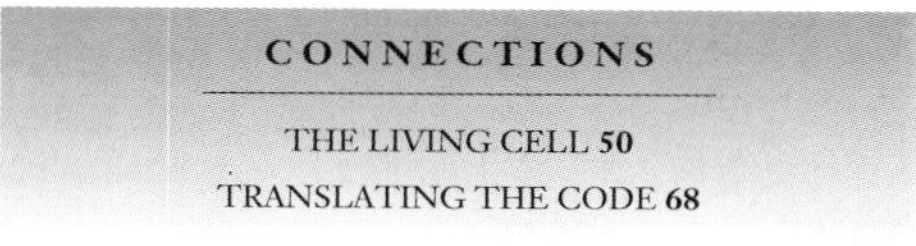

organizer
A part of the **embryo** that causes specific changes to occur in another adjacent part, thus organizing its development and differentiation.

origin
One or more of the special sites on the parent molecule at which the initiation of **DNA replication** occurs.

OPERON

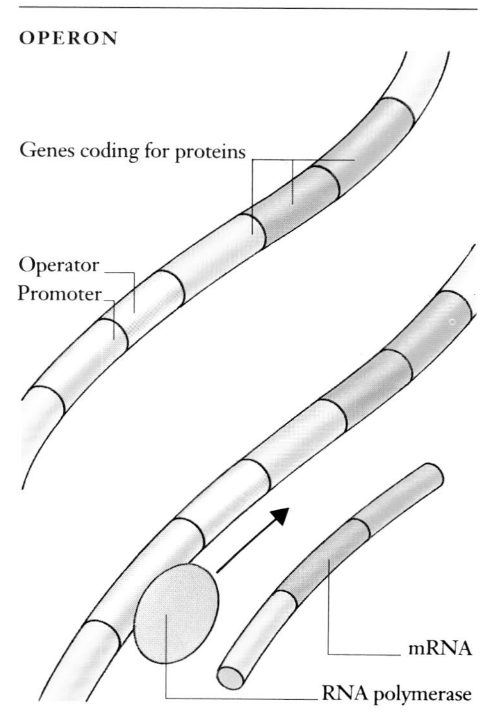

outbreeding
Sexual reproduction between unrelated or distantly related individuals. A population of outbreeding individuals shows more genetic **variation** than an inbreeding population and has greater potential for adapting to environmental changes. More of its genes occur as heterozygous **alleles**. *See* **inbreeding**.

ovum
The female **gamete** before **fertilization**. In animals it is called an egg and is produced in the ovaries. In plants, where it is also known as an egg cell or oosphere, the ovum is produced in an ovule. The ovum is nonmotile.

pairing (of chromosomes)
The association of **homologous chromosomes** during prophase I of **meiosis**. The process by which the chromosomes pair is known as synapsis. Each pair of homologous chromosomes constitutes a bivalent.

paleontology
The study of ancient life, encompassing the structure of organisms, their environment, evolution and ecology, as revealed by **fossils.**

parallel evolution
Evolution of similar characteristics in lineages of common ancestry.

parthenogenesis
A form of **asexual reproduction** in which a new individual develops from a single unfertilized **gamete**, usually an egg. It is the normal means of reproduction in a few plants (for example, dandelions) and animals (certain fish). Some sexually reproducing species, such as aphids, show parthenogenesis at some stage in their life cycle.

pecking order
A system of hierarchy in social groupings in which there is a linear order of precedence for access to food and mates. Gregarious birds such as chickens form pecking orders. Bird A is dominant to birds B, C and D; B is dominant to birds C and D, and so on.

pedogenesis
Sexual reproduction by a **larva** or immature animal.

peptide
A molecule of two or more **amino acid** molecules (not necessarily different) joined by condensation reactions which result in the formation of peptide bonds, by which the acid group of one amino acid is linked to the amino group of the other. The number of amino acid molecules in the peptide is indicated by referring to it as di-, tri- or polypeptide (two, three or many amino acids). **Proteins** are built up of interacting polypeptide chains with various types of bonds between the chains.

pH
The negative logarithm of the hydrogen ion concentration in an aqueous solution. A logarithmic scale numbered from 0 to 14 is used to show acidity or alkalinity. A pH of 7.0 indicates neutrality, below 7 is acid and above 7 is alkaline at 25°C.

phenetics
The study of the **phenotype** of an organism. Phenotypic classification takes no account of ancestral lineage. *See* **phylogeny** and **classification**.

phenotype
The observable traits displayed by an organism. It is not a direct reflection of the **genotype** because some **alleles** are masked by the presence of dominant alleles. It is further modified by the effects of the environment (for example, poor nutrition stunts growth). Identical phenotypes may not breed alike (*see* **true-breeding organism**).

CONNECTIONS
SWITCHING GENES ON AND OFF 70
LIFE'S BLUEPRINT UNFOLDS 72
THE LIMITS OF LIFE 74

photosynthesis
The use of light energy by a biological system to drive reactions that synthesize organic molecules from inorganic substances. The basis is the reduction of carbon dioxide to carbohydrates coupled to the oxidation of water or another inorganic compound. The light energy is usually absorbed by special-

PEPTIDE

Amino acids condense
Peptide bond
Water

ized pigment in the cells of living organisms. Photosynthesizing organisms include plants, algae and certain bacteria. *See* **chloroplast**.

phylogeny
The sequence of changes that occurs in a given species or other taxonomic group during the course of its evolution. *See* **ontogeny** and *see also* **recapitulation theory**.

phylum
A category of organisms that consists of one or more similar or closely related classes. Mammals, birds, reptiles, amphibians, fish and tunicates (sea squirts) belong to the phylum Chordata; the phylum Mollusca consists of snails, slugs, mussels, clams, squid and octopuses. There are nine plant phyla, including the Angiospermophyta, comprising all the flowering plants, the Gymnospermophyta or conifers, the Cycadophyta or cycads, Filicinophyta or ferns, Bryophyta or mosses and liverworts, and a number of smaller phyla. Related phyla are grouped together in a kingdom.

plasma membrane
See **cell membrane**.

plasmid
A small, independently replicating, circular, mobile piece of **DNA** found in bacteria. It is separate from the bacterial chromosome (*see* **bacterium**) but still multiplies during cell growth. Plasmids range from 3 percent to 20 percent of the size of the chromosome. There is usually only one copy of a single plasmid per cell, but occasionally several are found, and in a few cases 100 or more. Plasmids determine a variety of bacterial properties including resistance to antibiotics and the ability to produce toxins (*see* **immunity**). Some plasmids carry fertility genes (*see* **F factor**) that enable them to move between bacteria and transfer genetic information between strains. They are widely used in **recombinant DNA** technology (*see* **genetic engineering**).

CONNECTIONS

BACTERIA AND VIRUSES 60
REARRANGING DNA 126
FINDING THE GENES 128

pleiotropic
A **gene** or mutation whose expression can affect more than one characteristic.

ploidy
The number of sets of **chromosomes** in a cell. *See* **haploid, diploid** and **polyploid**.

POLARITY

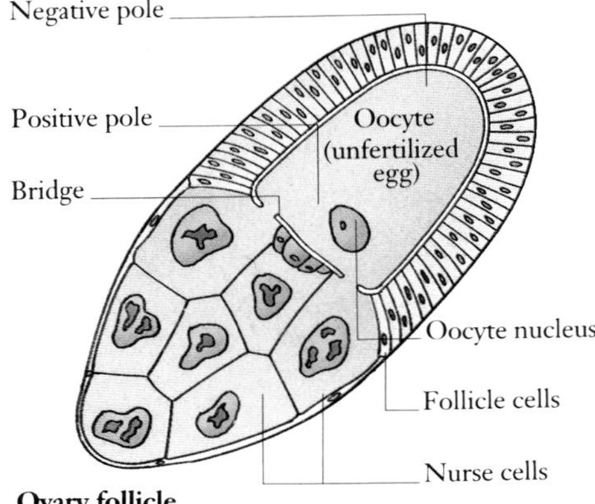

Ovary follicle

point mutation
1 A **mutation** in which a single **nucleotide** is replaced by a different nucleotide. A point mutation in a **structural gene** may result in a missense mutation (in which the **codon** now codes for a different **amino acid**), a nonsense mutation (in which the codon no longer codes for an amino acid – it may code for a stop or start signal instead), or a same sense mutation (in which a codon which codes for the same amino acid is produced). Point mutations may be induced by a number of chemical **mutagens** (agents causing mutations) such as 5-bromouracil and nitrous acid. **2** Any mutation involving a single nucleotide, including the loss or gain of a single nucleotide (resulting in a **frameshift mutation**).

polarity
In an egg or **embryo**, the existence of a definite axis along which a pattern of **differentiation** and organization of cellular material or cells takes place during development.

polar mutation
A **mutation** in a single gene which affects the expression of other genes nearby.

pollination
The transfer of pollen from the male pollen sacs of one plant to the receptive part of the female organ of another plant in flowering plants and conifers. *See* **cross-pollination** and **self-pollination**.

polyandry
The practice in animals of a female mating with more than one male during a breeding season. *See* **polygamy** and **polygyny**.

polycistronic RNA
RNA that contains the transcripts of two or more **genes**. It is also known as polygenic RNA. *See* **cistron, transcription** and **monocistronic RNA**.

polygamy
The practice in animals of having more than one mate during a breeding season. *See* **polyandry** and **polygyny**.

polygenic (multifactorial)
A characteristic, such as height, that is determined by contributions from a number of genes. *See* **gene** and **allele**.

polygyny
The practice in animals of a male mating with more than one female during a breeding season. *See* **polyandry**.

polymerase chain reaction
A technique of **gene** amplification by which selected **DNA** from a single cell can be duplicated indefinitely until there is a sufficient amount to analyze by conventional genetic laboratory techniques. The sample of DNA is mixed with a solution of enzymes (*see* **DNA polymerase**), which enable it to replicate with short single-stranded primers that flank the sequence to be amplified, and with a plentiful supply of **nucleotides**. The mixture is repeatedly heated and cooled. At each warming, the double-stranded DNA present in the mixture separates into two single strands, and with each cooling the polymerase assembles the free nucleotides into a new partner strand for each single strand. Each cycle takes approximately 30 minutes to complete, so that after 10 hours there is one million times more DNA present than at the start.

CONNECTIONS

FINDING THE GENES 128
CLINICAL AND FORENSIC GENETICS 138

polymerization
The chemical reaction in which two or more (usually small) molecules of the same chemical type join to form a new compound. When a simple molecule such as water is a byproduct, it is called a condensation reaction, as in the production of **polypeptides** by the polymerization of **amino acids**.

polymorphism
The coexistence of several different alleles of a particular gene or other DNA sequence in a group of plants or animals of one **species**. Examples of polymorphism include the alleles that affect blood groups in humans, and the different color forms found in some butterflies.

polypeptide
A long-chain molecule composed of three or more amino acids joined by peptide bonds. A **protein** may consist of one or more specific polypeptide chains.

polyploid
An individual with three (triploid), four (tetraploid) or more sets of **chromosomes** where the normal complement is two sets (diploid). Polyploidy is common in plants (mainly among flowering plants), but rare in animals. Many crop plants are natural polyploids, including wheat, which has four sets of chromosomes per cell (durum wheat) or six sets (common wheat). Plant breeders can induce the formation of polyploids by treatment with the chemical **colchicine**. Matings between polyploid individuals and normal diploid ones are invariably sterile; an individual that develops polyploidy through a genetic aberration can initially reproduce only vegetatively, by **parthenogenesis** or by **self-fertilization** (modes of **asexual reproduction** common only among plants). Once a polyploid population is established, its members can reproduce sexually.

population
A group of interbreeding individuals of the same **species** living in a certain area and sharing a common **gene pool**.

population genetics
The branch of genetics that studies how the frequencies of different **alleles** in **populations** of organisms change as a result of **natural selection** and other processes. The potential for change depends on the sum total of alleles available to the organisms (the gene pool). Estimates of the allele frequency (**gene frequency**) give an indication of response to a changing condition.

position effect
A situation in which the expression of a pair of **alleles** in the phenotype (observable characteristics) is affected by their position on the **chromosome** relative to other **genes**.

preadaptation
The chance possession of a characteristic that allows an organism to exploit a new situation. In many cases, it evolves to solve a problem that a species encounters in its preferred habitat, but once evolved it allows the organism to exploit an entirely different situation. The ability to extract oxygen directly from the air evolved in some early fish, probably in response to stagnant, deoxygenated pools; this made it possible for their descendants to spend time on land, so giving rise eventually to the air-breathing amphibians.

primary structure
The structure of a **protein** defined by the linear sequence of **amino acids** linked by peptide bonds in a **polypeptide** chain.

primer
A short segment of **nucleic acid** with a free $^{-}$OH group, that needs to be base-paired to a template DNA molecule in order to initiate polymerization during **DNA** synthesis. A short sequence of nucleotides, often of newly transcribed RNA, base-paired to part of a DNA molecule can initiate polymerization.

primitive traits
Traits possessed by an organism that have been inherited from an ancestral form and have remained through its evolution.

prion
An infectious agent, a hundred times smaller than a **virus**. It is thought to be composed of **protein** and to lack detectable amounts of nucleic acid (genetic material). Prions are believed to cause diseases such as scrapie in sheep (which can be passed to cattle and become bovine spongiform encephalopathy, "mad cow disease") and some degenerative diseases of the nervous system in humans.

PROTEIN

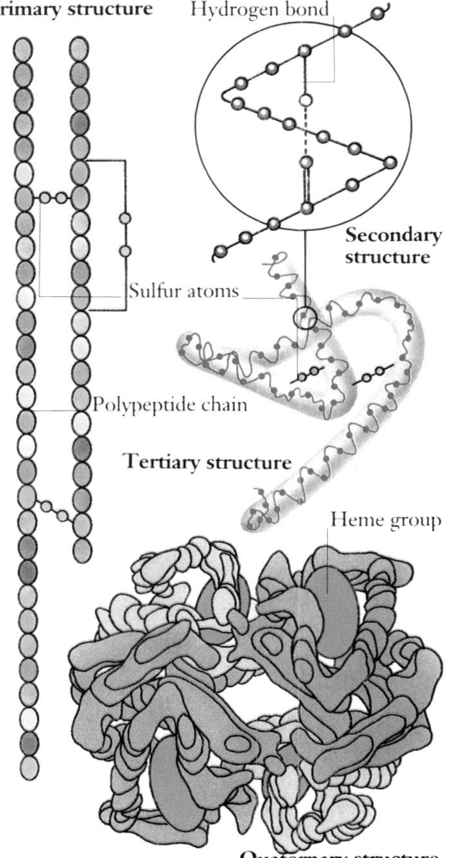

Some scientists think the protein in prions may be produced by an aberrant **gene**.

probe
A small segment of nucleic acid of known sequence that can be used to search for complementary sequences in a nucleic acid under investigation by hybridizing to them. Probes are often labeled with a radioactive isotope or fluorescent chemical so that their presence can be readily detected.

prokaryote
Any unicellular organism whose cells lack membrane-bounded **organelles**. Prokaryote **DNA** is not arranged in **chromosomes** enclosed within a nuclear membrane (*see* **nucleus**) but forms a coiled structure called a nucleoid. Prokaryotes comprise the bacteria and cyanobacteria (blue-green algae) and certain other single-celled microorganisms. Together they form the Kingdom Monera.

promoter
A sequence of **DNA** that directs **RNA polymerase** to bind to the transcriptional start site of a gene and initiate transcription. It may bind regulatory molecules that affect the expression of the gene.

prophage
A phage (*see* **bacteriophage**) **nucleic acid** or **genome** that is integrated into the host bacterium's **DNA**, replicates with it and is inherited by each of the host daughter cells when the bacterium reproduces (as when the bacterial cell divides). The phage nucleic acid may be DNA or **RNA** according to the particular phage involved. *See* **lysogeny**.

prophase
The initial stage in the division of the nucleus (*see* **mitosis** and **meiosis**), up to the arrival of the **chromosomes** at the equator of the **spindle**. The **nucleolus** becomes indistinct and a radial array of **microtubules** is formed from each of two pairs of **centrioles** when present. The chromosomes condense and become visible under a microscope.

protein
A complex, biologically important substance composed of **amino acids** linked together by peptide bonds (*see* **peptide** and **polypeptide**). Proteins are essential to all living organisms. As **enzymes** they regulate all aspects of metabolism. Structural proteins such as keratin and collagen make up the skin; muscle proteins such as myosin produce movement; hemoglobin transports oxygen; membrane proteins regulate the movement of substances into and out of cells (*see* **cell membrane**), and proteins such as

insulin act as chemical messengers between different parts of the body (hormones). The initial sequence of amino acids in the polypeptide chains (*see* **primary structure**) determines the shape of the molecule. The chains may be folded or twisted and held in place by other types of bonds (forming the **secondary structure**). This may result in a helical or sheet-like structure. Fibrous proteins, such as structural proteins, show little further folding (*see* **tertiary structure**), being composed of long parallel chains or polypeptides forming fibers or sheets. Globular proteins, such as enzymes and antibodies, have a distinct tertiary structure and are folded into spherical shapes. Conjugated proteins, such as hemoglobin, have nonprotein groups (prosthetic groups) associated with them. In hemoglobin the prosthetic group is the iron-containing pigment heme. Such associated structures form the **quaternary structure** of the protein. The genetic code works by coding for all the proteins needed, and these in turn govern the structure and functions of the organism.

CONNECTIONS

PROTEINS AND AMINO ACIDS **64**
THE GENETIC CODE **66**
TRANSLATING THE CODE **68**
SWITCHING GENES ON AND OFF **70**
LIFE'S BLUEPRINT UNFOLDS **72**

protein synthesis
The process of making **proteins** in the cell according to instructions contained in the **genetic code** on the **DNA**. In **eukaryote** cells, the DNA is located on **chromosomes** in the **nucleus**, while the structures that assemble proteins from their **amino acid** subunits, the **ribosomes**, are in the **cytoplasm**. Protein synthesis comprises two processes, transcription and translation. In transcription, a segment of DNA corresponding to a **gene** or **cistron** unwinds, and a strand of **RNA** complementary to the base sequence (*see* **base pairs**) on one of the exposed DNA strands is synthesized from free **nucleotides** using a polymerase enzyme. Any non-coding sections of RNA (**introns**) are then excised and the resulting messenger RNA leaves the nucleus through the pores in the nuclear membrane and enters the cytoplasm. Ribosomal subunits attach to it, forming one or more ribosomes. Amino acids in the cytoplasm are activated by the addition of phosphate groups that provide the energy for peptide bond formation. These amino acids are linked to molecules of **transfer RNA**, which transport them to the ribosomes. The transfer RNA molecules line up by complementary base pairing (*see* **base pairs**) with appropriate **codons** on the mRNA and peptide bonds form between the amino acids.

protoplasm
The contents of a living cell. It includes all the discrete structures (*see* **organelles**) in a cell, as well as the jellylike matrix in which these float. The contents of a cell outside the **nucleus** are called cytoplasm, so the protoplasm consists of nucleus plus cytoplasm.

protoplast
The naked cell of a plant or bacterium – the part of the cell enclosed by the **cell membrane**, but excluding any cell wall material.

protoplast fusion
The fusing of **protoplasts** from different plants (including plants not capable of interbreeding by **sexual reproduction**) to form somatic cell hybrids. *See* **somatic cell hybridization**.

provirus
Viral **DNA** that has become integrated into the chromosomal DNA of the host cell.

punctuated equilibrium
A pattern of **evolution** in which periods of comparative stability are interspersed with bursts of increased **variation** and the formation of new **species** (*see* **speciation**). The duration of the respective periods of stasis and bursts of evolutionary activity vary greatly under different circumstances. *See also* **gradualist theory**.

purine
An organic nitrogenous **base** that occurs in **DNA** and **RNA** (adenine and guanine in both). Purines pair with pyrimidines in base pairing. *See* **base pairs.**

pyrimidine
An organic nitrogenous **base** that occurs in **DNA** (as thymine and cytosine) and **RNA** (as uracil and cytosine). Pyrimidines pair with purines in base pairing. *See* **base pairs.**

quaternary structure
The three-dimensional structure of a globular **protein** made up of two or more **polypeptide** subunit chains, particularly the way in which the subunit chains fit together.

race
A nonspecific designation of a **population** of organisms within a **species** that are geographically, ecologically, physiologically or chromosomally distinct from other members of a species. The term is often used in the same context as subspecies.

radiometric dating
A method of dating rocks based on the rate of decay of certain radioactive elements.
random drift
See **genetic drift**.

random mutation
Mutation that occurs spontaneously in the absence of any apparent external **mutagens**. Such mutations usually arise as a result of errors in **DNA replication** and repair. Also known as background mutation. *See* **chromosomal aberration.**

reading frame
The particular groups of three in which the **nucleotides** that make up the **genetic code** of the **DNA** or **RNA** are "read" during **translation**. *See* **frameshift mutation** and **protein synthesis**.

reassociation of DNA
The association of single-stranded **DNA** chains at lowered temperatures following disassociation under raised temperatures. *See* **denaturation**.

recapitulation theory
The theory put forward by the German biologist Ernst Haeckel (1834–1919) that an animal passes through stages of embryonic development that resemble various stages in the evolution of its group – that is, **ontogeny** tends to recapitulate **phylogeny**. This theory is also known as Haeckel's law and biogenic law.

recessive allele
An allele (alternative form of a **gene**) that is expressed in the phenotype (observable characteristics of an individual) only if the individual inherits identical alleles from both parents (if it is homozygous recessive). Its expression will be wholly or partly masked if its partner allele is a dominant allele. Alleles for blue eyes in humans and shortness in pea plants are recessive. Many rare diseases such as hemophilia and sickle cell disease are due to recessive alleles. The term "recessive" is also used to describe the characteristic which results from the expression of a recessive allele. *See* **dominant allele**.

reciprocal translocation
The exchange of segments (*see* **recombination**) between two nonhomologous **chromosomes**. *See* **chromosomal aberration** and **meiosis**.

recombinant DNA
DNA molecules produced by cutting and joining DNA from different sources. They contain DNA from more than one individ-

ual (often from more than one species) or synthesized DNA. *See* **recombinant DNA technology** and **genetic engineering**.

recombinant DNA technology

A technique of **genetic engineering** that involves splicing together **DNA** molecules from more than one source, then multiplying the resulting **recombinant DNA** in a suitable host organism (often the spliced DNA is in the form of a **plasmid**, which is then multiplied in a bacterium host) in order to analyze the DNA or to obtain its protein products. The technology can be used to produce individuals with genetic properties not normally associated with that species (such as genetically engineered cows that produce human growth hormones).

CONNECTIONS

FINDING THE GENES 128
LIVING FACTORIES 130

recombination

Any process that recombines the genetic material, increasing genetic **variation** in the offspring. The two main processes both occur during **meiosis** (reduction division of cell nuclei). One is **crossing over**, in which **chromosome** pairs exchange segments; the other is the random reassortment of chromosomes that occurs when each gamete receives only one of each chromosome pair. The term sometimes refers only to recombination caused by crossing over.

regulator gene

Any **gene** responsible for the production of a **regulatory protein** that may serve to repress or activate the **transcription** of one or more **structural genes**. *See* **operon**.

release (termination) factors

Protein molecules that recognize specific stop **codons** during protein synthesis. Binding of a release factor to a termination codon causes the hydrolysis of the chemical bond between the **transfer RNA** and the growing **polypeptide** chain, releasing the polypeptide. *See* **protein synthesis** and **transcription**.

replication (DNA)

The replication of the genetic material, which usually occurs just before cell division. New strands of **DNA** are synthesized using pre-existing "parental" strands of DNA as templates. The DNA double helix unwinds from specific points called replication forks, and the resulting single strands act as templates for the synthesis of new strands. Free **nucleotide** bases pair (*see* **base pairs**) with complementary bases in the template strand and are sequentially polymerized (joined together) by a **DNA polymerase** (enzyme or enzyme complex). DNA replication results in new double-stranded DNA molecules each of which contains one "parental" strand (the template) and one new strand. This is called semi-conservative replication.

CONNECTIONS

MAKING THE MESSAGE 56
PASSING ON THE MESSAGE 58
SEXUAL REPRODUCTION 78

replicon

A segment of **DNA** that is replicated from a single point of origin (at which strand separation starts and polymerization begins). Most **prokaryote** cells have only one origin in the **genome** (the single circular DNA molecule that constitutes the genetic material) but in **eukaryotes** there may be several origins along each **chromosome**.

replisome

See **DNA replicase system**.

repression

The inhibition of the **transcription** of a **gene** as a result of a **repressor protein** binding to the regulatory DNA sequence (**promoter** or **operator**) for that gene. The repressor protein may be the product of a specific regulator gene; or, if the gene product is an **enzyme**, it may be the end product of a reaction in which this enzyme is involved. *See* **end-product inhibition**.

repressor protein

A protein produced by a **regulator gene** which prevents gene **transcription** by preventing **RNA polymerase** from binding to **DNA**. The repressor may act by binding with an operator gene, or with the **promoter** or **activator** of a **structural gene**. *See* **activator**.

CONNECTIONS

PROTEINS AND AMINO ACIDS 64
SWITCHING GENES ON AND OFF 70

reproductive isolation

The absence of interbreeding between members of two **populations** of the same species that are not geographically isolated. This phenomenon might be due to a lack of attraction (physical, chemical or behavioral) between males and females, or by physical differences in the genitalia which render them incompatible. In animals with elaborate courtship patterns, reproductive isolation may occur because the courtship behavior of one fails to stimulate the other. Such forms of behavioral incompatibility leading to reproductive isolation are sometimes known as behavioral isolation.

respiration

The sequence of biochemical reactions in living cells that break down organic substances and release of energy. Aerobic respiration, which utilizes oxygen, generates more energy than anaerobic respiration. Respiration releases energy in the form of ATP (adenosine triphosphate), a small molecule that contains a high-energy phosphate bond. ATP can travel around the cell and supply energy to other reactions: an **enzyme**-catalyzed reaction removes a phosphate group from ATP, releasing the energy stored in the phosphate bond. Other byproducts are water and carbon dioxide.

restriction endonuclease/restriction enzyme

Any of a large number of **enzymes** (endonucleases) that break the internal bonds of double-stranded **DNA** at highly specific **nucleotide** (base) sequences and then cleave the DNA. Several hundred restriction endonucleases are known, each cutting the DNA at a specific nucleotide sequence. Some make staggered cuts, leaving cut ends of DNA with single-stranded tails which can base pair (*see* **base pairs**) with the tails of any other DNA fragments cut by the same restriction endonuclease. These enzymes are important tools in **genetic engineering**. *See* **recombinant DNA technology** and **sticky ends**.

retrovirus

Any of a family (Retroviridae) of **viruses** containing single-stranded **RNA** rather than **DNA** as genetic material. For the virus to express itself and multiply within an infected cell, its RNA must be converted to DNA. It does this by using a built-in **enzyme** known as **reverse transcriptase** (the transfer of genetic information from DNA to RNA is known as transcription, and retroviruses do the reverse of this). Retroviruses cause **AIDS** and some forms of leukemia and other cancers. They can be used as **vectors** to introduce DNA sequences into **eukaryote** cells.

CONNECTIONS

BACTERIA AND VIRUSES 60
FINDING THE GENES 128

RHESUS FACTOR

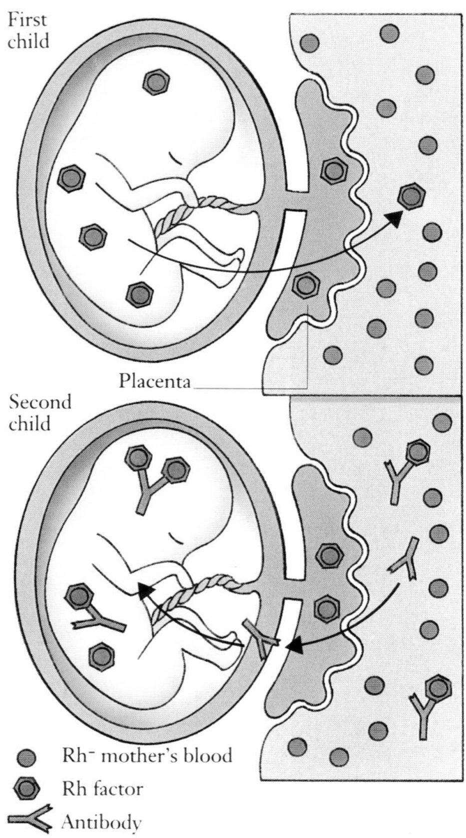

reverse transcriptase
An RNA-dependent **DNA polymerase** that synthesizes **DNA** from an **RNA** template. Reverse transcriptases are encoded by the **genomes** of **retroviruses** and certain similar elements. They are insensitive to many DNA and RNA polymerase inhibitors, but can be inhibited by drugs. Reverse transcriptases are widely used in **genetic engineering** to synthesize DNA from **messenger RNA (mRNA)**.

reverse transcription
The synthesis of **DNA** using an **RNA** template, which occurs in retroviruses (*see* **retrovirus**). This is the opposite of the usual process of DNA **replication** in other viruses and in eukaryote cells, and does not obey the central dogma, which states that genetic information always passes from DNA to RNA. *See* **reverse transcriptase**.

reversion
The process of restoring a mutant **phenotype** to the normal one by a further **mutation** of the **gene** involved (back-mutation) or by mutation of a gene at another locus (suppression). The resulting organism is known as a revertant.

rhesus factor
A group of **antigens** on the surface of red blood cells that characterize the rhesus blood group system. Most humans (85 percent of the population) possess the main rhesus factor (Rh^+), but those without this factor (Rh^-) produce **antibodies** if they come into contact with it. If an Rh^- mother carries an Rh^+ fetus, she may produce antibodies if fetal blood crosses the placenta. This is not normally a problem with the first baby because antibodies are produced only slowly. However, the antibodies continue to build up after birth, and a second Rh^+ child may be attacked by antibodies passing from mother to fetus, causing the child to contract anemia, heart failure or brain damage. In such cases, the blood of the infant has to be changed for Rh^- blood. The problem can be circumvented by giving the mother anti-Rh globulin just after the first pregnancy, preventing the formation of antibodies. *See* **immunity**.

RNA (ribonucleic acid)
The **nucleic acid** involved in the process of translating **DNA**, the genetic material, into proteins (*see* **protein synthesis**). It is usually single-stranded, unlike the double-stranded DNA, and consists of a large number of **nucleotides** strung together, each of which comprises the sugar ribose, a phosphate group, and one of four **bases** (uracil, cytosine, adenine or guanine). RNA is copied from DNA by the assemblage of free nucleotides against an unwound portion (a single strand) of the DNA, with DNA serving as the template (*see* **transcription**). In this process, uracil (instead of the thymine in DNA) is paired with adenine, and guanine with cytosine, forming **base pairs** that then separate. The RNA then travels to the **ribosomes** where it serves to assemble proteins from free **amino acids**.

RNA occurs in three major forms, each with a different function in the synthesis of protein. Messenger RNA (mRNA) is the template for protein synthesis. Each codon (a set of three bases) on the RNA molecule is matched with the corresponding amino acid, in accordance with the **genetic code**. This process (**translation**) takes place in the ribosomes, which are made up of proteins and ribosomal RNA (rRNA). Transfer RNA (tRNA) is responsible for combining with specific amino acids and matching up a special anticodon sequence of its own with a **codon** on the mRNA. This is how the genetic code is translated into proteins.

Although RNA is normally associated only with the process of protein synthesis, it also makes up the hereditary material itself in some viruses (*see* **retrovirus**).

RNAase/RNase/ribonuclease
Any of a group of **enzymes** that cleave RNA by **hydrolysis**. RNases recognize a specific **RNA** by its structure, and they play important roles in RNA processing, in various regulatory processes and in degrading RNA molecules.

CONNECTIONS

TRANSLATING THE CODE **68**
SWITCHING GENES ON AND OFF **70**
LIFE'S BLUEPRINT UNFOLDS **72**
FINDING THE GENES **128**

RNA polymerase
Any of a group of **enzymes** that are able to polymerize ribonucleotide triphosphates to form RNA using single-stranded DNA as a template.

ribosomal RNA (rRNA)
The kind of **RNA** that is present in the subunits of **ribosomes**. rRNA can form complex structures including hairpins and loops stabilized by base pairing (*see* **base pairs**). Certain regions of rRNA have been highly conserved during evolution and comparative sequence studies in ribosomal RNAs are used to indicate evolutionary relationships between organisms.

ribosome
The protein-making machinery of the cell. Ribosomes are located on the **endoplasmic reticulum** and in the **cytoplasm** of **eukaryote** cells, and in the cytoplasm of **prokaryote** cells. Each ribosome consists of two subunits composed of **ribosomal RNA** (rRNA) and various proteins. The ribosomes receive **messenger RNA** (copied from the **DNA**) and **amino acids**, and translate the messenger RNA by using its chemically coded instructions to link amino acids in a specific order to make a strand of a particular protein or polypeptide (*see* **protein synthesis** and **translation**). These reactions take place at specific sites on the ribosomes and involve ribosomal **enzymes**.

CONNECTIONS

PROTEINS AND AMINO ACIDS **64**
TRANSLATING THE CODE **68**

rough endoplasmic reticulum
Regions of the **endoplasmic reticulum** at which the outer surface of the organelle membrane that is in contact with the **cytoplasm** bears numerous **ribosomes**. *See* **smooth endoplasmic reticulum**.

rRNA
See **ribosomal RNA**.

satellite DNA
Regions of DNA in **eukaryote** cells that consist of repeating nucleotide sequences with a different base composition and different density from those found in other parts of the DNA. It does not appear to contain any specific genes and its function is unclear.

secondary sexual characteristic
An external feature of an organism, not including the reproductive organs themselves, that is indicative of its sex. These characteristics include facial hair in men and breasts in women, combs in cockerels, brightly colored plumage in many male birds and manes in male lions. In many cases, they are involved in displays and contests for mates and have evolved by **sexual selection**. Their development is stimulated by sex **hormones**.

secondary structure
The first level of three-dimensional structure in a **polypeptide** chain, in which the chain is folded into an alpha-helical structure or a beta-pleated sheet. The folding is stabilized by hydrogen bonds between the component **amino acids**. *See* **protein**.

segregation
The independent separation of pairs of **alleles** on **homologous chromosomes** into different daughter cells during cell division. A **heterozygous** parent may produce offspring of different **phenotypes**. The principle was fundamental to the work of Austrian biologist Gregor Mendel (*see* **Mendelian inheritance** and **Mendel's first law**).

selection
Any process that increases (positive selection) or decreases (negative selection) the probability of reproduction. *See* **natural selection, selection pressure** and **selective breeding**.

selection pressure
The evolutionary pressure exerted by environmental factors through **natural selection**. Strong selection pressure leads to many new adaptations; weak selection pressure to few. *See* **adaptation**.

selective breeding
Breeding from organisms with only desirable characteristics. It mimics **natural selection**, but the **selection pressure** is applied directly by humans. Selective breeding provides direct evidence that selection can give rise to specific characteristics and the production of distinct forms of **species**.

selfish gene
A term first proposed in 1976 by the British biologist Richard Dawkins to describe the hypothesis that organisms exist merely to replicate existing **genes**, rather than that genes function as the agents by which organisms survive and reproduce. This implies that **natural selection** acts on the genes rather than on the whole organism.

self-pollination
In plants, the transfer of pollen from the male reproductive organ (anther) to the receptive part of the female reproductive organ (stigma) on the same flower. *See* **apogamy** and **cross-pollination**.

semi-conservative replication
Replication of double-stranded **nucleic acid** so that each daughter duplex contains one of the original (conserved) sugar phosphate strands and one newly synthesized strand. *See* **replication (DNA)**.

sex chromosome
A **chromosome** that influences the determination of the sex of an individual. In humans, females have two similar sex chromosomes, termed the X chromosomes, while males have an X and a smaller Y chromosome. In fowl it is the females that have dissimilar sex chromosomes, designated Z and W chromosomes, while the males have two similar W chromosomes. *See* **heterogametic sex, homogametic sex** and **sex determination**.

CONNECTIONS

THE REASONS FOR SEX 98
CLINICAL AND FORENSIC GENETICS 138

sex determination
The process by which the sex of an organism is determined. In many species, the sex of an individual is dictated by the two **sex chromosomes** (X and Y or W and Z) it receives from its parents. In mammals, some plants, and a few insects, males are XY, and females XX; in birds, reptiles, some amphibians and butterflies the reverse is the case. In 1991 it was shown that human maleness is caused by a single gene on the Y chromosome. In bees and wasps, males are produced from unfertilized eggs and females from fertilized eggs. Environmental factors can affect some fish and reptiles, such as turtles, where sex is influenced by the temperature at which the eggs develop. Most fish have a very flexible system of sex determination, which can be affected by external factors. For example, in wrasse all individuals develop into females, but the largest individual in each area or school changes sex to become the local breeding male.

SEMI-CONSERVATIVE REPLICATION

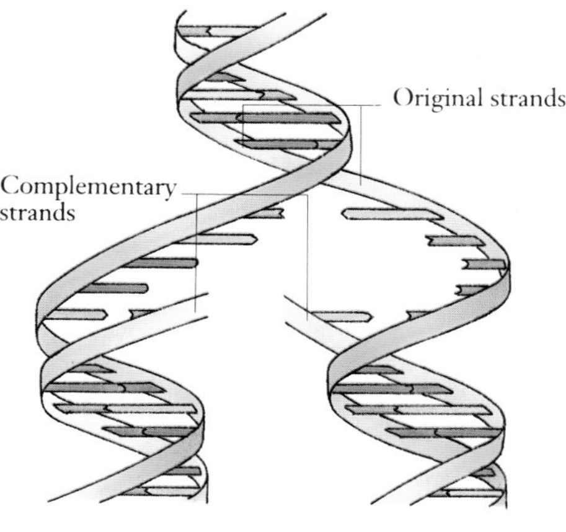

CONNECTIONS

SEXUAL REPRODUCTION 78
CROSSOVER AND LINKAGE 82

sex linkage
The tendency for some characteristics to occur exclusively or predominantly in one sex. Human examples include red-green color blindness and hemophilia, both found mostly in males. Both are recessive and are determined by **genes** on the X chromosome (*see* **sex chromosomes**). Since females possess two X chromosomes, a recessive **allele** on one is likely to be masked by the corresponding allele on the other. In males (who have one X chromosome and a largely inert Y chromosome) any gene on the X chromosome is automatically expressed. Color blindness and hemophilia can appear in females, but only if they are **homozygous** for these traits, due to **inbreeding**, for example.

sexual reproduction
Reproductive process in organisms that requires the union, or **fertilization**, of **gametes.** These are usually produced by two individuals, though **self-fertilization** occurs in a few **hermaphrodites**. Most organisms other than bacteria and cyanobacteria (blue-green algae) show some sort of sexual process. Except in some lower organisms, the gametes are of two distinct types: eggs and sperm. Eggs are produced by females, sperm by males. The fusion of a male and female gamete produces a zygote, from which a new individual develops. The alternatives to sexual reproduction are **parthenogenesis** and **asexual reproduction** by means of spores.

sexual selection
A process similar to **natural selection** but relating exclusively to success in finding a mate for the purpose of **sexual reproduction** and producing offspring. Sexual selection occurs when one sex (usually the male) competes for access to the opposite sex for the purpose of mating, or where one sex (usually the female) actively chooses a mate of the opposite sex. Sexual selection results in enhanced differences between the sexes: for example, to increase their ability to intimidate or fight other members of their sex or to increase their attractiveness to the opposite sex. Unlike natural selection, sexual selection promotes the breeding of the fittest members of a particular sex rather than of the fittest members of the whole population.

CONNECTIONS
EVOLUTION BY NATURAL SELECTION **88**
STRATEGIES FOR SURVIVAL **102**

silent mutation
Any **mutation** that does not affect the **phenotype** of an organism; for example, a **point mutation** in a **structural gene** that specifies the same **amino acid** as the original **codon** (a same-sense mutation).

sister chromatid exchange
The exchange of **chromatids** derived from the same **chromosome** during nuclear division by a mechanism similar to **crossing-over**. The rate of sister chromatid exchange induced by potential **mutagens** is widely used as a measure of their mutagenicity.

smooth endoplasmic reticulum
Regions of the **endoplasmic reticulum** at which the outer surface of the organelle membrane that is in contact with the **cytoplasm** lacks **ribosomes**. *See* **rough endoplasmic reticulum**.

somatic cell hybridization
The joining of **somatic cells** from two individuals or **species** to form a hybrid cell containing the **chromosomes** of both. *See* **hybridoma**.

somatic cells
All the cells of the body, other than the gametes (sex cells) and the cells from which they develop. *See* **germ cells.**

somatic mutation
A **mutation** that arises in a **somatic cell** and thus cannot be passed on to the progeny of the individual in which it occurs.

speciation
The separation of an interbreeding **population** into groups, members of which lose the ability to interbreed with members of the other groups, so that each group becomes genetically distinct. *See also* **allopatric evolution, evolution, species** and **sympatric speciation**.

species
A category of organisms that consists of groups of similar individuals that can interbreed among themselves and produce fertile offspring. Species are the lowest level in the system of biological classification. Related species are grouped together in a **genus**. A species is defined by two Latinized names, its genus name and its species name, both printed in italics. Thus the lion is *Panthera leo*. Within a species there are usually two or more separate populations, interbreeding groups of individuals which may in time become distinctive enough to be designated subspecies or varieties and could eventually give rise to new species through **speciation**.

sperm
Abbreviation of spermatozoon, a male **gamete**. A sperm cell usually has a head capsule containing a **nucleus** and a special **enzyme**-secreting region for penetrating the ovum (female gamete); a middle portion containing **mitochondria** (which provide energy); and a long tail (flagellum) for swimming to the ovum (*see* **sexual reproduction**). A few animals (such as crabs and lobsters) have nonmotile sperm. The term is commonly used for the male gametes of animals, and sometimes also for the motile male gametes (antherozoids) of lower plants.

S phase
The stage in the **cell cycle** when **DNA replication** takes place.

spindle
A structure formed from protein **microtubules** in the **cytoplasm** of cells during **metaphase** in nuclear division. They form a structural framework for the positioning and movement of **chromosomes**, which are attached by their **centromeres** (*see* **kinetochore**) to the spindle fibers at the widest part of the spindle (the equator). **Centrioles** are associated with the poles of the spindle.

splicing
1 Cutting a DNA molecule and joining it onto a different one. For example, particular sequences of **DNA** are spliced together to produce **recombinant DNA**. **2**. The removal of **introns** from a newly transcribed **messenger RNA** molecule and the rejoining of the remaining **exons** to form a mature mRNA molecule. *See* **protein synthesis** and **recombinant DNA technology**.

spontaneous mutation
Also known as a background **mutation, it** appears to occur naturally without any external **mutagens**, as from spontaneous errors in **DNA replication** and repair. Mutations caused by natural levels of gamma or ultraviolet radiation are also sometimes called spontaneous mutations, though this is not technically correct.

sporophyte
A phase of the life cycle of some plants that reproduce asexually by spores (produced by **meiosis**), characterized by the double (diploid) chromosome number in the **somatic cells**. *See* **alternation of generations**.

sticky ends
Complementary single-stranded ends of double-stranded **nucleic acid** that are produced by the action of certain **restriction endonucleases**. These **enzymes** cut the nucleic acid at specific base sequences, producing a staggered cleavage such that the resulting nucleic acid fragments have single-stranded tails. Different fragments produced by the action of the same endonucleases can be joined together (annealed) by base pairing (*see* **base pairs**) between their complementary single-stranded tails. Also known as cohesive ends. *See* **recombinant DNA technology**.

stop codon
Any of the three codons (sequences of three **bases** on a **messenger RNA** molecule) UAA, UAG and UGA that specify the termination of **polypeptide** synthesis during **translation**. Also called termination codon. *See* **protein synthesis**.

STICKY ENDS

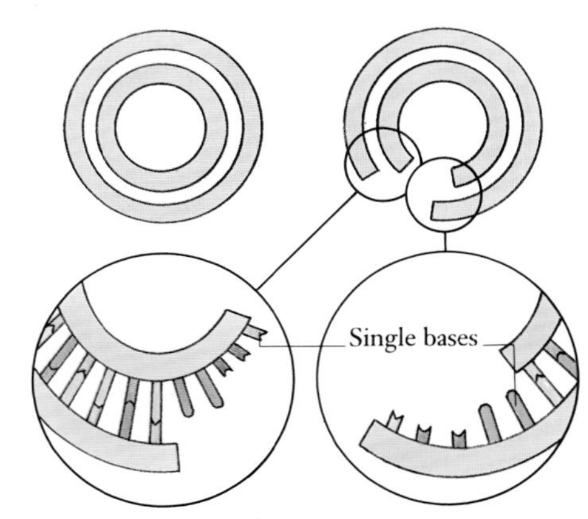

structural gene
A segment of **DNA** that codes for the specific **amino acid** sequence of a **polypeptide** chain or for a **transfer RNA** or **ribosomal RNA** molecule. *See* **regulator gene**.

survival of the fittest
A basic principle in classical evolutionary theory which postulates that those members of a **population** that are best adapted to a particular environment will be at a selective advantage in passing on their genes to the next generation. Evolutionary "fitness" refers not to health but to breeding success: those individuals that are better adapted have more chance of reaching reproductive age and passing on their favorable characteristics to their offspring. *See* **Darwinism, evolution** and **natural selection**.

CONNECTIONS

EVOLUTION BY NATURAL SELECTION 88
STRATEGIES FOR SURVIVAL 102

sympatric speciation
The **evolution** of new **species** within the same geographical range that was inhabited by their ancestors. Although not geographically isolated, the emerging species are at least partially reproductively isolated. *See* **allopatric speciation, reproductive isolation** and **speciation**.

synapsis
The pairing of homologous chromosomes that occurs during prophase I of **meiosis.** *See also* **diploid, eukaryote and homologous chromosome**.

syngamy
The fusion of the **haploid** nuclei of gametes to produce a **diploid zygote** nucleus during **sexual reproduction**. *See* **gamete**.

taxonomy
The describing, naming and classifying of living organisms into groups (taxa). *See* **classification**.

T cell
Also called a T **lymphocyte**, a T cell is a white blood cell of the immune system that plays several roles in the body's defenses. T cells are so called because they mature in the thymus – a gland composed mostly of lymphoid tissue and found beneath the level of the breastbone in humans. The thymus grows rapidly in an infant but then diminishes gradually in size throughout adulthood. There are three main types of T cells: T helper cells, which allow other immune cells to go into action; T suppressor cells, which prevent specific immune reactions from occurring; and T cytotoxic cells, which kill cells that are cancerous or infected with viruses. T cells have surface receptors that make them specific for particular **antigens**. *See also* **immunity.**

CONNECTIONS

BACTERIA AND VIRUSES 60
THE IMMUNE SYSTEM 140

telocentric chromosome
See **centromere**.

telomere
The specialized end section of a **eukaryote chromosome**. The telomere may be a few hundred base pairs long, and is involved in chromosomal stability and replication. A normal chromosome has two telomeres.

telophase
The fourth and final stage of nuclear division (**meiosis** or **mitosis**) in which the daughter nuclei are reconstructed. **Nuclear membranes** form around the newly separated daughter **chromosomes** and the chromosomes become less condensed and are therefore less visible.

temperate (phage)
Describing a phage (*see* **bacteriophage**) whose **DNA** can be incorporated into the **genome** (genetic material) of the host cell without being expressed. In this state the phage DNA can be replicated and passed on to the next generation of host bacteria. *See* **virulent.**

template
A large molecule that acts like a mold for synthesizing a complementary molecule. For example, during **DNA replication** and **messenger RNA** synthesis, one strand of the parent DNA molecule provides the pattern to guide the production of a complementary strand of DNA or of mRNA as free nucleotide bases pair up alongside their complementary bases (*see* **base pairs**) and are linked together. *See* **transcription**.

teratogen
Any substance that causes congenital malformations.

terminator
A segment of **DNA** that instructs **RNA polymerase** to stop the synthesis of an **RNA** molecule at a specific point during **transcription**.

tertiary structure
The three-dimensional structure of the individual **polypeptide** chains of a globular protein that comprises a stable folding of the chain. The tertiary structure is stabilized by a variety of bonds, including covalent bonds, sulfur–sulfur bridges and ionic attractions. *See* **protein**.

testcross
A breeding experiment used to discover the genotype (genetic make-up) of an individual organism. By crossing this organism with a double recessive individual (*see* **recessive allele**) of the same **species**, the offspring will reveal whether the test individual is homozygous (has similar alleles) or heterozygous (has different alleles) for the characteristic in question. In peas, a tall plant under investigation would be crossed with a double recessive short plant with known genotype tt. The results of the cross will be all tall plants if the test plant is TT. If the individual is in fact Tt then there will be some short plants (genotype tt) among the offspring. *See* **Mendelian inheritance**.

thymine
A **pyrimidine base** that occurs in **DNA** and pairs normally with **adenine**. *See* **base pairs**.

tissue culture
1 A method of cloning whole plants from small numbers of cells cultured in the laboratory. Tissue culture is an important technique for propagating new genetic strains of

TESTCROSS

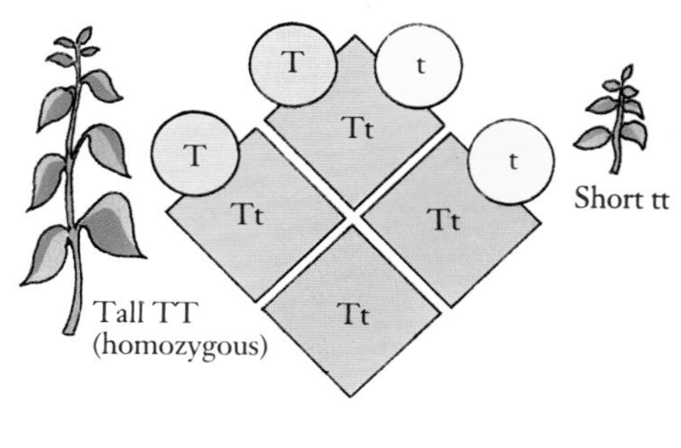

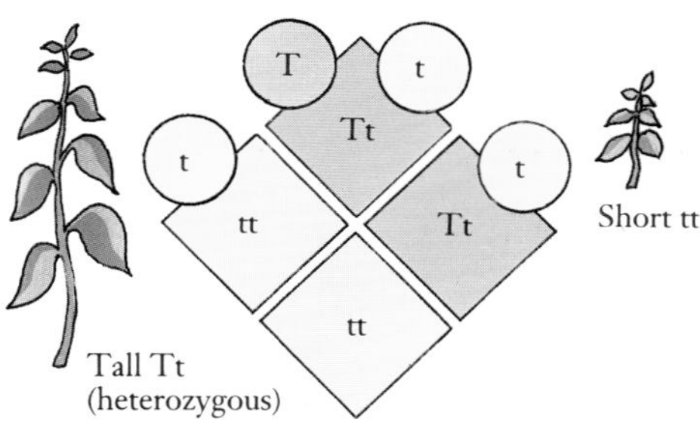

garden and crop plants, as it avoids the mixing of genetic characters that occurs with reproduction by seed (*see* **sexual reproduction** and **recombination**), and is also much faster. **2** The growth of cells and tissues outside the body on artificial media.

CONNECTIONS

LIVING FACTORIES **130**
THE NEW FARMING REVOLUTION **132**

tracer
A compound in which a stable atom is replaced by a radioactive **isotope** of the same element to enable its path through a biological system to be traced. These compounds are also called labeled compounds.

transcription
See **protein synthesis**.

transduction
The transfer of genetic material between cells by infectious mobile genetic elements such as viruses (especially **bacteriophages**). Transduction is used in **genetic engineering** to produce new varieties of bacteria. *See* **vector**.

transfer RNA
A small **RNA** molecule which combines with a specific **amino acid** and transports it to the **ribosome** during **polypeptide** synthesis (*see* **protein synthesis**). tRNA has a specific three-dimensional structure, which includes a triplet of bases at one end (the anticodon) and a specific attachment site for the corresponding amino acid. At the ribosome the tRNA is attracted to a specific **codon** on the **messenger RNA** in the ribosome, to which the three bases of its anticodon base pair (*see* **base pairs**), thus holding the tRNA in place while its amino acid is bonded to an amino acid on an adjacent tRNA molecule. The tRNA molecule then leaves the ribosome and returns to the cytoplasm.

CONNECTIONS

TRANSLATING THE CODE **68**
SWITCHING GENES ON AND OFF **70**

transformation (bacteria)
A change in the genetic make-up of a cell due to the uptake of foreign **DNA** either from a **vector** such as a virus or directly from the surrounding medium. The foreign DNA may be derived from another bacterium, or it may be purified DNA prepared in the laboratory. It becomes incorporated into the cell's **genome** by recombination. Transformation can occur naturally during certain growth phases in some bacteria; bacterial cells that can take up DNA are said to be competent.

TRANSFER RNA

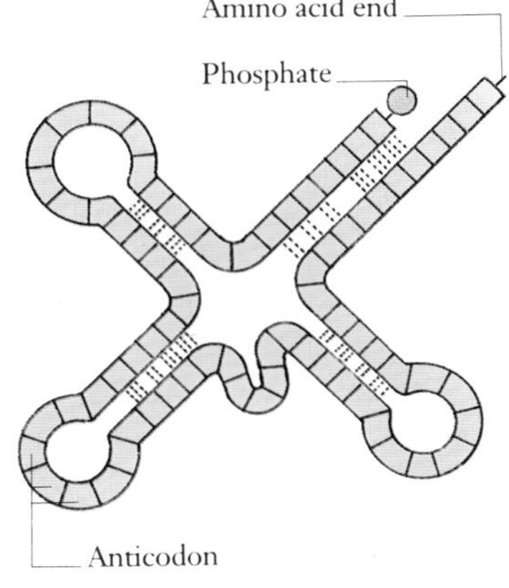

transformation (eukaryotic cells)
The change that occurs in **tissue culture** of certain cells in which the cells exhibit characteristics of tumor cells (such as unlimited *in vitro* growth and division, the development of new surface **antigens**, loss of adhesive properties). These changes may also be brought about by certain viruses.

transgenic
Describing an organism that has had a foreign **gene** or genes deliberately added to it by means of **genetic engineering**. The foreign DNA is present in both **germ cells** and **somatic cells**, and thus can be passed on to subsequent generations.

translation
See **protein synthesis**.

translocation
The movement of a portion of a **chromosome** to another part of the same chromosome or to an entirely different chromosome. *See also* **reciprocal translocation**.

transposition
The **translocation** of a **transposon** from one site to another (target) site.

transposon
A segment of **DNA** that can spontaneously move in and out of a **chromosome** or **plasmid**. If the transposon is inserted into a **structural gene** then an insertion **mutation** occurs, either inactivating the gene or resulting in a new **phenotype**; Transposons are found in both **eukaryotes** and **prokaryotes**. Also known as transposable elements or jumping genes.

transversion
A **mutation** occurring in **DNA** or **RNA** in which a **purine** base is substituted for a **pyrimidine** base or vice versa, resulting in a **point mutation**.

triplet code
The genetic code produced by successive groups of three **nucleotides** (triplets or codons) in **RNA** (or **DNA**), each of which specifies a particular **amino acid**. The codons are arranged in a linear order along the **nucleic acid**, thus specifying the linear order of amino acids in the resulting **polypeptide**. *See* **genetic code** and **protein synthesis**.

triploid
An organism, tissue or cell that contains three sets of **chromosomes** (3n). *See* **polyploid**.

trisomy
Three copies of a particular **chromosome** per cell. For example, Down's syndrome is the result of cells having three copies of chromosome 21.

tRNA
See **transfer RNA**.

true-breeding organism
1 A homozygous (having two identical **alleles** for a particular trait) organism that, when self-fertilized, produces offspring identical to the parent in respect of the **trait** under consideration. **2** A homozygous organism that, when crossed with a similar homozygote of the same **species**, produces offspring that are all identical to the parents in respect of a particular trait or traits. *See also* **Mendelian inheritance**.

unequal crossing-over
Crossing-over in which the two **chromosomes** do not receive equal lengths of **DNA**. This results in one **chromatid** having more than one copy of a certain **gene** or genes, which is or are now missing from the other.

uracil
A **pyrimidine base** that occurs in **RNA** but not in **DNA**. Uracil pairs with **adenine** in RNA. *See* **base pairs**.

variation
A difference between individuals of the same **species**, found in any sexually reproducing **population**. The cause of variation may be

genetic (inherited), environmental or more usually a combination of the two. The origins of variation can be traced to the **recombination** of the genetic material during the formation of the **gametes** and, more rarely, to **mutation**.

CONNECTIONS

variegation
The irregular coloration seen in the leaves and petals of some plants. Variegation may be the result of viral infection or mineral deficiency or it may be genetically determined. Genetic causes include genetically programmed patterns, the effects of chloroplast **genes** (*see* **extrachromosomal inheritance**), **transposons**, or the mixed genetic make-up of a **chimera**.

vector
A plasmid, virus or other vehicle used to transfer **DNA** from one organism to another to make **recombinant DNA** or to produce a **transgenic** organism.

vesicles
Small, membrane bound sacs within the **cytoplasm** of living cells. Vesicles are budded off from the **Golgi apparatus** and **endoplasmic reticulum**. They are used for transporting or storing substances.

virion
A complete mature virus particle, including both its genetic material and its protein coat. *See* **virus**.

viroid
An infective agent, smaller than a **virus**, consisting of a single strand of nucleic acid (usually a rod or circle of **RNA**) with no protein coat. Viroids cause stunting in plants and rare diseases in animals, including humans.

virology
The study of viruses. A Russian bacteriologist, Dmitry Iosifovich Ivanovsky (1864–1920), identified the first **virus** in 1892, after observing that tobacco mosaic disease could be transmitted through a filter that kept out bacteria; the causative agent was a virus, although it could not be seen until the electron microscope was introduced in 1940. The tobacco mosaic virus was the first to be crystallized (made into a pure form consisting of several thousand viruses and ideal for studying); poliomyelitis was the second.

virulent (phage)
Describing a phage that always destroys the host cell. *See* **temperate, bacteriophage** and **lysogeny**.

virus
An infectious microorganism consisting of a core of **nucleic acid** (DNA or RNA) enclosed in a protein coat (capsid). Viruses are non-cellular and are able to function and reproduce only if they can invade a living cell to use the cell's protein synthesis apparatus to replicate themselves. In the process they may disrupt or alter the host cell's own DNA (*see* **lysogeny**).

Bacteriophages are viruses that infect bacterial cells. Retroviruses are of special interest because they have an RNA **genome** and can produce DNA from this RNA by a process called **reverse transcription**. Viroids are infective agents even smaller than viruses, consisting only of nucleic acid. It is debatable whether viruses and viroids are truly living organisms, because they are incapable of an independent existence. *See also* AIDS, **bacteriophage, retrovirus** and **viroid**.

CONNECTIONS

Wallace's line
An imaginary line running down the Lombok Strait in southeast Asia, between the island of Bali and the islands of Lombok and Sulawesi. It was identified by the English naturalist Alfred Russel Wallace (1823–1913) as separating the southern Asian (Oriental) and Australian (Notogean) biogeographical regions, each of which has its own distinctive animals. It was while traveling in this region and making these observations that Wallace developed his theory of **natural selection**. Subsequently, others studying the area have placed the boundary between these two regions at different points in the Malay archipelago, owing to overlapping migration patterns. The zone of mixing is known as "Wallacea". *See also* **evolution, Darwinism** and **neo-Darwinism.**

wild type
The naturally occurring **gene** for a particular character that is typical of most individuals of a **species**, as distinct from new forms (**alleles**) that arise by **mutation**. Wild type characteristics are usually dominant.

X chromosome
The larger of the two mammalian **sex chromosomes**, the smaller being the Y chromosome. Female mammals have two X chromosomes, while males have an X and a Y. Genes carried on the X chromosome produce the phenomenon of **sex linkage**. *See* **sex determination**.

Y chromosome
The smaller of the two mammalian **sex chromosomes**. In male mammals it ispaired with the other type of sex chromosome (X), which carries far more **genes**. The Y chromosome is the smallest of all the mammalian chromosomes and is considered to be largely inert (that is, without direct effect on the physical body). *See* **sex determination**.

zygote
The ovum after **fertilization** but before it undergoes cleavage to begin embryonic development; that is, a diploid cell (having two sets of chromosomes) resulting from the fusion of two haploid **gametes** (each with only one set of chromosomes).

WALLACE'S LINE

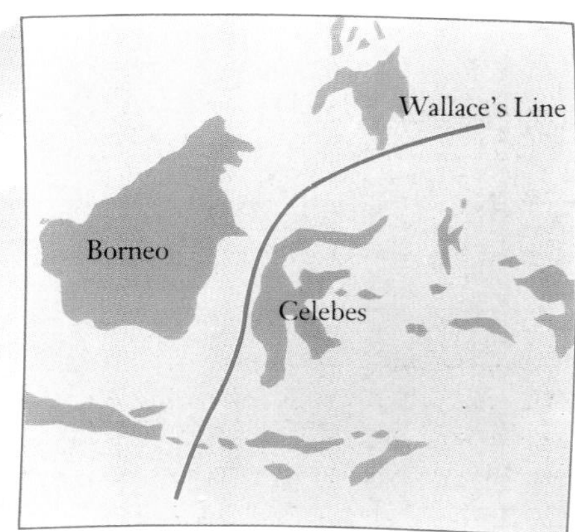

1

STRUCTURES *of Life*

HOW IS IT POSSIBLE to tell that something is alive? It is easy to recognize that animals are living – they are almost constantly moving when awake. Plants seldom move, but over a period of time they grow and set seed – they reproduce. Living things also respond to their environment in order to survive.

Growth, reproduction and responses to stimuli all require food (raw materials) and energy (which, for animals, is derived from food). Harnessing this energy requires multiple chemical reactions that take place inside the cells of a living organism. Among the most important are the reactions that release energy from food. These reactions are remarkably similar in all living organisms.

The great diversity of life is proof that there are many different ways of using energy to organize living material. Each kind of organism has a unique blueprint, which controls the ways in which its metabolic reactions build up its body and direct its lifestyle. This blueprint controls the timing of growth, development and reproduction, as well as short-term responses such as fear and aggression in higher animals. It even directs ageing and death: each species has a finite lifespan. Accurate copies of the blueprint must also be passed on to the next generation. The science of genetics aims to explain how this blueprint exerts its control on every aspect of life.

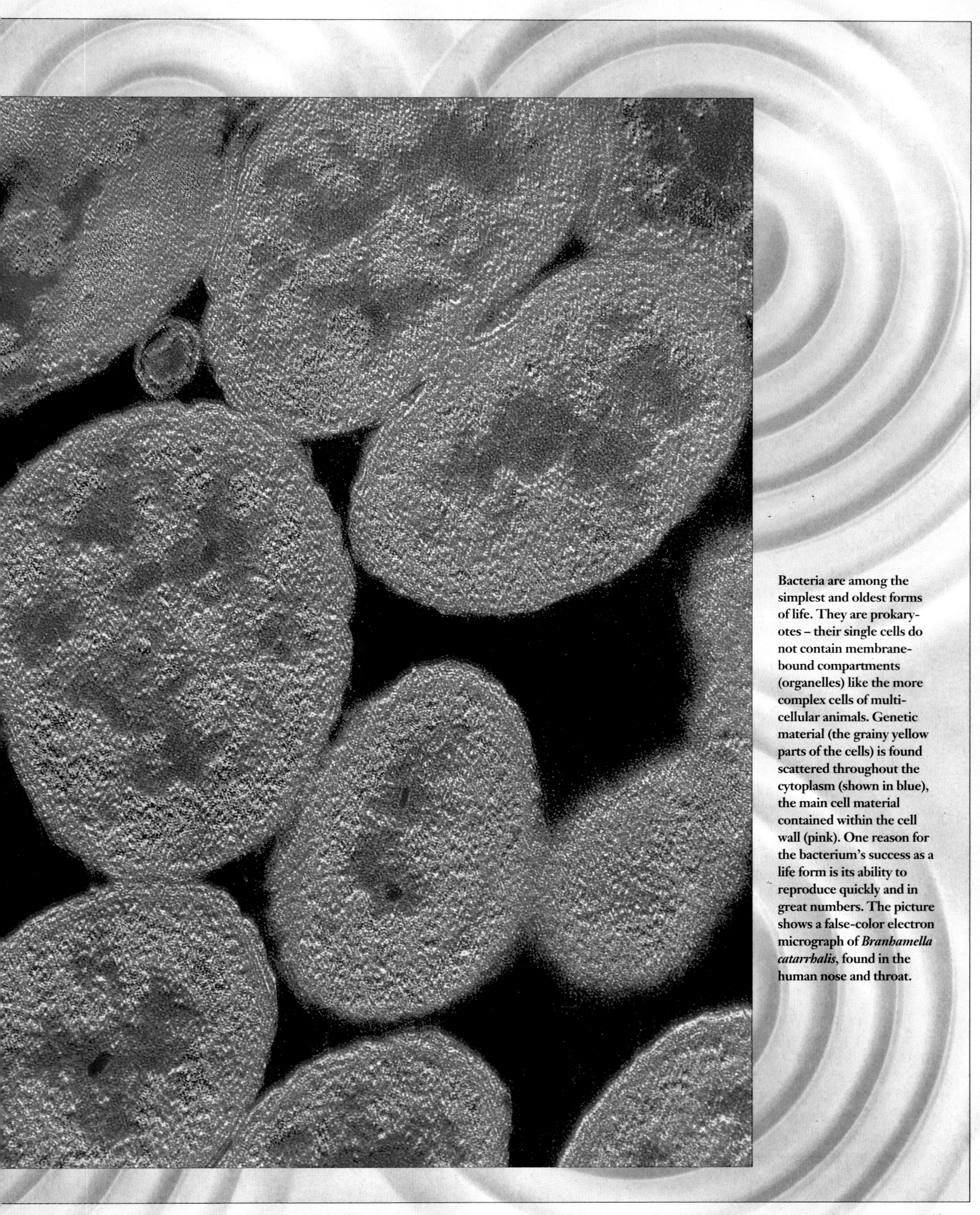

Bacteria are among the simplest and oldest forms of life. They are prokaryotes – their single cells do not contain membrane-bound compartments (organelles) like the more complex cells of multicellular animals. Genetic material (the grainy yellow parts of the cells) is found scattered throughout the cytoplasm (shown in blue), the main cell material contained within the cell wall (pink). One reason for the bacterium's success as a life form is its ability to reproduce quickly and in great numbers. The picture shows a false-color electron micrograph of *Branhamella catarrhalis*, found in the human nose and throat.

THE LIVING CELL

ALL living things are made up of one or more small compartments or cells. Cells are capable of maintaining and repairing themselves, and (usually) of reproducing. Every cell present in the world today has arisen from the division of a pre-existing cell.

A cell is a mass of living matter surrounded by a thin membrane (the plasma membrane), composed of various lipids (fats) and proteins. This membrane forms a barrier between the living matter and its surroundings, allowing the many reactions of life to proceed without interference from other chemicals in the environment. Materials can pass in and out of cells through the plasma membrane, but the cell can control which substances pass in each direction.

Recognition molecules on the surface of the plasma membrane allow cells to recognize each other and to sense their surroundings. They can distinguish between normal and foreign cells and substances, and can receive and respond to chemical messengers (hormones) from other parts of the body.

Cells vary greatly in size, but the average cell is invisible to the naked eye. They are usually measured in micrometers (thousandths of a millimeter). Most cells are between 10 and 30 micrometers in diameter. A few, such as a newly fertilized bird's egg, some frog and fish eggs and certain giant algal cells, are large enough to see with the naked eye. The size of most cells is restricted by the need to transport materials across the cell. This transport occurs mainly by diffusion.

KEYWORDS

CELL MEMBRANE
EUKARYOTE
NUCLEUS
ORGANELLE
VESICLE

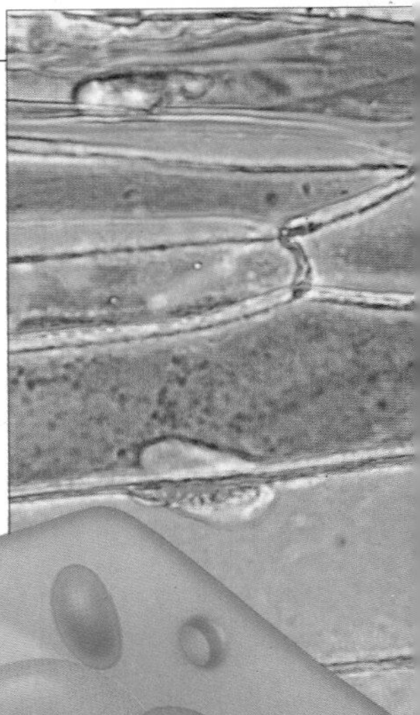

■ The cell wall of the plant cell BELOW gives it a definite shape. Many plant cells contain organelles called chloroplasts, in which photosynthesis takes place. Mature plant cells have a single large central vacuole (a fluid-filled membrane sac). The pressure of the fluid in the vacuole stretches the cell wall until it is rigid. In small plants this is the sole means of support. A micrograph of onion cells RIGHT indicates the small nuclei, and the rigid, angular shape of the cells.

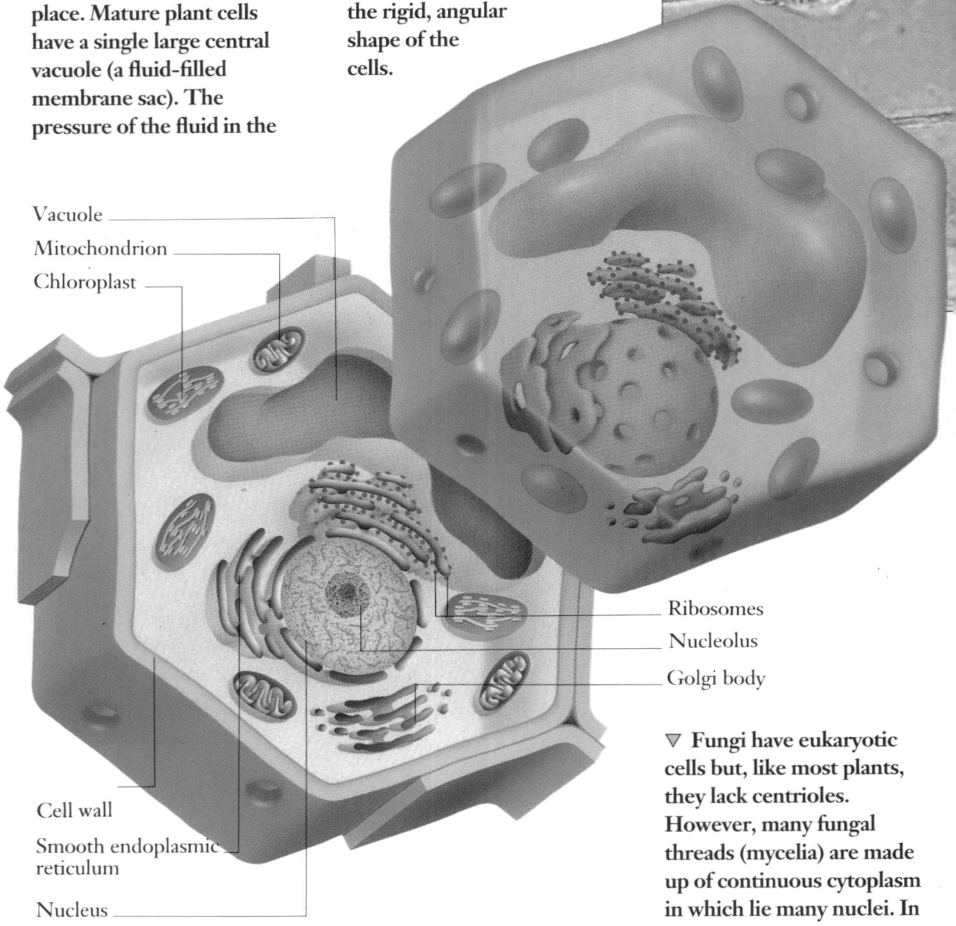

▽ Fungi have eukaryotic cells but, like most plants, they lack centrioles. However, many fungal threads (mycelia) are made up of continuous cytoplasm in which lie many nuclei. In some species there are occasional cross-walls. Materials are carried around the mycelium by streaming of the cytoplasm. The fungal cell wall is made up of a mixture of cellulose and chitin (a substance commonly found in invertebrate animals).

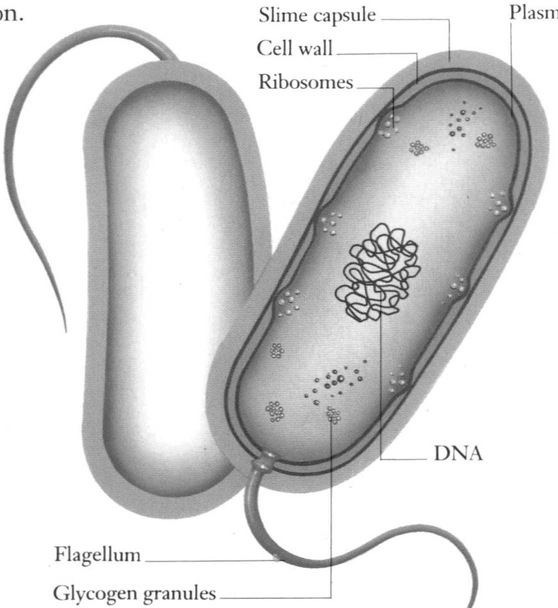

▷ A bacterium is a typical prokaryotic cell. The nucleus and organelles seen in the animal cell are absent. Instead, the DNA is confined to a certain part of the cytoplasm, the nucleoid. Ribosomes are scattered through the cytoplasm. A cell wall gives the cell a definite shape. The flagellum, used for propulsion, is made up of a complex arrangement of interlinked microfilaments. Other tiny filaments (pili) are used to recognize and to attach to other cells.

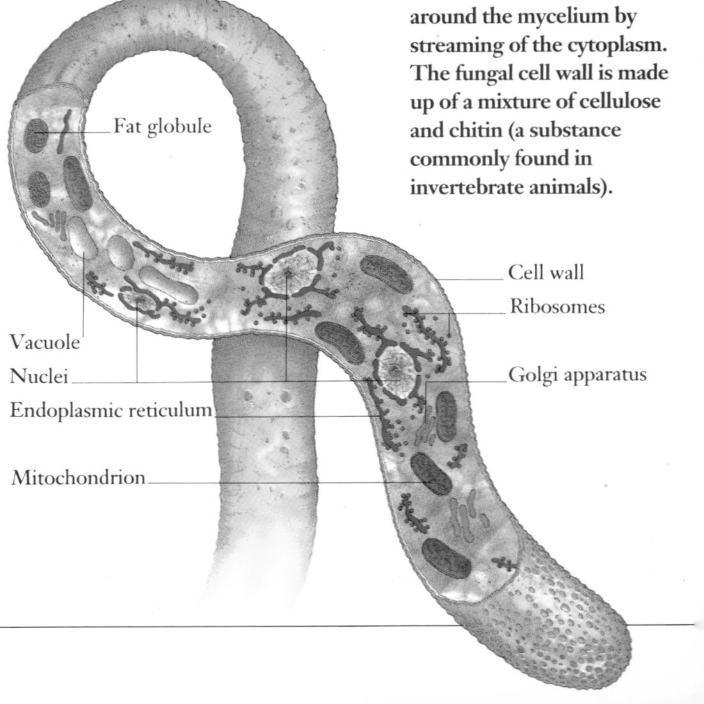

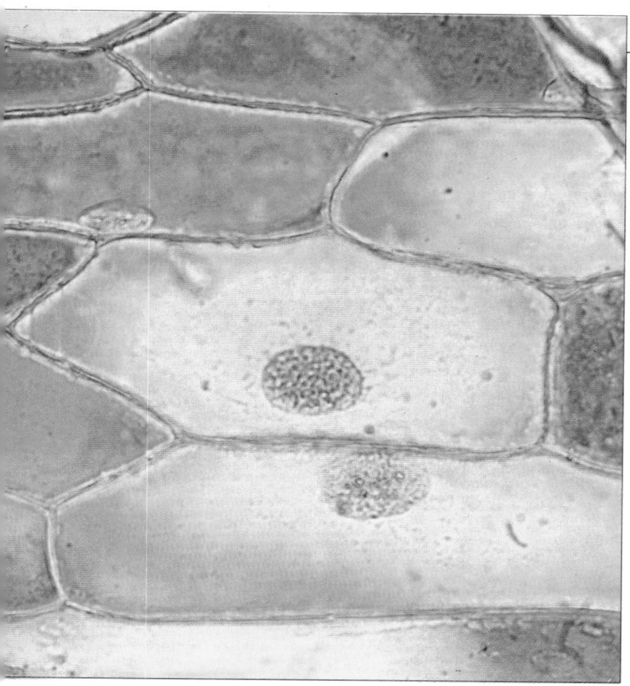

The larger the cell, the longer the diffusion path and the less efficient the transport.

Despite the great variety of living creatures, their component cells all have a great deal in common. There are two main kinds of cell. The simpler, such as bacteria, have a single membrane-enclosed compartment, a prokaryotic cell (from the Greek for "before nucleus"). Prokaryotic cells have no obvious structures or compartments in the cytoplasm, the jellylike material enclosed within the plasma membrane. All other living organisms have eukaryotic cells (from the Greek for "true nucleus"). These contain a number of specialized, membrane-bounded compartments called organelles, one of which – the nucleus – contains the genetic material. The organelles create a series of microenvironments within the cell, in which certain sequences of reactions can proceed at maximum efficiency. They separate different chemical reactions in space and time.

The organelles have the further function of increasing the area of membrane in the cell. Many reactions take place on membranes. Successive reactants can be arranged close together in the correct sequence, speeding up metabolic reactions. Membranes can control the rate of reaction by restricting the rate at which reactants enter the organelle or cell. Potentially harmful waste products of metabolism can be isolated from the rest of the cell in membrane bags and destroyed there if necessary.

Membranes are somewhat fluid structures. The endoplasmic reticulum and Golgi bodies form an interconnected series of membranes, sacs and bags (vesicles) and organelles, which provide a controlled environment for the synthesis and packaging of many cell products. Vesicles pinched off from the system carry the products to other parts of the cell, or fuse with the plasma membrane to release their contents on the cell surface.

The cell also has a skeleton, the cytoskeleton. Throughout the cell are many tiny tubules (microtubules and microfilaments) made up of proteins. Microfilaments, made of the elastic protein actin, enable cells to move and change shape, and sometimes help to hold cells together in tissues. Microtubules consist of parallel rows of globular proteins called tubulin.They can be disassembled and reassembled as needed. They cluster where new membrane is being organized, and form scaffolds that control the way the genetic material is partitioned during cell division. Microtubules may also be involved in the movement of vesicles in the cell.

The most prominent organelle in most cells is the nucleus. This contains the genetic blueprint of the cell, DNA (deoxyribonucleic acid). Even in prokaryotic cells, the DNA is found in a particular part of the cell, the nucleoid. This is the cell's control center. The nucleus contains not only the blueprint for making similar cells, but the blueprint for the whole organism. As a substance is needed by the cell, copies of the relevant part of the blueprint are made and passed into the cytoplasm, to be used as templates for synthesis.

▽ A section through an animal cell, a typical eukaryotic cell. The cell contains various organelles, such as the nucleus, which houses the cell's DNA (its genetic blueprint) and controls its activities; the mitochondria, sites of energy release; the endoplasmic reticulum, where proteins and lipids are made; the Golgi apparatus, where complex substances are made, and where materials are packaged into vesicles for transport; and the centrioles, which help control the distribution of the DNA during cell division. The lack of a rigid cell wall means the cell's shape depends on pressure from its surroundings.

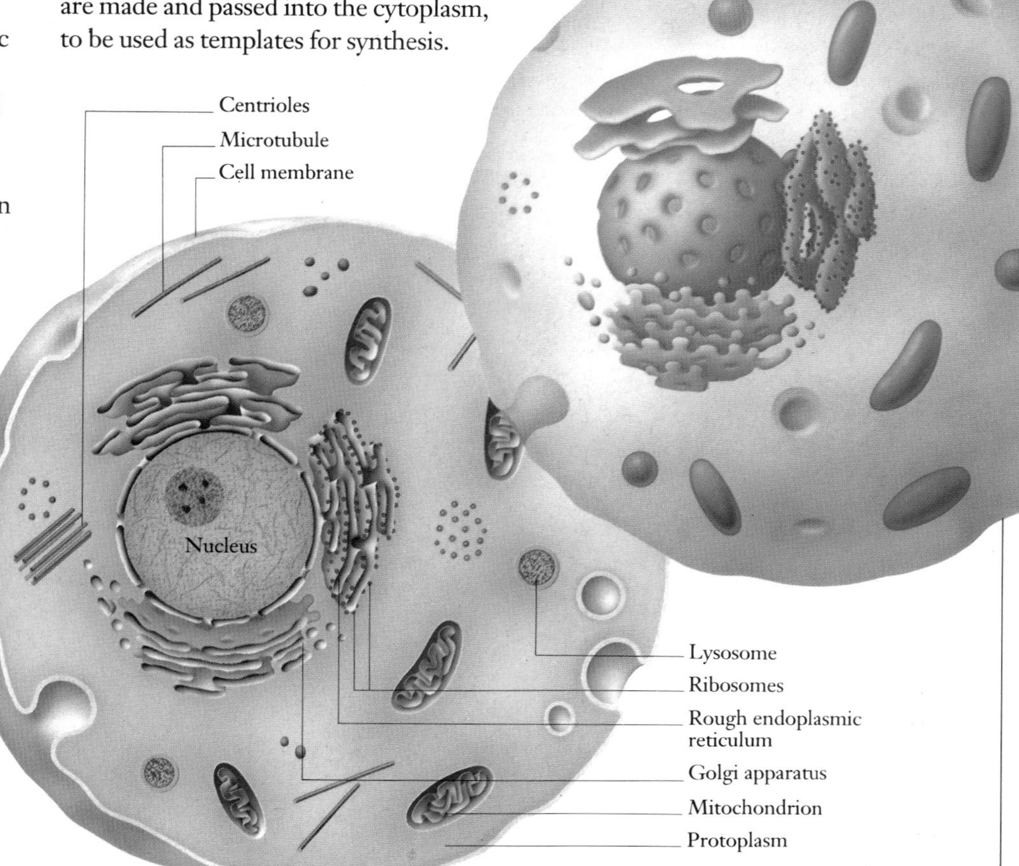

Inside the Nucleus

The nucleus is the control center of the cells of animals and plants. The combined activities of the nuclei of all the cells determine an organism's overall shape, size and behavior. The nucleus contains the genetic blueprint in the form of long molecules of DNA (deoxyribonucleic acid). One or more short stretches of the DNA, called genes, contain the instructions for producing a particular characteristic such as eye color, or a particular hormone. Every nucleus contains the complete blueprint for producing the whole organism. However, only part of the blueprint is active in any one cell – the part needed to produce that kind of cell and control its activities. In addition to DNA, the nucleus contains other molecules that are involved in reading the DNA and carrying its instructions to other parts of the cell.

KEYWORDS

CELL DIVISION
CHROMOSOME
DNA
EUKARYOTE
GENE
HISTONE
HOMOLOGOUS
KARYOTYPE
PROTEIN

The DNA must be kept apart from other chemicals in the cell to avoid altering it in any way. A double membrane called the nuclear envelope provides a barrier between the cytoplasm and the DNA. Pores in the membrane allow messenger molecules to travel across the barrier but keep the DNA in the nucleus.

When a cell divides, a complete error-free copy of its DNA must be passed to each daughter cell. In a human cell, 2 meters of DNA are packed into a nucleus with a diameter of just 0.01 mm.The total blueprint is divided into sections of DNA, each organized into a structure called a chromosome. Each species has a characteristic number of chromosomes. Humans have 46, horses 64 and fruit flies 8. Some plant nuclei have over 1000.

In a chromosome, the DNA is associated with proteins, especially small proteins called histones. Some histones act as spools for winding up short stretches of DNA. Each spool, called a nucleosome, bears two spirals of DNA encircling a core of eight histone molecules. An extended thread of DNA coiled around nucleosomes has a beaded appearance under the microscope. Usually, however, these threads are coiled into tight spirals, which in turn form loops that are stabilized by a "scaffold" of other proteins.

Most eukaryotic cells contain two copies of the genetic blueprint: their chromosomes occur in pairs. The members of a pair, called homologous chromosomes, contain similar DNA molecules. The chromosomes of each pair have a characteristic length. One of the pair is derived from the organism's mother, and one from its father. To describe the number, size and appearance of chromosomes of a species – its karyotype – a "photograph" is taken of the condensed chromosomes when they are spread out during cell division. Images of individual chromosomes are then cut out and arranged in pairs of increasing length.

There may be two unmatched chromosomes left over. These contain the blueprint for producing sexual characteristics and controlling sexual behavior. In most species there are two kinds of sex chromosomes, the larger ones called X and the smaller ones Y. The sex of the organism depends on which of these chromosomes it has inherited. A cell may have two Xs, an X and a Y, or just one X or Y. In humans, the cells of females contain two X chromosomes, and the cells of males contain one X and one Y. All other non-sex chromosomes are called autosomes.

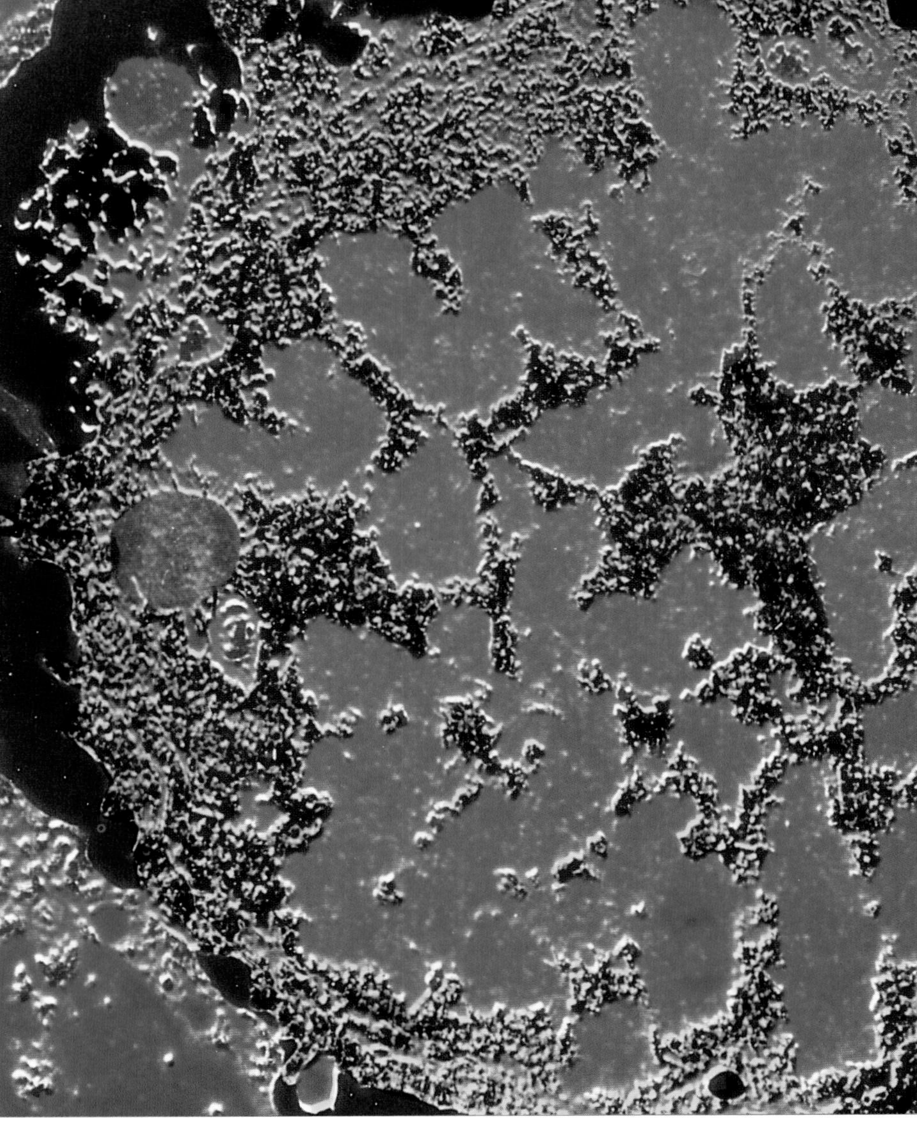

△ The nucleus of a cell contains the genetic material (DNA wrapped in histone proteins), falsely colored red in this electron micrograph of the nucleus of a human white blood cell. The picture was taken just before the nucleus divided, at a time when the tangle of threads of DNA and protein was condensing into tight coils, forming dense objects which impede the microscope's beam of electrons to show up dark (colored red here) in the picture.

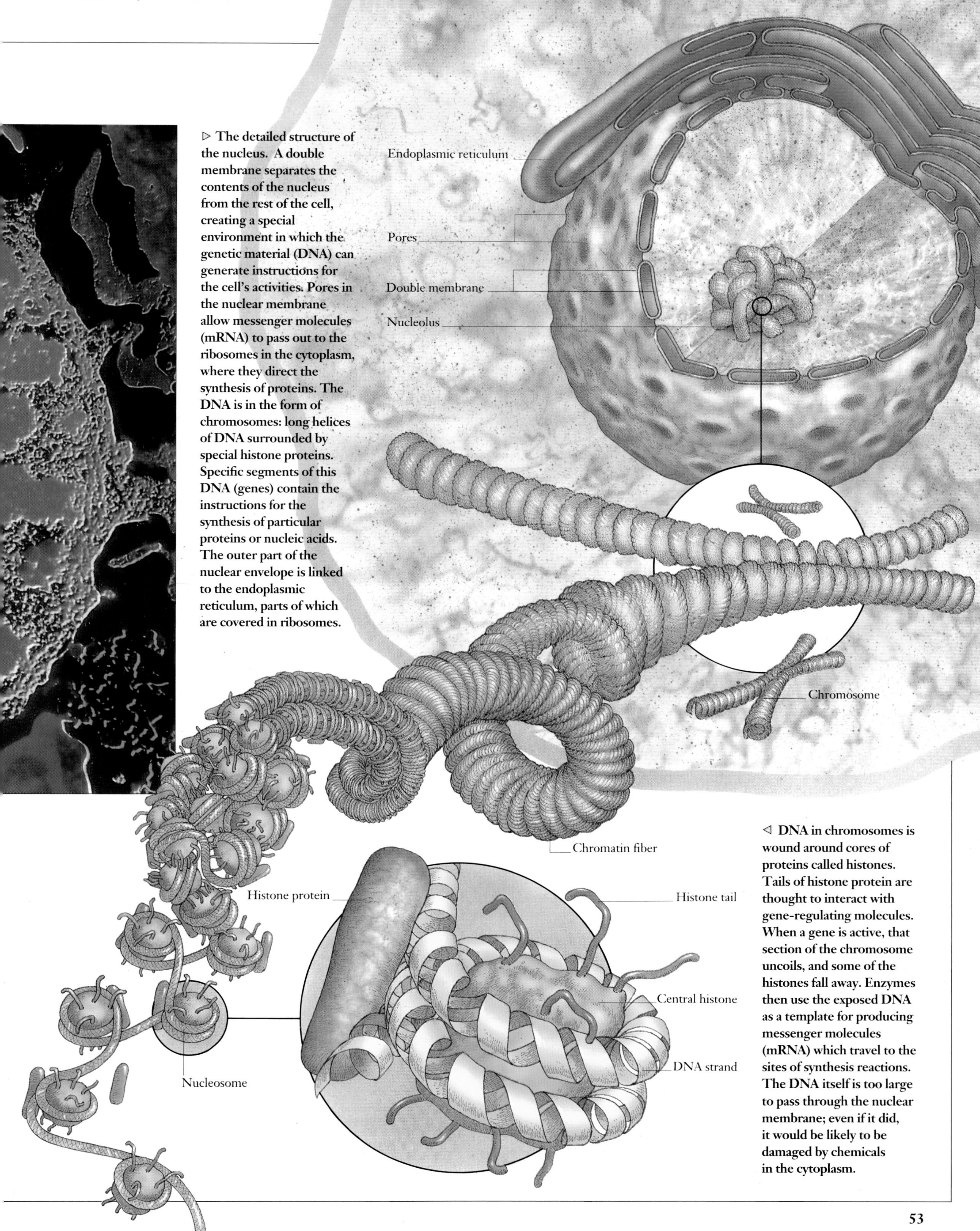

▷ **The detailed structure of the nucleus. A double membrane separates the contents of the nucleus from the rest of the cell, creating a special environment in which the genetic material (DNA) can generate instructions for the cell's activities. Pores in the nuclear membrane allow messenger molecules (mRNA) to pass out to the ribosomes in the cytoplasm, where they direct the synthesis of proteins. The DNA is in the form of chromosomes: long helices of DNA surrounded by special histone proteins. Specific segments of this DNA (genes) contain the instructions for the synthesis of particular proteins or nucleic acids. The outer part of the nuclear envelope is linked to the endoplasmic reticulum, parts of which are covered in ribosomes.**

◁ **DNA in chromosomes is wound around cores of proteins called histones. Tails of histone protein are thought to interact with gene-regulating molecules. When a gene is active, that section of the chromosome uncoils, and some of the histones fall away. Enzymes then use the exposed DNA as a template for producing messenger molecules (mRNA) which travel to the sites of synthesis reactions. The DNA itself is too large to pass through the nuclear membrane; even if it did, it would be likely to be damaged by chemicals in the cytoplasm.**

TRACKING DOWN THE MOLECULES

ONCE scientists realized that the hereditary material of cells is carried in the nucleus, the next question was which substance in the nucleus carries the genetic blueprint. The organized distribution of chromosomes between daughter nuclei during nuclear division made them the objects of intense scrutiny. Chromosomes are composed mainly of proteins and deoxyribonucleic acid (DNA). Both kinds of molecule are very large. DNA is relatively simple, with only four kinds of side-groups, but 20 or more different side-groups can be found in proteins. This made proteins the obvious place to begin looking.

KEYWORDS

BACTERIOPHAGE
BACTERIUM
BASE PAIRS
DNA
PROTEIN

An important breakthrough came from the study of bacteria. In 1928 the British bacteriologist Fred Griffith was trying to develop a vaccine against the bacterium *Streptococcus pneumoniae*, which causes pneumonia. He isolated two strains of *Streptococcus*, one with a smooth surface (S) and one with a rough coat (R). When injected into mice, the R bacteria did not cause pneumonia (the R strain is susceptible to attack by the host cell), but all the mice injected with live S cells died, and their blood was found to be teeming with S cells. Griffith found that heat-killed S cells, which by themselves could not kill the mice, caused pneumonia and death when mixed with harmless live R cells and injected into mice. Moreover, live S cells were then found in the mice's blood. The heat had not killed the substance causing pneumonia, and somehow this substance had been transferred to the R cells, transforming them into S cells. All successive generations of these cells were S cells – the transforming substance was inherited.

In 1944 the American chemists Avery, McCarty and MacLeod performed similar experiments. They found that they could block the transformation of harmless bacteria into pathogenic (disease-causing) ones by adding the enzyme deoxyribonuclease to the extracts of the dead S cells. Deoxyribonuclease destroys DNA but has no effect on proteins. This showed that it is DNA which is the transforming agent – the genetic material.

Further proof came from experiments by American biologists Alfred Hershey and Martha Chase in 1952,

Adenine

Guanine

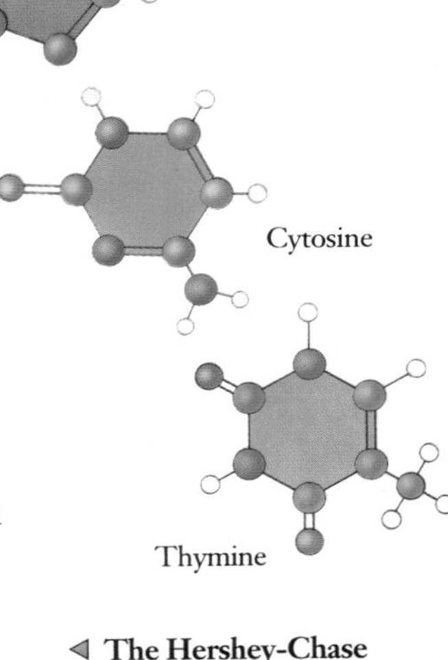

▼ **Adenine (A) and guanine (G), the upper and upper middle molecules, are large purine bases of DNA; cytosine (C) and thymine (T), the lower middle and lower molecules, are smaller pyrimidine bases. All are made of nitrogen, hydrogen, carbon and oxygen (but adenine has no oxygen).**

1 R No R
2 S S
3 Heat-killed S No S
4 R Heat-killed S S

◀ **Fred Griffith's 1928 experiments with vaccines against the pneumonia bacterium, *Streptococcus pneumoniae*, provided early insight into the way in which genetic material is passed on. 1 Bacteria of the rough-coated strain (R) did not cause pneumonia when injected into mice. 2 Bacteria of the smooth-coated strain (S) caused pneumonia; all the injected mice died. Their blood contained large numbers of bacterial cells. 3 Heat-killed S cells did not kill the mice. 4 Heat-killed S cells mixed with live R cells resulted in pneumonia and death. Live S cells were found in the mice's blood. From this, Griffith concluded that the pneumonia-causing substance was transferred from the heat killed S cells to the live R cells, transforming them into S cells.**

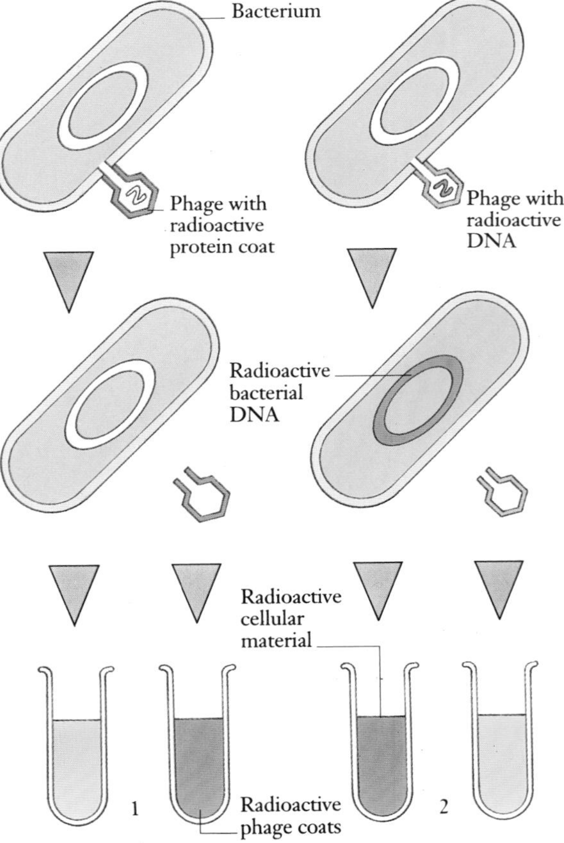

◀ **The Hershey-Chase experiment demonstrated that DNA, not protein, was the basic material of heredity. When bacteriophages infect bacteria, the phage bodies remain on the surface of the bacteria, but something is injected into the bacteria. This substance causes the bacteria to make new phages. Bacteria were infected with phages which had been radioactively labelled with either sulfur (S-35) to tag their protein coat or phosphorus (P-32) to tag their DNA. The cells were then centrifuged to separate the bacterial cells from the phage bodies. 1 The S-35 (protein) label remained in the fluid with the phage coats. 2 The P-32 (DNA) label remained in the cells, showing that it was the DNA that contained the instructions for producing new phages.**

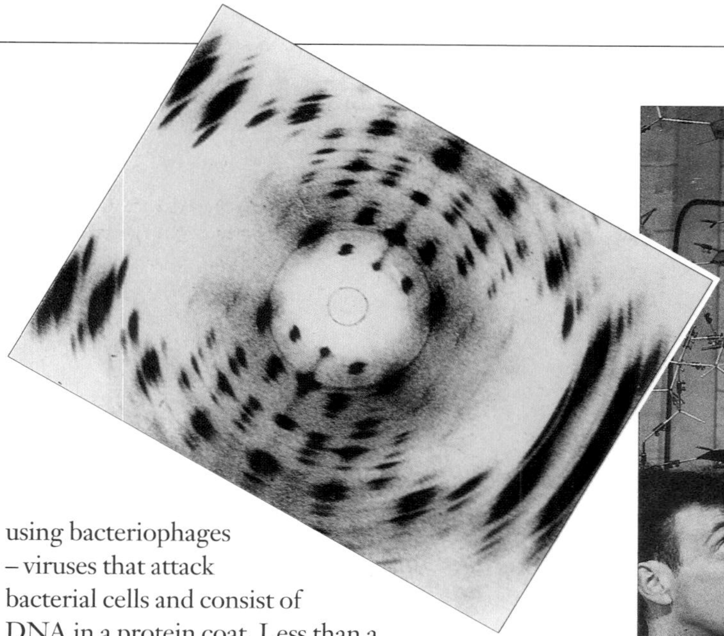

using bacteriophages – viruses that attack bacterial cells and consist of DNA in a protein coat. Less than a minute after a phage has attached to a bacterium, the host cell begins to produce the nucleic acids and proteins to build new phages. Proteins contain the element sulfur but not phosphorus, while DNA contains phosphorus but not sulfur. Using radioactive forms of sulfur and phosphorus, Hershey and Chase were able to label the protein coat and the DNA of the phages. These experiments showed that only the DNA entered the bacterial cells, and it must therefore carry the genetic message.

The next challenge was to find out the detailed structure of DNA, and how the genetic message was encoded in it. Chemical analysis showed that DNA is made up of the sugar deoxyribose, phosphate groups and varying amounts of four small organic molecules called nucleotide bases – adenine, thymine, cytosine and guanine. Cytosine and thymine are pyrimidines, whereas adenine and guanine are purines, which are considerably larger molecules. By the early 1950s Edwin Chargaff and his colleagues in the United States had discovered that the amounts of these four bases differ from species to species, but that the amount of adenine always equals the amount of thymine, and that guanine and cytosine also occur in identical amounts.

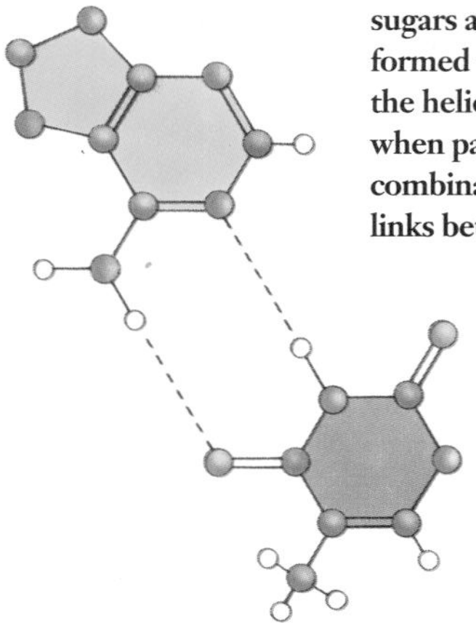

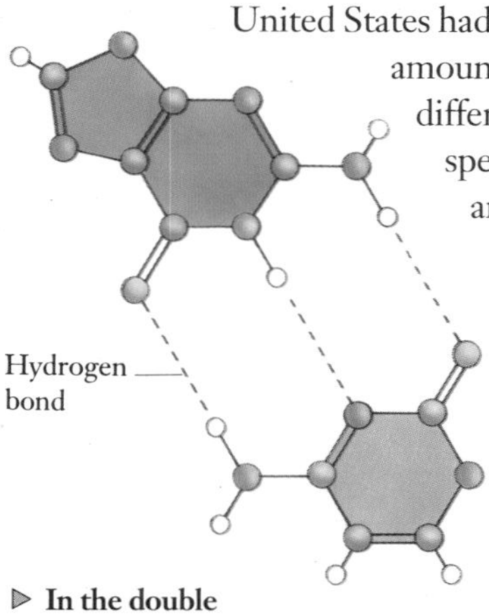

The next clue came from the X-ray crystallography studies of British biophysicists Maurice Wilkins and Rosalind Franklin. These showed that the DNA molecules consist of two strands joined together, the strands being twisted into a helix with a constant diameter of about 2 nanometers (billionths of a meter), and each complete turn of the helix is 3.4 nanometers long.

How could the various bases, sugars and phosphate groups be fitted together to produce such a shape? Two postgraduate students at Cambridge University, American James Watson and British student Francis Crick, used cutout cardboard shapes to work out the possible chemical bonds between the bases, sugars and phosphates. They tried fitting the shapes together, assuming that the sugars and phosphates formed a backbone of the DNA. They realized that if the small purine bases were paired opposite the larger purines, this would give a chain of fairly constant diameter. Further, they proposed that adenine always pairs with thymine, and cytosine with guanine. When arranged at a certain angle, hydrogen bonds form between the pairs of bases. The final solution turned out to be two clockwise spirals of DNA joined together, running in opposite directions – the double helix. Crick, Watson and Wilkins shared a Nobel Prize for this discovery.

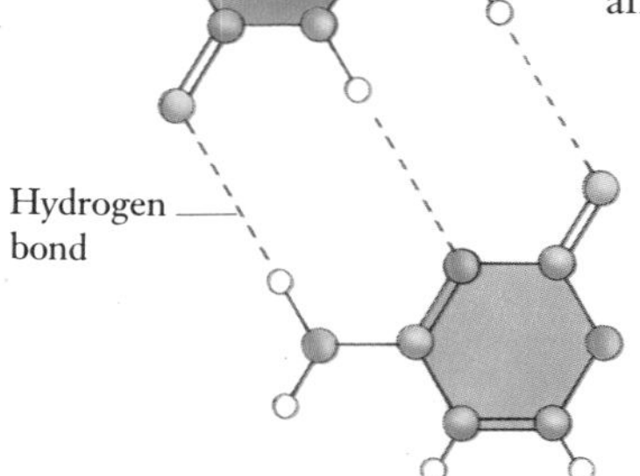

▷ **In the double strands of DNA, adenine bonds with thymine, and guanine with cytosine. The GC pair is stronger because it has three hydrogen bonds compared with two in AT.**

■ **The clues to how DNA controls inheritance lie in its structure. The first indication of this structure came from X-ray diffraction studies of DNA crystals INSET. Analysis of the pattern indicated that the DNA consists of two parallel strands twisted into a helix. Chemical analysis had revealed that DNA was made up of deoxyribose sugars, phosphate groups and four different kinds of organic bases. James Watson and Francis Crick ABOVE showed that the sugars and phosphates formed the backbones of the helices while the bases, when paired in particular combinations, formed the links between them.**

MAKING THE MESSAGE

ALTHOUGH DNA is not a particularly complex molecule, it holds all the genetic information for a particular species. This information is in the form of a code which can be "read" by the cell and used to produce the chemicals that make up the cell's structure and control its activities. Nucleotide bases along the DNA molecule act as the code. A mistake in the sequence may prevent the synthesis of a chemical vital to the cell's survival, so it is essential that when the cell divides, it produces exact copies of the DNA to pass on to every daughter cell.

KEYWORDS

BASE PAIR
DNA
GENE
GENETIC CODE
PROTEIN
REPLICATION

Part of the DNA contains the code that determines when the DNA starts to replicate. DNA replication is controlled by a series of special protein molecules. Some of these are enzymes – proteins that act as biological catalysts, helping to speed up reactions. The key to DNA replication lies in the pairs of nucleotide bases. The base pairs are joined together by weak hydrogen bonds. If these are broken, matching bases in the surrounding solution are attracted to pair with the now unpaired bases. The energy to form these bonds is provided by phosphate groups. The unattached bases in the nucleus are in the form of triphosphates – nucleotide bases with three phosphate groups attached. When these bases join with exposed bases on the DNA chain, some of the phosphates are removed by the enzyme DNA polymerase. The energy released forms new bonds to link the bases. The remaining phosphates join the sugar-phosphate DNA "backbone".

The DNA bases become exposed when the histone proteins that hold the DNA in a tight spiral dissociate, causing the double-stranded DNA spiral to unwind and split. The single strands act as templates for the synthesis of new strands with matching bases. Binding proteins attach themselves to the single DNA strands to prevent them rejoining. The enzyme DNA polymerase joins the new nucleotide bases to the exposed bases on the single strand to form a new double-stranded molecule. Energy for unwinding the spiral comes from another molecule with three phosphate groups, adenosine triphosphate (ATP). In eukaryotic cells (in which the DNA is contained in a nucleus), unwinding begins at several points along the DNA molecule and spreads in both directions, until eventually the newly synthesized sections join up. This process results in daughter DNA molecules, each of which contains one of the original parent strands and one newly synthesized strand. It is known as semiconservative replication.

The nucleus has its own mechanism for correcting mistakes in the copying of DNA. A recognition enzyme can detect where a damaged or wrongly inserted base upsets the spiral shape of the DNA. Other enzymes remove it, and DNA polymerase replaces it with the correct base. On average, for every 100 million nucleotides added to a growing DNA strand, only one mistake escapes correction.

Bacteria have a single, circular, double-stranded DNA molecule. During replication, unwinding begins at a single point on the DNA, and continues until the two new circular strands are complete.

▷ The structure of DNA resembles the shape of a twisted ladder – the famous "double helix". The sides of the ladder are made up of a sugar (deoxyribose) and phosphate groups – hence the name deoxyribose nucleic acid (DNA). The "rungs" of the DNA ladder are made of pairs of bases. Thymine links to adenine by two hydrogen bonds, and cytosine and guanine are joined by three hydrogen bonds. No other or different pairings of nucleotide bases can occur in DNA.

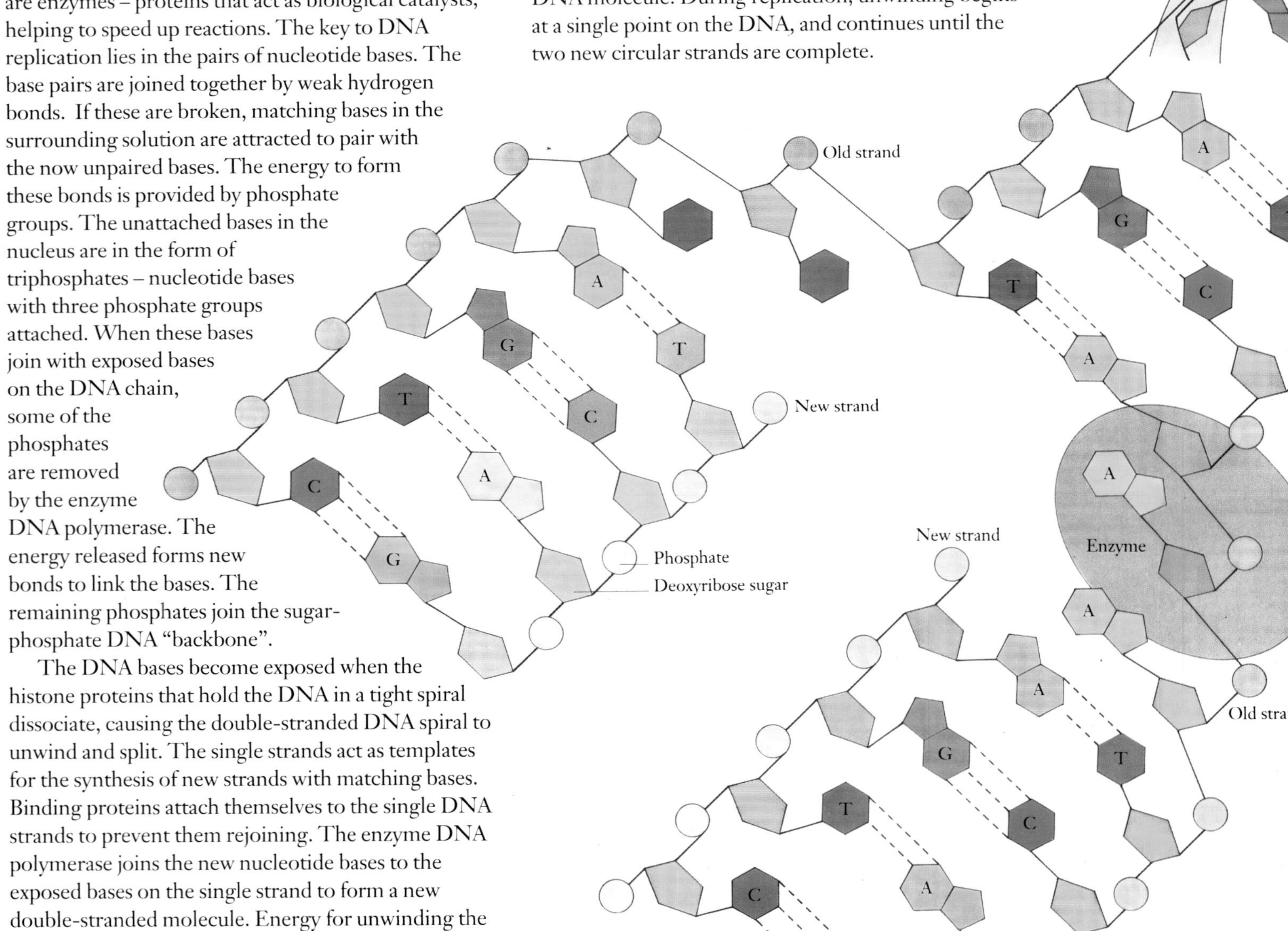

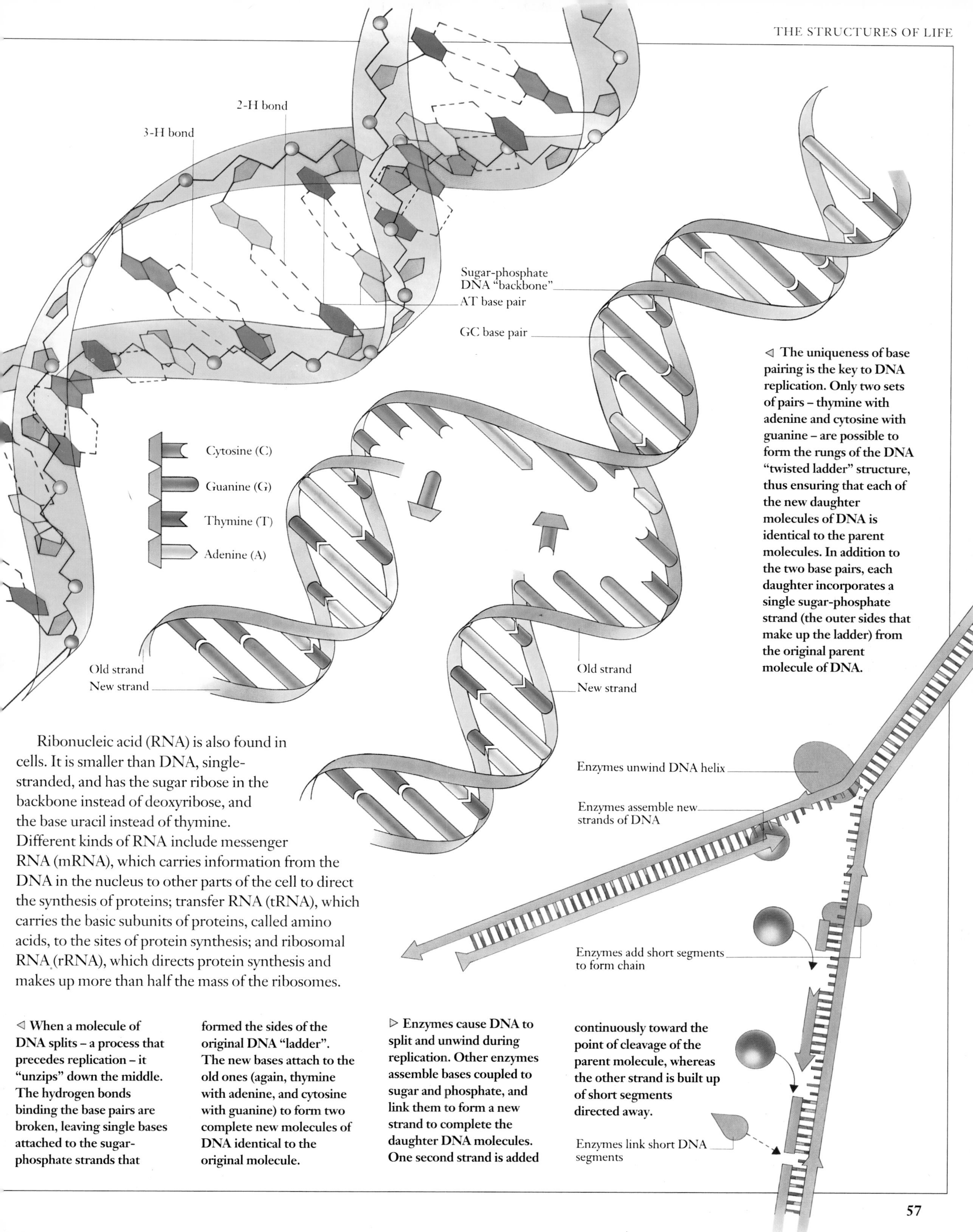

◁ **The uniqueness of base pairing is the key to DNA replication. Only two sets of pairs – thymine with adenine and cytosine with guanine – are possible to form the rungs of the DNA "twisted ladder" structure, thus ensuring that each of the new daughter molecules of DNA is identical to the parent molecules. In addition to the two base pairs, each daughter incorporates a single sugar-phosphate strand (the outer sides that make up the ladder) from the original parent molecule of DNA.**

Ribonucleic acid (RNA) is also found in cells. It is smaller than DNA, single-stranded, and has the sugar ribose in the backbone instead of deoxyribose, and the base uracil instead of thymine. Different kinds of RNA include messenger RNA (mRNA), which carries information from the DNA in the nucleus to other parts of the cell to direct the synthesis of proteins; transfer RNA (tRNA), which carries the basic subunits of proteins, called amino acids, to the sites of protein synthesis; and ribosomal RNA (rRNA), which directs protein synthesis and makes up more than half the mass of the ribosomes.

◁ **When a molecule of DNA splits – a process that precedes replication – it "unzips" down the middle. The hydrogen bonds binding the base pairs are broken, leaving single bases attached to the sugar-phosphate strands that formed the sides of the original DNA "ladder". The new bases attach to the old ones (again, thymine with adenine, and cytosine with guanine) to form two complete new molecules of DNA identical to the original molecule.**

▷ **Enzymes cause DNA to split and unwind during replication. Other enzymes assemble bases coupled to sugar and phosphate, and link them to form a new strand to complete the daughter DNA molecules. One second strand is added continuously toward the point of cleavage of the parent molecule, whereas the other strand is built up of short segments directed away.**

PASSING ON THE MESSAGE

THE adult human body contains some 65 trillion cells, yet each person originates as a single fertilized egg cell. Repeated divisions of this cell and its descendants have produced all 65 trillion cells – some at a rate of two million per second. Division continues in many parts of the body throughout life, although some types of cells lose their ability to divide after they have become differentiated (changed into specialized cell types). These include nerve cells of the human brain, and most plant cells.

KEYWORDS

CELL CYCLE
CELL DIVISION
CHROMOSOME
DNA
MITOSIS

The DNA, the genetic blueprint, is capable of replicating itself very accurately, but if daughter cells are to be viable, the replicated DNA molecules must be distributed accurately between the nuclei of daughter cells. Each daughter cell ends up with the same number of chromosomes and exactly the same genetic information as its parent. In eukaryotes, this is achieved by mitosis (from the Greek word for threads). It is used not only to produce new cells and repair old ones, but in simple organisms it may also be used for "asexual" reproduction, to produce identical offspring.

Before a cell divides, it synthesizes new organelles to distribute between the daughter cells. Most organelles are made under instructions from the DNA in the nucleus, but mitochondria and chloroplasts have their own DNA. They do not act completely independently – the timing of their replication is controlled by nuclear DNA, and some of their components are also synthesized under instructions from the nucleus. Large amounts of RNA are produced to transmit the instructions from the DNA to the ribosomes, and to control the synthesis of proteins by the ribosomes. The nucleolus consists of parts of several chromosomes involved in directing the synthesis of ribosome subunits; it becomes prominent at this time as the DNA unwinds to allow its message to be read.

The stages in the life cycle of a cell are described in the cell cycle. Nuclear division, or mitosis, occupies only a small fraction of the cell's life. Once mitosis starts,

▷ The last phases in mitosis are metaphase (chromatids attach to the centromeres), anaphase (they separate and move to opposite poles), and telophase (two new daughter cells are formed).

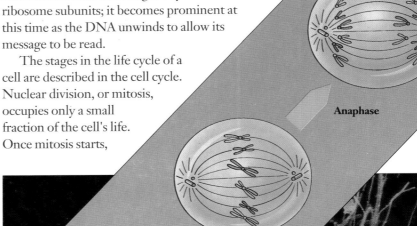

▷ Mitosis in an animal cell takes place in several stages. It begins with the interphase – often misleadingly called the "resting phase". Interphase is a period of growth, increase in size and synthesis of organelles and other new cell components. The nucleoli direct synthesis of ribosome subunits. In late interphase, the DNA and histones of each chromosome replicate. During the next stage, prophase, the chromosomes shorten (condense) to 4% of their original length by spiralling tighter. They show up in stained microscope preparations, but the centromeres remain unstained.

The centrioles move to opposite poles of the cell and short microtubules radiate from them to form asters. The nucleoli decrease in size as the chromatids to which they are linked condense. In late prophase the nuclear envelope fragments into small vesicles and the spindle starts to form.

Late interphase
Cell membrane
Nuclear membrane
Centrioles
Chromosomes
Nucleolus

Early prophase
Developing spindle
Aster
Centromere

Late prophase

Metaphase

Anaphase

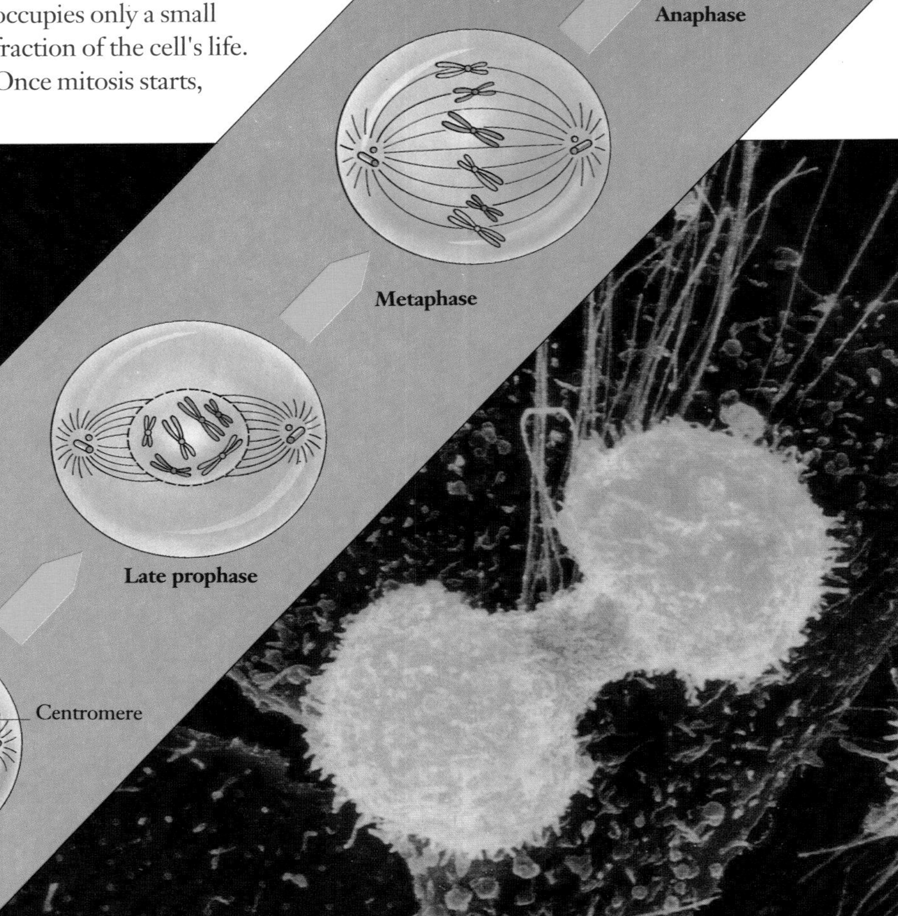

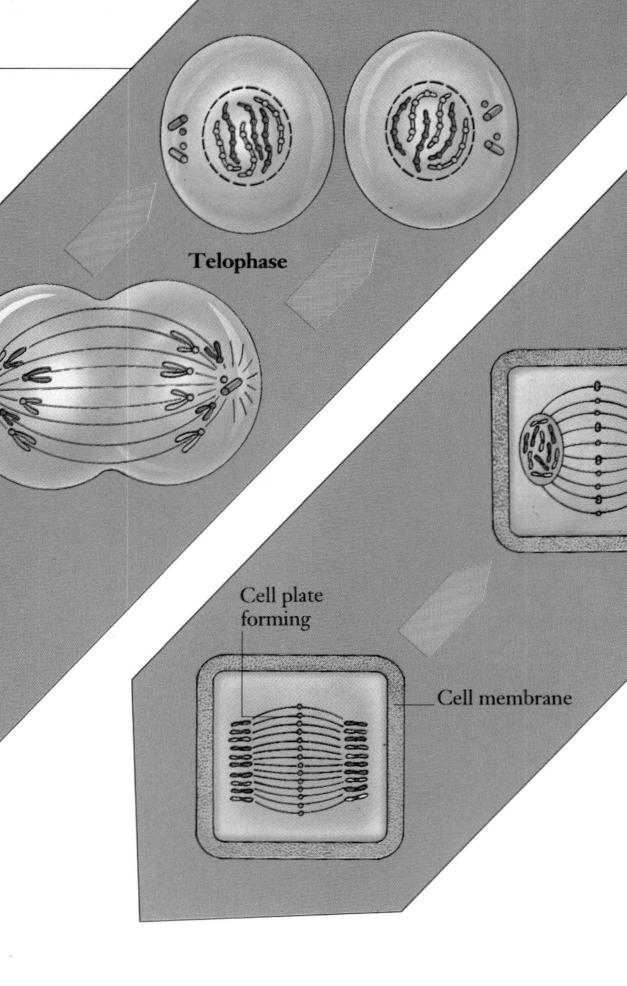

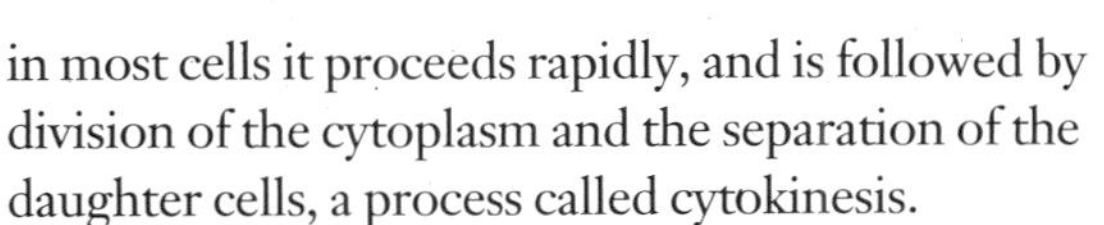

◻ In mitosis in plant cells LEFT no centrioles are involved. Because of the rigid cell wall, the cell membrane cannot simply pinch inward to separate the two nuclei. Instead, a partition called a cell plate, consisting of microtubules and associated common vesicles, begins to split the parent cell after two new daughter nuclei form. As the new membrane is organized, lamellar matrix is laid down between the daughter nuclei, and cellulose is then deposited to form the primary walls of the daughter cells.

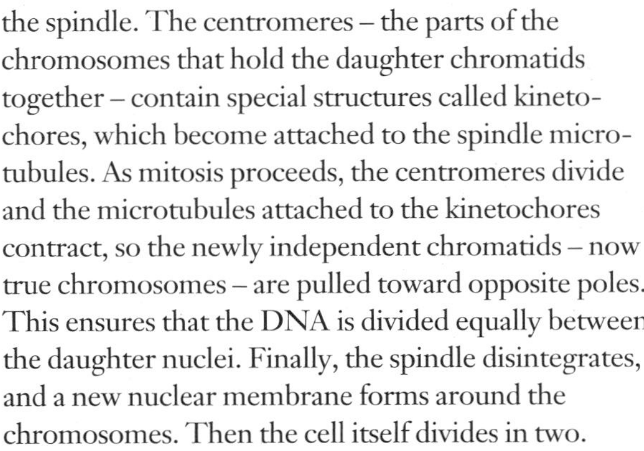

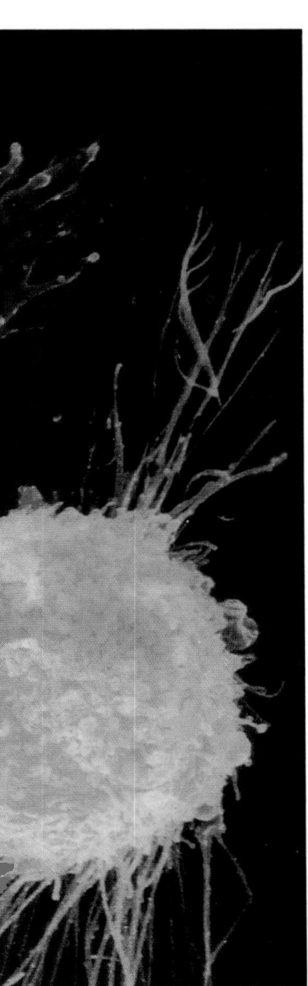

◁ A micrograph shows the division of ovary cells by mitosis – one cell at anaphase and another just before it splits at telophase. The daughter cells, still connected, have already received their chromosomes from their parent cell at this stage.

in most cells it proceeds rapidly, and is followed by division of the cytoplasm and the separation of the daughter cells, a process called cytokinesis.

Mitosis itself is concerned with manipulating the chromosomes. DNA replication occurs before there are any visible changes in the nucleus. The histones reassemble around the daughter DNA strands, which remain connected to each other at the centromere. Each chromosome is now in two parts, called chromatids, consisting of a replicated DNA molecule and associated proteins. As mitosis begins, the chromosomes spiral more tightly; they become more visible under the microscope, and appear to be double. The nuclear membrane disintegrates, forming a series of scattered membrane vesicles. A spindle-shaped scaffold of microtubules forms, assembled from subunits of the protein tubulin in the nucleoplasm. The chromosomes move to the center, or equator, of the spindle. The centromeres – the parts of the chromosomes that hold the daughter chromatids together – contain special structures called kinetochores, which become attached to the spindle microtubules. As mitosis proceeds, the centromeres divide and the microtubules attached to the kinetochores contract, so the newly independent chromatids – now true chromosomes – are pulled toward opposite poles. This ensures that the DNA is divided equally between the daughter nuclei. Finally, the spindle disintegrates, and a new nuclear membrane forms around the chromosomes. Then the cell itself divides in two.

There are differences in mitosis between plant and animal cells. For instance, plant cells have no centrioles, which were once thought to play a role in organizing the spindle; but plant cells still form spindles. Animal cells have centrioles, but if they are removed from a cell, it can still form a spindle.

BACTERIA AND VIRUSES

TRILLIONS of tiny bacteria – each one a few micrometers across – may live in the gut of a cow, and tens of billions are found in a handful of soil. These vast numbers reflect the great ability of bacteria to multiply. Their genetic systems are much more flexible than in eukaryotes. Genes can be transferred between organisms in many ways, and in some cases they can even be transferred between organisms of different species. Bacteria and blue-green algae (cyanobacteria) are prokaryotes – their cells do not have a distinct nucleus. Their genetic blueprint is contained in a single circular DNA molecule. The total DNA is only about one-fifth of that in a eukaryote cell, and contains only a few thousand genes.

KEYWORDS

BACTERIOPHAGE
BACTERIUM
BINARY FISSION
DNA
LYSIS
PLASMID
PROKARYOTE
TEMPERATE PHAGE
VIRUS

Bacteria may have other genetic information in the form of small circular DNA molecules called plasmids, which contain from a few to several hundred genes. A bacterial cell may contain more than one kind of plasmid, and up to 100 copies of each. Plasmids can replicate independently of the main bacterial DNA, and some (called episomes) can insert themselves into the bacterial DNA. Plasmids can be transferred from one bacterium to another during mating, and are sometimes transferred between bacteria of different species. Because of this, plasmids are important tools in the techniques of genetic engineering. They are also transmitted by viruses.

Bacteria do not have chromosomes, but their circular DNA molecule is often referred to as the bacterial chromosome. When this DNA replicates it becomes attached to an infolding of the plasma membrane. When the two daughter molecules of DNA are complete, each attaches to the plasma membrane, which stretches until they are widely separated. New plasma membrane and cell wall then form between them, ensuring that each cell receives a copy of the bacterial DNA. In some bacteria, the daughter cells remain stuck to each other after division, forming chainlike colonies. Simple division into two daughter cells is called binary fission. Occasionally bacteria can reproduce sexually and thus exchange genetic material. Bacteria are also capable of taking in DNA from a surrounding solution, a process called transformation.

Viruses are even smaller than bacteria (they are measured in nanometers, or millionths of millimeters, rather than micrometers or thousandths of millimeters). They consist simply of a molecule of DNA or RNA, either single- or double-stranded, surrounded by a protein or protein-and-lipid (fat) coat called a capsid. Outside of a living cell they are incapable of replication or any activity. However, when their genetic material enters a host cell, it rapidly causes the host cell to produce new viruses.

Viruses are the cause of many diseases, including chickenpox, influenza, warts and cancers, as well as more than a thousand diseases of

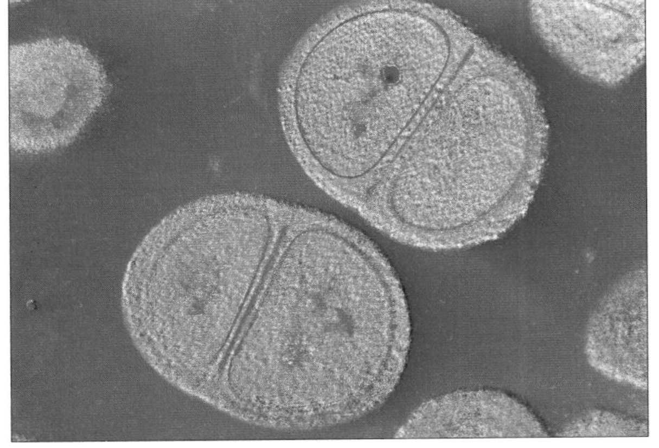

◁ **Most bacteria, such as this common *Staphylococcus* found in human mucus and on skin, reproduce by binary fission (splitting into two identical daughter cells). Bacteria can reproduce very quickly: in half a day, a single bacterium can produce over a billion descendants. Unless there is a mistake during DNA replication, every daughter cell is an exact copy of its parent.**

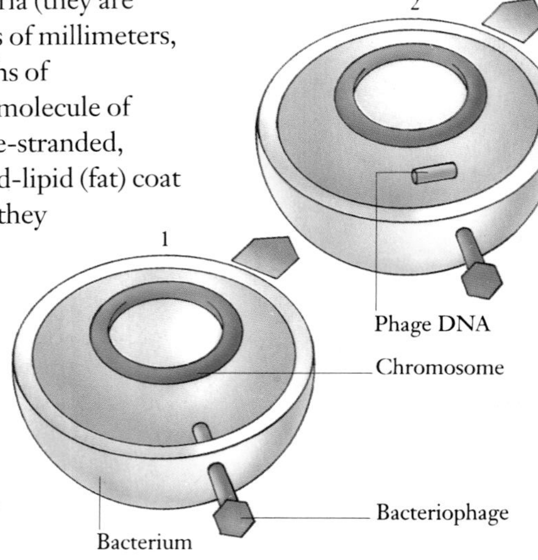

▽ **The life cycle of a virus may follow different patterns. 1 Phage particles recognize chemicals on the surface of the host bacterium; 2 they attach to this surface and inject their DNA. These two beginning stages are found in all types of viruses.**

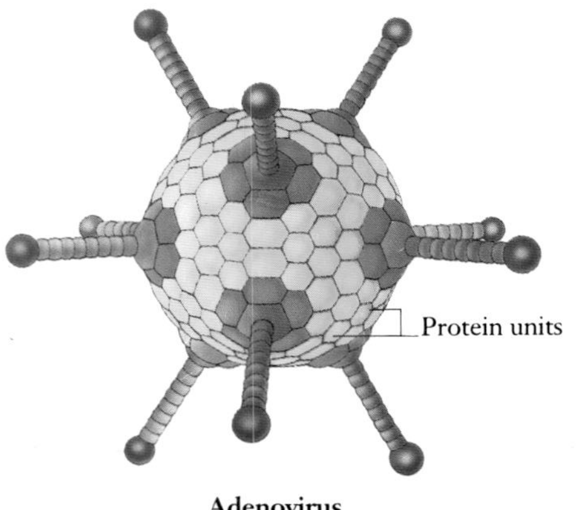

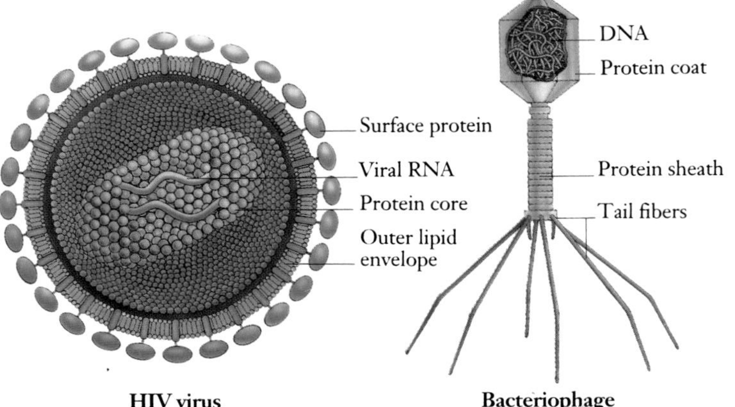

◁ **Viruses consist of DNA or RNA in protein coats. In adenoviruses the DNA is surrounded by tiny protein units. The HIV virus has a lipid coat derived from its host, embedded with proteins that help it recognize and interact with cells. The T4 bacteriophage has tail fibers to support it on the surface of the host. It injects DNA with a spike housed in a protein sheath.**

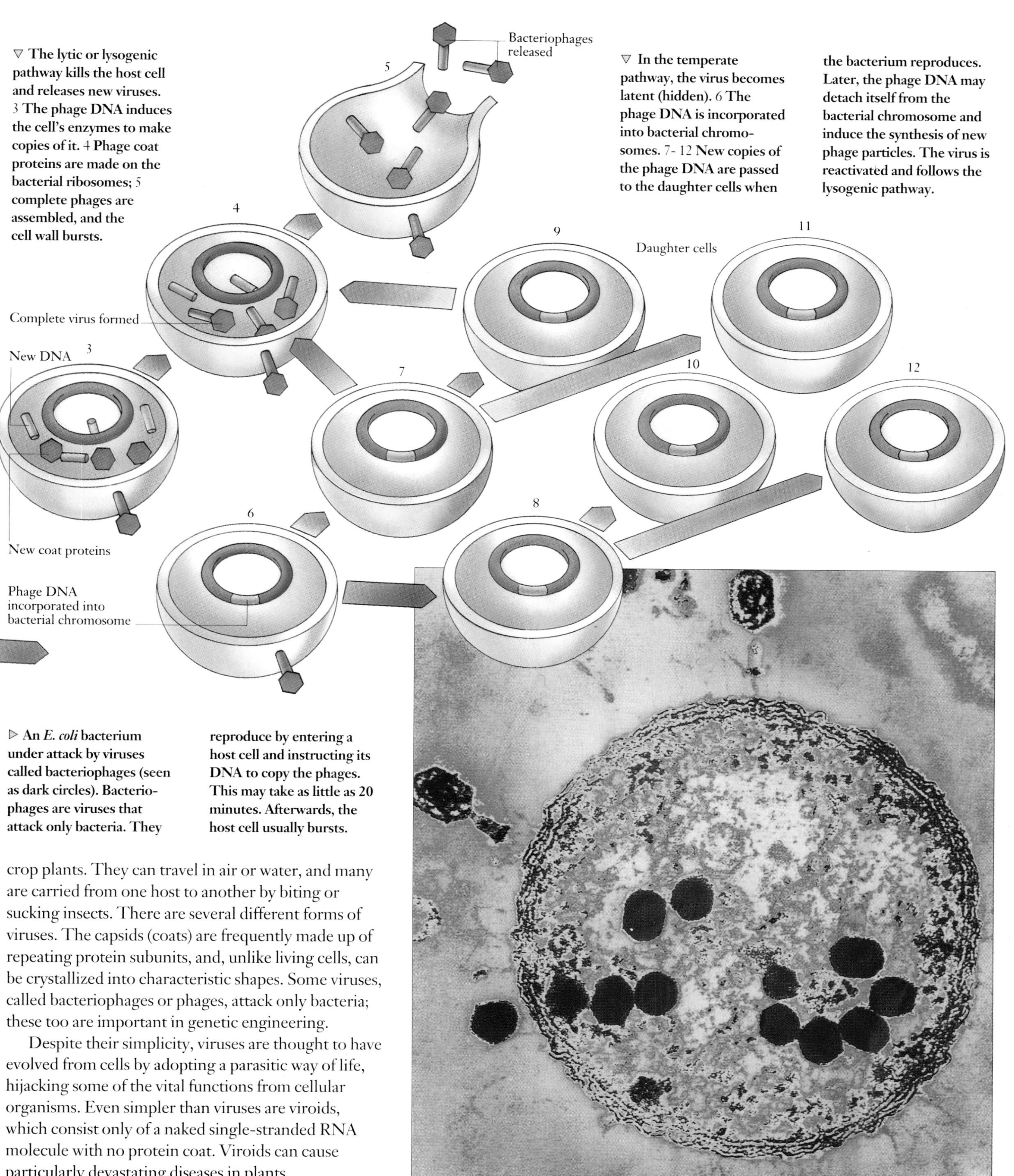

▽ **The lytic or lysogenic pathway kills the host cell and releases new viruses. 3 The phage DNA induces the cell's enzymes to make copies of it. 4 Phage coat proteins are made on the bacterial ribosomes; 5 complete phages are assembled, and the cell wall bursts.**

▽ **In the temperate pathway, the virus becomes latent (hidden). 6 The phage DNA is incorporated into bacterial chromosomes. 7- 12 New copies of the phage DNA are passed to the daughter cells when the bacterium reproduces. Later, the phage DNA may detach itself from the bacterial chromosome and induce the synthesis of new phage particles. The virus is reactivated and follows the lysogenic pathway.**

▷ **An *E. coli* bacterium under attack by viruses called bacteriophages (seen as dark circles). Bacteriophages are viruses that attack only bacteria. They reproduce by entering a host cell and instructing its DNA to copy the phages. This may take as little as 20 minutes. Afterwards, the host cell usually bursts.**

crop plants. They can travel in air or water, and many are carried from one host to another by biting or sucking insects. There are several different forms of viruses. The capsids (coats) are frequently made up of repeating protein subunits, and, unlike living cells, can be crystallized into characteristic shapes. Some viruses, called bacteriophages or phages, attack only bacteria; these too are important in genetic engineering.

Despite their simplicity, viruses are thought to have evolved from cells by adopting a parasitic way of life, hijacking some of the vital functions from cellular organisms. Even simpler than viruses are viroids, which consist only of a naked single-stranded RNA molecule with no protein coat. Viroids can cause particularly devastating diseases in plants.

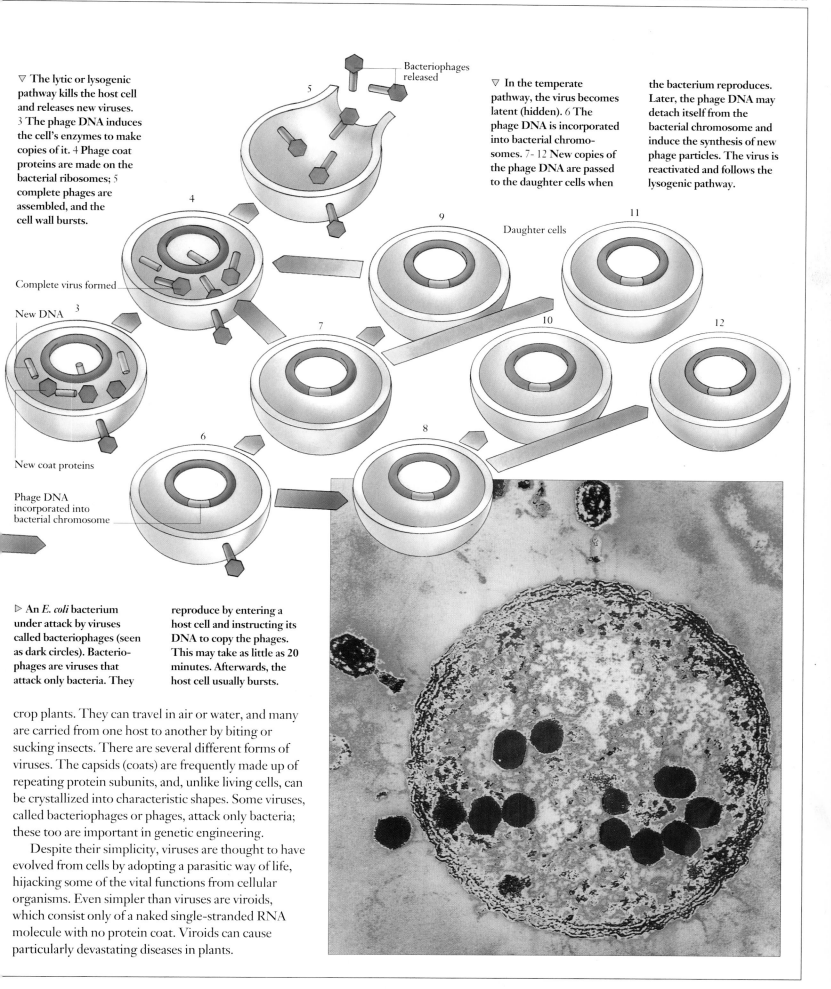

2

CODING *for Life*

THE GENETIC BLUEPRINT of an organism, carried by the DNA molecules in its cells, is a set of instructions ("code") for producing every characteristic of that species and organizing its growth and reproduction. DNA consists of segments called genes, which contain the instructions for making chemicals and for controlling the activity of other genes. Many genes code for particular proteins – large organic molecules made up of long chains of subunits called amino acids. Amino acids can be linked in long chains called polypeptides. Each protein molecule is made up of one or more polypeptides, each coded for by a different gene.

Proteins play many different roles. Structural proteins are involved in cell architecture; some, such as collagen, strengthen tissues such as tendons. Hemoglobin, found in red blood cells, is the main oxygen-carrying substance in the blood. A few proteins, like insulin, act as chemical messengers. Almost all metabolic reactions depend upon proteins called enzymes; without them, these reactions would proceed far too slowly to sustain life. Their control is highly specific, each enzyme catalyzing only one reaction. Compounds other than proteins are made in the cell by processes that require the presence of an enzyme. Thus, by directing the synthesis of proteins, DNA controls the production of every chemical in the body.

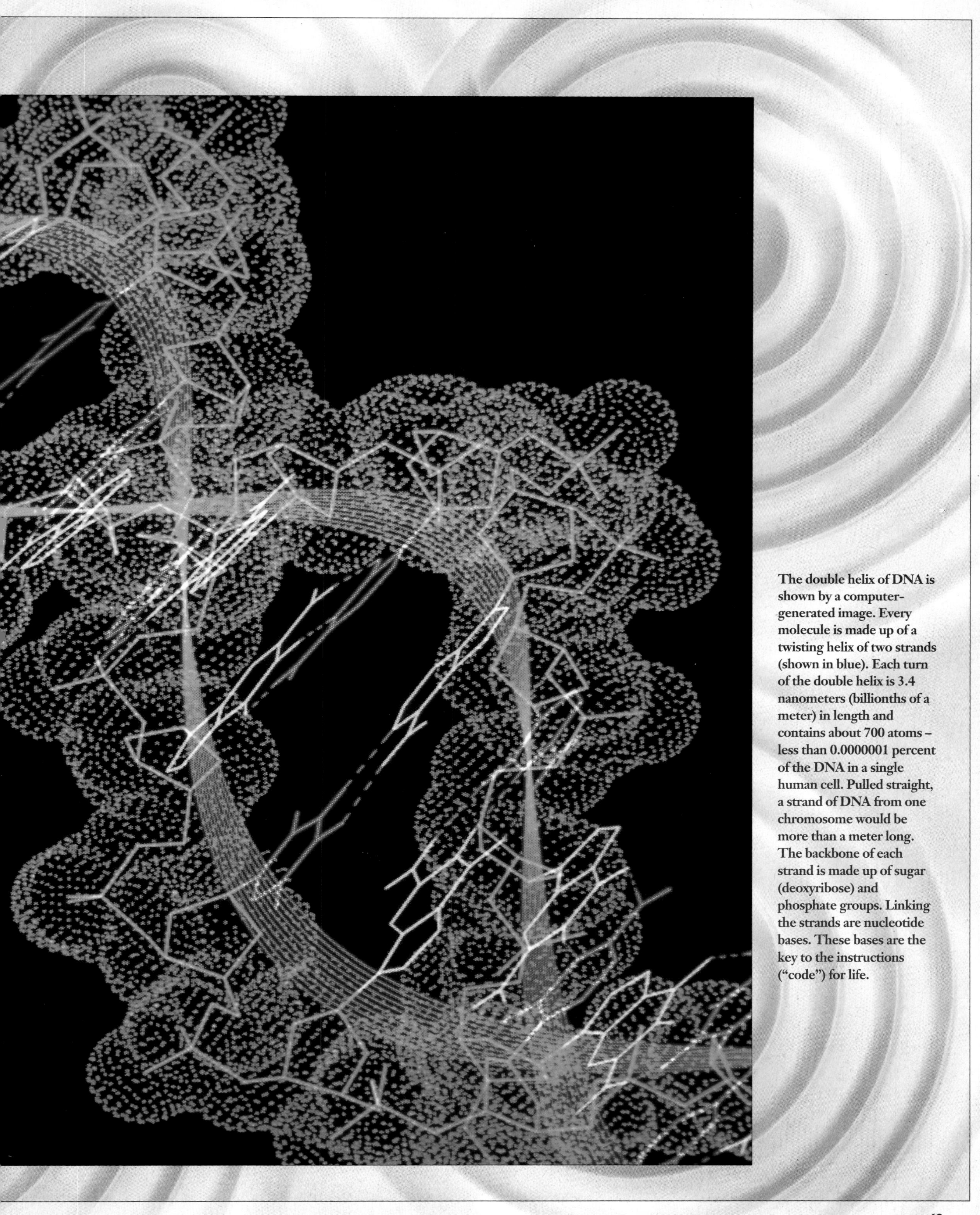

The double helix of DNA is shown by a computer-generated image. Every molecule is made up of a twisting helix of two strands (shown in blue). Each turn of the double helix is 3.4 nanometers (billionths of a meter) in length and contains about 700 atoms – less than 0.0000001 percent of the DNA in a single human cell. Pulled straight, a strand of DNA from one chromosome would be more than a meter long. The backbone of each strand is made up of sugar (deoxyribose) and phosphate groups. Linking the strands are nucleotide bases. These bases are the key to the instructions ("code") for life.

PROTEINS AND AMINO ACIDS

THE 10,000 or so proteins found in the human body all have a special role to play. Besides controlling the rate of metabolic reactions and even whether these reactions occur at all, proteins are involved in processes such as regulating which substances pass through the membranes of the cell; acting as messengers in cell communication; breaking down food into soluble products that can be absorbed by the body; contracting and relaxing muscles; carrying oxygen; transporting electrons in metabolic reactions; forming the hair, nails and bone; providing strength for tendons and ligaments; supplying food for embryos in eggs; forming the basic network of a blood clot in a wound; wrapping up the nucleic acids of viruses; and constituting the active ingredient in snake venom and bacterial toxins. Even more important, the proteins associated with the DNA in chromosomes may permit or prevent certain lengths of DNA being read and acted upon. Certain proteins may attach to particular genes to prevent their instructions being read or to activate them. These are produced by so-called regulator genes. Major developmental changes such as those associated with puberty in mammals, or with the breeding behavior in birds, owe their timing to the activity of such regulator genes.

KEYWORDS

ACTIVE SITE
AMINO ACID
CHROMOSOME
DNA
ENZYME
POLYPEPTIDE
PROTEIN
PROTEIN SYNTHESIS
REGULATOR GENE

Proteins are made up of long chains of amino acids called polypeptides. An amino acid is a small molecule characterized by having two particular groups of atoms: an amino group comprising a nitrogen atom with two hydrogen atoms attached, and a carboxylic acid group consisting of a carbon atom linked to an oxygen atom and an oxygen-hydrogen combination. The remainder of the amino acid molecule may consist of chains or ring of carbon atoms, with various side chains of other atoms attached. Many proteins contain more than 100 amino acids. The largest proteins are found in the coats of viruses. That of tobacco mosaic virus, for instance, contains some 336,500 amino acids in 2,130 polypeptide chains.

The particular sequence of amino acids in the polypeptide chains (the protein's primary structure) determines the structure of the protein. The chain may be folded into a kind of pleated sheet, or twisted into a spiral or helix (the protein's secondary structure). These in turn may be folded in various ways (tertiary structure), and two or more polypeptides may be linked together (quaternary structure), perhaps enclosing other atoms such as iron or magnesium. The twists and turns of the polypeptide chains are stabilized by various kinds of chemical bonds.

The shape of the protein is particularly important in the case of enzymes. Enzymes are globular proteins which have a highly specific region called the active site. Each enzyme catalyzes one particular chemical reaction. The chemicals on which an enzyme works are called its substrates. They fit into the enzyme's active site and bond to it to speed up the reaction or to cause it to happen. For example, in a breakdown reaction, the enzyme may bond to the substrate, then change shape slightly so that the bonds holding the

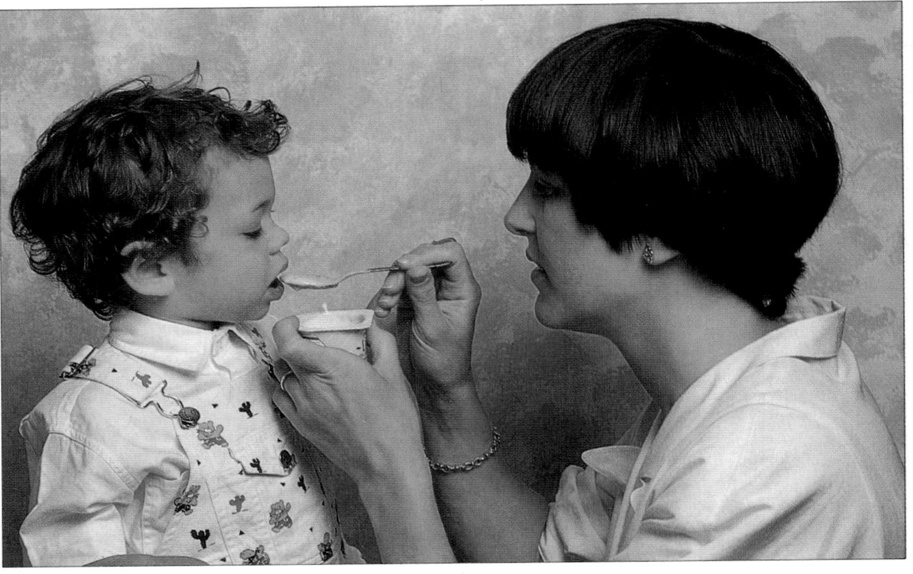

△ **A mother feeding yogurt to her young child is contributing protein to his diet. Proteins are made up of various combinations of 20 amino acids; nine of these cannot be made in the human body, so they must be supplied by proteins in food. Proteins literally build the body. Because of this, they can be said to be the most important factor in the "survival of the fittest" on which evolution by natural selection is based.**

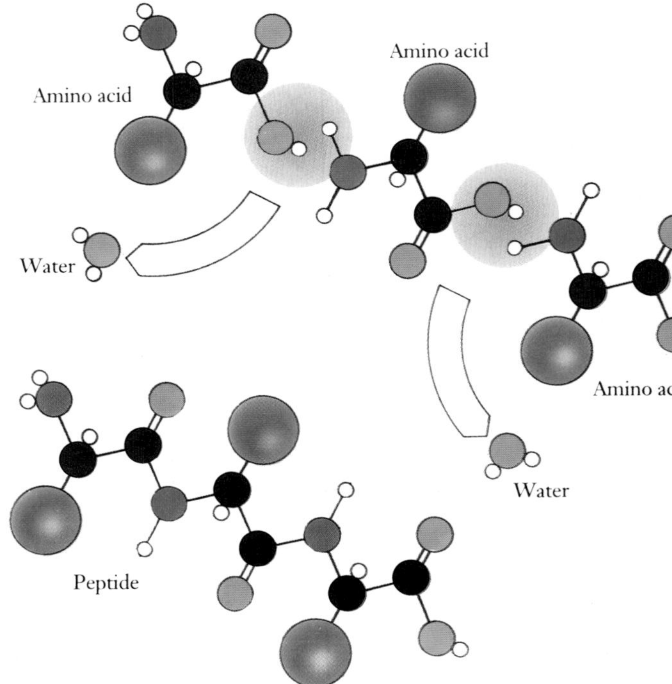

▷ **Amino acids are joined by peptide bonds, which form by condensation – a reaction that eliminates water molecules. The carboxyl groups of the amino acids carry a small negative electric charge; the amino groups are slightly positive. The hydroxyl (OH-) group of the carboxylic acid reacts with a hydrogen atom from the amino group to form water, and the amino acids link. In cells, this reaction is catalyzed by a specific enzyme. The newly-formed dipeptide molecule has an amino group and a carboxyl group, so it can build up a chain of amino acids.**

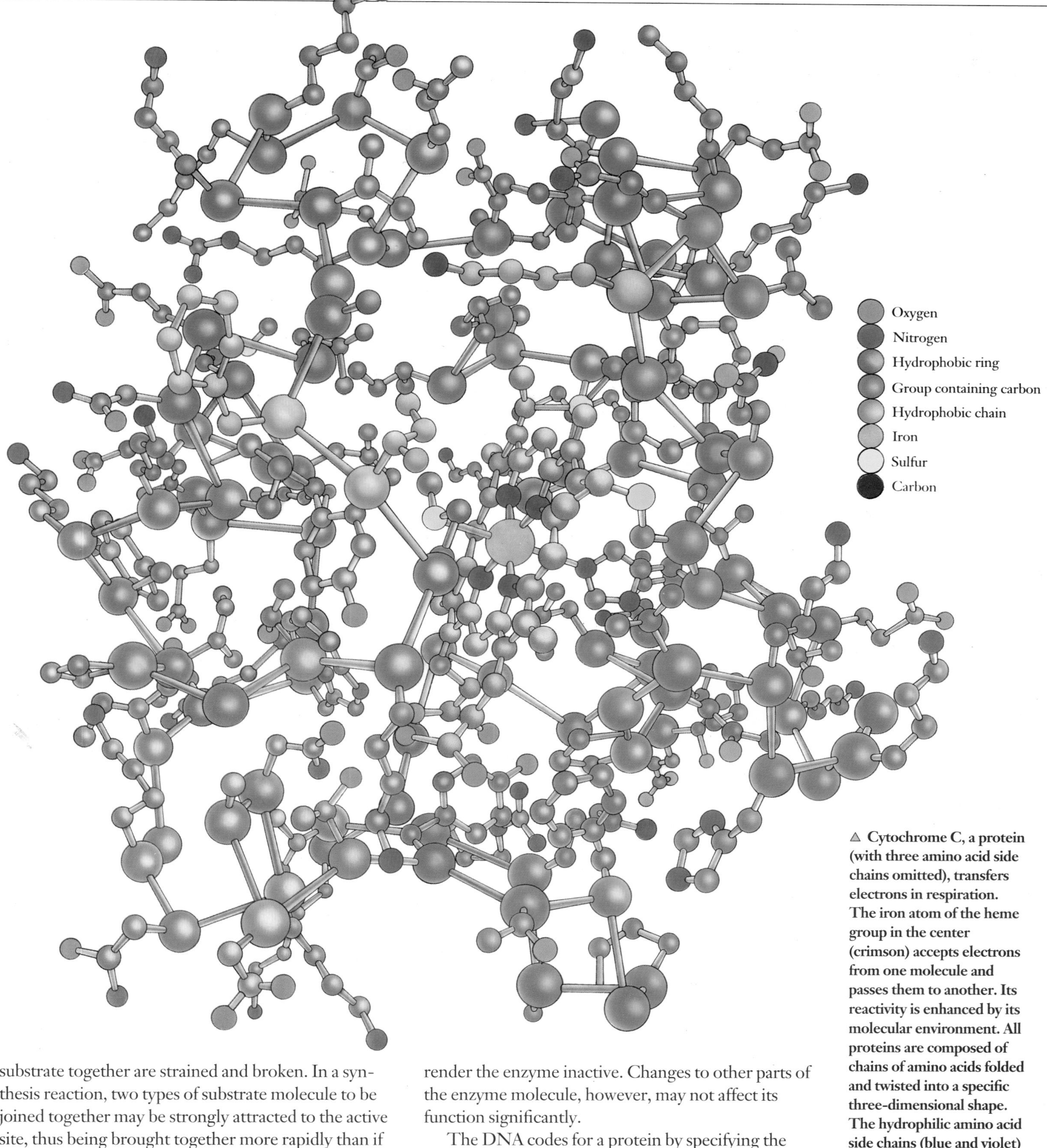

△ Cytochrome C, a protein (with three amino acid side chains omitted), transfers electrons in respiration. The iron atom of the heme group in the center (crimson) accepts electrons from one molecule and passes them to another. Its reactivity is enhanced by its molecular environment. All proteins are composed of chains of amino acids folded and twisted into a specific three-dimensional shape. The hydrophilic amino acid side chains (blue and violet) lie outside the molecule, in contact with the aqueous solution of the cell. Hydrophobic chains (red and orange) are found in the interior, especially around the heme group.

substrate together are strained and broken. In a synthesis reaction, two types of substrate molecule to be joined together may be strongly attracted to the active site, thus being brought together more rapidly than if they relied on bumping into each other by chance in the solution. The substrate fits into the active site like a key fitting a lock; hence the size and shape of the active site and the pattern of electrical charges on its surface are crucial. The slightest change in the DNA instructions for making this part of the enzyme molecule may render the enzyme inactive. Changes to other parts of the enzyme molecule, however, may not affect its function significantly.

The DNA codes for a protein by specifying the sequence of amino acids in its primary structure. The information for this is conveyed in the linear sequence of nucleotide bases in the DNA molecule. The bases are "read" in groups of three, each trio coding for a single amino acid. There are also sequences of bases which mark the start and end of a gene.

THE GENETIC CODE

THE genetic code is the key to the language of the genes. The individual bases on the DNA and RNA molecules are like the letters of an alphabet, making up words that are used as instructions for synthesizing proteins, which determine the structure and function of an organism. The total information of the genetic code for an organism is its genome.

Genes are stretches of DNA with specific linear sequences of nucleotide base pairs. The sequence of bases in a gene specifies the sequence of amino acids that must be joined together to form a protein, or one of the polypeptide chains in a protein. In fact, the code is made up of triplets of bases, called codons. Each codon specifies one amino acid. Four bases provide a possible 64 (4^3) codons, more than is needed to make 20 different amino acids. The code is said to be "degenerate", because some amino acids are specified by more than one codon. Some codons have other roles, for example as "start" and "stop" codons to signal the beginning and end of the polypeptide chain.

KEYWORDS

ALLELE
AMINO ACID
BASE PAIR
CHROMOSOME
CISTRON
CODON
DNA
GENE
GENETIC CODE
POLYPEPTIDE
PROTEIN
RIBOSOME

Only a small fraction of the DNA sequence in the nucleus of a eukaryote cell (between one and 10 percent) provides information for the synthesis of protein. The remainder, often known as "junk" DNA, consists of seemingly meaningless sequences found between and within genes. Stretches of "junk" DNA found in genes are called introns, and the stretches of coding sequence are called exons.

Prokaryotes generally lack introns, which are the only parts of a gene that are not involved in coding for a polypeptide chain. Part of the DNA code is involved with controlling the gene – helping to determine whether it is switched on or off. Controlling sequences, called promoters and enhancers, are generally found "upstream" from the start codon for the polypeptide chain, and in the case of enhancers may be hundreds of bases away from the start site. For a gene to be turned "on", its control sequences must form a complex with various regulatory proteins. The production of these proteins may be triggered by hormones or other chemical signals, often involving regulatory genes.

The code of the DNA sequence is translated into protein in a two-step process. First the DNA is used as a template for the synthesis of a complementary strand of RNA in the nucleus. Then the introns are removed from the RNA by means of enzymes in a process called "splicing", producing a molecule of messenger RNA (mRNA) which can travel to the cytoplasm and direct the synthesis of proteins. The genetic codes usually quoted are those of the mRNA molecule. mRNA also has four different bases: like DNA, it contains adenine (A), cytosine (C) and guanine (G), but uracil (U) substitutes for the thymine (T) found in DNA. Most mRNA molecules also gain a tail of 100-200 adenine-containing molecules at the other end, which seems to prevent the molecule being degraded in the cytoplasm before it reaches the ribosomes.

The genetic code is non-overlapping. This means that each base belongs to only one codon. For instance, the mRNA sequence AGCCAACUG will be "read" as AGC–CAA–CUG, coding for serine-glutamine-leucine, not as AGC–GCC–AAC or any other combination.

The genetic code is the same for almost all known organisms (some of the exceptions are certain protozoa and mitochondrial DNA). If human mRNA coding for hemoglobin is added to a cell extract from a bacterium, hemoglobin will be produced: the bacterium's protein synthesizing apparatus is able to "read" the human DNA.

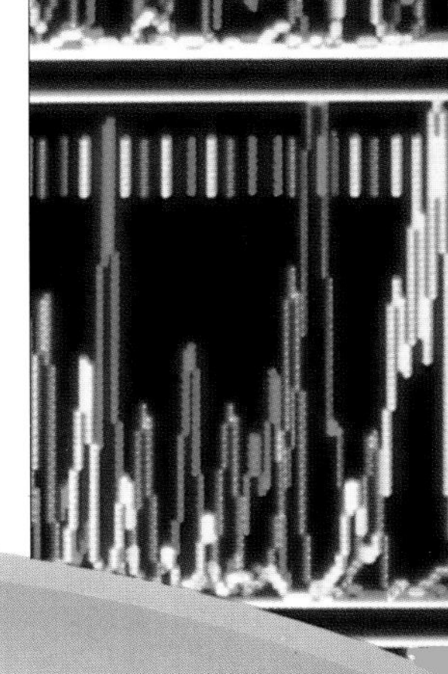

▷ Not all the DNA in a gene codes for the protein. There are many "junk" segments of apparently meaningless sequences called introns. These, too, are initially copied onto the mRNA; before it leaves the nucleus, the introns are edited out by a process called splicing. Enzymes cut out the unwanted sections and join together the remaining segments to form a smaller, "mature"

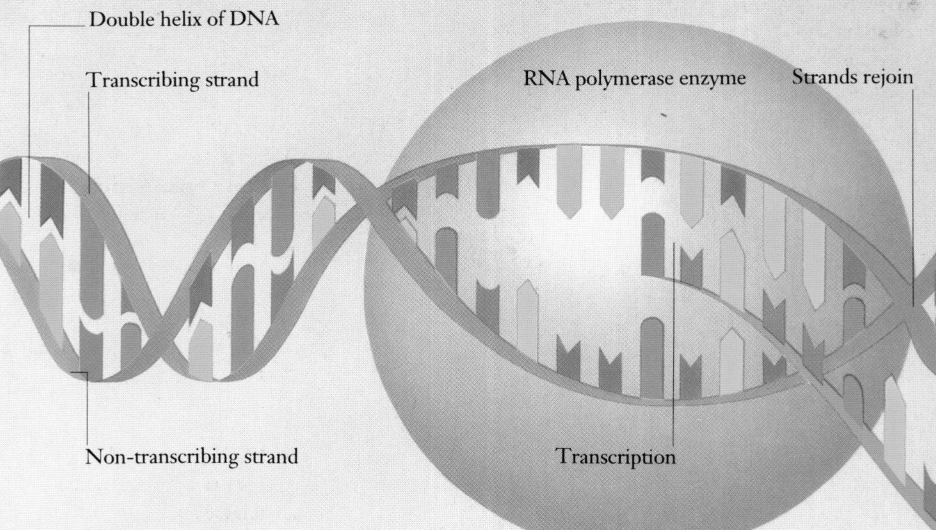

△ The coded instructions for producing a particular protein or polypeptide lie in a segment of DNA called a gene. The first stage in protein synthesis is called transcription: copying the gene's message onto a molecule of messenger RNA (mRNA). With the help of enzymes, the DNA unwinds, starting from a specific point near the start of the gene. One of the single DNA strands is used as a template to synthesize mRNA. Activated nucleotide bases pair up with corresponding bases on the DNA strand, but in mRNA the base uracil (instead of thymine) pairs with adenine. These bases are then joined together by the enzyme RNA polymerase, forming a single strand of mRNA.

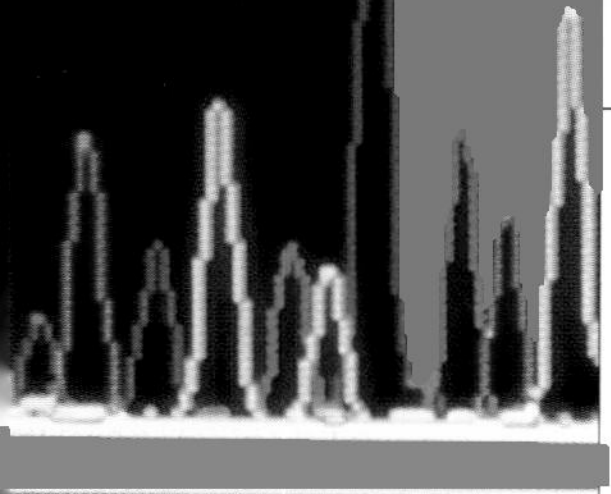

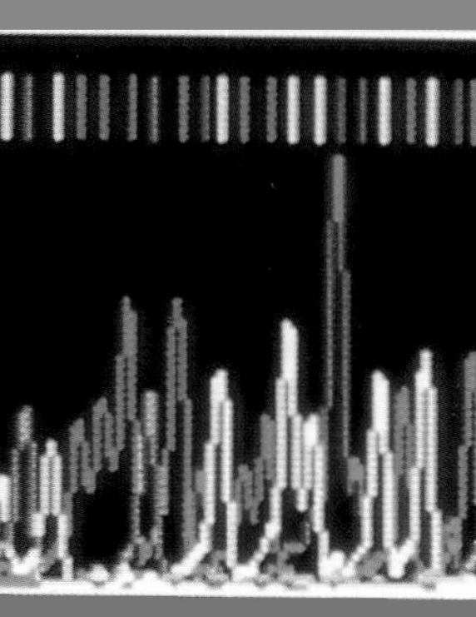

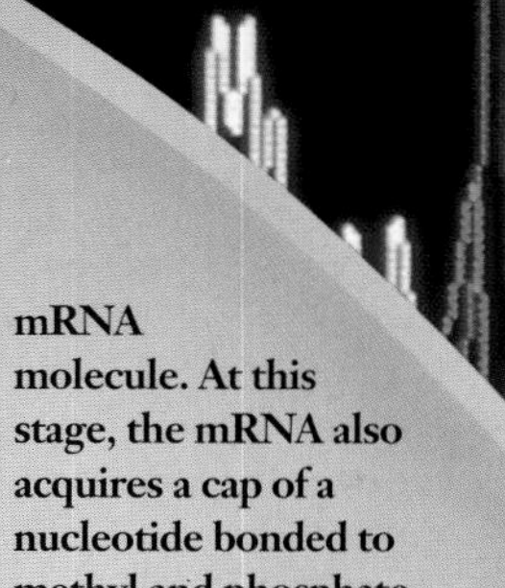

◁ A computer displays an analysis of the sequence of nucleotide bases in a segment of DNA – in this case, the human gene cluster HL-A, which plays an important role in immunology. The bases are represented by letters and colors: adenine (A, red), thymine (T, blue), cytosine (C, green) and guanine (G, yellow). The picture was taken at a French hospital participating in the international Human Genome Project, which has been set up to study the entire assortment of human genes worldwide.

mRNA molecule. At this stage, the mRNA also acquires a cap of a nucleotide bonded to methyl and phosphate groups at its starting end. This cap appears to help the mRNA to be recognized by other molecules involved in the initiation of polypeptide synthesis.

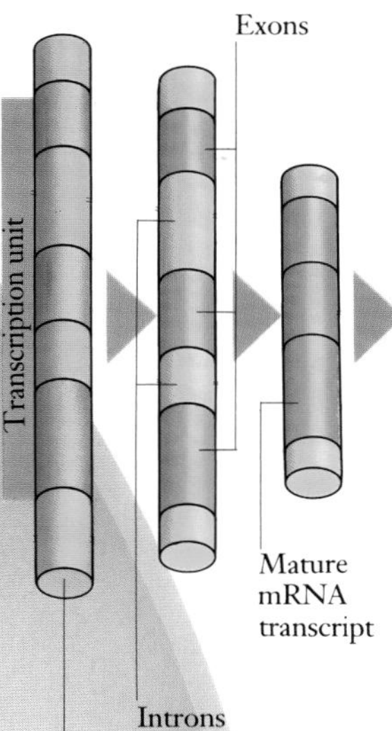

First base	Second base: Uracil (U)	Second base: Cytosine (C)	Second base: Adenine (A)	Second base: Guanine (G)	Third base
Uracil (U)	Phenylalanine	Serine	Tyrosine	Cysteine	U
	Phenylalanine	Serine	Tyrosine	Cysteine	C
	Leucine	Serine	STOP	STOP	A
	Leucine	Serine	STOP	Tryptophan	G
Cytosine (C)	Leucine	Proline	Histidine	Arginine	U
	Leucine	Proline	Histidine	Arginine	C
	Leucine	Proline	Glutamine	Arginine	A
	Leucine	Proline	Glutamine	Arginine	G
Adenine (A)	Isoleucine	Threonine	Asparagine	Serine	U
	Isoleucine	Threonine	Asparagine	Serine	C
	Isoleucine	Threonine	Lysine	Arginine	A
	Methionine	Threonine	Lysine	Arginine	G
Guanine (G)	Valine	Alanine	Aspartic acid	Glycine	U
	Valine	Alanine	Aspartic acid	Glycine	C
	Valine	Alanine	Glutamic acid	Glycine	A
	Valine	Alanine	Glutamic acid	Glycine	G

△ The triplets of nucleotide bases on mRNA code for specific amino acids. There are four bases: adenine (A), cytosine (C), guanine (G) and uracil (U). The ribosomes read three bases at a time. A triplet of bases (codon) usually specifies one amino acid to be added to the ribosome's polypeptide chain. Some amino acids are coded for by more than one codon. Not all codons code for amino acids; nonsense codons have other functions. UAA, UGA and UAG are stop signals which cause the ribosome to stop the growing polypeptide chain at this point. AUG codes for the amino acid methionine and acts as a start signal, ensuring that the ribosome "knows" where to start counting.

Single strand of mRNA

▷ The messenger RNA passes out of the nucleus through the pores in the nuclear envelope and becomes attached to a ribosome. Here, the amino acids corresponding to the codes in the triplet codons on the mRNA are brought together and peptide bonds form between them under the influence of specific enzymes, producing a growing polypeptide chain.

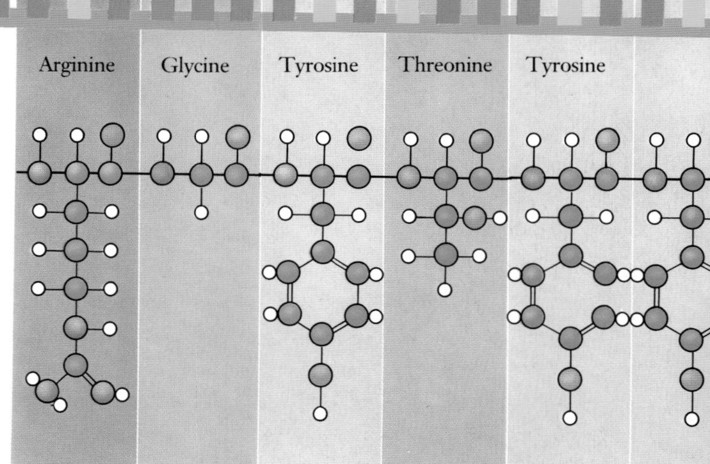

TRANSLATING THE CODE

THERE are probably well over 125,000 genes that code just for the polypeptide chains that make up the 10,000 or so different proteins in the human body. By comparison, about 10,000 genes are involved in directing the growth and development of any one kind of cell. The information in these genes must be "translated" into cell proteins and other vital substances in order to be acted upon. Translation is part of protein synthesis, one of the most fundamental biochemical processes of life. These processes are the same for all eukaryotic cells – that is, all cells that have a nucleus.

KEYWORDS

AMINO ACID
ANTICODON
BASE PAIRS
CODING STRAND
CODON
DNA
GENETIC CODE
NUCLEOTIDE
PROTEIN SYNTHESIS
RIBOSOME
RNA
RNA POLYMERASE
SPLICING
STOP CODON

Most eukaryotic cells contain many tens of thousands of the tiny particles that carry out protein synthesis – the ribosomes. Even bacteria (which are prokaryotes rather than eukaryotes) may have about 10,000 ribosomes. In bacteria the ribosomes start translating the messenger RNA (mRNA) molecules as they peel off the DNA, but in eukaryote cells the ribosomes are in the cytoplasm, whereas the DNA molecules are confined to the nucleus. If the DNA were to venture into the cytoplasm, it would risk being damaged by contact with other chemicals. This is avoided by using a messenger molecule, messenger RNA.

The synthesis of a mRNA molecule is very similar to the synthesis of new DNA during DNA replication. The DNA unwinds and a strand of RNA is synthesized, using one of the exposed DNA strands as a template; this strand is called the coding strand. Just as in DNA replication, matching bases are added to each of the newly exposed bases, which one exception – instead of thymine, the nucleotide base uracil is used. The synthesis of RNA from a DNA template is called transcription. It is a very rapid process – new bases are added to the growing RNA strand at the rate of about 30 nucleotides a second.

The nucleotides of the RNA are joined together by the enzyme RNA polymerase. The DNA unwinds as the enzyme moves along it, rewinding behind it. Once the RNA polymerase reaches the endpoint of the gene, it releases the RNA from the template and may then start all over again. In the lifetime of a cell, thousands of RNA copies of the same genes may be made. In a single silk gland cell, for instance, in just four days the gene which codes for fibroin (the main protein in silk) may make 10,000 copies of its RNA, each directing the synthesis of 100,000 molecules of fibroin – a total of one billion molecules of fibroin.

After transcription, the newly synthesized RNA is trimmed to remove its introns (apparently useless pieces of DNA along an RNA strand) in the process called splicing: just as a film editor cuts out strips of unwanted film, then joins the remaining pieces together, so the RNA splicing enzymes cut out introns to produce a shorter segment of mRNA. The mRNA then passes out of the nucleus through the nuclear membrane into the cytoplasm.

Ribosomes consist of specific proteins and a special type of RNA called ribosomal RNA (rRNA). Each ribosome is made up of two subunits, a small one and a larger one. When the two subunits are combined to form a ribosome, they provide exactly the right environment for protein synthesis, as well as special binding sites for the amino acid carriers and for the mRNA strand. Enzymes built into the ribosome catalyze the joining together of amino acids in the cytoplasm to form polypeptide chains. The amino acids are brought to the ribosome by another form of RNA, transfer RNA (tRNA). There is at least one kind of tRNA molecule for each kind of amino acid. Each tRNA molecule has at one end a sequence of three bases called the anticodon. These pair with the bases (codons) on the mRNA that code for the amino acid carried by this tRNA. Thus the tRNAs act like adapters, bringing the correct amino acids specified by the mRNA codons bound to the ribosome.

Translation starts when a special initiator tRNA binds to a small ribosome subunit. Its anticodon then binds to the start codon on the mRNA. A large subunit then binds to the small one, forming a functional ribosome. As each succeeding amino acid is brought to the ribosome by its tRNA, a ribosome enzyme catalyzes the formation of a peptide bond between it and the amino acid bound to the preceding tRNA, building up the polypeptide chain. Translation proceeds until a stop codon is reached; then the whole amino acid chain is released from the ribosome, and the two subunits separate. A single strand of mRNA may have more than one ribosome moving along it at a given time. A cluster of ribosomes on an mRNA molecule is called a polysome.

The polypeptide chain may be stored in the cytoplasm of the cell, or transported to the nucleus or another organelle; or it may enter the endoplasmic reticulum or Golgi apparatus to be processed further. Special amino acid sequences on the peptide help it to recognize its correct destination.

▷ Clusters of messenger RNA molecules (magnified 6700 times) form a fernlike structure around a backbone of DNA molecules, which are undergoing transcription. Transcription begins at one end, and the mRNA molecules become longer as the process continues.

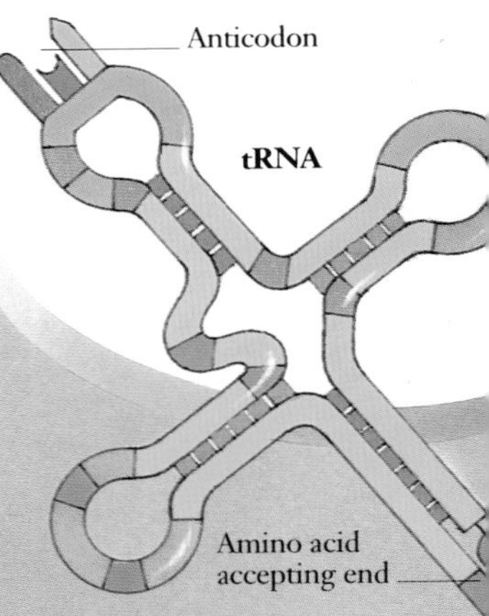

△ Transfer RNA carries a specific amino acid to the ribosome for protein synthesis. There are 31 different kinds of tRNA in eukaryotic cells, held in shape by hydrogen bonds. The amino acid attaches to the unpaired part of the tRNA "tail". The anticodon comprises three nucleotide bases complement ary to those of the codon on the

▷ Before a protein or polypeptide is synthesized, the DNA unwinds to expose the gene that codes for it. The DNA is a template for the synthesis of RNA: the code on the DNA is represented by complementary bases on the RNA. This RNA may be messenger RNA (which carries instructions for the sequence of amino acids in a polypeptide), transfer RNA (which transports a specific amino acid to the ribosomes to be used in the polypeptide), or ribosomal RNA (which is a major

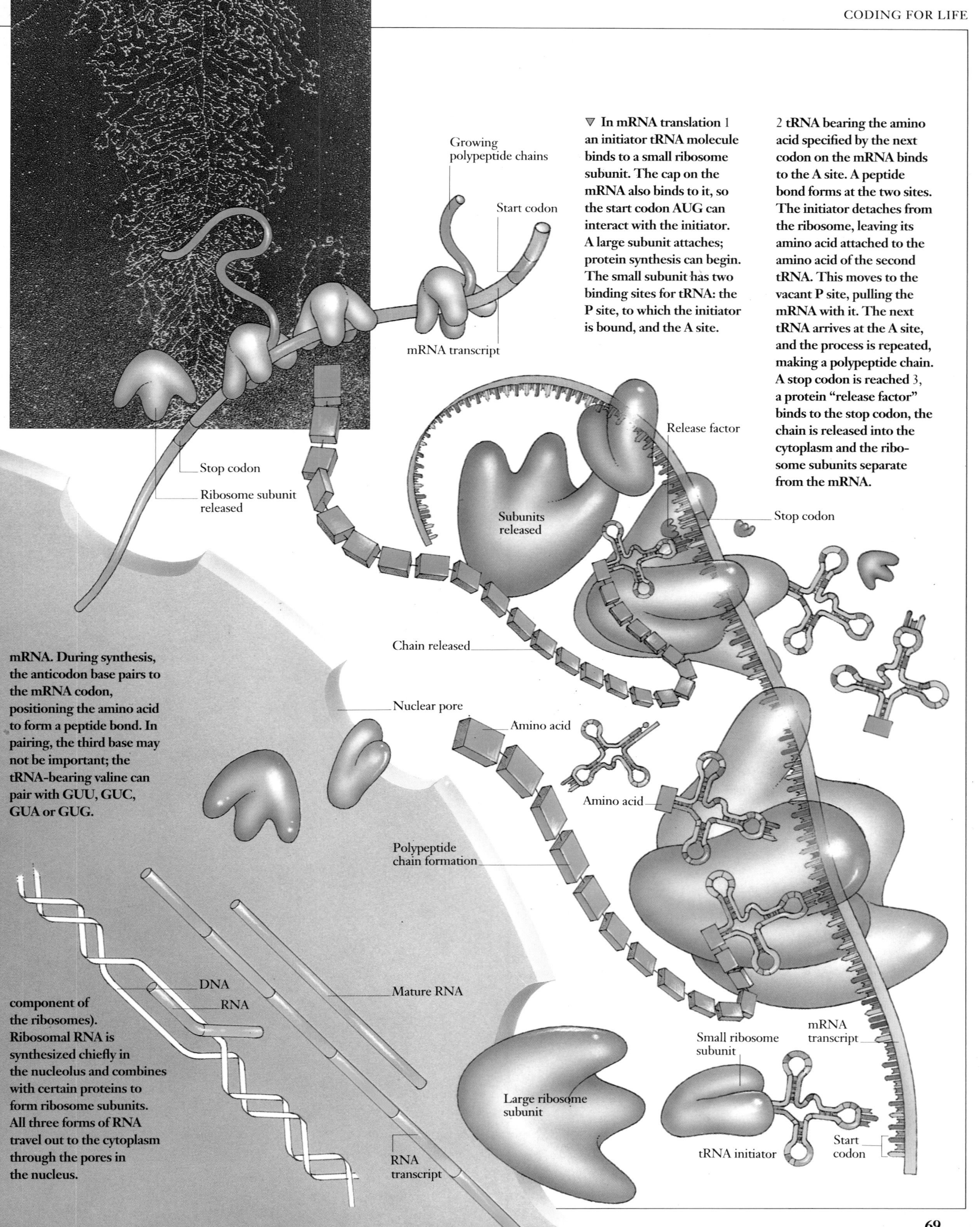

▽ In mRNA translation 1 an initiator tRNA molecule binds to a small ribosome subunit. The cap on the mRNA also binds to it, so the start codon AUG can interact with the initiator. A large subunit attaches; protein synthesis can begin. The small subunit has two binding sites for tRNA: the P site, to which the initiator is bound, and the A site. 2 tRNA bearing the amino acid specified by the next codon on the mRNA binds to the A site. A peptide bond forms at the two sites. The initiator detaches from the ribosome, leaving its amino acid attached to the amino acid of the second tRNA. This moves to the vacant P site, pulling the mRNA with it. The next tRNA arrives at the A site, and the process is repeated, making a polypeptide chain. A stop codon is reached 3, a protein "release factor" binds to the stop codon, the chain is released into the cytoplasm and the ribosome subunits separate from the mRNA.

mRNA. During synthesis, the anticodon base pairs to the mRNA codon, positioning the amino acid to form a peptide bond. In pairing, the third base may not be important; the tRNA-bearing valine can pair with GUU, GUC, GUA or GUG.

component of the ribosomes). Ribosomal RNA is synthesized chiefly in the nucleolus and combines with certain proteins to form ribosome subunits. All three forms of RNA travel out to the cytoplasm through the pores in the nucleus.

SWITCHING GENES ON AND OFF

SOME of the most dramatic transformations in nature occur when plants and animals approach the age for reproduction. Such changes are brought about by major changes in the pattern of gene expression, with some genes being switched off and others becoming active. Similar changes occur during normal growth and development, as cells differentiate and become specialized for different functions. The control of gene activity is extremely complex, and scientists still do not fully understand it.

KEYWORDS

ACTIVATOR
BASE PAIRS
DNA
ENZYME
EUKARYOTE
INTRON
MESSENGER RNA
OPERON
PROMOTER
PROTEIN SYNTHESIS
REPRESSION
RNA POLYMERASE

Genes are switched on and off daily according to the needs of the cell, enabling it to cope with changing food supplies, cell division, defense against invading bacteria, or the need to repair damage. The switch may be triggered by local signals such as changing concentrations of chemicals inside the cell, or by external signals such as hormones. Both signals stimulate regulator genes to produce proteins that bind to particular parts of the DNA molecule, or to other proteins associated with it in the chromosome. The most common regulators change the rate at which particular genes are transcribed (copied onto a messenger RNA molecule for transport to protein-synthesizing ribosomes in the cytoplasm). Repressor proteins prevent the transcription enzyme RNA polymerase from binding to the DNA, whereas activator proteins stimulate the enzyme to bind.

Before the RNA polymerase can start to transcribe a section of DNA (a gene), it must bind to a particular sequence of bases, the promoter, at the start of the gene. This has been studied in detail in bacteria, which have relatively simple control systems. In bacteria, there is another base sequence, the operator, between the promoter and the start point, which may be blocked by a regulator protein. Studies of bacteria have shown how this works for controlling the production of lactase, an enzyme that breaks down lactose, a common sugar. In the bacterium *Escherichia coli* (*E. coli*), an inhabitant of the human gut, the genes coding for the various enzymes involved in producing lactose lie next to each other on the DNA, and are preceded by an operator and a promoter. The whole unit of promoter, operator and genes is called an operon. Another gene some distance away on the

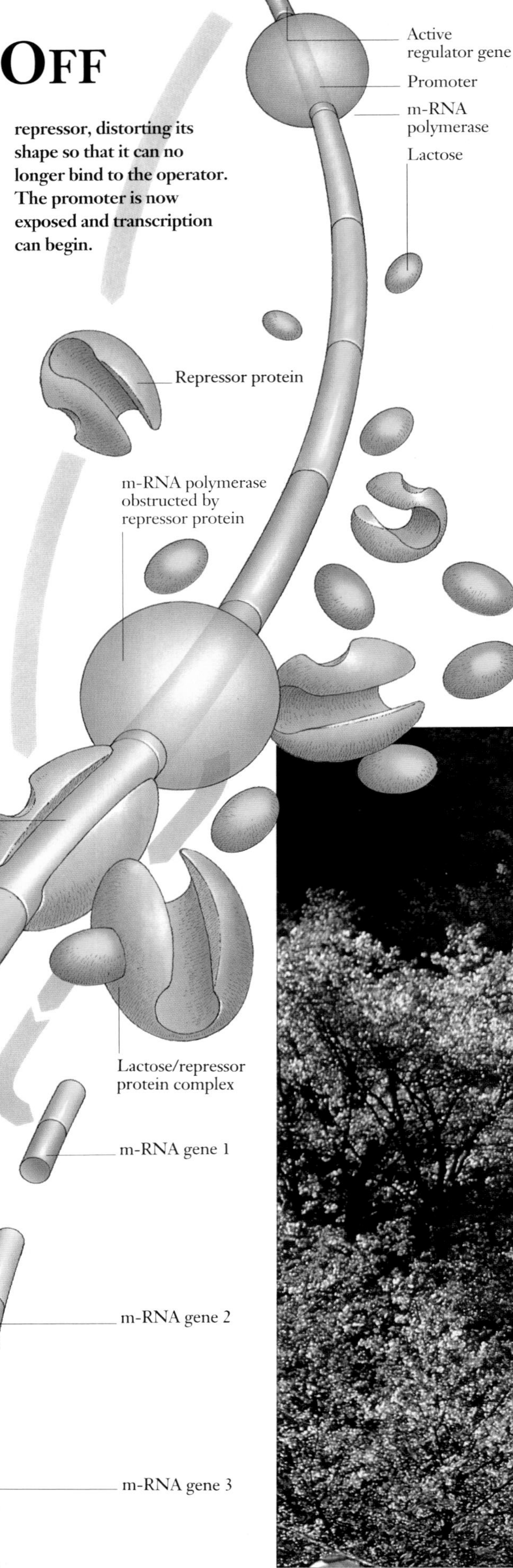

Breakdown of the sugar lactose in bacteria is controlled by a segment of DNA called the lactose operon. The process involves three enzymes: beta-galactosidase splits lactose into glucose and galactose; permease transports lactose into the cell; and acetylase takes part in lactose metabolism. The genes coding for these enzymes lie adjacent to each other on the DNA. A regulator gene codes for a repressor protein which, in the absence of lactose, binds to the operator, overlapping the promoter and preventing RNA polymerase from binding to the DNA and initiating transcription. When lactose is present, it binds to the repressor, distorting its shape so that it can no longer bind to the operator. The promoter is now exposed and transcription can begin.

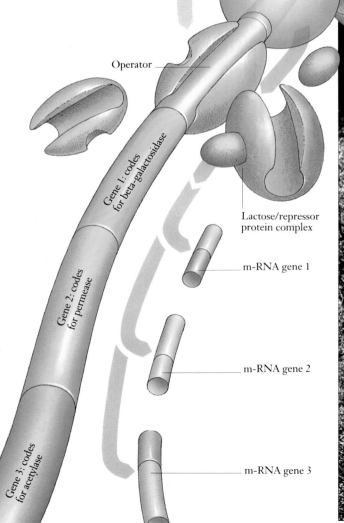

DNA acts as a code for a repressor protein. This protein can bind to either the operator of the lactose genes or to lactose itself. When bound to the operator, it prevents RNA polymerase binding to transcribe the lactose genes. If there is a lot of lactose in the cell, the repressor binds to it instead, and the lactose operon is then activated.

The opposite happens with genes that control the intake of nitrogen from food by *E. coli*. The RNA polymerase binds only weakly to the nitrogen operon promoter. It needs help from an activator protein. If nitrogen is in short supply, this switches on genes that activate an activator protein: the genes produce an enzyme that adds a phosphate group to the activator protein, enabling it to stimulate the RNA polymerase to bind to the nitrogen operon promoter. When nitrogen is abundant, the same enzyme works in the opposite direction, removing the phosphate from the activator, so switching off the nitrogen operon.

In eukaryote cells, control is more complex – regulator proteins may prevent the DNA uncoiling and becoming available for transcription. They may also prevent the RNA polymerase from binding to the DNA, or they may interfere in the transport of mRNA out of the nucleus, its binding to the ribosomes or the further processing of the proteins that are produced. Often regulation involves many different combinations of proteins bound to multiple control sites.

One fascinating form of control only recently studied is control of the gene splicing that may occur when introns are removed from the RNA transcribed from the DNA before it leaves the nucleus. By deleting different sections of the RNA, it is sometimes possible to produce different proteins. Patterns of splicing of the same gene transcript may differ from one type of cell to another.

These regulatory systems allow a multicellular organism to produce thousands of different types of cells, tissues and organs, and to respond to changes in the environment around it.

△ Many invertebrate animals – and some vertebrates – change form as they mature. The free-swimming larva TOP grows into a slow-moving bottom-dwelling starfish ABOVE. Changes in gene activities cause this metamorphosis. The pattern of change is itself controlled by other genes, in response to both internal and external signals.

◁ Environmental signals and genetic programming interact, causing flowers of the same species to blossom at the same time each year. This provides the best opportunity for cross-pollination, enhancing variation in offspring and contributing to evolution. Each species is programmed to respond to signals that trigger changes in gene activity.

LIFE'S BLUEPRINT UNFOLDS

THE TRANSFORMATION of a cygnet into a swan looks dramatic, but it is much less complex than the transformation of a caterpillar into a butterfly or a maggot into a fly. Metamorphosis – changes in color; body shape; the number, position and even the existence of appendages such as legs, wings and antennae; compound eyes instead of simple ones; and a complete change in diet – call for extremely complex changes in the pattern of gene switching, and in the types of cells and organs needed in different parts of the body. The cells involved must be instructed what changes to make, and how to go about performing them. These changes have been studied in depth in animals, especially in vertebrates and insects.

KEYWORDS

AMINO ACID
DIFFERENTIATION
EMBRYO
EVOLUTION
GENE
GENETIC ENGINEERING
HOMEOBOX
HOMEOTIC GENE
INSERTION
METAMORPHOSIS
MUTATION
REGULATOR GENE
STRUCTURAL GENE
ZYGOTE

A new organism is formed when an egg and a sperm cell fuse to form a zygote. Further divisions of the zygote form the embryo, which in each species follows a specific pattern of development and growth, programmed by its genes.

The information to begin development is contained in the DNA of the zygote and in the cytoplasm of the fertilized egg, which is inherited from the mother. In most animal embryos, the first divisions of the zygote produce large numbers of daughter nuclei or daughter cells, which migrate to the outside of the developing embryo, eventually forming a hollow ball of cells called a blastula. These may divide to form two or more layers. Infolding of these layers forms structures that later give rise to particular parts of the animal's body, with a range of different cell types and arrangements. The embryo at this stage is called a gastrula.

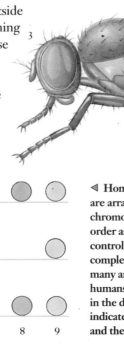

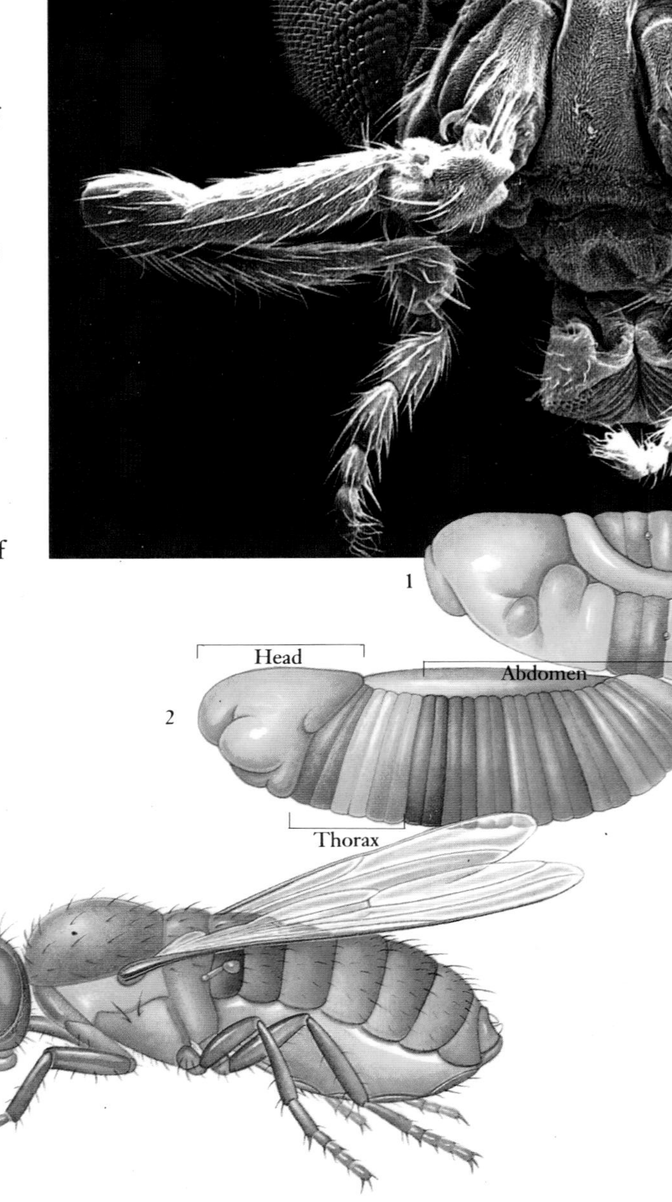

▲ The stages of development of a fruitfly (*Drosophila*). The body segments are color-coded. 1 At an early larval stage, certain regions of the embryo are committed to forming specific structures in the adult, even though the clusters of cells derived from them later change position 2. In the adult fly 3 the origins of structures are masked by the hard cuticle, which is derived from imaginal disks – infolded pouches of cells in the body of the larva that act as organizers. Linear sequences of homeobox genes have been shown to control this process.

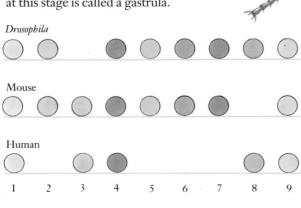

Drosophila

Mouse

Human

1 2 3 4 5 6 7 8 9

◀ Homeobox genes are arranged on the chromosome in the same order as the segments they control. Similar gene complexes are found in many animals, ranging from humans to mice, as shown in the diagram; gaps indicate the missing genes and their related body parts (most notably the thorax, which humans and mice both lack). DNA analysis has shown them to be remarkably similar in both composition and spatial arrangement in different groups of animals, which suggests that they originated very early in the history of evolution.

◀ **A fruitfly with a mutant *Antennapedia* gene, which has resulted in legs developing on its head in place of antennae. The genes that control development are found in the DNA of all the cells, but are not active in all the cells; this mutation is often caused by the *Antennapedia* gene becoming active in a place where it is normally not active.**

During the process, individual cells and clusters acquire a kind of address, which tells them which part of the body they are destined to give rise to. This identity is partly a result of the "history" (cell lineage) of the cells and their position in the embryo. In some animals, such as fruitflies and some amphibians, identification begins in the unfertilized egg. Gradients of chemical and physical factors in the mother's ovaries (the result of the activities of her genes) confer upon the egg a polarity, so that the cytoplasm differs in composition in different parts of the egg. In these animals, cells acquire an identity because of their position in the blastula. In mammal embryos, the cells do not acquire an "address" until much later.

Deciphering the programming of developing embryos has relied mainly on two lines of research. By removing or displacing sections of the early embryo and observing the resulting changes in the pattern of development, scientists have discovered which parts signal to each other and what structures form as a result. By performing experiments at different stages of development, they can learn at what stage the "addresses" become fixed. Microlasers have been used to remove individual cells from the blastula of fruitfly embryos. By noting which segments or appendages fail to develop in the adult insect, scientists can produce a "fate map", showing which cells in the embryo give rise to which structures in the adult.

Another important source of information is the study of mutations in the controlling genes. There are groups of genes called homeotic genes which respond to the positional cues and signals and direct the development of particular body structures. Mutations in these genes can result in the transformation of one body part into another, or in the loss or doubling up of certain segments or structures. Homeotic genes have been found in plants as well as in animals.

One group of homeotic genes, called homeobox genes, code for proteins that contain a characteristic region of 60 amino acids called the homeodomain. The part of the gene that codes for the homeodomain is called the homeobox. The homeodomain binds DNA, so these proteins act as switches for the genes controlling development. These sequences are so similar, even in very different animals, that scientists believe they evolved at least 600 million and possibly a billion years ago. Some homeobox genes are arranged on the DNA in clusters, in the same order as the body parts they direct. Examples include the genes that control the identity of structures in the hindbrain of vertebrates which are important in the development of the head and neck and associated nerves.

Homeotic genes have also been found in plants. Geneticists have successfully cloned some of the genes involved in the pattern of formation of flowers, roots and root hairs. Some of these genes contain sequences similar to those found in animals and yeasts. Mutations in these genes can cause dramatic changes in developmental pattern, such as transforming petals into sepals.

■ **The weed *Xanthium strumarium* LEFT is also known as cocklebur. A highly magnified shoot tip BELOW shows bumplike "initials" (also called primordia) arranged in a pattern characteristic of the species. These develop into buds and new side shoots, each in a position specified by the plant's genes. At a certain stage in the life cycle, determined by genetically programmed responses to daylength, temperature, and the plant's state of nutrition (especially the levels of nitrogen in relation to other nutrients), the pattern and nature of the initials at the shoot tip change BELOW RIGHT for flower production.**

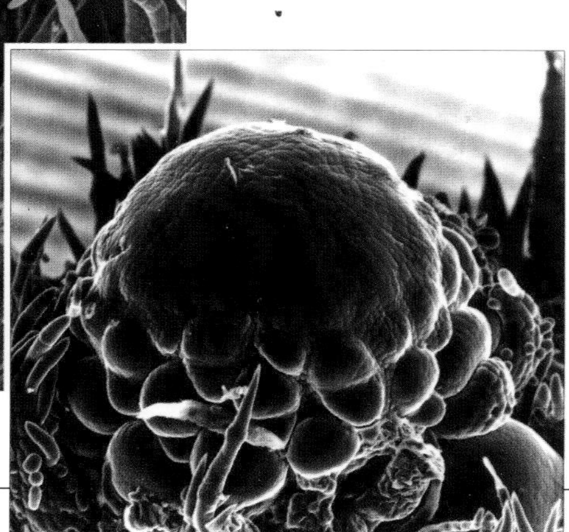

◀ **In a flowering apex, sepals, petals, stamens and carpels are produced instead of leaves. The arrangement of these is specific to each species and is determined by hormones and developmental genes. Mutations produce the wrong parts of flowers, or flowers in the wrong place.**

THE LIMITS OF LIFE

THE timing of major changes in the pattern of development varies greatly in different organisms. In insects, for instance, growth occurs in spurts after each molt of the hard outer skeleton or cuticle, when the soft inner cuticle is free to expand. In insects such as locusts, the wings develop in steps, becoming a little bigger after each molt. Butterfly caterpillars simply get bigger after each molt, but stay the same shape. But the final change from caterpillar to butterfly is very dramatic, involving the absorption and complete rearrangement of tissues. Such a marked change in body form from young to adult is called metamorphosis. It is also seen in toads and frogs. Mammals, on the other hand, simply change in proportion as they grow and mature: human babies and children have much larger heads in proportion to the rest of their bodies than do adults.

KEYWORDS

CELL DIVISION
DIFFERENTIATION
DNA
EMBRYO
GENE
HORMONE
METAMORPHOSIS
PROTEIN
PROTEIN SYNTHESIS

Environmental factors can have a marked influence on the pattern of gene activity, and hence on the pattern and timing of growth. Humans who are well-nourished when young grow taller, and often fatter, than malnourished individuals. The genes simply set limits to this growth. Furthermore, well-fed humans attain puberty (sexual maturity) earlier. Trees growing in exposed sites often become twisted and bent in a direction away from the prevailing wind. Leaves growing in the shade tend to be larger and thinner than leaves on the same plant that are in sunlight, in order to gather as much light as possible.

Even after they have become specialized, most animal cells can still divide again, to repair damage to the tissues or contribute to growth. The liver of a mammal, for example has remarkable powers of repair: if two thirds of it are removed, it can regenerate its original size and shape in just three weeks. Some cells, however, never divide again. Cells of the brain and nervous system are unable to divide, probably because the complex network of interconnections is set up under direction from chemical gradients present in early life and it would be difficult to reestablish them. Red blood cells lose their nuclei during development; on death, they have to be replaced by new cells produced in the bone marrow and spleen.

In plants, by contrast, growth is usually confined to the tips of the shoots and roots and, in woody plants, also to bands of dividing cells (cambium) that lie in a circle just below the outer layers of stems and roots. The cambium layers contribute to the increase in girth

◁ Baby blackbirds hatch while featherless and blind. Programmed cell death plays an important part in their development: eventually death of the cells along the faint line just visible on their eyelids will allow the eyelids to open and the baby birds to see for the first time.

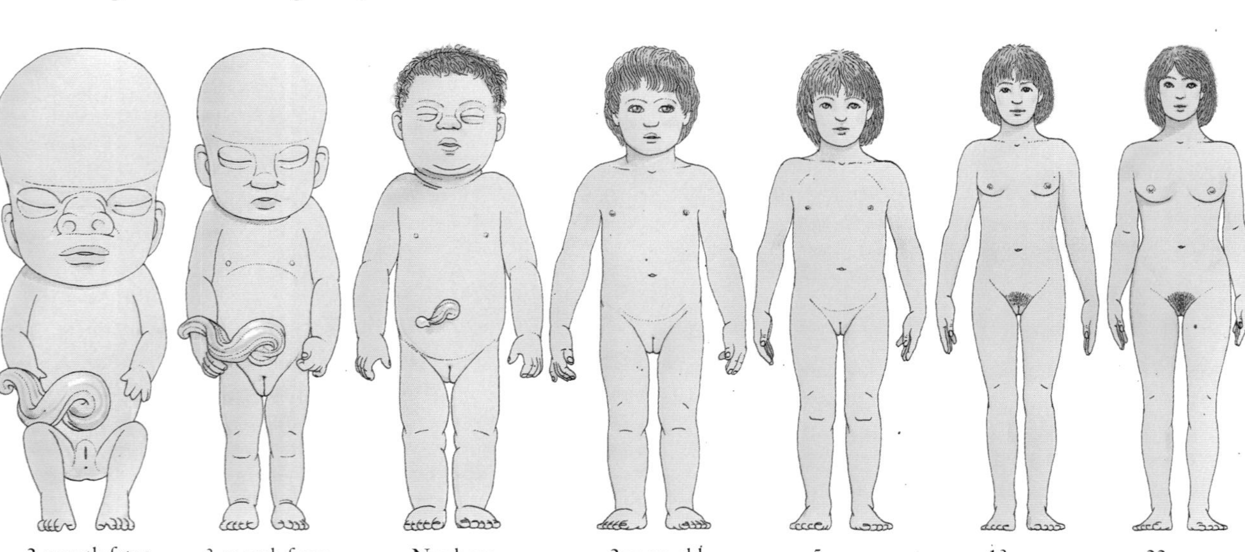

◁ In humans, the change from newborn baby to adult is not simply a case of increase in size. There are big changes in the ratio of the head to the rest of the body (many other mammals, such as dogs and cats, also have proportionally larger heads at birth, though not to the same degree). The most dramatic changes take place in the first few years of life, and again at puberty, when secondary sexual structures appear, and differences in height and shape arise between boys and girls.

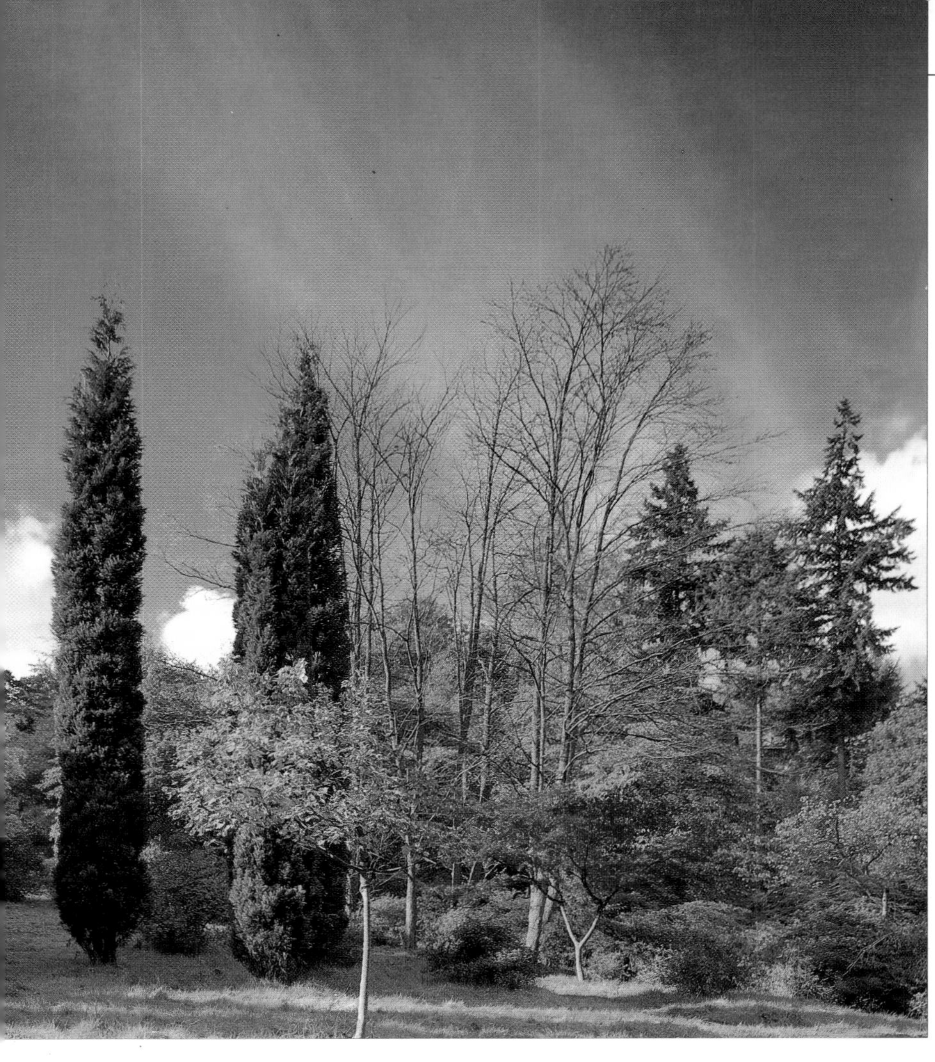

progressive loss of tissues, and a consequent loss of efficiency in the body's functions – sight and hearing become less acute, reaction times slow, digestion becomes less efficient, bones break more easily, and so on. There are many theories as to how and why aging occurs. Some scientists think cells gradually lose the ability to repair DNA, so damage slowly accumulates, affecting protein synthesis. This in turn may upset metabolism, affect the transport of materials around the body, and cause changes in hormone levels. Aging in women, for instance, can be slowed by taking certain hormones. If the proteins of the immune system are affected, the body may become less able to fight off disease and cope with stress. There is also some evidence that certain chemical byproducts of metabolic reactions, called free radicals, accumulate in the body as time goes by, and have a destructive effect.

Scientists still do not know for sure if aging and death are genetically programmed. In terms of survival of the species, a long life is not necessary, or even desirable. Once an organism has survived long enough to produce sufficient offspring to perpetuate the species, it is unnecessary to maintain its body systems any more. So there is no reason why we should have evolved ways of avoiding aging and death.

as the plant grows taller. Plant tissues that keep the ability to divide are called meristems. Other plant cells, once they have become specialized for a particular purpose, are incapable of dividing.

Sooner or later, in both plants and animals, growth slows down or ceases; the body deteriorates and death ensues. For each species or kind of creature, the maximum lifespan appears to be genetically predetermined. Humans live on average for 70 to 80 years, although a few individuals live for over 100 years. Mice and shrews have much shorter lives, whereas tortoises may live even longer than humans. Annual plants live for less than a year, often for only two or three months. Trying to discover why growth stops, and why all organisms age and eventually die, scientists have found ways of isolating cells from humans and culturing them in the laboratory. Even in ideal conditions, most cell cultures stop dividing after about 50 generations. The older the human from whom the cells are taken, the fewer are the cell generations produced. Programmed cell death is part of the growth and development process itself. The human embryo, for example, is blind until shortly before birth. Then the cells joining its eyelids die and the eyelids separate.

During aging, cells in most of the body's tissues appear to divide more slowly, so that there is

△ Trees grow in a variety of forms, all genetically programmed. Their lifespans also vary; oak trees may live for a few hundred years, bristlecone pines to 5100 years; but this is often restricted by environmental factors such as disease or drought. Slow-growing species live the longest.

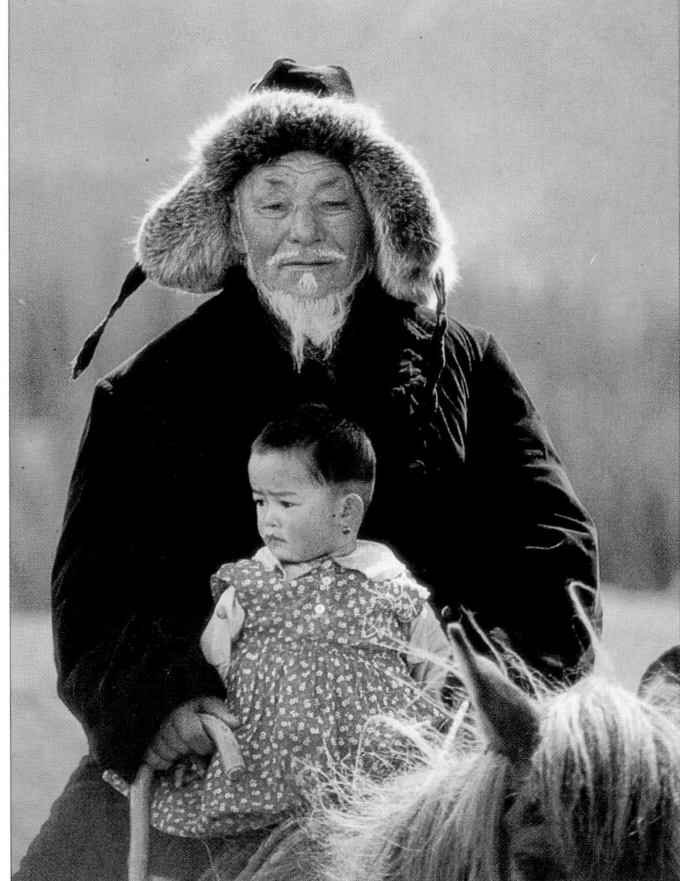

▷ In old age, a decline in the efficiency of cell division and differentiation, and a reduction in the ability to repair damaged genetic material, leads to visible changes in the tissues – drying and wrinkling of the skin, loss of color in the cheeks and hair. Cells are thought to divide more slowly with age, so tissues are progressively lost, which causes deterioration of the major body functions such as sight, hearing, reaction times, digestion and repair of damaged tissues.

3

PATTERNS *of Inheritance*

HUMANS VARY IN HEIGHT and build, weight, skin color, hair color, eye color and other characteristics. Differences between domestic dogs are even more striking, yet any kind of dog can breed with any other kind; like humans, they are all the same species. The variations between different individuals of the same species are due to differences in their genes.

When a man and a woman have children, the children (unless they are identical twins) are not alike, nor are they exactly like either of their parents. A man with brown hair and blue eyes who marries a woman with red hair and brown eyes may have a child with brown hair and brown eyes: the characteristics of the parents are mixed up when they are passed on to the offspring. This is because humans – and dogs – reproduce by sexual reproduction. Individuals of two different sexes come together, their sex cells (sperm and egg) fuse, then divide to produce a new individual, so the cells of the offspring contain genes from both parents.

However, there are additional factors. Even if both parents have brown eyes, the children may not; there are rules governing the pattern of inheritance of different versions (alleles) of the same genes. These rules impose limits on the degree of variation in the offspring, and hence on the evolution of new species and varieties.

Animal behavior is intimately linked to genetic inheritance: each animal acts in a way that attempts to ensure that its own genes will be passed on to future generations. Suricates (meercats), for example, assign adult members of a group to take turns protecting the young from predators while others look for food. There is often a family relationship between offspring and minders; thus the family's genes are the common interest. This cooperative system also allows the favor of protecting non-kin young to be exchanged among a diverse social group, improving every animal's chances of survival.

Sexual Reproduction

During sexual reproduction, sex cells (sperm and egg) from two individuals fuse to form a cell with chromosomes from both parents, the zygote. This cell divides, giving rise to a new individual with characteristics derived from both parents. If the sperm and eggs were produced by normal cell division – mitosis – the number of chromosomes would double every generation. This does not happen. The sex cells (gametes) are produced by reduction division, or meiosis, in which the chromosome number is halved.

KEYWORDS

CHROMOSOME
DIPLOID
GAMETE
MEIOSIS
SEXUAL REPRODUCTION
ZYGOTE

The normal body cells of most animals and vascular plants contain two copies (a homologous pair) of each kind of chromosome: they are said to be diploid. One member of each pair was derived from the female parent, and the other from the male parent. During meiosis, daughter chromosomes are distributed in a very exact way between the daughter nuclei such that each daughter nucleus receives one chromosome from each homologous pair.

Meiosis involves two nuclear divisions. In the first, the homologous chromosomes, already divided into sister chromatids joined at the centromere, pair up and align themselves at the equator of the spindle in such a way that the members of each pair lie on opposite sides of the equator, as if repelled by their centromeres. Unlike mitosis, the centromeres do not divide during this first division. Instead, only one member of each homologous pair passes to each daughter nucleus. Which member of the pair passes to which pole is quite random: each pair of homologous chromosomes is assorted into gametes independently of the other pair present in the cell (independent assortment). So the gametes end up with different mixes of maternal and paternal chromosomes.

The second division is more like mitosis: the chromosomes line up along the equator, the centromeres divide and the sister chromatids, now true chromosomes, move to opposite poles, one into each daughter nucleus. In this way the chromosome number is halved. Each gamete contains only one member of each homologous pair of chromosomes – it is a haploid cell.

Another important thing happens during meiosis. As the spindle forms for the first division, the homologous pairs of chromosomes line up closely alongside each other, a process called synapsis. At certain points adjacent non-sister chromatids break in one or more places along their length and exchange corresponding segments. This process is called crossing over. It mixes the genes from the maternal and paternal chromatids into new combinations. Different chromatids may have different versions (alleles) of the same genes, so this increases variation in the offspring.

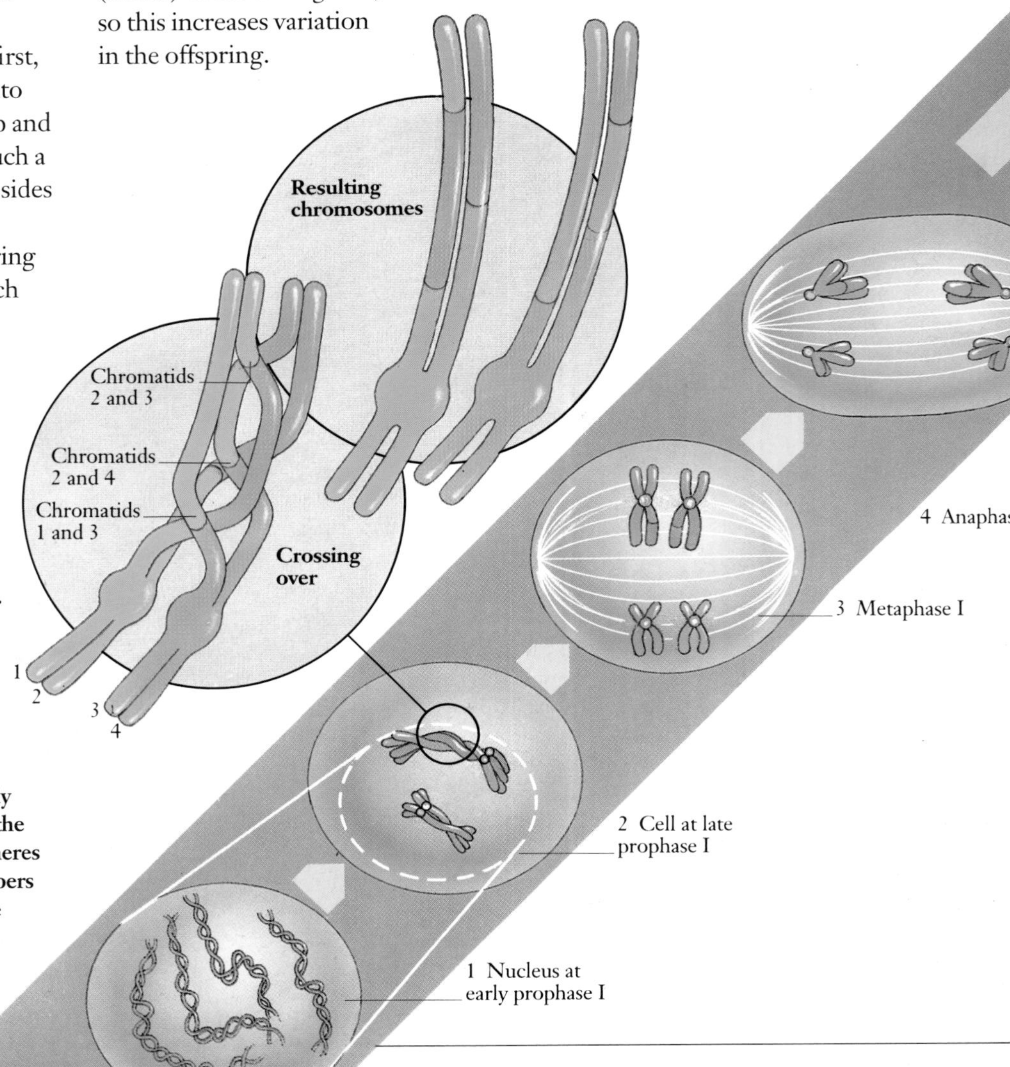

▷ In the interphase of meiosis – as in mitosis – DNA replicates and the chromosomes are duplicated, forming pairs of sister chromatids joined at the centromere. In prophase I, the spindle starts to form. 1 and 2 The chromosomes condense, and homologous pairs form bivalents. Crossing over occurs: the homologous chromosomes repel each other and separate, but they remain joined at crossover points (chiasmata) where breakage and rejoining occur. When the chromatids separate, they have new combinations of alleles. The centrioles (if any are present) migrate to the poles and the nuclear envelope disperses. 3 In metaphase I, the chromosomes randomly align at the equator of the spindle. Their centromeres repel, so that the members of a pair lie on opposite sides, pulled by the spindle fibers from opposite poles.

▽ In anaphase I 4, the centromeres do not divide. Spindle fibers pull the centromeres and associated sister chromatids toward the poles: each chromosome is separated from its homolog, moving to the opposite pole, to be incorporated into a daughter nucleus. 5 By telophase I, the chromosome number has reduced. Each chromosome consists of two sister chromatids, but owing to crossing over these are not identical. The spindle disappears. In animals and some plants

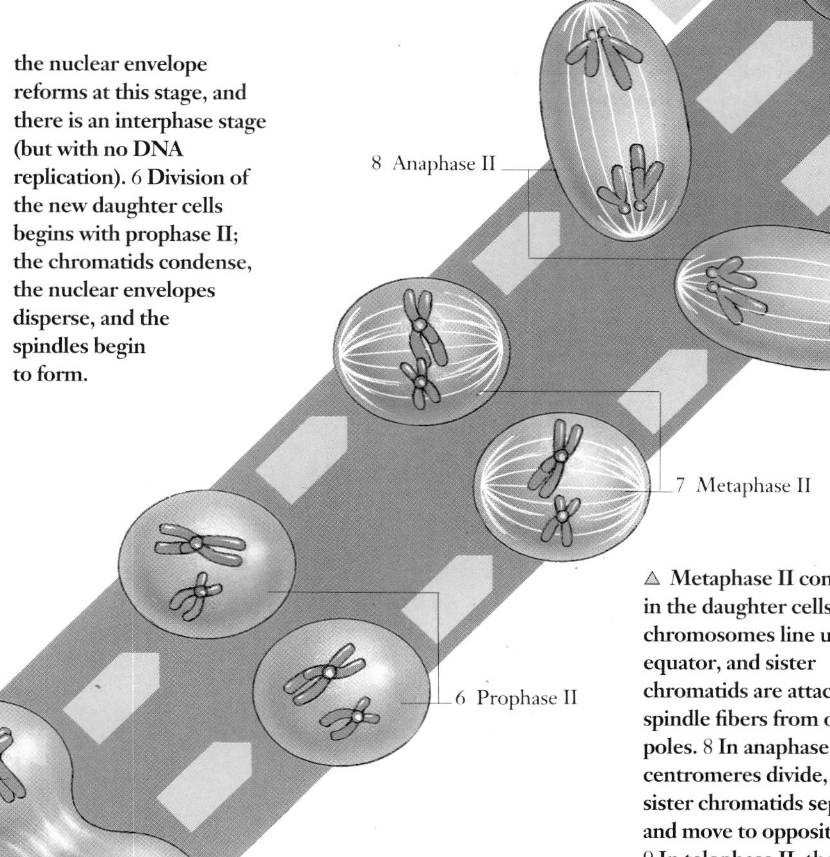

the nuclear envelope reforms at this stage, and there is an interphase stage (but with no DNA replication). 6 Division of the new daughter cells begins with prophase II; the chromatids condense, the nuclear envelopes disperse, and the spindles begin to form.

△ Metaphase II continues in the daughter cells 7. The chromosomes line up at the equator, and sister chromatids are attached to spindle fibers from opposite poles. 8 In anaphase II, the centromeres divide, and sister chromatids separate and move to opposite poles. 9 In telophase II, the spindle disappears and a nuclear envelope forms around each nucleus. The new nuclei have the haploid number of chromosomes.

Meiosis therefore has two functions: to halve the chromosome number, and to bring about new combinations of alleles in the offspring. Not only does the zygote receive chromosomes from both parents; those chromosomes contain a mixture of alleles from both sets of grandparents.

Bacteria have no nuclei, and they do not produce gametes or undergo fertilization. But they do have a kind of sexual reproduction in which genetic recombination occurs. Part of the DNA from a donor cell is transferred to a recipient cell whose DNA is different. As in crossing over of meiosis, breakage and reunion of part of both donor and recipient DNA occur in the recipient, with exchange of DNA, resulting in variation in the offspring.

This exchange takes place in several ways. The DNA may simply be released by the donor and taken in by the recipient (transformation), or it may be transferred from one to the other by a bacteriophage (transduction). Transfer by direct contact between bacteria (conjugation) requires the presence of a small circular DNA fragment, the F (fertility) factor. This converts its owner into a donor, by coding for a protein that enables it to make contact with another bacterium and transfer a section of its DNA. In all cases, homologous parts of donor and recipient DNA associate, break at certain points and part of the donor DNA is exchanged for part of the recipient DNA.

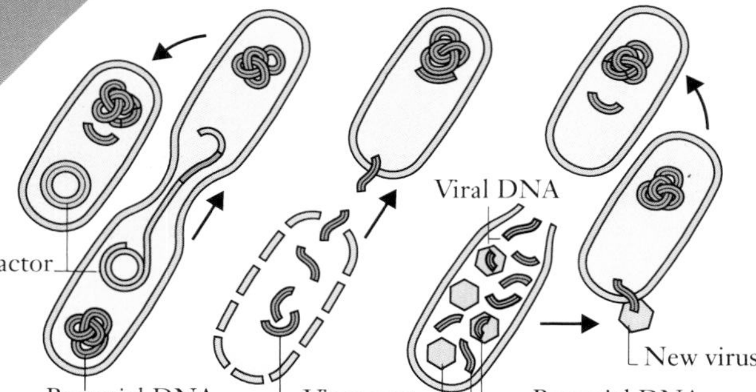

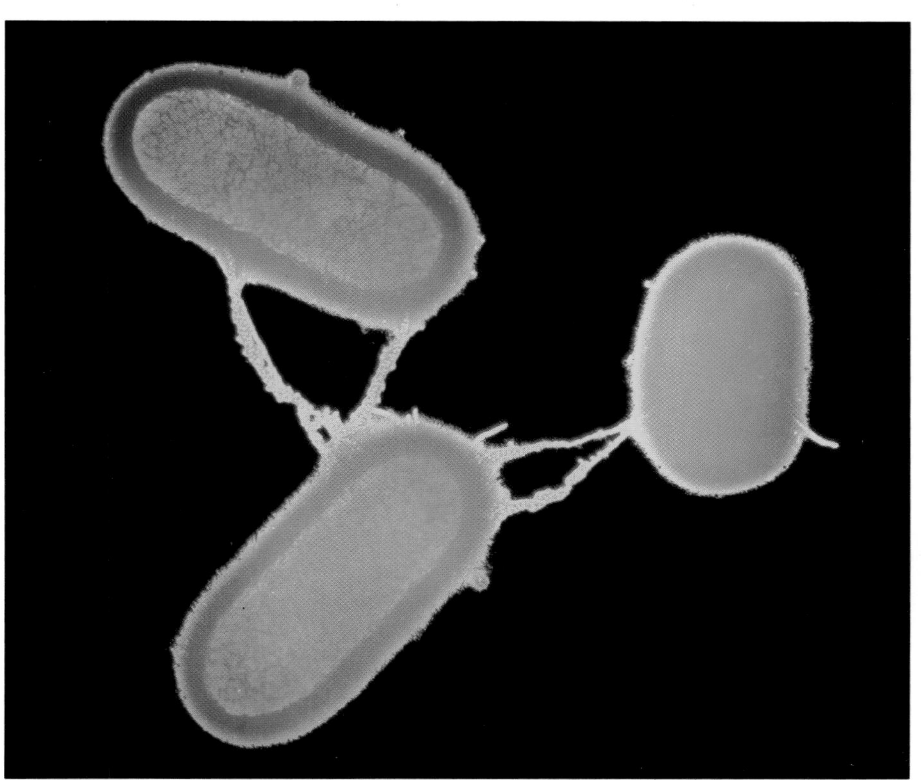

□ Bacteria interchange genetic material in three ways. Conjugation is the most common form of sexual reproduction. Cells come together and DNA passes from one to another. In transformation, a short piece of DNA is "donated" from one to another. In transduction, the DNA is transferred from donor to recipient by a bacteriophage (virus). In all cases, donor DNA is exchanged with host DNA, resulting in variation in the offspring. RIGHT Bacteria undergoing conjugation. Along with the main "chromosome", donor cells have a circle of double-stranded DNA called the F (fertility) factor. It unwinds, and one strand of it passes into the recipient cell, which then in turn becomes able to act as a donor cell.

MENDEL'S BREAKTHROUGH

LONG before chromosomes or DNA had been discovered, an Austrian monk, Gregor Mendel (1822-84), was experimenting with artificial breeding of plants, studying the inheritance of individual characteristics. He was not the first, but he had one great advantage: he understood mathematics.

Mendel chose for his studies the garden pea, *Pisum sativum*. Peas can fertilize themselves as well as other pea plants, and their flowers have both male and female parts, so every possible combination of parent can be used. Mendel studied contrasting characteristics, which he called traits, such as different flower colors or stem lengths, or smooth versus wrinkled seeds.

KEYWORDS

ALLELE
CHROMOSOME
DIPLOID
DOMINANT
HEREDITY
HOMOLOGOUS
MENDELIAN INHERITANCE
RECESSIVE ALLELE
TESTCROSS

Mendel knew that inherited traits were passed on in the gametes (pollen and eggs). He kept his plants isolated from insects and pollinated them by hand, brushing pollen from selected plants onto the stigmas (female sex organs) of other plants from which he had removed the stamens so that they could not fertilize themselves. He started by crossing pure-breeding plants with contrasting traits. When bred with each other, pure-breeding plants consistently produce the same characters for many generations. Because they were pure-breeding, Mendel knew which parent had contributed to a particular trait in the offspring. In his first experiments, the parents (P) were true-breeding for a single trait. Mendel traced the trait through two generations of offspring, the first generation (F_1) and the second (F_2). A cross between a white-flowered plant and a purple-flowered one produced an F_1 generation that were 100 percent purple. But when Mendel allowed the F_1 plant to self-fertilize, their offspring (the F_2 generation) had purple flowers and white flowers in a ratio of 705:224, or approximately 3:1.

Mendel interpreted this to mean that each plant inherits two "factors" (now known as genes) for flower color which retain their identity from generation to generation. Each parent passes on only one factor to each of its offspring. The F_1 generation would each have inherited one purple factor and one white one. Because the purple color masked the white, the purple factor must be the dominant form of the trait: the trait associated with the dominant factor is expressed, even when the recessive factor is also present. During fertilization, every male sex cell (sperm or male

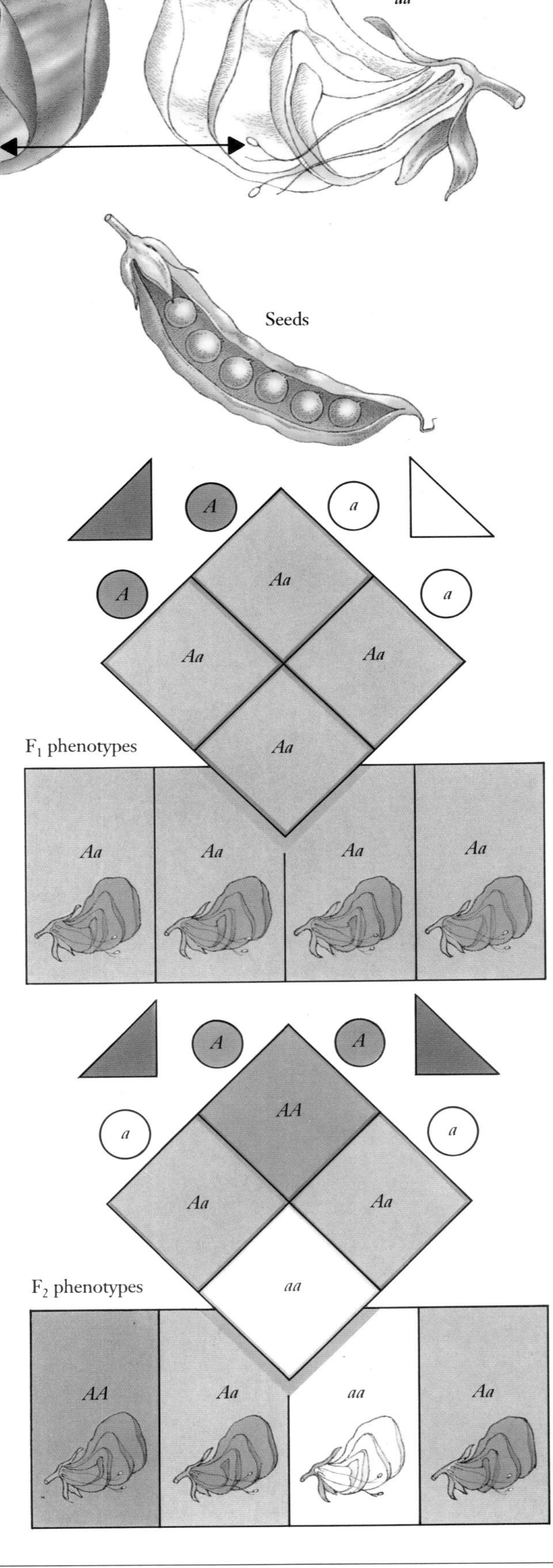

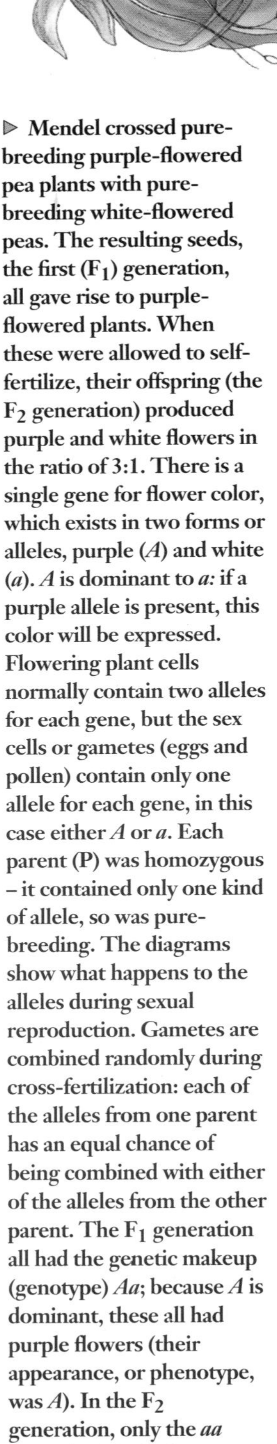

▷ **Mendel crossed pure-breeding purple-flowered pea plants with pure-breeding white-flowered peas. The resulting seeds, the first (F_1) generation, all gave rise to purple-flowered plants. When these were allowed to self-fertilize, their offspring (the F_2 generation) produced purple and white flowers in the ratio of 3:1. There is a single gene for flower color, which exists in two forms or alleles, purple (*A*) and white (*a*). *A* is dominant to *a*: if a purple allele is present, this color will be expressed. Flowering plant cells normally contain two alleles for each gene, but the sex cells or gametes (eggs and pollen) contain only one allele for each gene, in this case either *A* or *a*. Each parent (P) was homozygous – it contained only one kind of allele, so was pure-breeding. The diagrams show what happens to the alleles during sexual reproduction. Gametes are combined randomly during cross-fertilization: each of the alleles from one parent has an equal chance of being combined with either of the alleles from the other parent. The F_1 generation all had the genetic makeup (genotype) *Aa*; because *A* is dominant, these all had purple flowers (their appearance, or phenotype, was *A*). In the F_2 generation, only the *aa* individuals had white flowers, because all the others contained at least one *A* allele.**

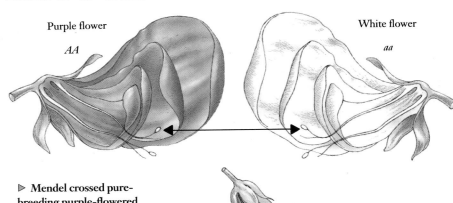

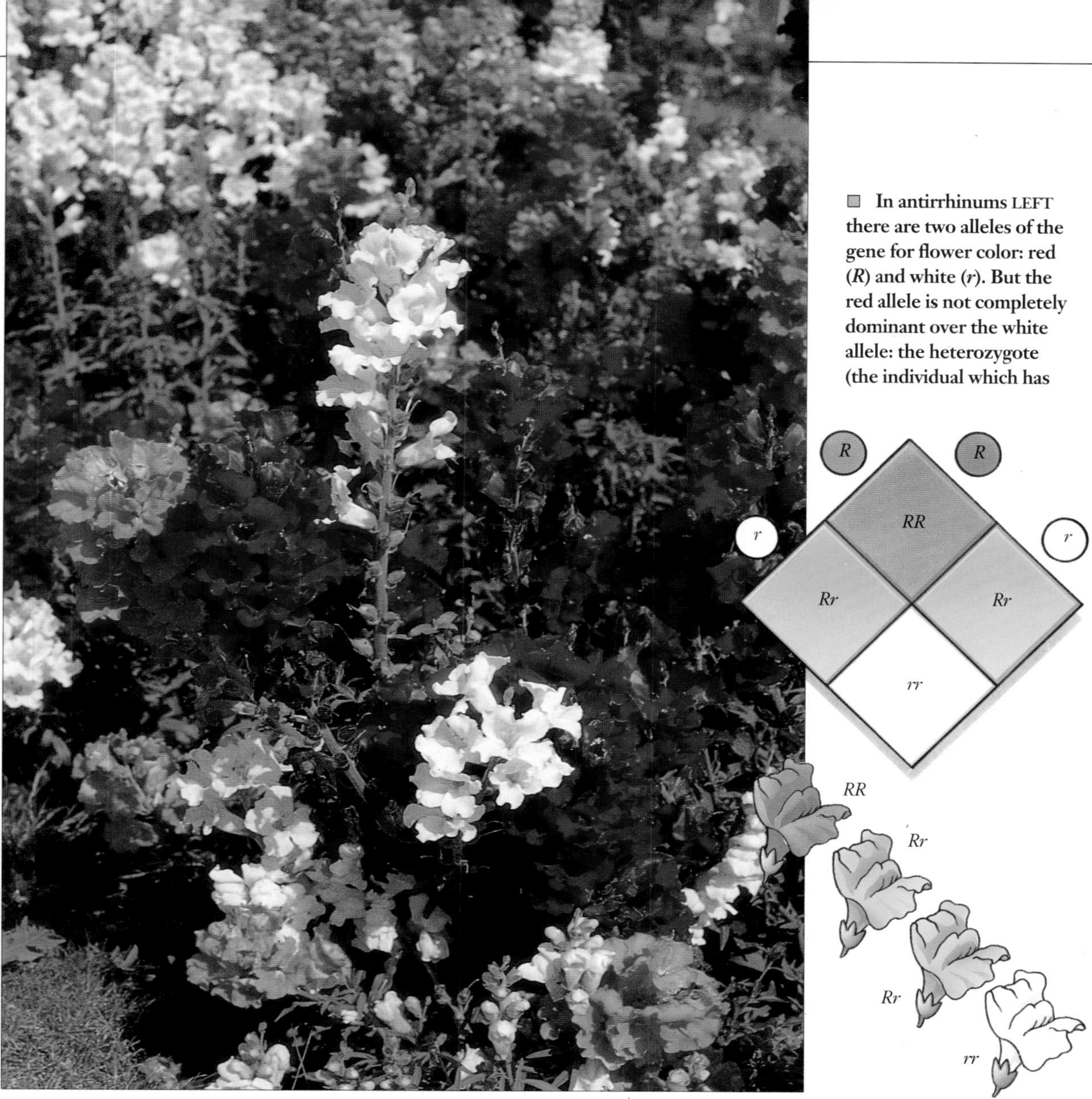

■ In antirrhinums LEFT **there are two alleles of the gene for flower color: red (*R*) and white (*r*). But the red allele is not completely dominant over the white allele: the heterozygote (the individual which has one of each allele) shows a pink intermediate phenotype. When a pure-breeding red flower is crossed with a pure-breeding white flower** RIGHT, **the F_1 generation are all pink, while the F_2 generation are red, pink and white in the ratio 1:2:1. The dominant allele codes for the production or deposition of a red pigment, while the white allele does not, but with only one dominant allele present, insufficient pigment is produced for a true red color.**

▽ Sickle-cell anemia, found in tropical areas where malaria is rife, is due to a single recessive gene that must be inherited from both parents to cause the disease. It produces a defective form of the oxygen-carrying pigment hemoglobin. The red blood cells become sickle-shaped and clump together, impeding blood flow, oxygen transport and gaseous exchange in the tissues, which causes tissue damage and often death. The same allele provides resistance to malaria: in affected areas the sickle-cell individual is more likely to survive; this explains the geographical connection.

gamete) has an equal chance of combining with every female sex cell (egg): fertilization is a random event. By calculating the probability of different patterns of recombination occurring in the offspring, Mendel determined that with a large enough number of crosses he would indeed get the results outlined above.

These crosses can be explained by genetics. Flowering plants are diploid: each nucleus has pairs of homologous chromosomes. The traits are determined by genes at specific positions on these chromosomes. Each gene may occur in more than one form (allele), some of which may be dominant over others. Each nucleus thus contains two copies (alleles) of every gene. The genetic make-up of the individual is called its genotype, its actual appearance its phenotype. The dominant allele is represented by a capital letter, and the nondominant or recessive allele by a lower case letter. In this cross a purple pure-breeding dominant parent (*AA*) was crossed with a white recessive parent (*aa*). After meiosis, each gamete contains only one of each type of homologous chromosome, hence only one allele for that trait. When male and female gametes combine at fertilization, only one combination is possible, *Aa*; when *Aa* offspring self-fertilize, more combinations are possible.

This demonstrates Mendel's law of segregation – the two alleles of a particular gene (located on a pair of homologous chromosomes) segregate from each other at meiosis, so each gamete formed after meiosis has an equal chance of receiving one or the other allele, but not both. In peas, a double recessive gene for seed-coat type produces wrinkled coats; coats are smooth when the dominant allele is present. This gene has been isolated, and it has been shown that the recessive allele does not code for any protein, whereas the dominant allele codes for a protein involved in producing a smooth coat. In other genes, one allele may code for a protein that blocks the activity of the protein produced by another allele of the same gene.

CROSSOVER AND LINKAGE

THE discovery of genes as the transmitters of individual characteristics, made by the Austrian monk Gregor Mendel, came from studying the inheritance of more than one pair of alleles at a time. With two pairs of alleles, such as flower color and stem length, the first (F_1) generation are all as expected: when a plant homozygous for the dominant allele of both traits is crossed with a homozygous recessive plant, all the second (F_2) generation express the dominant traits – purple flowers and tall stems. In the F_2 generation, there are nine possible genotypes, resulting in four possible phenotypes in a ratio of 9:3:3:1.

KEYWORDS

DOMINANT
EPISTASIS
GENOTYPE
HOMOLOGOUS
PHENOTYPE
RECESSIVE ALLELE

This can happen only if the genes for flower color and the genes for stem length are passed independently of each other into the gametes. This is Mendel's principle of independent assortment. However, it works only if the gene pairs are located on different pairs of homologous chromosomes. If the genes for both traits are on the same pair, they do not travel independently. Mendel's law must be modified: each gene pair tends to assort into gametes independently of other gene pairs that are located on nonhomologous chromosomes. Genes on the same chromosome tend to be inherited together – "linkage" – unless they are transferred to another chromosome by crossing over during meiosis.

Some genes, such as those that determine blood group have more than two alleles. Blood groups are important because if a person receives a transfusion of blood of a different group from his or her own, the body may reject the blood cells, which provokes a very dangerous reaction. There are three alleles: I^A, I^B and i. I^A and I^B are codominant when paired with each other – neither allele is dominant. I^A and I^B are dominant to i.

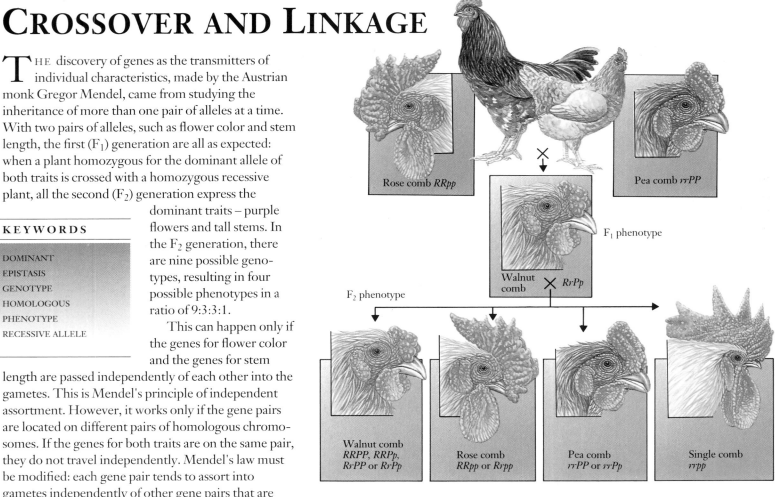

Some traits are determined by more than one gene. Some of the genes modify the expression of others. In some cases, two genes acting together can produce a phenotype that neither can produce alone. Where very large numbers of genes are involved in the expression of a particular trait, an almost continuous range of variation may occur (continuous variation). This is seen in hair color in Europeans and North Americans, and in eye color and height.

Sometimes one gene may completely mask the expression of another gene, so that some expected phenotypes do not occur at all. This is called epistasis. In some dogs, for instance, a number of different genes control the synthesis of the pigment melanin by controlling the metabolic pathways involved. Some affect how much melanin is produced, so the animal's coat may be black or brown. If no melanin is produced, the individual is albino, with a white coat and pink eyes. Other genes affect the deposition of melanin; if none is deposited, the coat is yellow. Gene interactions are not the only factors controlling gene expression – signals from the organism's external or internal environment, often mediated by hormones, also regulate the expression of many genes.

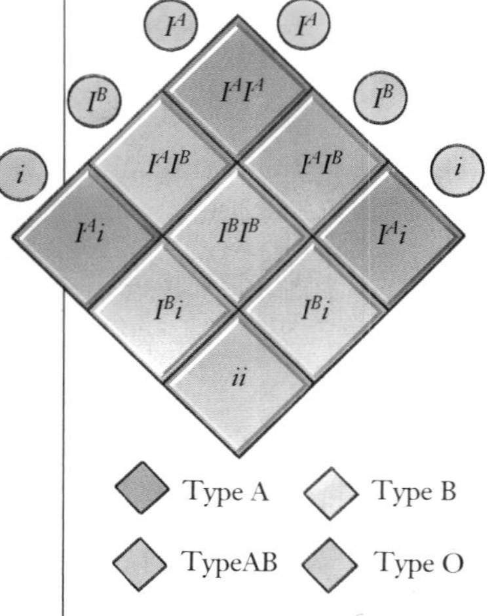

◁ **The ABO blood group system classifies blood according to the presence or absence of certain proteins (^{A} and ^{B}). Three alleles of the same gene are involved. I^A and I^B are both dominant to i; when paired with each other, I^A and I^B are codominant – neither is dominant over the other – and i is recessive to both. Thus there are four blood types: A, B, AB and O. Neither ^{A} nor ^{B} protein is present in type O.**

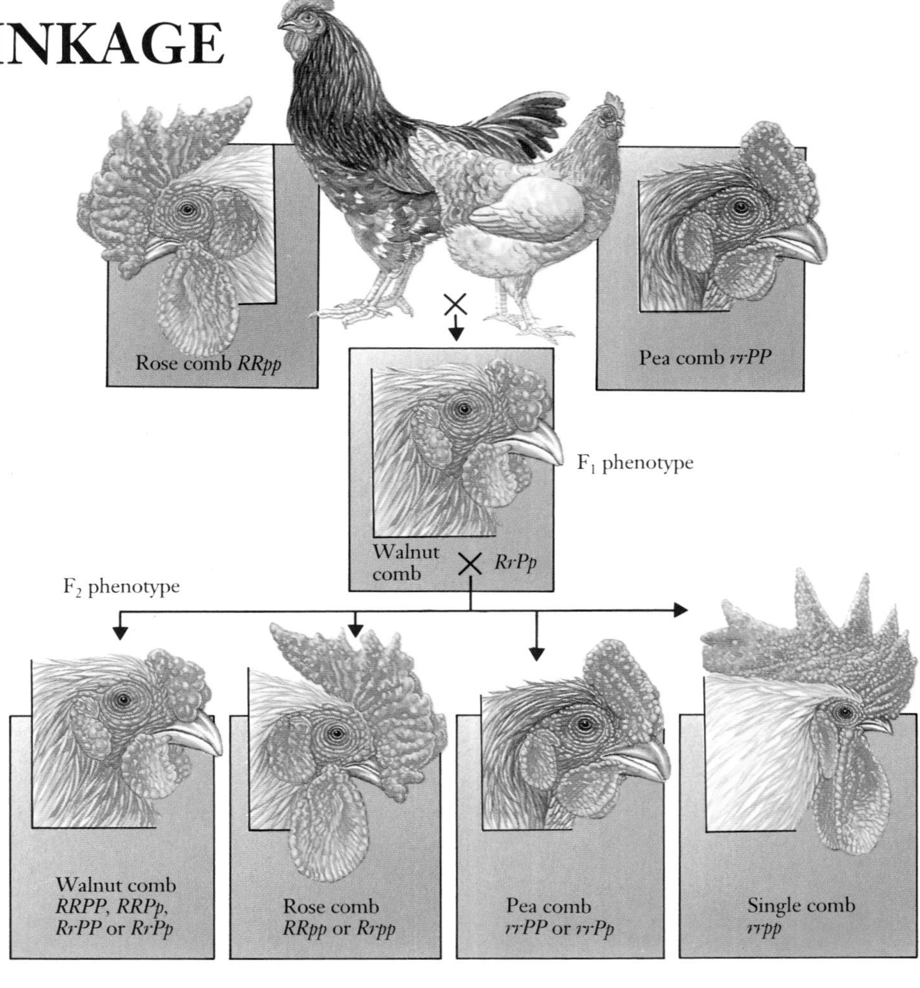

△ **Comb shape depends on two genes, *R* and *P*, which interact to produce a walnut comb – not produced by either gene alone; *rr* and *pp* combine to produce a single comb.**

▷ **Color blindness is an inherited condition whose gene is on the X chromosome. The recessive form results in lack of light-sensitive pigments in the retina. Red-green color blindness is the most common form, in which a green table and red balls appear much the same color. This is common in men, who have only one X chromosome;** FAR RIGHT **a single recessive allele (X^cY) causes the condition to be expressed. A woman is colorblind only if she has recessive alleles from both parents (X^cX^c), but she may be a carrier (X^CX^c).**

Certain alleles may be lethal to the offspring. Alleles that suppress or fail to activate the production of chlorophyll in plants result in death of seedlings once they have used up their food reserves. Such mutations are often recessive. They upset the expected phenotype ratios in cross-breeding experiments.

A sex-linked gene is located on the sex chromosomes. In some cases it may be expressed only in one sex. If it is on the Y chromosome, it is expressed only in the sex with genotype XY; in these individuals it is expressed whether it is dominant or recessive. Recessive alleles carried only on the X chromosome are always expressed in the XY sex, but expressed in the XX sex only if both alleles are recessive. Hemophilia and color blindness are far more common in men than in women. Their alleles are recessive, and are located on the X chromosome, so they are readily expressed in XY males. Only double recessive females express these alleles. A heterozygous female can be a carrier, and may have hemophiliac or colorblind sons.

▷ **The color of these Labrador retrievers is an example of epistasis – interaction between different genes. Alleles of the *B* gene determine how much of the dark pigment melanin is produced: *B* (black) is dominant to *b* (brown). But alleles of another gene, *D*, determine whether or not the pigment is deposited in the fur. *D* allows deposition, but the recessive allele *d* does not, so the genotype *dd* prevents its deposition, resulting in yellow fur. For either *B* or *b* to be expressed, the dominant *D* allele must be present.**

■ **A calico cat** TOP **is always female.** CENTER LEFT **The gene for black and ginger pigments is on the X chromosome. Males have only one X, so they can be only black or ginger. Black (*B*) is dominant over ginger (*b*). *Bb* produces the patchy coat in females. In the embryo, one of the X chromosomes is activated at random in each of the cells. In all their descendants, the same X chromosome remains active, giving rise to patches of yellow or black. (The white patches are due to another gene.)** CENTER LEFT **A calico female and a ginger male produce a calico female (*Bb*); a black male (*B*); a ginger female (*bb*); and a ginger male (*b*). Like color blindness** BOTTOM LEFT, **a calico coat is an example of sex linkage.**

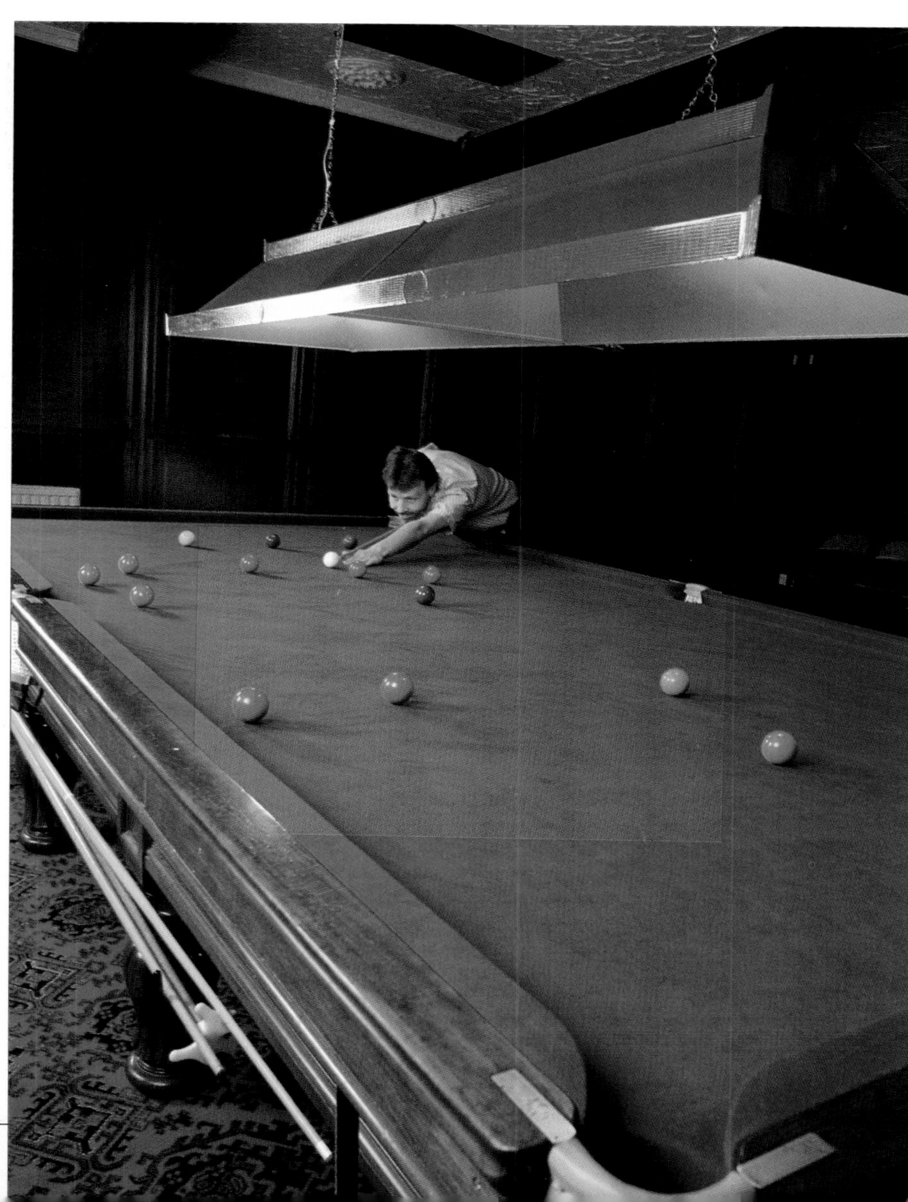

PATTERNS TO ORDER

In nature, the outcome of generations of Mendelian inheritance depends upon how well-suited individual combinations of characteristics are to their environment. Those that survive to breed and produce large numbers of healthy young pass on their characteristics. In an artificial environment, such as a laboratory or a farm, humans impose their own environment, and by various techniques can change the outcome of plant or animal breeding.

KEYWORDS

HOMOLOGOUS CHROMOSOME
HYBRID
INBREEDING
MEIOSIS
MENDELIAN INHERITANCE
OUTBREEDING
PLOIDY
SELECTIVE BREEDING

Mendel, for instance, hand-pollinated plants so that he could perform exactly the crosses he wanted to. Artificial insemination – the injecting of sperm from a selected male animal into the vagina of the female – can be used when breeding mammals. In this way, humans can select for particular combinations of characteristics in the offspring. Over many, many generations such artificial selection in breeding can produce dramatic changes. The many breeds of dogs are an example. Many of these would not have survived in nature. The bulldog, for example, in acquiring its flattened face has stored up considerable breathing problems. Charles Darwin was impressed by the many races of domestic pigeons, all descended from the wild rock dove, and still capable of interbreeding with it – still the same species. Selective breeding is most successful in species that reach sexual maturity relatively quickly, so that many successive generations can be obtained.

▲ A prize bull is the result of selective breeding that aims to produce desirable characteristics – size (to produce the maximum meat) and quality of meat. Its parents will have been chosen carefully, but they may never have met; much livestock breeding is now by artificial insemination. With this technique, a single bull may impregnate tens of thousands of cows.

When individuals of the same species from two different lines are crossed, the offspring often show enhanced fertility or vigor. This is known as hybrid vigor. It also occurs in hybrids produced by crossing individuals of two different species.

Sometimes it may be desirable to combine the features of two different species. If they are very closely related, this may be possible: a horse and a donkey can breed, but the resulting hybrid offspring is infertile. This is because the chromosomes from the two parents are not exactly homologous, so they do not pair properly during meiosis. This interferes with the apportioning of chromosomes into daughter nuclei during gamete formation.

The outcome of a hybrid cross may depend upon characters carried on the sex chromosomes. For instance, a mule is the offspring of a jack donkey and a mare; the offspring of a jenny donkey and a stallion is a

■ Sometimes two species may be sufficiently closely related to be able to breed together. For example, a horse can breed with a donkey BELOW to produce a mule LEFT, and a tiger can breed with a lion to produce a tigon. However, the offspring of such cross-breeding are sterile, because the chromosomes from the two parents do not match and cannot pair properly during meiosis; as a result, chromosomes are not distributed equally to daughter cells during gamete formation.

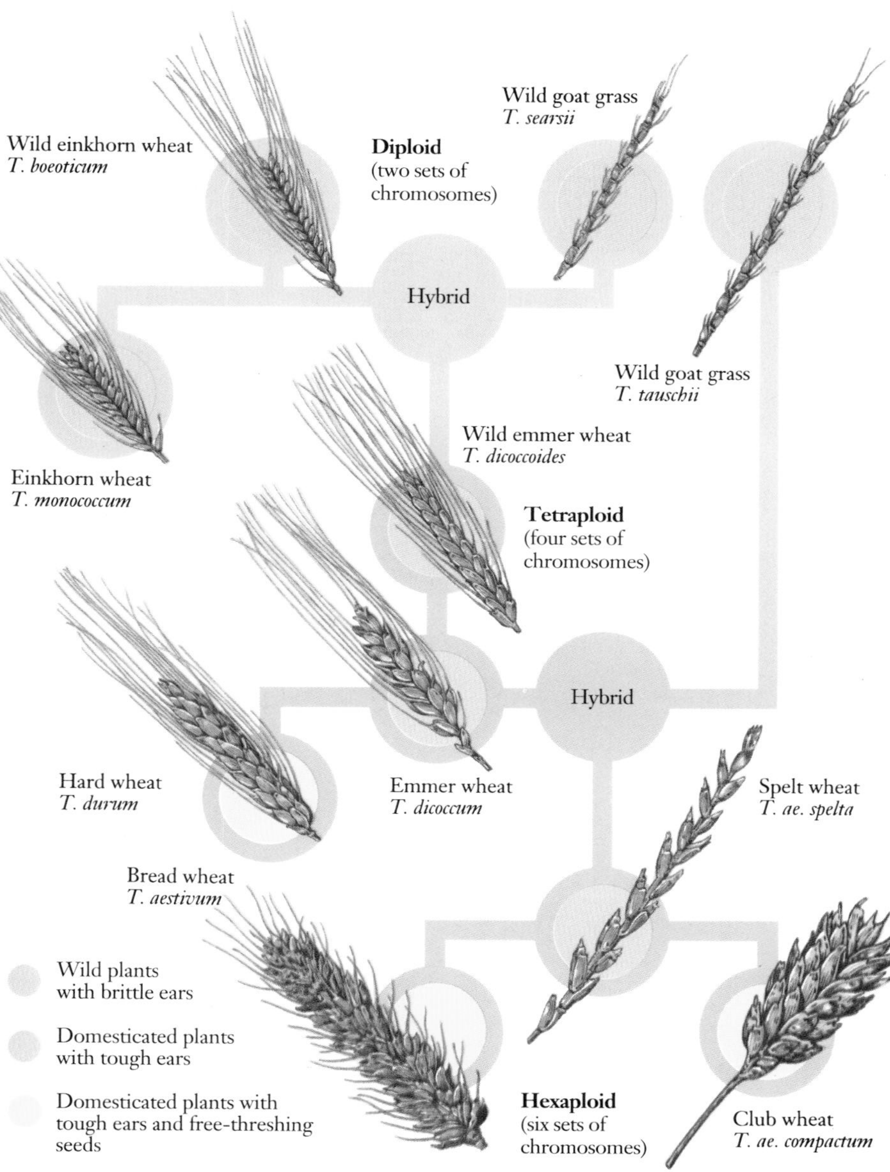

△ Analysis of modern bread wheat (*Triticum aestivum*) shows that each nucleus contains six sets of chromosomes (42 in all), which fall into three groups, each containing seven matching pairs of chromosomes. It is thought that *T. monococcum*, a diploid wheat, hybridized with an unknown wild species, also diploid, to form a hybrid. Because this contained one set of chromosomes from each of two different parents, it was sterile; the chromosomes could not pair up properly at meiosis. At a later stage, failed meiosis produced gametes containing two sets of chromosomes. The resulting zygote was tetraploid and fertile. Later still, this tetraploid crossed with another wild diploid wheat (*T. tauschi*), forming a hexaploid wheat, again fertile – *T. aestivum*.

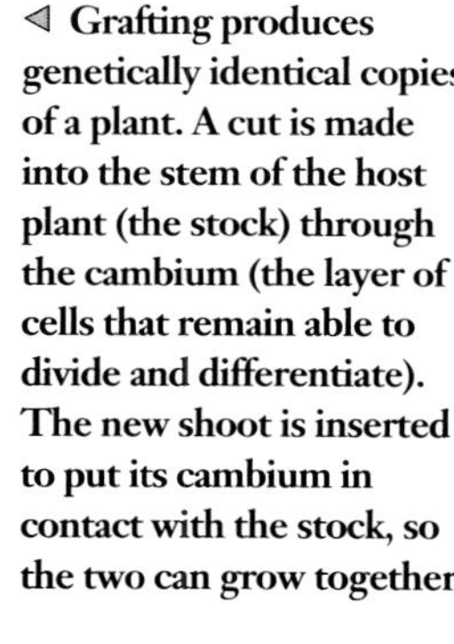

◁ Grafting produces genetically identical copies of a plant. A cut is made into the stem of the host plant (the stock) through the cambium (the layer of cells that remain able to divide and differentiate). The new shoot is inserted to put its cambium in contact with the stock, so the two can grow together.

hinny. The difference is due to alleles carried on the Y chromosome of the male.

Plant and animal breeders usually have one of two goals. They may seek to combine two different breeding stocks to obtain offspring with a new combination of features; this is called outbreeding. Alternatively, a breeder may wish to preserve an existing combination of features. Sexual reproduction results in a mixing up of existing combinations of alleles. Not all plants and animals are capable of asexual reproduction, but by crossing closely related individuals the desirable features may be maintained. This is called inbreeding.

The problems of sexual reproduction can be avoided altogether by certain breeding techniques. The grafting of fruit trees is an example. A twig from the desired fruit tree, perhaps a high-cropping variety, is grafted onto another tree, perhaps of a variety which has vigorous root growth. Sometimes multiple grafts may be made – for instance, with the root system of a species well adapted to the local soil, a trunk which is unusually short and therefore suitable for mechanical harvesting, and a crown of the desired fruit variety. Culturing buds and leaves and taking cuttings are ways of maintaining existing stocks and avoiding the variation that occurs during seed production. The use of natural asexual plant parts is another method. Tubers, bulbs, corms, rhizomes and so on produce new plants identical to their parents – clones of their parents. Plant cells can also be grown in cultures in the laboratory, and eventually develop into entire plants. This is another way of cloning plants. In both plant and animal cultures, modern techniques allow direct manipulation of the cells, permitting the introduction of nuclei from another individual, or the insertion of foreign cells into the developing embryo.

In plants, new features are often produced both in nature and artificially by polyploidy – the doubling of the chromosome number. This is usually done in cell cultures, by applying the chemical colchicine, which prevents spindle formation during nuclear division. Nuclei with double the normal number of chromosomes – tetraploid nuclei – are obtained. Tetraploids are often larger and more vigorous than their diploid ancestors. They are fertile, because they have two complete sets of homologous chromosomes which can pair during gamete production. Infertile hybrids formed by crossing two different species (interspecific hybrids) can be rendered fertile by this treatment, thus creating a new species. However, if a normal diploid species is crossed with a tetraploid, the result is an infertile triploid; again, the chromosomes are unable to pair during meiosis.

4

EVOLUTION *and Variation*

IN 1831 A YOUNG ENGLISH NATURALIST set out to sail around the world, studying the plants and animals he found on the voyage. Charles Darwin observed that in the natural world, reproduction roughly balances death from illness, accident and old age. He noted the wide variation in characteristics between members of the same species, and observed that many of these variations were inherited. He suggested that individuals whose characteristics give them a better chance of surviving to reproduce would leave behind more offspring than less well adapted individuals; consequently the successful characteristics are more widespread in the next generation. This is the concept of natural selection. Darwin proposed that over many generations the characteristics of a population can change so substantially that a new species is formed. This process of change is called evolution.

Another naturalist, Alfred Russel Wallace, studying the flora and fauna of South America, Malaya and the East Indies, had come up with the same theory. In 1858 he sent an essay to Darwin which prompted Darwin to make the theory public. Darwin and Wallace knew nothing of genes and chromosomes, but they provided an explanation for both the diversity of life and the similarities between living organisms.

A meadow of wild flowers is an example of the great diversity of life. The English naturalists Charles Darwin and Alfred Russel Wallace independently proposed the theory of evolution by natural selection to explain how such a variety of life forms arose from simple beginnings. This theory is based on the idea that the pressures of environmental stresses and competition from other living creatures determine which individuals of a particular species – and hence which characteristics – survive to give rise to the next generation. Wild plants – or weeds – are among the most successful life forms.

EVOLUTION BY NATURAL SELECTION

THE idea of evolution was not completely new to biologists in the mid-19th century. Many had read *Essay on the Principles of Population* written by the English clergyman Thomas Malthus in 1798, in which he surmised that population increase is limited by the availability of food – in other words, by competition for food. Also familiar were plant and animal breeding, or "artificial selection", by which breeders could produce plants and animals with new characteristics which would be passed on from generation to generation. In 1753 the Swedish botanist Carl von Linné (Carolus Linnaeus) had published *Systema Naturae*, in which he attempted to classify plants and animals by grouping them together on the basis of shared characteristics. This had revealed that animals with widely different forms and habits, such as whales and monkeys, were often fundamentally similar in structure and development, a puzzle readily explained by evolution from a common ancestor. But the theory of evolution was not widely accepted for several decades, until theories for its underlying mechanism were available.

At the time, the concept of evolution shocked the general public, many of whom believed in the biblical story of creation. As far as they were concerned, the Bible taught that every species had been created as

KEYWORDS

ACQUIRED CHARACTERISTICS
DARWINISM
EVOLUTION
GERM CELLS
NATURAL SELECTION

◁ The English peppered moth is well camouflaged against the lichen-covered tree bark on which it rests. If placed against a non-matching background, it is more frequently preyed upon by birds – "natural selection" acts against it. From time to time a dark mutant form spontaneously arises in the population. This is not camouflaged, and is soon eliminated by predation. However, during the Industrial Revolution, trees became darkened by deposits of soot. The dark form now had an advantage, and the proportion of dark moths in the population increased. As air quality improved, trees reverted to their original color, and the mottled moth again became the dominant form.

▽ The 19th century saw two rival explanations for the giraffe's long neck. According to Darwin: giraffe ancestors had short necks 1. Some giraffes with chance mutations that produced longer necks were able to avoid competition with other animals (including giraffes with shorter necks) 2. They obtained plenty of food and survived to reproduce. The longer necks were inherited by their offspring. Continued selection pressure led to enhanced survival of individuals with very long necks 3, which therefore increased in the population. Competition for food led to the extinction of short-necked giraffes, which failed to survive long enough to produce offspring.

1

2

3

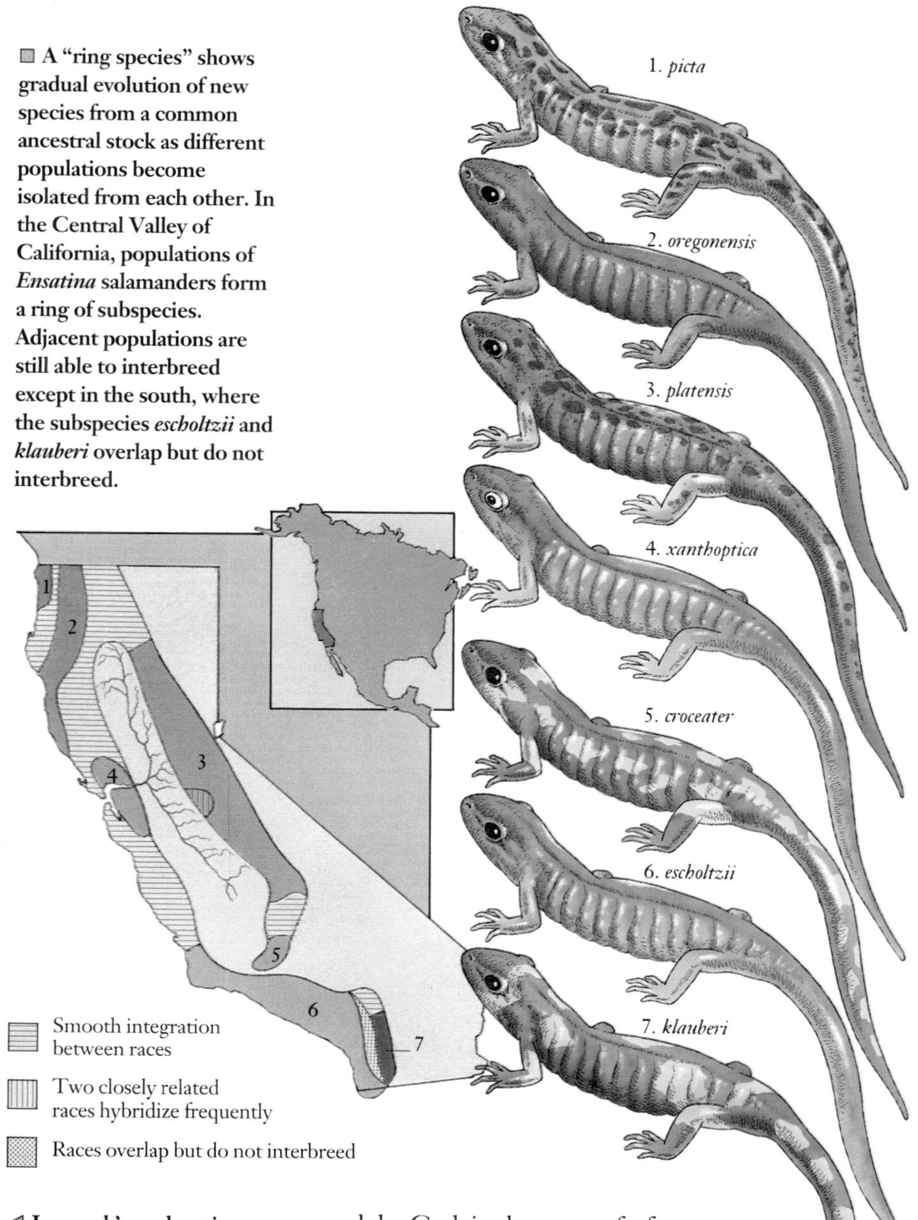

■ A "ring species" shows gradual evolution of new species from a common ancestral stock as different populations become isolated from each other. In the Central Valley of California, populations of *Ensatina* salamanders form a ring of subspecies. Adjacent populations are still able to interbreed except in the south, where the subspecies *escholtzii* and *klauberi* overlap but do not interbreed.

◁ Lamarck's explanation for the giraffe's neck differed from that of Darwin. He accepted that ancestral giraffes had short necks 1, but argued that, because some giraffes kept stretching their necks, the necks grew longer 2. The longer neck was inherited by their offspring. The short-necked giraffes did not try to stretch their necks, so they failed to increase in length and died out as a result of competition 3.

such by God, in the space of a few days, and had not changed since. This is the doctrine known as creationism. Creationists have trouble explaining many known facts. For instance, why are there no modern animals preserved in the rocks as fossils? How can new species which are evolving at the present time be explained? And why should the fossil record show a gradual progression from simple to more complex forms over millions of years? The theory of evolution does not deny God a role in creation, but it does recognize that species can change over time.

One popular theory of the early 19th century was Lamarckism. In 1809 the French scientist Jean Baptiste de Lamarck proposed that the characteristics that an animal acquires during its lifetime in response to life's pressures can be passed on to the offspring. He thought that if certain structures were not used, they would disappear, and that if a structure was used a lot it would develop further. His most famous example was the giraffe's neck: at some time in the past giraffes found it advantageous to browse on higher vegetation. By constantly stretching their necks, they came to have longer and longer necks, and this characteristic was passed to their offspring.

Scientists now know that changes that occur in normal body cells ("acquired characters") are not usually inherited. It is changes to the genes in the germ cells – the cells that give rise to sperm and eggs – that produce inheritable variations, a rule first proposed by the German biologist August Weismann in 1893. Acquired characters cannot be inherited, because information cannot pass from proteins to DNA, but only from DNA to protein.

Since the first half of the 19th century when Charles Darwin was working, many discoveries have reinforced his ideas and suggested mechanisms by which evolution could take place. Chromosome and DNA structure explain how characteristics are passed on from generation to generation, and the principles of inheritance laid down by the Austrian monk Gregor Mendel provide a basis for the action of natural selection on the inheritance of different variants (alleles) of particular characteristics. Mutations provide the raw material – the variation – upon which natural selection can work. Natural selection then changes the frequency of different genes or gene combinations in natural populations.

Some of the strongest evidence for evolution comes from studies of selection in action at the present time. This is best seen in bacteria and insects, which have short life cycles and can be studied over many generations. When bacteria are grown in the presence of an antibiotic which is known to kill them, a few small colonies may survive. A few individuals acquire mutations that confer resistance. These have then multiplied to produce resistant colonies. Antibiotic resistance is often caused by a gene mutation which produces an enzyme that breaks down the antibiotic.

Disease-carrying insects such as mosquitoes have become resistant to some insecticides, bacteria such as the tuberculosis bacterium have become resistant to a wide range of antibiotics, and rats have not only become resistant to many poisons, but have evolved races capable of detecting a poison and avoiding it altogether. Plants can evolve rapidly, too. Many spoil heaps containing waste from coal mines, with toxic levels of lead, tin, copper and nickel, are colonized by various grasses which have become genetically adapted to survive high levels of these metals.

THE RECORD IN THE ROCKS

THE 19th century was a century of collectors – of butterflies, beetles, birds and mammals, shells and fossils. Fossils are the remains of ancient organ--isms now preserved in rocks. They usually occur in sedimentary rocks, formed from deposits of mud and silt. The oldest are at the bottom, the youngest at the top. The rocks can be dated by a process called radio-isotope dating, which uses the rate of decay of radio-active minerals in the rocks as a kind of calendar. Many fossils indicate how life forms have changed over time. New species appear, increase in numbers, then vanish – they become extinct. Looking at the fossil record over the whole period of geological time, in the oldest rocks only very simple forms of algae and bacteria are found. The fossils become more complex as the rocks become younger. This supports the theory of evolution, by which simple organisms have diversi-fied in response to new competition pressures (selection pressures) or changing environments.

KEYWORDS

EVOLUTION
EXTINCTION
FOSSIL
FOSSIL RECORD
SELECTION PRESSURE
SPECIATION

Often there are missing links in the sequence for a particular fossil group. Some of the intermediate forms may not have been fossilized, their fossils have not yet been discovered, or the rocks in which they were preserved have been destroyed through erosion. Most dead organisms, especially soft-bodied forms, decompose rapidly; only in rare situations are they so rapidly buried under sediment that decomposition is arrested. Often scientists are left trying to reconstruct an evolutionary sequence from fossils separated in time by thousands or even millions of years.

The discovery of missing links between major groups of animals and plants is always exciting. The amphibianlike *Seymouria* also has many reptilian features, and perhaps is related to the ancestors of the reptiles. The earliest birdlike fossil, *Archaeopteryx*, shows many reptilian features, confirming suspicions that birds are descended from reptiles. *Cynognathus*, on the other hand, is a mammal-like reptile, related to the group of reptiles that gave rise to the mammals.

Some scientists have proposed a theory of "punctuated equilibrium" to account for gaps in the fossil record. They suggest that evolution may occur in short, rapid bursts which occupy so short a period that there is little opportunity for intermediate forms to be fossilized. The bursts of evolution may occur in only a small sub-population of the species, in one particular location, from which the new, more competitive species may rapidly invade the rest of the old species' distribution range.

The fossil record contains evidence of both gradual evolution and punctuated equilibrium. Many families of trilobites (marine arthropods similar to modern horseshoe crabs) show gradual transitions between species over time, whereas among fossil snails in Lake Turkana in Africa, rapid bursts of evolution occur simultaneously in unrelated groups of fossil mollusks, and appear to coincide with changes in the water level.

■ Mollusk fossils have been found at Lake Turkana, Kenya ABOVE. They come from two locations. In the first sequence RIGHT, sedimentation has been interrupted or there has been a period of erosion of sediments at some stage, so the fossil record is incomplete; it appears to be a case of punctuated equilibrium – short, rapid bursts of evolution. However, a sequence of the same species from another location FAR RIGHT reveals that change has been gradual; intermediate forms of fossil are present.

▷ The horseshoe crab is an example of a living fossil – a descendant of a group that was once much more widespread, abundant and diverse, but is now almost extinct. Such living fossils have often changed very little over millions of years. The fossil horseshoe crab dates from the Jurassic period, which was some 190 million years ago.

Another source of apparently rapid evolution results from changes in the regulator genes that control animal development. Very small numbers of mutations in these genes can produce large changes in the size and shape of an animal's body.

Sedimentary rocks and their fossils provide evidence of past climates. They show great changes in climate, which can often be explained by the theory of continental drift. According to this concept – which is backed up by strong scientific evidence – the continents lie on plates of the Earth's crust which slowly move around on the surface of the planet, driven by convection currents in the hot mantle rocks below. These movements have carried the continents through various latitudes, and hence climates. From time to time plates have collided or separated, creating or destroying land links between land masses (and sea links between oceans) and pushing up mountain barriers, so affecting the spread of animal and plant species.

The distribution of certain groups and species of animals and plants in the present can also provide evidence of evolution. Lungfish are found only in Africa, Australia and South America. In Devonian times, between 408 and 360 million years ago, these continents were all joined together in a single giant supercontinent, Gondwanaland, which later broke up to form South America, Africa, Antarctica, Australia and the Indian subcontinent. The lungfish evolved after Gondwanaland had become separated from the northern land masses, but before it broke up. The proteas, a family of flowering plants, have a similar distribution.

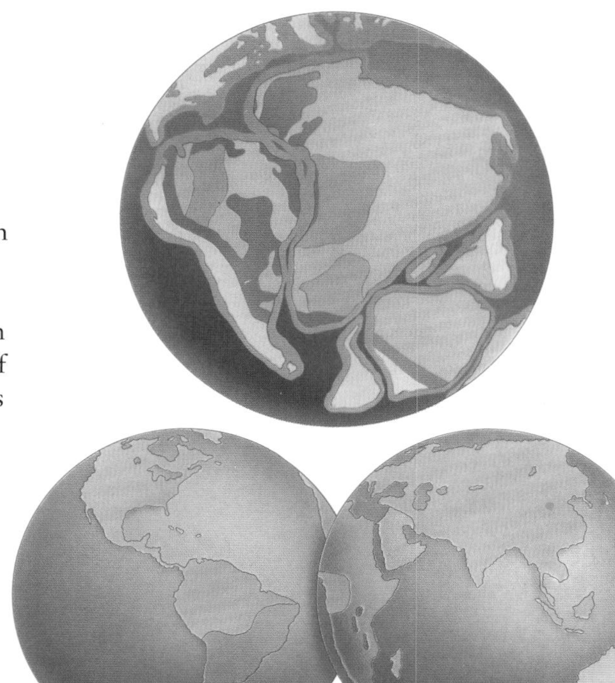

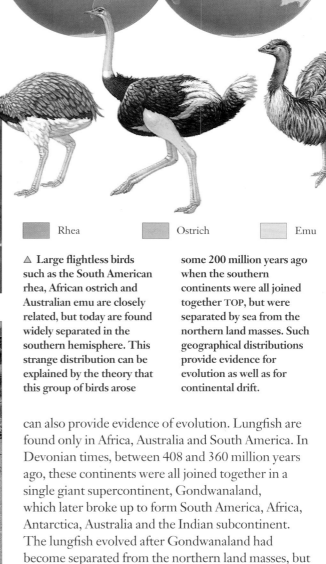

△ Large flightless birds such as the South American rhea, African ostrich and Australian emu are closely related, but today are found widely separated in the southern hemisphere. This strange distribution can be explained by the theory that this group of birds arose some 200 million years ago when the southern continents were all joined together TOP, but were separated by sea from the northern land masses. Such geographical distributions provide evidence for evolution as well as for continental drift.

▷ Tropical velvet worms, which have characteristics of both annelid worms and arthropods, were once considered to be the "missing link" between the annelids and the arthropods, but they probably arose from an ancestor of the annelids. Fossils of similar animals have been found in rocks that date back more than 500 million years.

HIDDEN CLUES TO THE PAST

MANY clues to the evolutionary relationships between species (their phylogeny) can be found by studying their anatomy. Animals that look very different may be built to the same basic body plan. Whales, dogs and humans are a good example. All are mammals: they share many features, such as a common skeleton plan, with a bony backbone, and shoulder (pectoral) and hip (pelvic) girdles which link the limbs to the backbone. In a whale the limbs have been greatly reduced in adaptation to the streamlining required for an aquatic existence, but the basic bone structures are still there. The same basic bones are found in amphibians, reptiles, birds and mammals. Their presence suggests that these animals share a common ancestor.

KEYWORDS

DNA
EMBRYO
HOMOLOGOUS STRUCTURE
NATURAL SELECTION
NEOTENY
ONTOGENY
PHYLOGENY
RECAPITULATION THEORY

A whale has no hind limbs, but the pelvic girdle is still present, although greatly reduced. The pelvic bones are used to support the whale's sex organs. Such reduced organs, which now have no obvious function, or have a different function from that of the original, are called vestigial organs. Snakes, similarly, have reduced pectoral and pelvic girdles. They are thought to be descended from lizardlike ancestors. The human coccyx is homologous with the tail of other mammals, and the human appendix, which has no obvious function, is homologous with the appendix of plant-eating mammals, in which it contains bacteria that break down plant fibers.

Many of the evolutionary changes that lead to new species take place during growth and development, so embryonic development may be quite similar in groups that share a common ancestry. Comparison of the embryos of the major vertebrate classes shows that the earliest stages are almost indistinguishable from each other: all have a large head, a tail, a simple heart and gill slits. In general, the longer the resemblance between two embryos persists during development, the more closely they are related. Because the ancestors of these groups resembled more closely the embryos of modern forms – for instance, amphibians are descended from fish ancestors, and both embryo and tadpole stages are fishlike – some scientists have proposed that the stages of embryo development mimic the stages of evolution. This is the theory of recapitulation. A simpler explanation is that natural selection acts on the sexually mature adult stage rather than on the embryo, so the main changes affect the form of the adult.

Fish

Amphibian

Bird

Rabbit

Human

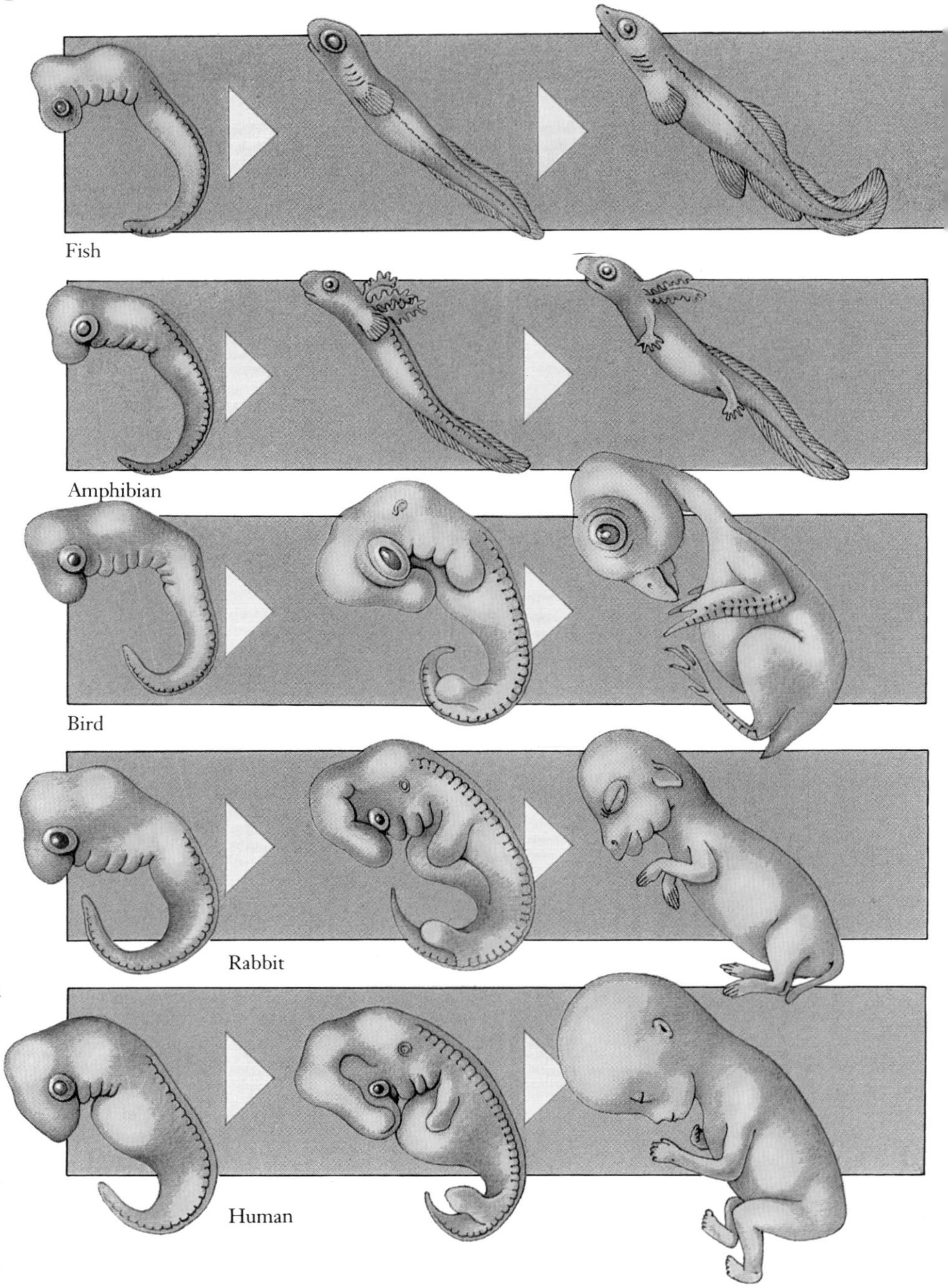

△ **The similarities between embryos of vertebrates (five groups are shown here) reveal a common ancestry: closely related genes specify the development of body parts along the vertical axis. The embryos all have a segmented tail, a two-chambered heart and gill clefts. In fish, the gill clefts form the gill slits. In other groups, one slit develops into the auditory (ear) canal and Eustachian tube.**

In some species, under certain circumstances the juvenile form may become sexually mature, a phenomenon known as neoteny. Mexican axolotls (species of salamanders) in certain lakes do not normally undergo the transition to the adult, lung-breathing salamander. Instead, they attain sexual maturity while retaining such larval features as gills, tail fins and pale coloration. This is due to a failure of the pituitary gland to secrete sufficient thyroid stimulating hormone because of low iodine levels in the lake water. Addition of thyroxin to the water induces the axolotls to turn into adult salamanders. Many species are

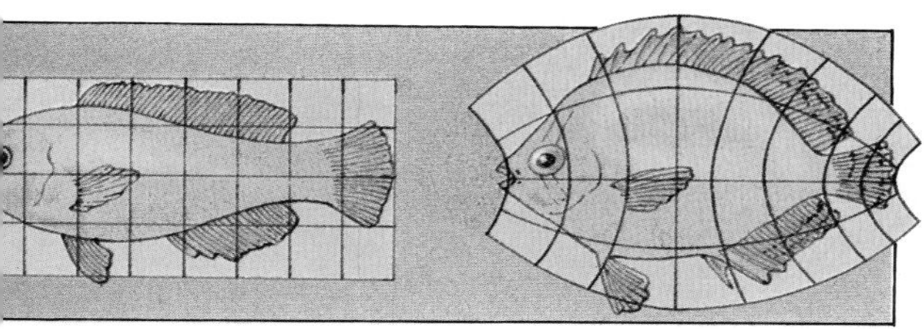

△ These graphs illustrate shape differences between species. One species may evolve from another by changes in the growth rates of different body parts. However, this does not indicate which of the two species is the ancestral one.

▽ The outward form of animals may change during evolution, but internal patterns of organization are often more conservative. The recurrent laryngeal nerve of the giraffe follows an apparently illogical route from the brain down to the heart and back up to the larynx, which requires the nerve to be some 4.5 m (15 ft) long. This nerve has evolved from the fourth branchial branch of the vagus nerve in the giraffe's fish ancestors, where it was looped around the remnant of one of the arterial arches, now surviving as the ductus arteriosus.

thought to have arisen by permanent retention of the larval or juvenile form. The chordates, the phylum to which humans and other mammals belong, are thought to be descended from neotenous forms of sea squirts, whose tadpoles have a cartilaginous backbone. Island birds may become flightless by retaining the juvenile flightless form. There is even a suggestion that insects may be descended from myriapods (millipedes and centipedes), which are born with only six legs. Neoteny allows the relatively unspecialized larval form to diversify and acquire new features which could not easily evolve from the already specialized adult form.

The amino acid sequences of complex proteins required for basic cell processes show small differences between species. The more closely related the species, the fewer differences between their proteins. Such relationships are studied by immunology. Serum (blood plasma) from animal A is injected into an animal of species B. B forms antibodies against the proteins in A's serum. When B's serum is mixed with serum from a third species, C, the antibodies combine with their specific proteins, causing the proteins to precipitate (come out of solution). If C has the identical proteins to A, all the protein precipitates. The fewer similar proteins, the less precipitation.

The most definitive biochemical studies are the sequencing of the DNA, the genetic blueprint itself. Comparative studies of DNA exons (coding sequences which are essential for protein synthesis) provide the best clue to evolutionary relationships.

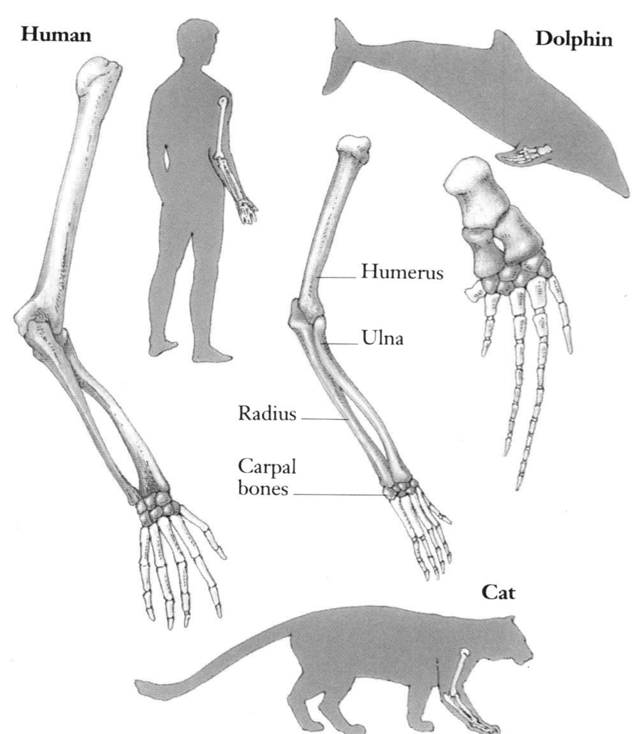

△ The so-called pentadactyl (five-fingered) limb of vertebrates has retained its basic pattern of bones through evolution, although the actual lengths and thicknesses in different species have changed with time as different animal groups have evolved. In some, the bones have become fused together, whereas in others, they have been lost. The changes in the relative sizes and strengths of the various bones indicates a change in function. For example, humans use their hands for grasping, while cats walk on theirs (more accurately, on their toes). Porpoise limbs have been modified to form powerful flippers.

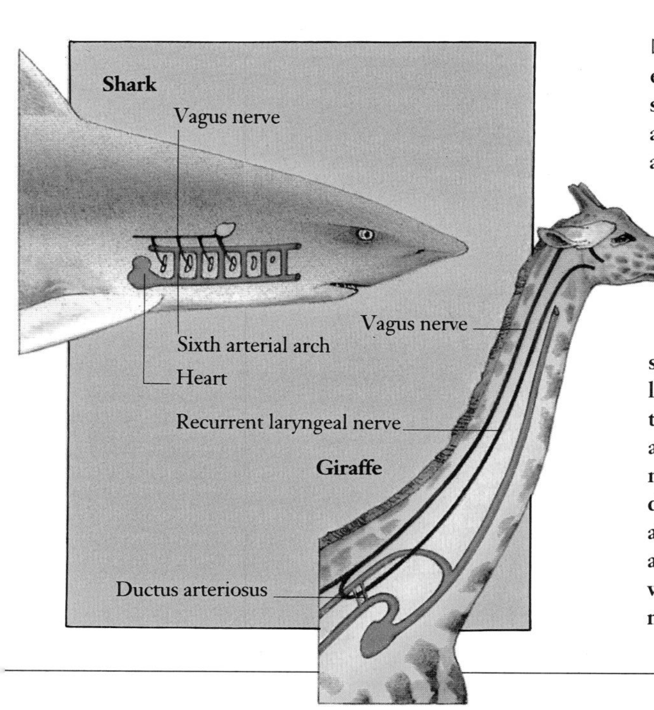

▷ Evidence of past evolutionary history can sometimes be found in the anatomy of modern animals. Snakes evolved millions of years ago from four-legged reptiles. Pythons, which are relatively primitive among snake species, retain traces of the limbs of their ancestors: they have a vestigial pelvis and tiny claws, used by the males to caress females during courtship. Pythons also have two lungs; more advanced snake species, which comprise the majority, have only one.

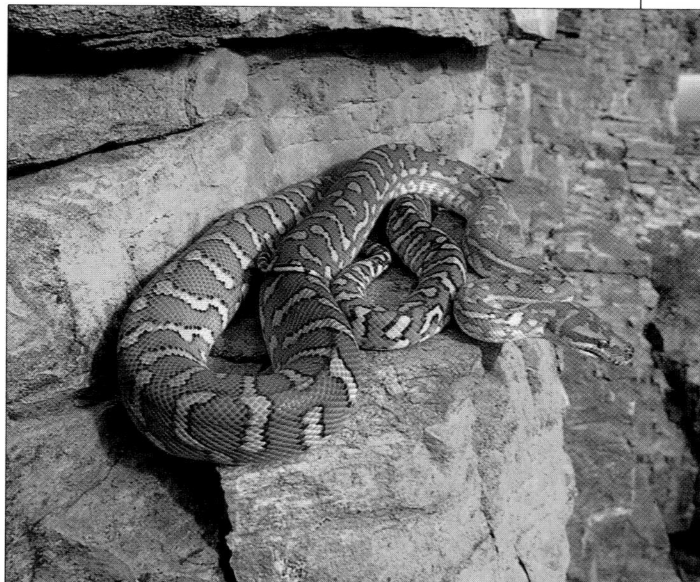

RELATED OR ADAPTED?

APPEARANCES can be deceptive. Animals that look the same may have very different origins: moles in the Americas, Europe and Asia, which are placental mammals, resemble moles in Australia, which are marsupials (pouched mammals). This also applies to body structures. The wings of insects are formed of thin hard cuticle made of a substance called chitin, supported by chitin-reinforced veins. These have similar function and form to the wings of birds, which are modified vertebrate forelimbs – bony skeletons covered in feathers. Such structures are called analogous.

KEYWORDS

ADAPTIVE RADIATION
ANALOGOUS STRUCTURES
COMPETITION
CONVERGENT EVOLUTION
DIVERGENT EVOLUTION
ENDEMIC
EVOLUTION
ISOLATING MECHANISM
NICHE
PARALLEL EVOLUTION
SPECIES

Animals with similar lifestyles often look very similar, even though they may live on different continents whose animals have evolved in isolation for millions of years. The Australian marsupials are a typical example. Australia became separated from the other continents some 145 million years ago. Elsewhere in the world, the placental mammals – most of which evolved after Australia became isolated – are the most numerous. Yet many placental mammals have counterparts among the Australian marsupials. For rabbits, there are rabbit-eared bandicoots; for insect-eating hedgehogs, there are echidnas (spiny anteaters); for hyenas, the extinct Tasmanian wolf. Where whole groups of animals have undergone convergent evolution to the same ecological niches (roles in the community and habitat) in different parts of the world, such evolution is called parallel evolution.

The process by which the early marsupials diversified to occupy different habitats and fulfill different roles is known as adaptive radiation. Some of the best examples of adaptive radiation are found on islands. Islands become isolated in one of two ways: they become separated from the mainland by earth movements or erosion, or they arise in the middle of oceans and are gradually colonized by animals and plants that cross the sea. In both cases, a limited number of species form the ancestral populations. Isolated from the competition of other species, but under increasing competition from members of their own species as their numbers grow, they evolve to exploit a variety of resources and habitats. The more diverse the habitats on the islands, the greater the adaptive radiation. As a result, islands often have a large number of species found nowhere else. These are called endemic species. On the island of Madagascar, for example, 90 percent of its animal species, including all 30 lemurs, and 80 percent of its 10,000 plant species are endemic.

The English naturalist Charles Darwin (1809-82) was particularly impressed by the variety of finches on the Galapagos Islands, 1000 kilometers from the South American coast. He was struck by both their similarities and their differences. The finches resembled finches from the South American mainland, but Darwin noticed that the Galapagos finches had adopted diets other than the typical finch diet of seeds. Different islands had different species of finches, and many were confined to a single island or group of islands – they had evolved in the isolation of those islands. He concluded that they were all descended from a small number of colonizing finches from the mainland, probably of only one species. They had

◁ Eight species of Galapagos finches illustrate how one species can evolve into several. They are found only on the Galapagos Islands, 600 miles west of South America. The main difference is in the size and shape of their bills, which are related to their different diets. It is thought that their common ancestors originally came from the mainland. From this single species, populations gradually diversified, adapting to different food sources and habitats which on the mainland would have been occupied by other species. Such evolutionary divergence is called adaptive radiation. By becoming more specialized, the finches colonized new parts of the islands and expanded their food base: different species could co-exist without competing. Even in modern species, the average size of finches' bills fluctuates

Anteater

△ Anteaters' features – long snouts with tough skins; long, sticky tongues; and sharp claws – are shared by species around the world, descended from different ancestors. But the true anteater species are found only in Central and South America, whereas echidnas are found only in Australia and New Zealand; aardvarks only in Africa; and pangolins only in Africa and Asia. All are mammals, but anteaters and pangolins give birth to live young, whereas echidnas lay eggs. The same features have evolved in these animals in the same ecological niches, a phenomenon known as convergent evolution.

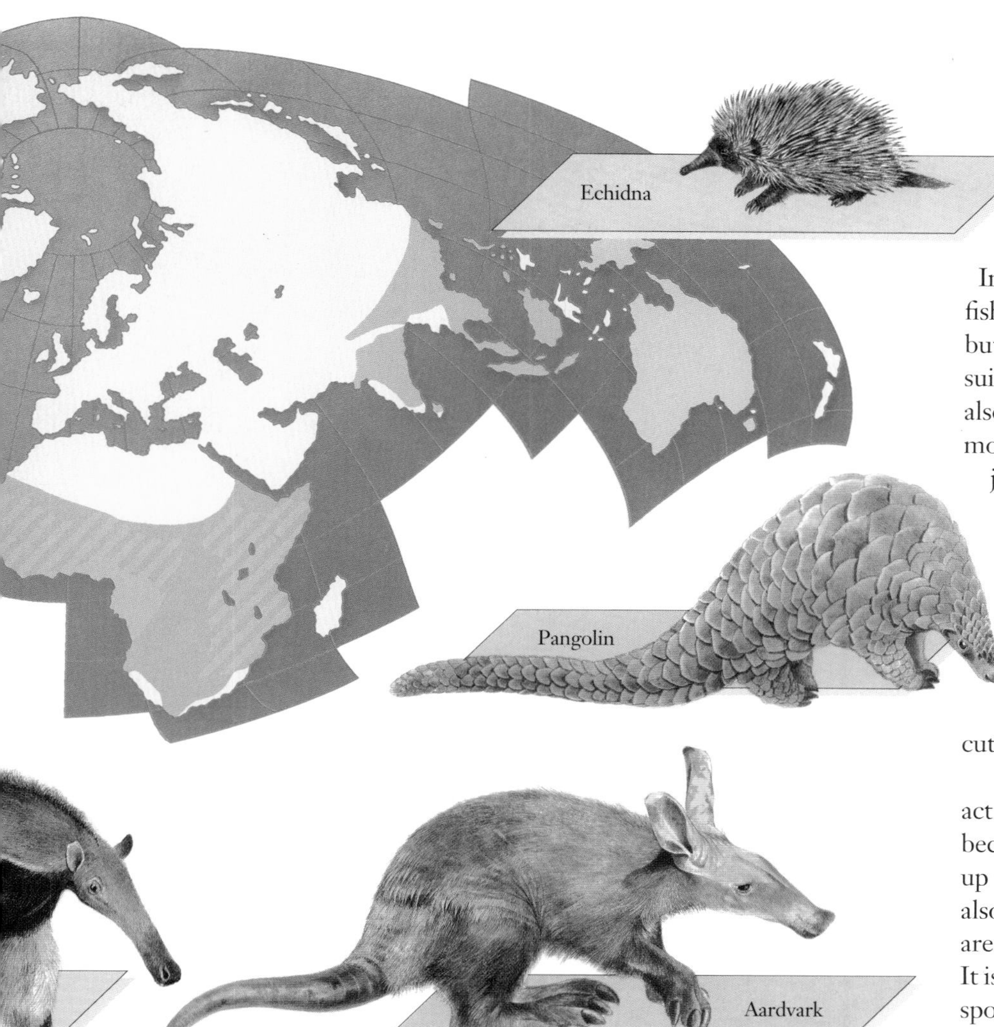

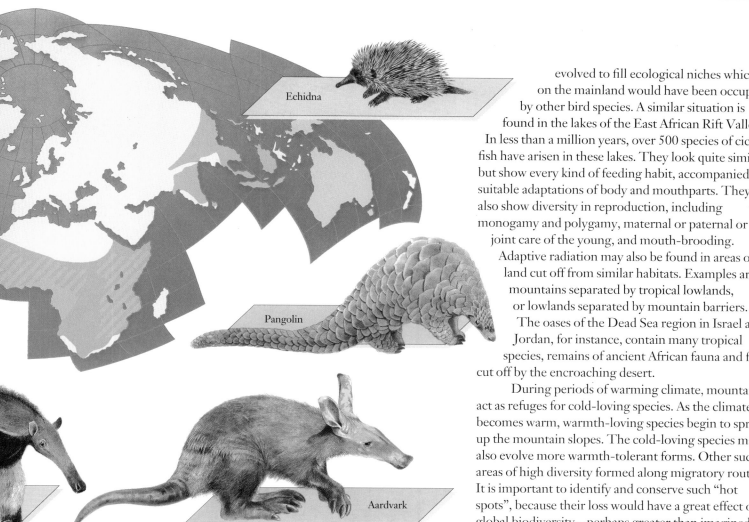

evolved to fill ecological niches which on the mainland would have been occupied by other bird species. A similar situation is found in the lakes of the East African Rift Valley. In less than a million years, over 500 species of cichlid fish have arisen in these lakes. They look quite similar, but show every kind of feeding habit, accompanied by suitable adaptations of body and mouthparts. They also show diversity in reproduction, including monogamy and polygamy, maternal or paternal or joint care of the young, and mouth-brooding.

Adaptive radiation may also be found in areas of land cut off from similar habitats. Examples are mountains separated by tropical lowlands, or lowlands separated by mountain barriers. The oases of the Dead Sea region in Israel and Jordan, for instance, contain many tropical species, remains of ancient African fauna and flora cut off by the encroaching desert.

During periods of warming climate, mountains act as refuges for cold-loving species. As the climate becomes warm, warmth-loving species begin to spread up the mountain slopes. The cold-loving species may also evolve more warmth-tolerant forms. Other such areas of high diversity formed along migratory routes. It is important to identify and conserve such "hot spots", because their loss would have a great effect on global biodiversity – perhaps greater than imagined.

▷ **The Cape region of South Africa is a "hot spot" of diversity: it has a high number of species. There are many species of proteas, seen here flowering. The many table mountains provide an isolated environment in which new species evolve. They have also acted as refuges in periods of climate change, from which species could migrate back to the plains under more favorable conditions, there to interbreed with and increase the variation in the species already present. Proteas are also found in Australia, having evolved at a time when Australia and Africa formed part of a giant continent.**

VARIATION IN THE GENETIC CODE

THE process of evolution depends on environmental pressures acting on the inheritable variations in a population. In sexually reproducing species, existing variations make new combinations. Some of these may be adapted more than others. But the evolution of new life forms depends ultimately on new versions (alleles) of genes and also on completely new genes.

KEYWORDS

BASE PAIR
CHROMOSOME
MEIOSIS
MUTATION
NONDISJUNCTION
POINT MUTATION

Sudden changes in the DNA are called mutations. They may arise spontaneously as mistakes during the replication of DNA or during meiosis, or they may be induced by harmful chemicals or radiation. The average natural rate of mutation is one or two mutations per 100,000 genes per generation. Species with short life cycles, and therefore more frequent meiosis, show greater rates.

The simplest mutation is point mutation, a change in a single base pair. Because the genetic code is read three bases (one codon) at a time, the effect of point mutation depends on the sense of the new codon. If it codes for the same amino acid, it has little effect. If it codes for a different amino acid, its effect depends on how important that amino acid is in the protein. For example, mutations to the active site of an enzyme have a greater effect than mutations elsewhere in the molecule. Mutation to a stop codon shortens the protein or peptide being produced. Changes in the genes involved in development can affect the position and structure of whole organs. In rare cases, mutation may enhance the efficiency of the protein.

Even larger effects are produced by chromosome mutations, which most often occur during breakage and rejoining of chromosomes during meiosis (gamete formation). Whole sections of chromatids and their associated genes (and eventually chromosomes) may be lost, duplicated, inverted or transferred to an unrelated chromosome. This may be fatal, because the chromosomes fail to segregate at the next nuclear division. It can also upset the action of groups of adjacent genes which are usually transcribed together.

Duplications have interesting effects. The genomes of most eukaryotes contain lengths of repeated DNA sequences, often nonfunctional. Where several copies of a functional gene occur and only one is required, the other copies may continue to mutate at random,

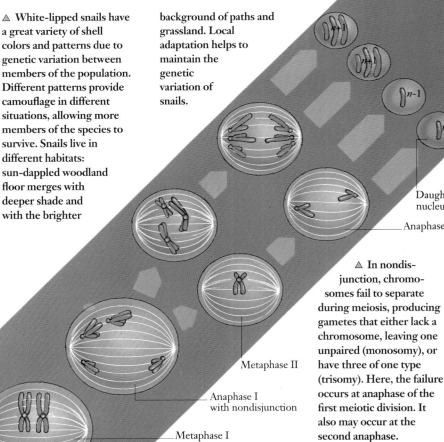

△ White-lipped snails have a great variety of shell colors and patterns due to genetic variation between members of the population. Different patterns provide camouflage in different situations, allowing more members of the species to survive. Snails live in different habitats: sun-dappled woodland floor merges with deeper shade and with the brighter background of paths and grassland. Local adaptation helps to maintain the genetic variation of snails.

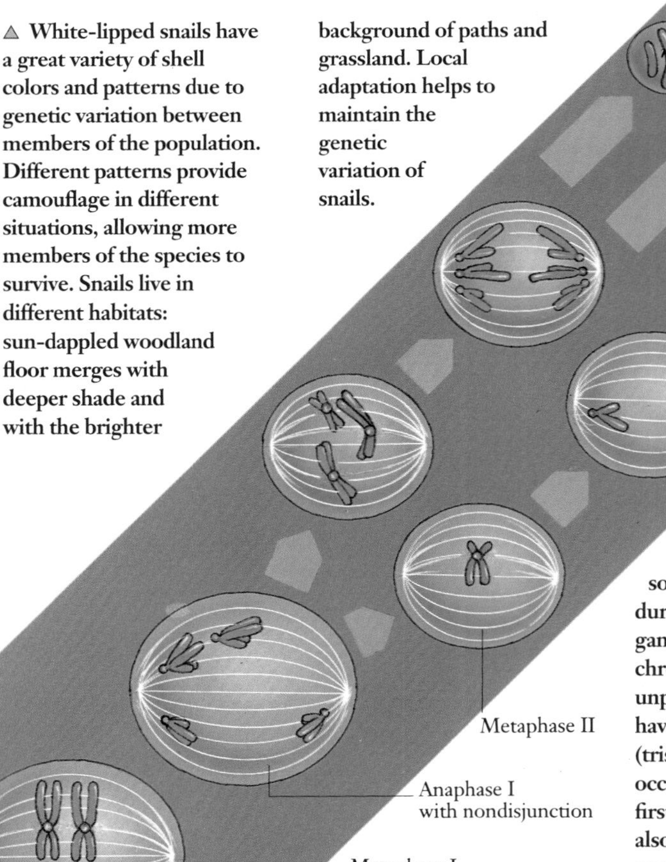

△ In nondisjunction, chromosomes fail to separate during meiosis, producing gametes that either lack a chromosome, leaving one unpaired (monosomy), or have three of one type (trisomy). Here, the failure occurs at anaphase of the first meiotic division. It also may occur at the second anaphase.

so that the nature of the protein gradually changes with no immediate effect. Cumulative mutations eventually lead to new or modified proteins. If the spindle malfunctions, the number of chromosomes itself may change. Some daughter cells may have too many chromosomes, with multiple copies of some; others lack certain chromosomes. Down's syndrome in humans is caused by an extra chromosome.

Some stretches of DNA appear to be able to jump from one chromosome to another, not necessarily of the same homologous pair, sometimes duplicating in the process. These transposons contain special DNA sequences that include the instructions for transposition. Retroposons work by producing an RNA copy of themselves, which is copied by reverse transcriptase, an enzyme that copies RNA to DNA. The arrival of a transposon causes breakage of the recipient chromosome, and often leads to rearrangement of the DNA. Transposons are common in bacteria, in which they can affect gene expression.

Reshuffling of alleles occurs in gamete formation and fertilization. Over 10^{600} combinations of genes are possible in human gametes, yet there are not even 10^{10} humans alive. No two people (except identical twins) are likely to have the same genetic makeup as anyone else alive today or in the past, or even in the future.

▽ A single purple flower has appeared in the middle of this double pink African violet as the result of a "jumping gene" or transposon, a stretch of DNA that jumps from one chromosome to another. The recipient chromosome breaks and the transposon is inserted, disrupting gene action and often leading to further rearrangement of the DNA. In this case, the coding for color and petal number is affected.

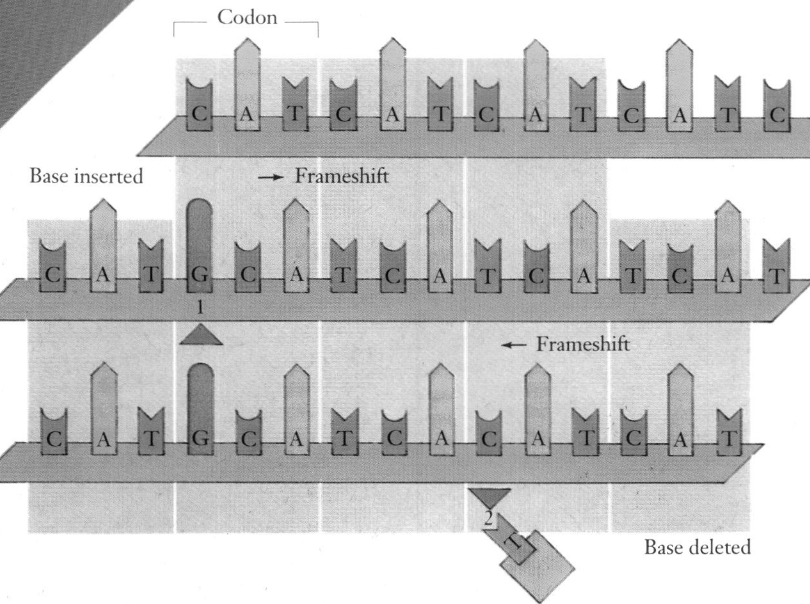

◁ Frameshift mutations involve the addition or removal of one or more bases that shift the "reading frame" of the genetic code, so that subsequent codons (triplets of bases) are misread. These mutations may arise during chromosome replication, or they may be due to damage by chemicals or ionizing radiation. In this example, an extra G base 1 has been inserted into the codon CAT for histidine. The codon now reads GCA, which codes for alanine. The last base of the original codon is now read as the first base of the next codon, and so on for the remainder of the gene. Removal of a T base 2 causes TCA (for serine) to become CAT; the second base of the codon is now read as the first, and so on.

▷ Chromosome breakage may occur during meiosis or (rarely) mitosis, or it may be induced by radiation or chemicals. Whole blocks of genes may be rearranged. Serious disruption results from breakage in the middle of a gene or between a gene and its controlling DNA sequence. An even more serious problem arises in meiosis, when the resulting chromosomes are unable to pair with their homologs, so the organism is unable to produce viable gametes.

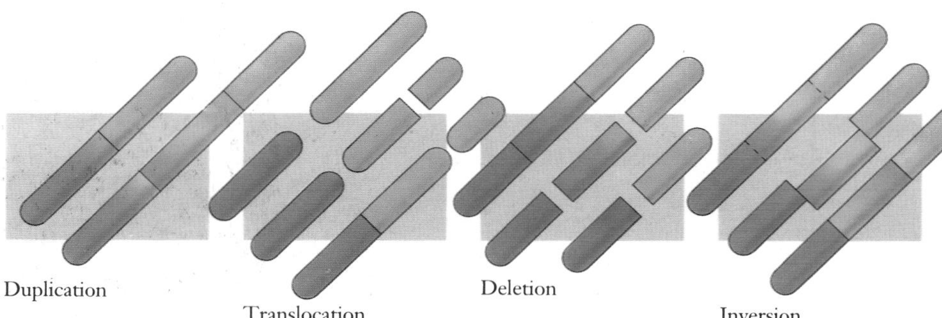

The Reasons For Sex

For most plants and animals, sexual reproduction is a major source of the variation upon which natural selection can work to produce evolution. Not only does it reshuffle existing alleles into new combinations, but it also provides a means of testing the effects of new alleles in different genetic environments. During sexual reproduction, the alleles are first mixed into new combinations in the chromosomes during meiosis, and then the chromosomes from two different individuals, male and female, are randomly pooled in the offspring. The more distantly related the two partners are, the more their genes are likely to differ and the greater the variation produced by sexual reproduction.

KEYWORDS

ALLELE
DIPLOID
EUKARYOTE
FERTILIZATION
GAMETE
HAPLOID
SEX DETERMINATION
SEXUAL REPRODUCTION
SPERM

Sexual reproduction occurs only in eukaryotes, whose DNA is arranged in chromosomes. Bacteria have diverse methods of exchanging DNA including, in some species, the pairing of individuals in conjugation, but there is no meiosis or gamete production.

Sexual differences have become more extreme as evolution has progressed. In very simple creatures, such as protozoans, algae and fungi, some difference between gametes is programmed by alleles at certain points on the chromosomes, and the organisms are described in terms of different mating strains. In more complex organisms, there is a gradual transition from gametes of different sizes, in which the larger one is deemed the female gamete, to gametes of different forms – a large egg containing food reserves and a much smaller swimming sperm. This conserves energy: the egg need not provide for movement; the sperm carries less weight while moving. In diploid animals and plants, the differences also extend to the parent organism. Male and female organs have evolved for specialist methods of fertilization, and the bodies of the two sexes are adapted for sexual attraction, competition for mates or parental care.

Sex determination is genetically based, but its expression may be controlled by internal and external factors. In humans, a distinctive pair of chromosomes – the sex chromosomes – carry genes that influence the sex of the individual. There are two kinds of human sex chromosome, a large X chromosome and a smaller Y chromosome. Individuals with two X chromosomes (XX) are female, whereas those with an X and a Y chromosome (XY) are male. Humans are female by default – a sex-determining gene *SRY* on the Y chromosome overrides femaleness to produce a male. This *SRY* gene is the primary switch that affects the many genes scattered throughout the genome that are involved in the pathways of sexual differentiation.It is the presence or absence of the Y chromosome that is important (abnormal XXY humans are male, XO female). This system of sex determination is common in both the animal and plant kingdoms, but sometimes it is the female that is XY and the male that is XX. In some species, however, the ratio of sex chromosomes to all other chromosomes is the crucial factor.

In a few species, sex is determined by whether an animal has one set of chromosomes (is haploid) or two (is diploid). Honeybee males (drones) develop from unfertilized eggs, whereas the female workers and queens develop from fertilized eggs. This system of sex determination is found only in invertebrates.

The genes that determine sex switch on at various stages of development. In some species of plants and

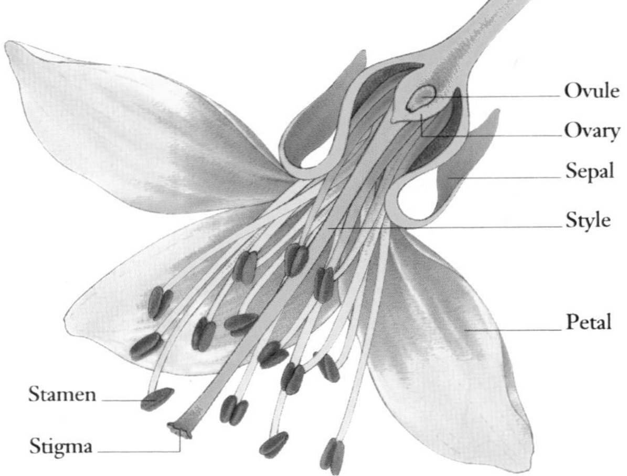

▷ **Most flowering plants are hermaphrodite: they contain both male (stamens) and female organs (ovaries, stigmas and styles). Stamens develop further from the center than the female parts, suggesting that gradients of hormones control the expression of sex .**

▽ **Sexual reproduction is the main source of genetic variation in populations: the genes of the parents mingle in the offspring. Animals must be able to recognize members of their own species and to distinguish between the sexes. Among mammals, this is often based on scents produced by hormones related to sexual activity. Differences in size between the sexes may also occur, especially where males compete for females. This competition is especially pronounced among lions, in which the male may be distinguished not only by his size but also by his abundant mane.**

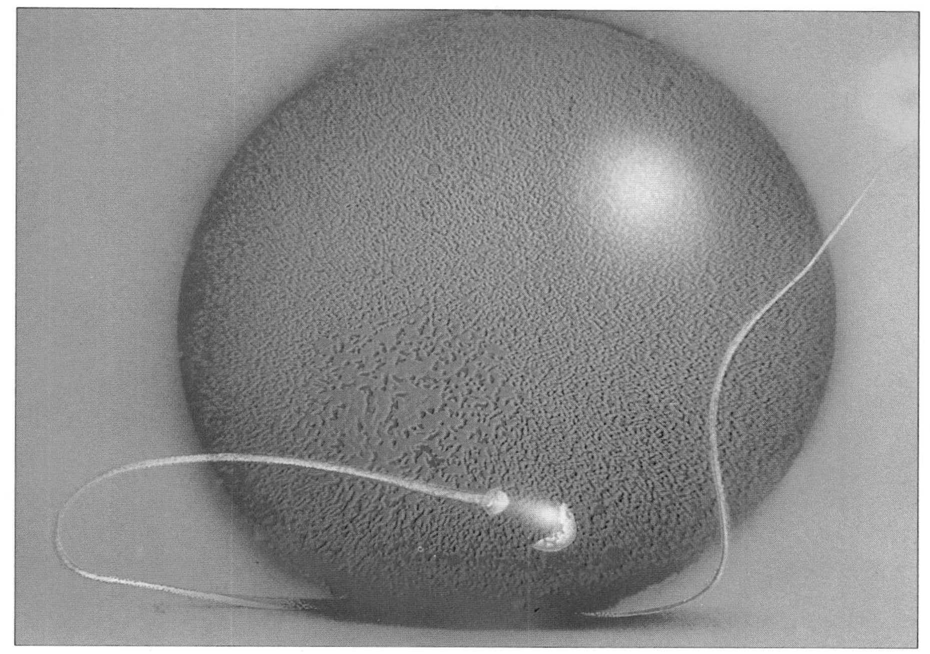

△ **Human sperm, released several hundred million at a time, are much smaller than the single egg they seek to fertilize. Only several hundred complete the journey to the egg in the woman's fallopian tube, propelled by whipping movements of their tails; of these, only one can fertilize the egg. Releasing so many sperm at once improves the chances of fertilization.**

△ **Sea slugs are hermaphrodites: each partner has both male and female sex organs. During mating, both partners exchange sperm and eggs. This means that any sea slug can mate with any other, ensuring that very few of the species go unmated. In organisms with separate sexes, more specialization of reproductive functions is possible: the female may be adapted for egg-laying (and for providing nutrients and protection for the egg/embryo); the male for traveling in search of non-related females (thus increasing the variation in his offspring), or for competition for access to females, thus ensuring that his offspring outnumber the offspring of his rivals in the next generation.**

animals, factors such as the temperature of the environment, the organism's nutritional state or the levels of certain hormones can determine which sex develops. The sex of crocodiles and turtle embryos is determined by the temperature at which the eggs are incubated. Flowering plants in particular are flexible, especially those that produce separate male and female flowers on the same shoot apex: the pattern of organizers in the growing shoot apex switches to producing male or female flowers according to daylength.

A few animal species change sex during their lifetime. In a school of blue-headed wrasse, all the fish are female except for the dominant fish, which is male. If he dies, the dominant female becomes a male within hours. If another male appears, she reverts to female again. This ensures that the reproductive potential of the females is not wasted if males are in short supply, and economizes on production of males. Many flowering plants regularly change sex – they produce both stigmas and stamens in the same flower, but (according to species) either the stigmas or the stamens ripen first, thus avoiding self-fertilization.

▽ **In mice, sex-related characteristics are affected by the concentration of sex hormones in the womb. Female embryos with males on both sides are exposed to relatively high levels of testosterone; on reaching adulthood they have a slightly masculine anatomy, are less attractive to males and behave aggressively. The most attractive females have female embryos on either side. Male embryos with females on either side grow up to develop some female characteristics.**

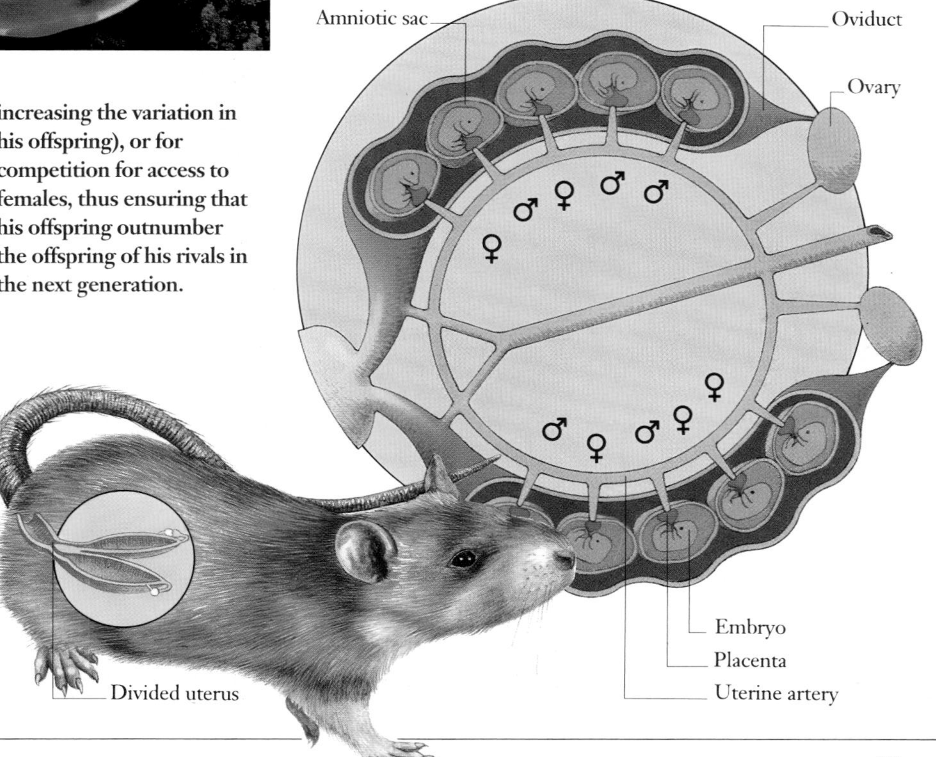

Reproduction Without Sex

Sexual reproduction provides the genetic variation that allows adaptability in a population. However, if a population or individual is already well adapted, some advantage may be lost if the genetic makeup continues to vary through sexual reproduction. Only asexual reproduction results in offspring that are genetically identical to their parents. For this reason, many species of plants and invertebrates reproduce asexually as well as sexually.

KEYWORDS

ASEXUAL REPRODUCTION
CLONE
EMBRYO
FERTILIZATION
MEIOSIS
MITOSIS
NONDISJUNCTION
PARTHENOGENESIS
PEDOGENESIS
POLYPLOID
SEXUAL REPRODUCTION
ZYGOTE

Grasses are some of the most successful flowering plants. They reproduce asexually by producing new shoots from their lowermost nodes. Eventually the connection between old and new shoots disintegrates and a new, genetically identical grass plant – a clone – is established. A field of grass is a mosaic of clones of various species. There are many other types of asexual reproduction in plants – the formation of daughter bulbs and corms, the rooting of arching stems that happen to touch the ground, the production of overground runners or underground rhizomes (buried stems) or tubers, which produce new shoots, then disintegrate, and even, in the case of some succulent plants, budding off tiny plantlets along the edges of leaves. Dandelions spread rapidly by producing seeds without the need for fertilization: one of the normal diploid cells of the ovule develops into an embryo and eventually a seed. This form of reproduction is particularly important for plants such as polyploids which are often unable to reproduce sexually, and is also found in many plants of the Arctic, where there are few insects to act as pollinators.

Single-celled creatures such as protozoans and many algae can simply divide in two by mitosis, a process known as binary fission. Simple fragmentation into new organisms occurs in many algae and simple invertebrates such as flatworms, sponges and corals. Flatworms split in two and regrow their "other half", whereas some sea anemones slowly pinch themselves into a figure eight, then separate into two new animals. Other organisms, such as yeasts, hydras and sea anemones, produce new individuals by budding.

All these creatures from time to time also undergo sexual reproduction, thus maintaining the variation in the population. Often there is a regular cycle of asexual reproduction for rapid population spread during a favorable season, followed by sexual reproduction at the onset of winter or a dry season, when rapid reproduction is no longer an option. Sexual reproduction in these species often produces a zygote (fertilized egg) in a tough cyst, able to lie dormant until conditions improve, or perhaps even be blown about and help to disperse the species. Hydra is an example.

More complex invertebrates are unable simply to divide in two, but they show some quite extraordinary forms of asexual reproduction. Spreading as rapidly as dandelions, aphids (greenfly) infest garden plants and crops in summer. These aphids are all females, which

▽ The ability to reproduce asexually means that plants need not rely on insects to pollinate them. Dandelions, one of the most successful examples, are able to produce seeds without fertilization; instead, seeds develop from one of the diploid cells of the ovule – a structure in a plant ovary that contains egg cells – which in other plant species require fertilization in order to produce seeds.

▷ In the summer, water fleas reproduce very rapidly by parthenogenesis: 10 to 12 unfertilized eggs develop inside a special brood pouch on the back of the female (shown here) until they hatch. The young water fleas (also female) are then released into the water. Males are produced only in conditions of overcrowding or food shortage; fertilized females lay eggs protected in tough coatings than can survive winter or drought.

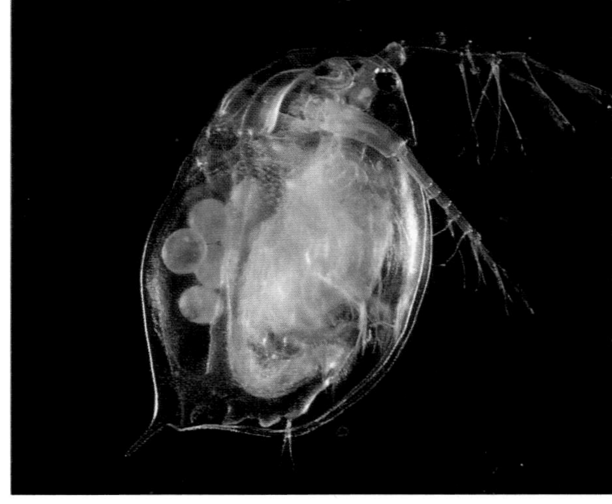

◁ **Certain sea anemones, such as these snakelocks anemones, can reproduce asexually by simply splitting in two, a process called binary fission. This is most common in one-celled organisms, though it also occurs in simple multicellular organisms such as anemones. The two offspring produced in this way (which are always called daughters) are genetically identical to their parent. This form of reproduction is ideal for organisms that live in a stable environment and so would not benefit – or may even be adversely affected – by the genetic variation that sexual reproduction causes.**

give birth to female offspring without the need for mating. Instead of producing haploid eggs to be fertilized, the egg-producing cells of the female aphid undergo a special form of meiosis in which nondisjunction of chromosomes occurs (all the chromosomes go into one daughter cell), to produce diploid eggs which are chemically stimulated to develop into female embryos. In aphids this parthenogenesis (virgin birth) occurs so rapidly that the young aphids are born pregnant, already bearing developing embryos. In autumn, winged males and females are produced. Sexually produced eggs are capable of surviving the winter. Water fleas have a similar lifecycle, giving birth to live daughters from unfertilized eggs all summer. Overcrowding or food shortage induces production of males. Fertilized females lay eggs in a protective covering to enable them to survive winter or drought.

Parthenogenesis is also found in a number of other invertebrates which have little opportunity to meet mates, but it is rare in vertebrates. All these species have evolved from sexually reproducing species. The Amazon molly, a parthenogenetic fish, still needs the stimulation of sperm in order to lay eggs, so the females lure males of a related species into a false mating act in order to acquire the sperm.

Parthenogenesis may also be used to produce particular members of a social group, as seen in social insects such as bees. The queen honeybee lays fertilized eggs which develop into females (queens and workers) and unfertilized eggs which develop into males (drones), which produce sperm by mitosis.

▽ **A braconid wasp has laid her eggs in this sphinx moth caterpillar. As the eggs developed, the early mass of embryo cells gave rise to many embryos. The larvae fed on the caterpillar tissues and eventually emerged through the body wall.**

△ **This whiptail lizard from the United States is a female – as are all its relations. This is one of the few vertebrates that reproduce asexually by laying unfertilized eggs (parthenogenesis). Because the species was formed by hybridization between two other species, this is the only way it can reproduce. In the short term, it has the advantage of being able to reproduce without having to find a mate.**

Some tiny gall midges produce large parthenogenetic eggs which hatch into larvae, each of which produces more eggs while proceeding to devour their parent from the inside. Each of these eggs in turn devours its parent while producing more parthenogenetic eggs, and so on, until several generations have passed before a generation of wasps finally reaches adulthood. This is called pedogenesis. Parasitic chalcid wasps go one step further: the eggs themselves reproduce, in a process called polyembryony.

Strategies for Survival

Long-term survival of a species requires as much genetic variation as possible in its populations, allowing them to adapt to changing conditions. Thus it is preferable for unrelated individuals to mate. This is called outbreeding. The dispersal of offspring enhances variation by increasing chance meetings between unrelated individuals; plants cross-pollinating is one example. Some animal species gather in breeding colonies which contain animals that normally live far apart. Ants and termites from different colonies usually swarm on the same day, increasing the chance meetings of individuals from different colonies. In many mammal societies, young males, or more rarely young females, are driven away from the group at adolescence and join unrelated groups. Winged insects such as butterflies disperse as adults, while the young of many sedentary animals living on the seabed – such as mussels, barnacles, crabs, starfish and corals – are free-swimming larvae that drift with the plankton. Although mating occurs between gametes from near neighbors, those neighbors have come from many different places.

KEYWORDS

BREEDING SYSTEM
CROSS-POLLINATION
HETEROSTYLY
INBREEDING
OUTBREEDING
SURVIVAL OF THE FITTEST

Chemical incompatibility prevents self-fertilization and inbreeding in many flowering plants: their pollen does not germinate on closely related plants. Others prevent self-pollination by producing ripe stamens and stigmas at different times, or produce male and female flowers on separate plants.

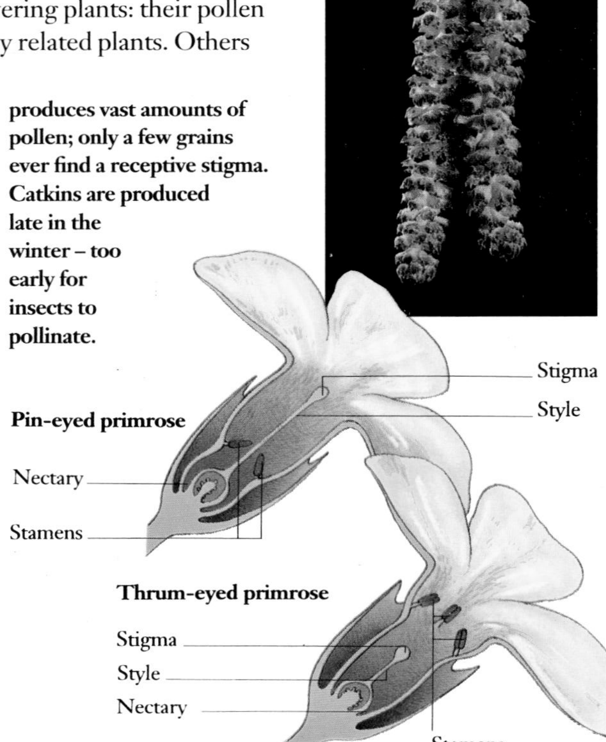

□ In the primrose BELOW RIGHT, cross-pollination is promoted by heterostyly, the existence of two kinds of flowers: pin-eyed flowers with long styles and short stamens, and thrum-eyed flowers with short styles and long stamens. Insects have to probe deep to reach the nectaries at the base of the flowers. Pollen brushes off on an insect's body when it visits a flower; when it visits the other kind of flower, the pollen rubs off on the stigma. ABOVE RIGHT Separate male (catkins) and female flowers (tufts of feathery red stigmas) are found on the same hazel plant. Hazel is wind-pollinated and produces vast amounts of pollen; only a few grains ever find a receptive stigma. Catkins are produced late in the winter – too early for insects to pollinate.

Natural selection acts directly on the individual, which selects the healthiest mate to give its offspring the best chance of survival. Many breeding systems have evolved for this purpose. In species where the young need care from both parents, monogamy is often the rule, with pairs staying together for the breeding season, or even for life. If the mother can bring up the young alone, monogamy is unnecessary, especially if large litters or numbers of eggs can be produced – it is in the interests of both male and female to mate with as many partners as possible.

Where smaller numbers of young are produced, the male needs to breed with as many females as possible, but the female needs to select the fittest male: there is little point in having several mates to produce only one or two young. The males may fight for possession of females or mating territories, as in deer and fur seals, so a small number of very fit males get to mate with most of the females. Alternatively, the female chooses her mate. In these species males often evolve spectacular ways of impressing the females, from showy plumage in birds to "dancing" in fish. Female frogs have been shown to select the males with the loudest, deepest croak – the males which are also the largest and fittest specimens.

◁ Many seabirds, such as penguins, nest in very large colonies, as do some marine mammals such as seals and sea lions. Such animals may be widely dispersed over different feeding grounds during most of the year. If they were not brought together in large numbers for courtship, nesting and breeding, the chances for genetic variation in their offspring would be greatly reduced, and the species as a whole would suffer.

△ This female deep-sea anglerfish has two parasitic dwarf males permanently attached to her. In the deep there are few opportunities for mating; when a male finds to female, he clings to her. Their blood supplies fuse, and he obtains nutrients and oxygen. His body shrinks until little is left but the reproductive organs, which the female can utilize at any time.

Sometimes evolutionary self-interest is taken to brutal lengths. From time to time young lions fight for possession of a pride of females, ousting the aging owners. If the pride has any cubs, they are killed by the newcomers. The loss of their cubs brings the lionesses into breeding condition very quickly, so the new lions are able to sire their own young at the expense of their rivals'. Lion prides show another unusual feature: the females often suckle and look after each other's cubs. This is still self-interest: they are usually sisters, sharing many of their genes. Sharing care of the young in closely related groups is also found in hunting dogs and many species of primates and birds.

In some social animals, such as wolves and mongooses, only one pair in the group is allowed to breed; the rest act as helpers. The breeding pair are the largest, fittest animals in the group. Although this may improve the fitness of successive generations of the group as a whole, it does little for variation. It is difficult to see how it this in the interests of other members of the group, unless the young require the care of more than two adults in order to survive.

▽ It is in the interest of females that only the fittest males be allowed to sire their young. In kangaroos and many other mammals, the males compete for access to the females. In such species, males are often much larger than females, having evolved for their fighting ability. Ritual fighting, such as boxing, ensures that injuries are seldom fatal and the whole population is thus not at risk of losing good genes.

△ Female grouse can take their pick of mates. Male black grouse display in a group on special territory; within it, each male defends his own spot. The dominant males hold the center and engage in the most intense displays and fights. The females fly to the center to select the fittest males.

How Species Arise

Evolution is concerned with the creation of new species – organisms belonging to the same group that can interbreed under natural conditions and produce fertile offspring. An understanding of how new species arise begins with the alleles (different versions of genes) found in a population, and the frequencies with which each allele occurs. The total alleles in a population make up its gene pool. Natural selection acts by changing the relative frequencies of different alleles in successive generations. It acts on the end product of these alleles – on the phenotype, traits such as beak size, flowering time, and so on.

KEYWORDS

GENE POOL
HYBRID
PHENOTYPE
POLYPLOID
SELECTION
SPECIATION

For any trait, most members of the population have one of a limited range of phenotypes, close to the optimum for the prevailing conditions. The more the phenotype diverges from this ideal, the smaller the number of individuals showing it. If conditions have remained constant for a long time, most of the population have adapted to them; a very high proportion have phenotypes near the ideal. This is called stabilizing selection. It has happened in "living fossils", species which have remained virtually unchanged for millions, sometimes hundreds of millions, of years. However, such a narrow range of phenotypes reflects a very small gene pool, so such species are extremely vulnerable to extinction if the environment changes.

When the environment is changing, natural selection may favor phenotypes nearer the edge of the range. The average phenotype shifts in one direction: this is directional selection. In the northwestern Pacific, the increasing use by fishermen of gill nets, which take the largest fish and allow the smaller ones to escape, has led to a 30 percent reduction in the average weight of the catch: selection favors salmon which reach sexual maturity at a lower weight.

The direction in which natural selection acts may be different for different populations of the same species, according to local pressures. Over time, these populations may come to have quite different gene pools. This is common, for instance, where plants are found in several different habitats. These populations retain their distinctive phenotypes even when grown together under identical conditions. Normally this divergence is countered by movement of individuals between populations. But if populations become isolated, for instance by a new geographical barrier, the populations may become so different that, even if they were to make contact again, they could no longer interbreed: they have become two separate species. This has happened to some species of fish in the Caribbean and Pacific Oceans, whose populations became separated when the sea level fell and the isthmus of Panama was formed.

Species that colonize newly formed islands are isolated from other populations of the same species right from the start, which is why many unique and rare species are found on islands. Speciation due to such geographical isolation is called allopatric speciation. Sometimes species arise without such separation, perhaps where a population at the extreme edge of a species' range becomes highly adapted to local conditions. Initially, there may be an almost continuous gradation of gene pools (a cline) along an environmental gradient – for instance, up a mountain. Eventually populations at the extremes of the range may diverge in traits which lead to reproductive isolation – the inability to interbreed. Such speciation, which does not involve geographical isolation, is called sympatric speciation. There may be many causes.

▽ Species can change and new species arise under the influence of environmental factors. This tends to occur in three different ways. 1 In directional selection, the optimal characteristics are shifted in one direction by changing environmental factors, and individuals that would not have been successful in previous generations are now fit for the new conditions. 2 In disruptive selection there are two sets of optimal characteristics. This may arise near the boundary between two habitats, or where a new area is colonized. 3 In stabilizing selection, in a stable environment, the range of variation in the population decreases as the most common (best adapted) forms become even more common, and the less common forms become even less successful.

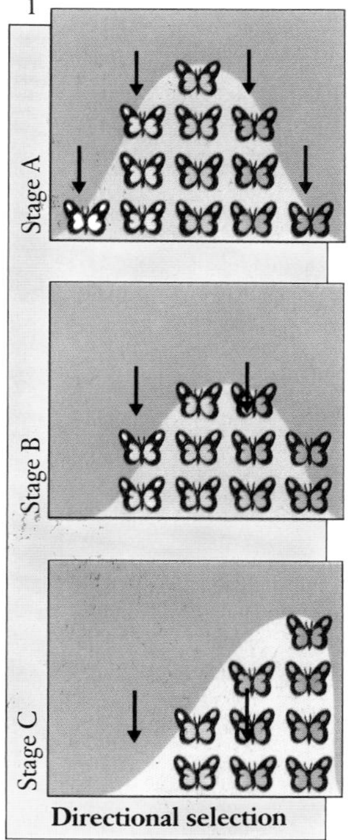

Directional selection

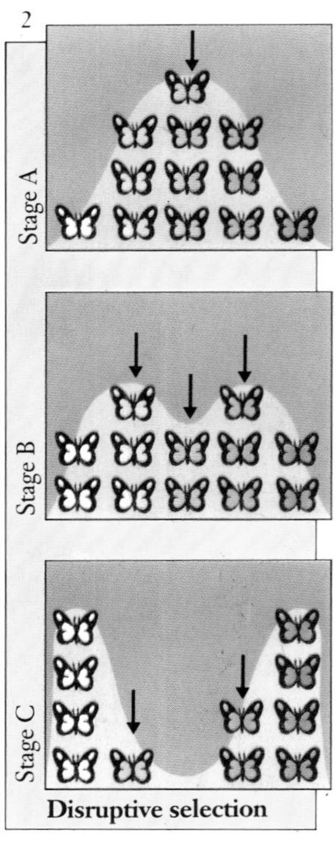

Disruptive selection

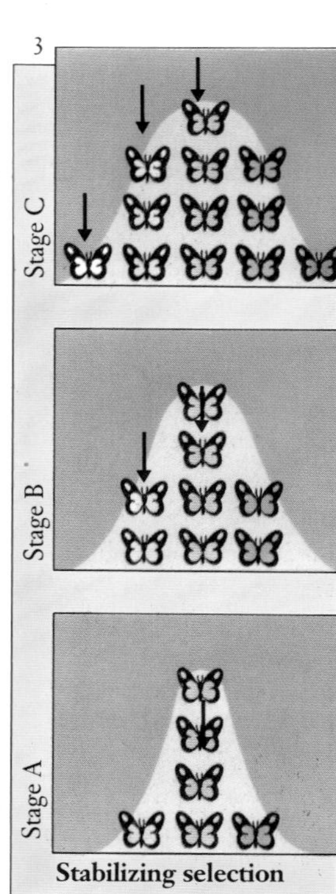

Stabilizing selection

■ The domestic German shepherd dog LEFT has evolved from its ancestor, the grey (timber) wolf ABOVE, through selective breeding techniques, managed by humans, which began about 10,000 years ago. Most domestic dogs are subspecies of the timber wolf species, and the two remain sufficiently closely related to be capable of interbreeding. In other dog species, such as Alaskan huskies, the resemblance to the ancestral wolf may be even more marked.

▽ Populations of the California yarrow plant, *Achillea lanulosa*, grow at different altitudes. They show continual gradation in stem height according to where they grow. 1 Genetically identical plants were grown at different locations. The change in altitude could be observed in their growth. 2 When individuals from each population were grown near sea level in an experiment, differences in height were maintained, showing a genetic basis – part of the yarrow's general adaptation to changing climate and soil conditions and distance from the sea.

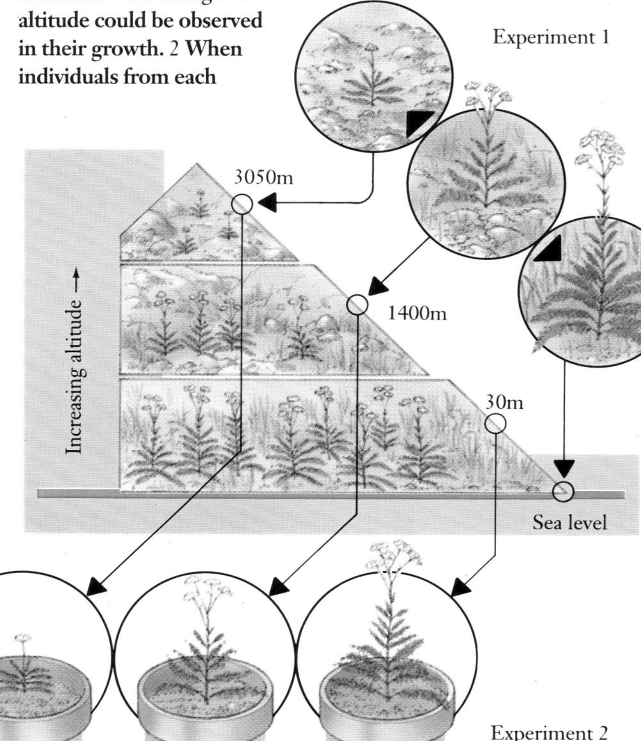

▷ Living fossils, such as this nautilus, survive where selection pressures are weak and do not change. Such stabilizing selection preserves a very narrow range of genetic diversity, with little scope for evolution. Nautilus, found in the deep ocean waters of the tropics, has changed little in 300 million years. It owes its survival to its persistent and relatively unchanging environment and an absence of strongly competing species. Hundreds of species of nautiloids and their close relatives, the ammonites, once dominated shallow water, but failed to evolve as new predators appeared.

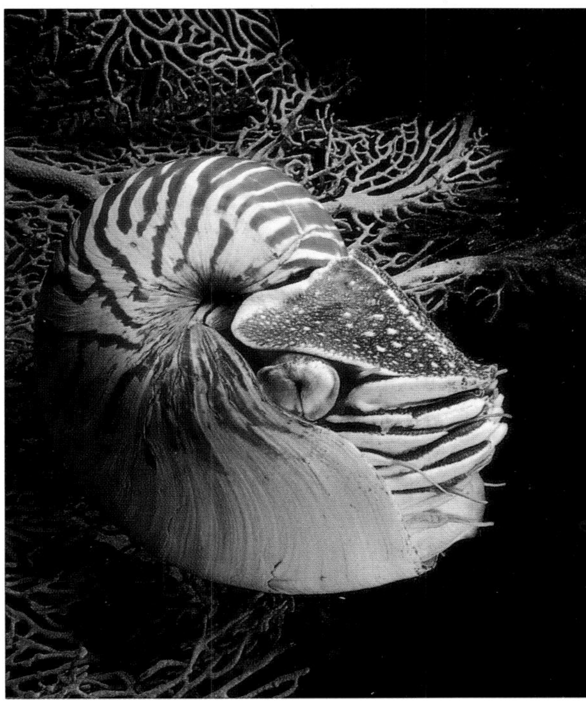

Climate differences may lead to populations diverging genetically with regard to breeding season or flowering time; or, in plants, flowers may become selectively adapted for different pollinators.

Among animals, changes in courtship behavior are a common cause of reproductive isolation. On the island of Hawaii, more than 1000 different species of the "picture-wing flies" (*Drosophila*) have evolved, probably from a single ancestral species. These often form very small populations, isolated from each other by lava flows until vegetation eventually colonizes the lava. Changes in the courtship antics of the male flies is a major cause of incompatibility between species.

Polyploidy is another cause of speciation. Failure of the chromosomes to separate during meiosis leads to a doubling of the chromosome number. Hybrids with the original species are sterile, but may form large populations and spread over a wide area if they possess some form of asexual reproduction. If these hybrids then undergo further chromosome doubling, fertility is restored and a new species has arisen.

Species and Other Kin

In 1735 the Swedish botanist and explorer Carl von Linné (Carolus Linnaeus) published his *Systema Naturae*, in which he classified living organisms according to the characters they have in common. The more features they have in common, and the more exclusive those features are, the more closely they are related. Linnaeus' s system is still in use today. The lowest unit of this classification system is the species, the interbreeding unit. Members of the same species have more in common than members of different species.

KEYWORDS

CLADISTICS
CLADOGRAM
CLASSIFICATION
COMPARATIVE BIOLOGY
EVOLUTIONARY TREE
FOSSIL RECORD
LINNAEAN CLASSIFICATION
SPECIES

Linnaeus gave two Latin names to each species. The second name (species) is unique; the first name (genus) refers to a group of closely related species to which that species belongs. Thus the tiger, *Panthera tigris*, belongs to the genus *Panthera*, which includes the other big cats; the lion, a different species, is *Panthera leo*. Linnaeus used Latin names so that scientists would all use the same language for classification, and could be sure they were talking about the same species. The process of grouping species into related categories, or taxa, is called taxonomy. Only the species is a natural biological grouping, and only the two names that define the species are printed in italics – all other taxa are expressed in normal type.

There are many ways of grouping species with similar features. Classification must not confuse genuine species with different populations of the same species that happen to differ in appearance. Features should be constant in any location and at any time. An ideal classification reflects the evolutionary history of the species. Members of the genus *Panthera* are all thought to be descended from a single ancestral species; cats of the genus *Felis*, which includes the domestic cat, are descended from a different ancestor. Both genera belong to the family Felidae, so are descended from an even older ancestral species.

It is often difficult to select the right characteristics without knowing the evolutionary history of the group. Horses and zebras, which have only one toe, are considered closely related because the evolution of the single toe occurred relatively recently. Humans and gorillas have five toes, but then so do lizards and frogs, so this is not such a useful feature to use. Five toes is in fact the primitive state. The features used to define groups should be those that produce least confusion, and ideally the groups should also share as many other features as possible. Modern statistical techniques and the use of computers have enabled large numbers of features to be quantified.

There is another kind of classification whose goal is purely to show evolutionary relationships. This is cladism – the construction of evolutionary trees. Species are grouped according to how recently they shared a common ancestor. In most cases, the two processes have the same outcome, but sometimes creatures with very different phenotypes may be closely related: sea squirts and humans are more closely related than barnacles and limpets. The ultimate test of cladism lies in an organism's genetic code, and the sequencing of DNA and of proteins has revealed many evolutionary relationships.

SPECIES	***Panthera leo***	(lion)
GENUS	***Panthera***	(lion, tiger, leopard, jaguar, snow leopard)
FAMILY	**Felidae**	(lion, cheetah, clouded leopard, wild cat)
ORDER	**Carnivora**	(lion, wolf, bear, raccoon, weasel, mongoose, hyena)
CLASS	**Mammalia**	(lion, elephant, whale, monkey, rat, kangaroo, platypus)
PHYLUM	**Chordata**	(lion, parrot, crocodile, frog, tuna, shark, sea squirt, lancelet)
KINGDOM	**Animalia**	(lion, octopus, crab, ant, earthworm, jellyfish, ameba)

▲ According to the Linnaean system, organisms are classified into seven different groups in order of common characteristics. The base unit is the species, the group which is capable of interbreeding. Each species is defined by two Latinized names. The first name is the genus, the next largest classification group; the second name is the species name. Members of the same species share more characteristics than members of the same genus; larger groupings contain progressively more diverse kinds of organisms.

▷ The process of separating organisms into related groups on the basis of shared characteristics is called cladistics. The first stage in attempting a cladistic classification is to list the features which are shared by some (but not all) of the group. In this table, the most obvious features have been listed first; in practice, a very large number of features would be used. The next step is to use this data to construct a branching tree of relationships – a cladogram – using the simple rule that an organism can be placed only at the tips of the branches, not at the forks. Fifteen possible trees can be drawn to connect four animals. Five are shown below. The diamonds at each fork indicate which characteristics are shared by all the animals above the fork.

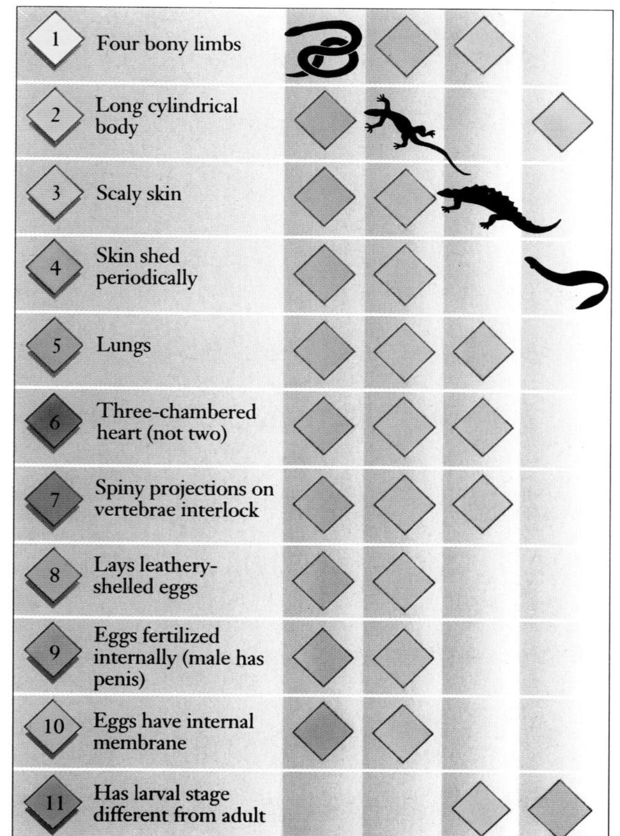

1 Four bony limbs
2 Long cylindrical body
3 Scaly skin
4 Skin shed periodically
5 Lungs
6 Three-chambered heart (not two)
7 Spiny projections on vertebrae interlock
8 Lays leathery-shelled eggs
9 Eggs fertilized internally (male has penis)
10 Eggs have internal membrane
11 Has larval stage different from adult

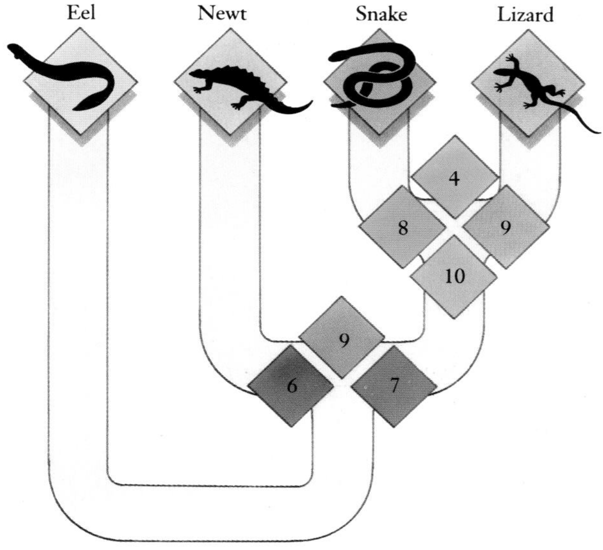

▲ A good cladogram leaves the fewest similarities unexplained. This one explains only seven characteristics. However, the remaining four can be accounted for. The skeleton of the snake contains a vestigial pelvic girdle, indicating the presence of limbs in its ancestors. Its long body has arisen by loss of limbs, unlike the eel, which never had limbs in the first place. The fossil record shows that ancestral amphibians had scales. The embryos of snakes and lizards have larval stages inside the egg.

▷ Cladograms show relationships based on arbitrarily selected sets of characteristics; they do not necessarily show evolutionary relationships, which can only be determined by analysis of DNA samples.

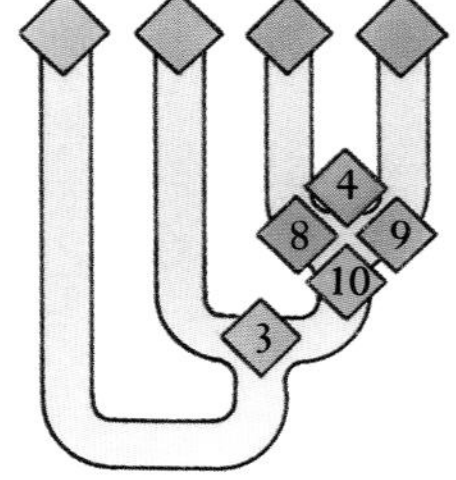

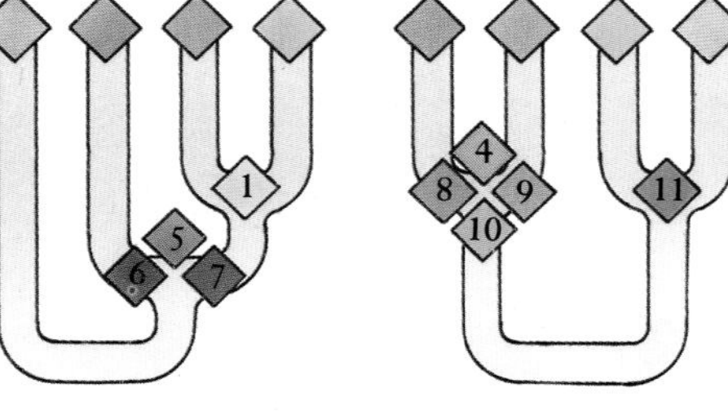

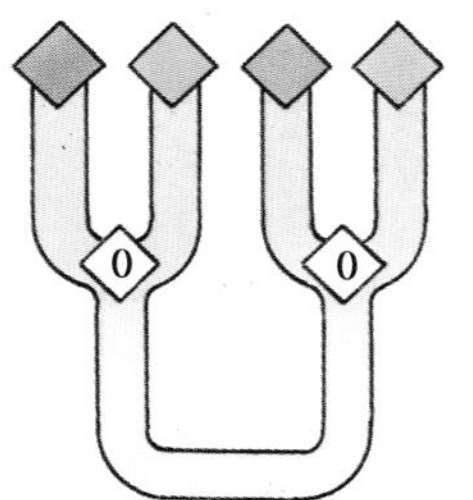

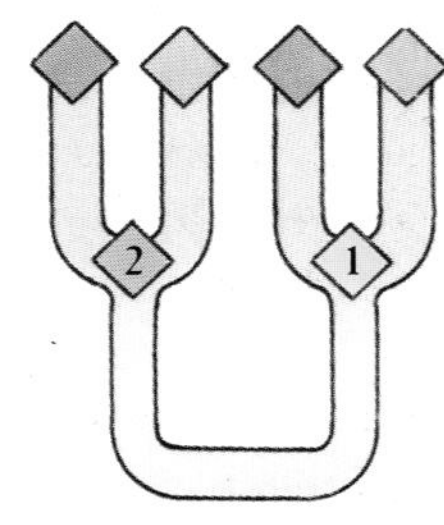

Cladism is not necessarily the most practical tool for identification purposes, because it may require complex and expensive techniques to explain relationships. Nor can it adequately classify species formed from hybrids. If the two parents of a hybrid species are from two different genera, then according to cladism the hybrid belongs to a higher taxon than its parents. "Jumping" genes (transposons) – which cross from one species to another, creating a new species, as in many bacteria – also upset this system.

Even if these problems were overcome, parts of the evolutionary tree are so complex that a classification system based purely on cladistics would have so many taxa that it would be unworkable in practice. Nonetheless, most modern classification systems aim to come as close to the evolutionary tree as is practical.

◁ The classification of incomplete fossils poses considerable problems. *Anomalocaris*, a meter-long shrimplike creature 570 million years old, is one example. Early fossil discoveries were fragmented; different parts of the body were seen in isolation and classified as different animals. The name *Anomalocaris* was originally given to pieces of abdomen; the round mouthparts were thought to be a fossil jellyfish, and the curved feeding limbs a wormlike creature.

THE GENETICS OF POPULATIONS

NATURAL selection is not the only cause of changes in the gene pools of populations. Over a long period of time, the effects of chance matings and deaths and of random mutations can produce considerable changes. This random fluctuation in allele frequencies with time, due entirely to chance, is called genetic drift. Genetic drift is most rapid in small populations, where each individual carries a higher proportion of the total gene pool than in a large population. The result is to increase the variation between different populations.

KEYWORDS

ALLELE
GENETIC DRIFT
GENETIC LOAD
PHENOTYPE
POLYMERASE CHAIN REACTION

Most dramatic changes in the gene pool occur where a new population is started by a small number of individuals who colonize a new area or become isolated from the main population. If the number of individuals is small, they may have a different balance of alleles from that of their parent population, and the selective pressures may well be different, too. This "'founder effect" is a common occurrence when new volcanic islands are colonized. It is also seen in the incidence of the human disease porphyria variegata, which causes severe or lethal reactions to barbiturates. Among South African Afrikaners, there is an unusually high frequency of this disease, and all 30,000 carriers can be traced back to one immigrant couple who arrived from Holland in 1685 and 1688.

A similar thing happens when a population suffers from disease or catastrophe: the chance survivors have a limited gene pool whose frequencies may be quite different from those of the original population. This is called a bottleneck. Another process is gene flow, whereby the gene pool of a population is altered by individuals leaving or coming into the population.

The problem of small gene pools particularly affects endangered species with small surviving populations. Not only do they have little variation for coping with environmental changes, such as those imposed by human activities, but inbreeding between closely related individuals tends to further reduce variation, as recessive alleles more frequently show in the phenotype and can be eliminated by natural selection, so that the species is accelerated towards extinction. Inbreeding also tends to reduce fertility, for reasons not fully understood. Many captive breeding programs designed to rescue threatened species involve keeping a stud book, with the genetic history of each individual, with the aim of minimizing inbreeding as far as possible. While extreme cases of inbreeding are usually fatal, this is not always the case: the Chatham Island black robin of New Zealand has made a successful comeback from just four individuals. Populations which contain a lot of variation in their gene pools have a good potential for long-term survival. However, carrying so much variation imposes a strain on the population, many of whose members do not have optimal genetic makeups – the population is considered to carry a high "genetic load". This is the hidden cost of natural selection: the higher the intensity of the selection pressure, the more nonoptimal individuals will die as allele frequencies shift closer to the optimum for the prevailing

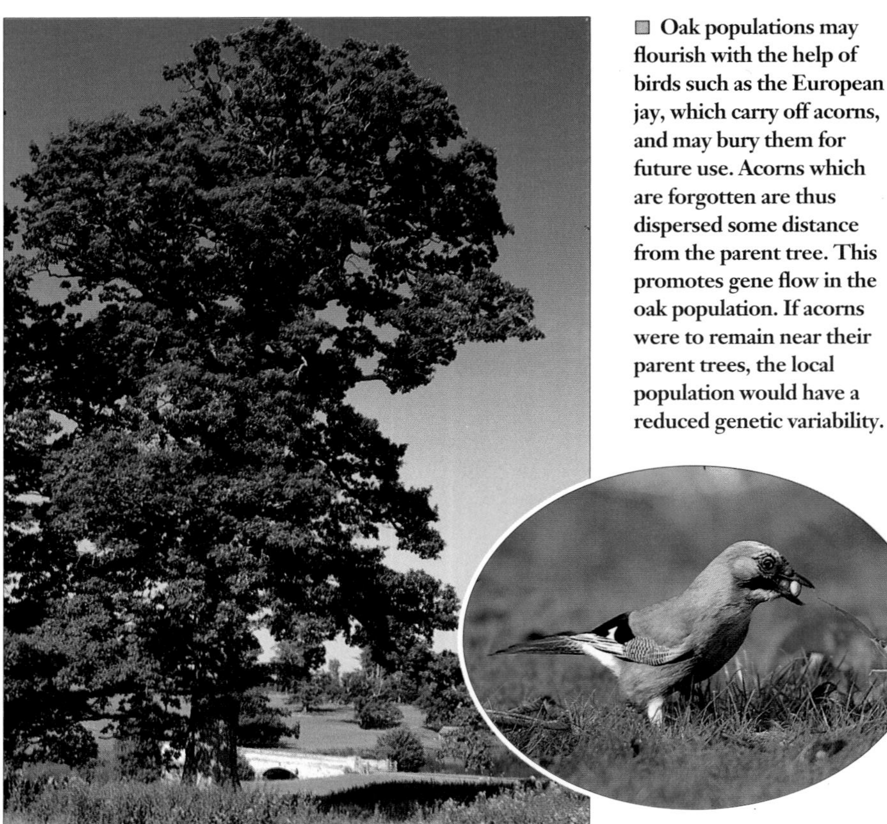

Oak populations may flourish with the help of birds such as the European jay, which carry off acorns, and may bury them for future use. Acorns which are forgotten are thus dispersed some distance from the parent tree. This promotes gene flow in the oak population. If acorns were to remain near their parent trees, the local population would have a reduced genetic variability.

◁ A lone cheetah surveys its territory. Attempts to increase the population by captive breeding have met with little success. The population contains very little genetic variability; about 10–13,000 years ago it probably came close to extinction, so the present population is descended from only a few individuals. Breeding between closely related animals is rarely very successful, and the low reproduction rate is threatening the survival of the species today.

conditions. Where conditions continue to change so the optimal balance is never achieved, this load can be considerable.

Some scientists believe that, at the molecular level, evolution is driven mainly by the random processes of genetic drift and gene flow and not by natural selection. This is the neutral theory. According to this theory, many mutations are neither beneficial nor harmful – they are neutral, and will therefore not be selected against. Most evolutionary changes in the DNA are therefore not adaptive. The main effect of natural selection is to select for adaptive features. There is indeed a great deal of small-scale variation in protein sequences which is not reflected in the phenotype, so is not susceptible to natural selection.

In human populations yet another process is acting on gene pools – cultural evolution. In many human societies, reproductive patterns are no longer geared towards maximizing the number of offspring: new, cultural goals such as career satisfaction and the acquisition of wealth often affect the timing and extent of reproduction.

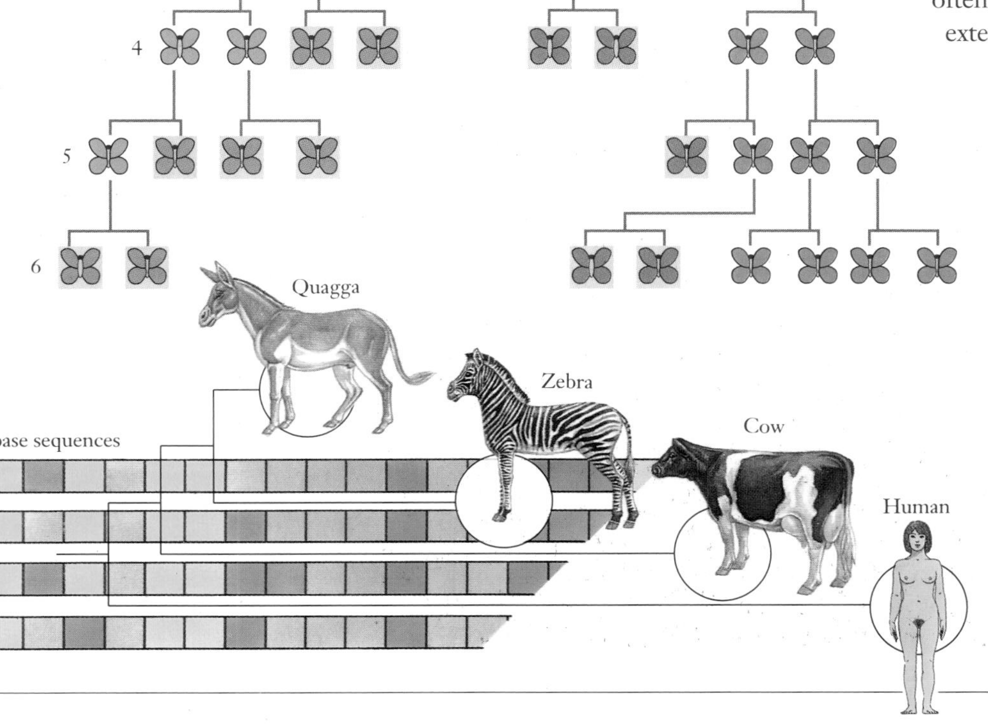

▽ The quagga was hunted to extinction in 1883. DNA studies of skin from stuffed specimens have shown that the quagga was probably a subspecies of zebra, and could probably interbreed with zebras. Even tiny fragments of DNA present in long-dead animals can be amplified by the polymerase chain reaction to provide samples for analysis. When the base sequences of certain DNA fragments from different species are compared, the degree of similarity gives an indication of how closely related the species are. From these studies, an evolutionary tree has been worked out, showing how the quagga and mountain zebra are descended from a common ancestor. They were more distantly related to cattle, and even more distantly to humans.

◁ This diagram shows what happens to two different alleles of a gene, through several generations of the same population. In each generation half the individuals, selected arbitrarily, died without reproducing (gray squares). The bottom line shows the changed proportion after six generations. This difference has arisen not through natural selection but purely by chance – by random matings, and by random individuals dying before mating: the process of genetic drift.

SHARED EVOLUTION

SOME of the most bizarre relationships in nature are the result of coevolution – the evolution of one species in response to changes in another. The shapes and sizes of flowers and their many, highly specialized pollinators are familiar examples. Even the different species of plants and animals living together in the same habitat are all interdependent to some extent.

Coevolution also occurs between predators and prey. The first abundant fossils are of sea bed animals such as trilobites that had evolved shells to protect them from predators. Other arthropods such as sea scorpions then evolved crushing pincers and mouthparts for dealing with the shells. Then came fish with more powerful jaws and teeth, and so on. Modern mammal predators usually have larger brains than their prey, but the brain sizes of both predators and prey have increased through time, a pattern of evolution called escalation.

KEYWORDS

CHLOROPLAST
COEVOLUTION
COMPETITION
EUKARYOTE
FOSSIL
MITOCHONDRION
NATURAL SELECTION
SELECTION PRESSURE
SPECIATION

Escalation does not necessarily lead to more efficient species. Lions have evolved powerful feet and claws, jaws and teeth for dealing with their prey, but they probably do not catch any more prey than formerly, because zebra and antelopes have become fleeter of foot, with more highly-developed senses of smell and hearing.

◁ Cinnabar moth caterpillars feed on ragwort, which produces toxic chemicals in its tissues to discourage grazing animals from eating it. The caterpillars take in these toxic compounds and retain them as adult moths – advertised by their bright colors in both stages of life, which warn predators not to eat them.

▷ The yucca plant of the California desert is pollinated by a single species of moth, which lays eggs in the flower's ovary. The plant's eggs are successfully fertilized and develop into seeds, some of which are eaten by the moth's larvae.

▽ A deep-sea anglerfish uses a luminous lure and chin barbels to attract prey in the dark ocean depths. The light in the lure is produced by the biochemical activities of symbiotic bacteria in the anglerfish's tissues.

Other species have coevolved to their mutual benefit – they have formed relationships called symbioses. Many deep sea animals contain pockets of light-emitting bacteria or algae in their tissues. The microorganisms gain protection and a ready supply of nutrients, while their hosts gain a source of illumination, which they can use for hunting, or for signalling to each other. Even more widespread are the pouches of bacteria in the guts of many mammals and some insects. The bacteria are able to digest the

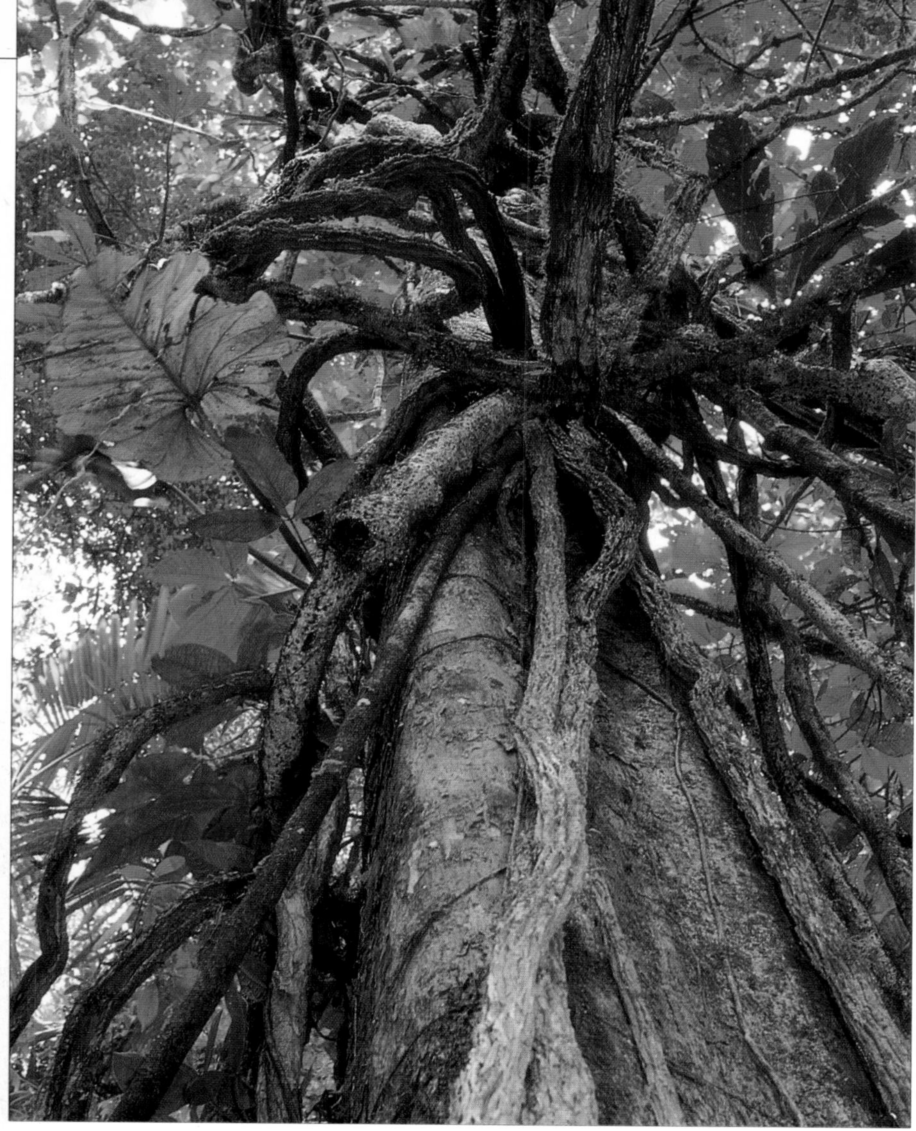

▲ **Competing for light, many tropical tree species evolved very tall trunks, sometimes 100 meters or more high. Woody vines called lianas grow up along their trunks to the crown of the tree, where there is enough light for the lianas to flower. More light and space are made for lianas when a tree falls.**

▲ **The giant flowering *Rafflesia* is a parasite that has lost its leaves, stem and roots, and obtains all its nutrients from the sap of giant tropical forest lianas. The flowers smell of rotting meat, attracting flies for pollination.**

cellulose of plant fibers and make the products available to their hosts. The digestive system of herbivores such as cows, sheep, deer and antelope depend on this relationship. Symbiotic protozoans and bacteria enable termites to digest wood. Many trees are heavily dependent on a similar relationship with fungi: fungal threads called mycorrhizae ("fungus roots") inside or sheathing their roots supply them with minerals from the soil. In return, the tree supplies the fungus with carbohydrates.

Another plant/fungus symbiosis is the lichen, which is made up of fungal filaments interspersed with cells of cyanobacteria (blue-green algae). Products of the bacteria's photosynthesis are exchanged for protection against desiccation and physical damage. The pollination and seed or fruit dispersal of many plants depends on particular animals. Plants have evolved "rewards" such as nectar and pollen, or the juicy flesh of fruit, to entice animals to disperse them. Animals in turn have evolved specialized mouthparts such as a nectar-sucking proboscis or hovering flight to exploit these food sources. Perhaps the most important coevolution event was the symbiosis of certain bacterial cells (which later became mitochondria and chloroplasts) with others to form the eukaryotic cell. The evolution of mycorrhizae and various pollination symbioses made possible other great evolutionary leaps forward.

Some symbioses may well have evolved from parasitic relationships, in which originally one species benefited at the expense, or even the death, of the other. It is in the interest of many other parasites to keep their hosts alive. A fungus attacking the roots of a plant, for instance, might gain by supplying it with nutrients to keep it alive. In turn, the tree would find it advantageous to "encourage" the fungus by supplying it with other nutrients. As both partners become more specialized for the relationship, they also become more mutually dependent.

Even true parasites coevolved with their hosts. If the host population becomes fragmented and begins to evolve independently from other populations of that host species, the parasite may also become isolated from other populations of its species and being to speciate. Most specialism for parasitism leads to loss of independence, often to the extent of loss of organs in the parasite which it would be difficult to evolve again. In other words, parasitism is a virtual guarantee of dependency on a particular host species.

Some parasite adaptations involve extremely complex genetic changes. For example, parasites such as the fluke that causes schistosomiasis pass very different parts of their lifecycles in snails and in humans. Large but distinct sections of its genome (its total genetic information) must be switched on in sequence, adapted to different hosts and different stages of penetration, multiplication and escape. Yet these parasites are very successful, infecting hundreds of millions of people with the diseases they cause.

Many plants produce toxic substances or spines to deter attack by herbivorous insects or mammals. In turn, the herbivores have evolved ways of overcoming these deterrents.

5

THE HISTORY *of Life on Earth*

IN A LITTLE MORE than 4.5 billion years the Earth has become home to perhaps 30 million species. The story of how life developed from self-replicating nucleic acid molecules to its present complexity is a fragmented one. Yet sufficient evidence has survived to explain the main events of largescale evolution.

As life evolved, it modified the Earth which gave birth to it. Photosynthesis put free oxygen into the atmosphere; forests trapped moisture and changed the rainfall over continents. Animals evolved to consume the oxygen and replace it with carbon dioxide, and billions of microscopic organisms in the oceans absorbed that carbon dioxide and used it to create new rocks. Not only have living things had to adapt to these changing global and local environments, but they have also had to adapt to living with each other, and to the evolutionary changes occurring in the species that share their habitats. This world of continual change has spurred on evolution, yet a few species – "living fossils" – seem to have remained almost unchanged for hundreds of millions of years, while countless others have faded into extinction. At different times the Earth has been dominated by fish, amphibians and giant reptiles, but never have the dominant species created such rapid and dramatic changes as have humans, relative newcomers to the evolutionary stage.

Fossils of ammonites lie on a beach. These marine organisms, relatives of squid and octopus, were successful in the Paleozoic period (beginning about 590 million years ago). They were able to float in the water, propelling themselves by jet propulsion, because their bodies had chambers filled with gas rather than water (like other early marine animals). Tough shells protected them against predators. Some grew to 4 meters long – the world's first very large animals – and dominated the seas. However, they became extinct about 65 million years ago, at the same time as the dinosaurs.

The Earliest Life Forms

SURPRISING as it may seem, whereas most living creatures cannot survive without oxygen, life itself could not have evolved in the presence of oxygen. The oldest evidence of life comes from rocks some four billion years old. The world was a very different place then. The atmosphere contained very little free oxygen (not combined with other elements) and very little carbon dioxide. There was no ozone layer to keep out the intense ultraviolet radiation from the Sun. The atmosphere was rich in ammonia and the gas methane, which contains carbon and hydrogen, as well as some hydrogen sulfide, water vapor, nitrogen, hydrogen and carbon monoxide. These gases dissolved in the waters of the early oceans, rivers and lakes.

KEYWORDS

AMINO ACID
BACTERIUM
CHLOROPLAST
DNA
EUBACTERIA
EUKARYOTE
EVOLUTION
MITOCHONDRION
NUCLEUS
NUCLEOTIDE
PHOTOSYNTHESIS
PROKARYOTE

Laboratory experiments, especially those of the American chemist Stanley Miller, have created artificial mixtures of these gases in water and exposed them to lightning discharges or strong ultraviolet radiation, and have shown that complex organic compounds such as carbohydrates, amino acids and even nucleotides (the building blocks of nucleic acids) can be formed in this way. If some of the fatty compounds formed sheets on the water which were then broken into droplets by wind-driven ripples and waves, DNA and other chemicals might be trapped in membranes – life might begin. But this is speculation.

Molecular evolution provides a good basis for deducing what the first living organisms were. There are two main groups of living prokaryotes (cells without nuclei): eubacteria, which include most bacteria and show a wide range of lifestyles and biochemical adaptations, and archaebacteria, which live in hot mineral springs, salt flats, deep sea "smokers" (mineral-rich steam vents), and in the intestines of animals. The archaebacteria are by far the older. They still live in anaerobic (oxygen-less) conditions similar to those of the early Earth. They derive their carbon from methane or other organic molecules, their hydrogen from hydrogen sulfide and their oxygen from the minerals around them. If exposed to free oxygen, they die. Instead of respiring carbon dioxide, many respire hydrogen sulfide.

Most of the early evolution of bacteria was chemical – new methods of obtaining energy, using new substrates. Bacteria have many ways of exchanging DNA, short life cycles and great potential for evolution. Some of them evolved pigments – colored molecules capable of absorbing sunlight. The captured energy was used to break apart simple molecules and extract hydrogen, carbon and oxygen to build cell materials in a primitive kind of photosynthesis. Mutation rates were probably high, because there was far more ultraviolet radiation reaching the Earth's surface in those days. Eventually the bacteria evolved enzymes capable of extracting the oxygen from water. This step changed the Earth forever, allowing the evolution of photosynthesis using water as a source of hydrogen, and releasing free oxygen into the atmosphere. Photosynthetic cyanobacteria (blue-green algae) are among the most abundant fossils in Precambrian rocks, dating back 3.5 billion years, and are still numerous today.

As the amount of oxygen in the atmosphere increased, other bacteria began using it to release energy from their food by the process of aerobic respiration. This was a much more efficient method of obtaining energy than those used in the absence of oxygen. However, the anaerobic (non-oxygen-using) bacteria could not cope with the oxygen, and today they are confined to habitats where there is very little oxygen, such as the bottom mud of ponds and lakes, and the intestines of animals.

From these aerobic bacteria evolved the eukaryote cells, with specialized organelles and DNA housed in chromosomes in a membrane-bound nucleus. Among the organelles, mitochondria are specialized for energy release, and chloroplasts for photosynthesis.

▷ Life probably evolved in an environment similar to these mineral springs in Yellowstone National Park in the United States. Bacteria still live in such places today. The colors in the spring are due not only to bacteria, but also to cyanobacteria (blue-green algae), which use colored pigments to make food by photosynthesis. This activity eventually built up enough oxygen in the air to allow other life to evolve.

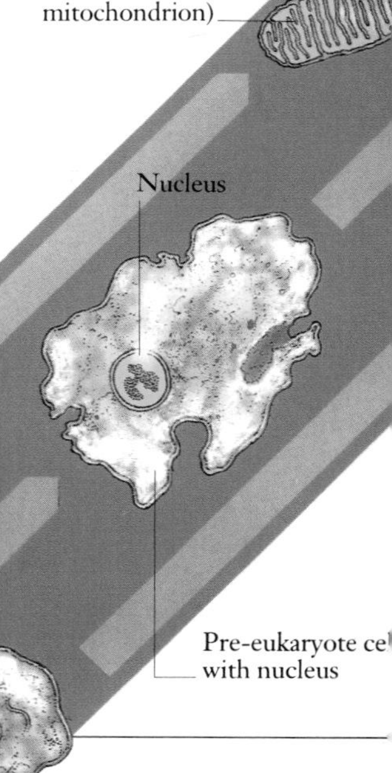

▷ The evolution of the eukaryote cell began with primitive prokaryote cells of the earliest bacteria, which diversified into a variety of forms. In these cells, different reactions all took place in the main compartment of the cell. The first specialized compartment to develop was the nucleus, bounded by a membrane, which reflected a more sophisticated system of gene replication and activation. At this stage, the cells were still pre-eukaryotes.

▷ As photosynthetic bacteria evolved, oxygen in the atmosphere increased and oxygen-using bacteria appeared. Some of the more advanced aerobic bacteria, in which the enzymes of respiration were highly organized on folded sheets of membranes, then invaded the eukaryotic cells. They formed symbiotic relationships and eventually lost their independence and became mitochondria. The ancestral cell of all modern animal cells, with a mitochondrion and

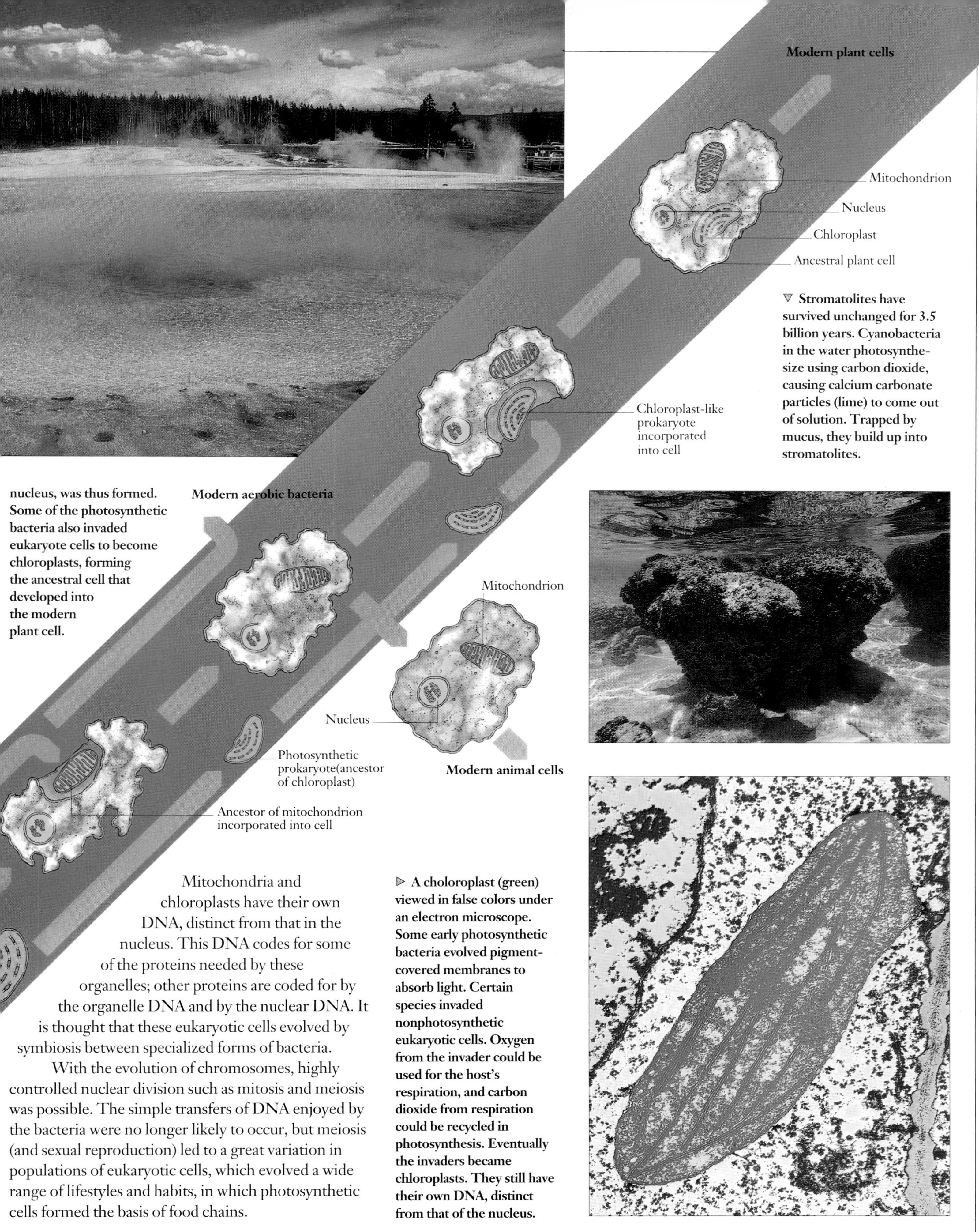

nucleus, was thus formed. Some of the photosynthetic bacteria also invaded eukaryote cells to become chloroplasts, forming the ancestral cell that developed into the modern plant cell.

▽ Stromatolites have survived unchanged for 3.5 billion years. Cyanobacteria in the water photosynthesize using carbon dioxide, causing calcium carbonate particles (lime) to come out of solution. Trapped by mucus, they build up into stromatolites.

Mitochondria and chloroplasts have their own DNA, distinct from that in the nucleus. This DNA codes for some of the proteins needed by these organelles; other proteins are coded for by the organelle DNA and by the nuclear DNA. It is thought that these eukaryotic cells evolved by symbiosis between specialized forms of bacteria.

With the evolution of chromosomes, highly controlled nuclear division such as mitosis and meiosis was possible. The simple transfers of DNA enjoyed by the bacteria were no longer likely to occur, but meiosis (and sexual reproduction) led to a great variation in populations of eukaryotic cells, which evolved a wide range of lifestyles and habits, in which photosynthetic cells formed the basis of food chains.

▷ A choloroplast (green) viewed in false colors under an electron microscope. Some early photosynthetic bacteria evolved pigment-covered membranes to absorb light. Certain species invaded nonphotosynthetic eukaryotic cells. Oxygen from the invader could be used for the host's respiration, and carbon dioxide from respiration could be recycled in photosynthesis. Eventually the invaders became chloroplasts. They still have their own DNA, distinct from that of the nucleus.

AN EXPLOSION OF LIFE

IT TOOK perhaps 2.5 billion years for eukaryotic cells to evolve from primitive prokaryotic cells, then another 700 million years for multicellular animals to appear. Nobody knows for sure how multicelled organisms evolved, but we can gain several clues from living organisms. Algae and many other simpler organisms form new cells by mitosis. In many algae these cells fail to separate, giving rise to long chains, plates or spherical colonies of cells. Within these colonies, some cells may become specialized for particular functions, such as reproduction.

KEYWORDS

BACTERIUM
CAMBRIAN EXPLOSION
EUKARYOTE
EVOLUTION
FOSSIL
MITOSIS
NATURAL SELECTION
PROKARYOTE
SELECTION PRESSURE

Sponges are a special case. Normally a sponge functions like a single multicellular animal, in which different groups of cells have different functions. But if the sponge is damaged, the component cells are able to reorganize themselves into a new sponge remarkably quickly, forming chambers and branching canals. Such events are a normal part of the lifecycle of cellular slime molds, which regularly spend part of their lives as independent unicells, and part as a single coordinated organism made up of millions of individual cells.

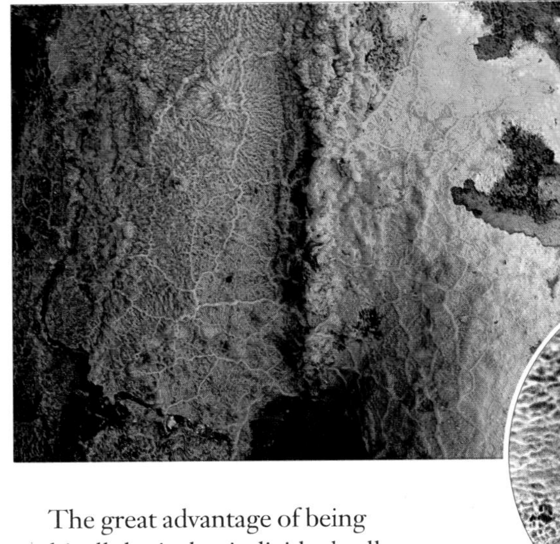

◁ Slime molds are among the earliest life forms. Many are capable of living separately, but some are found clinging together in a colorful blob that responds to the presence of chemicals and light.

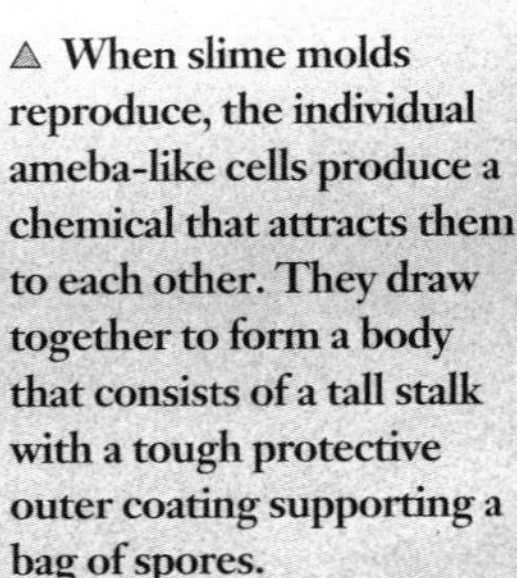

△ When slime molds reproduce, the individual ameba-like cells produce a chemical that attracts them to each other. They draw together to form a body that consists of a tall stalk with a tough protective outer coating supporting a bag of spores.

The great advantage of being multicellular is that individual cells can specialize in a particular function, such as digestion, locomotion or reproduction, and develop adaptations which would be impossible if the cell had to carry out all the other bodily functions at the same time. The result is a more efficient organism, and the possibility of a wide range of body forms and modes of life. Multicellular animals require a partitioning of genetic activity between different parts of the body: different genes are switched on in different cells and tissues, often in response to signals (themselves the product of gene activity) from cells in other parts of the body. The more complex the animal

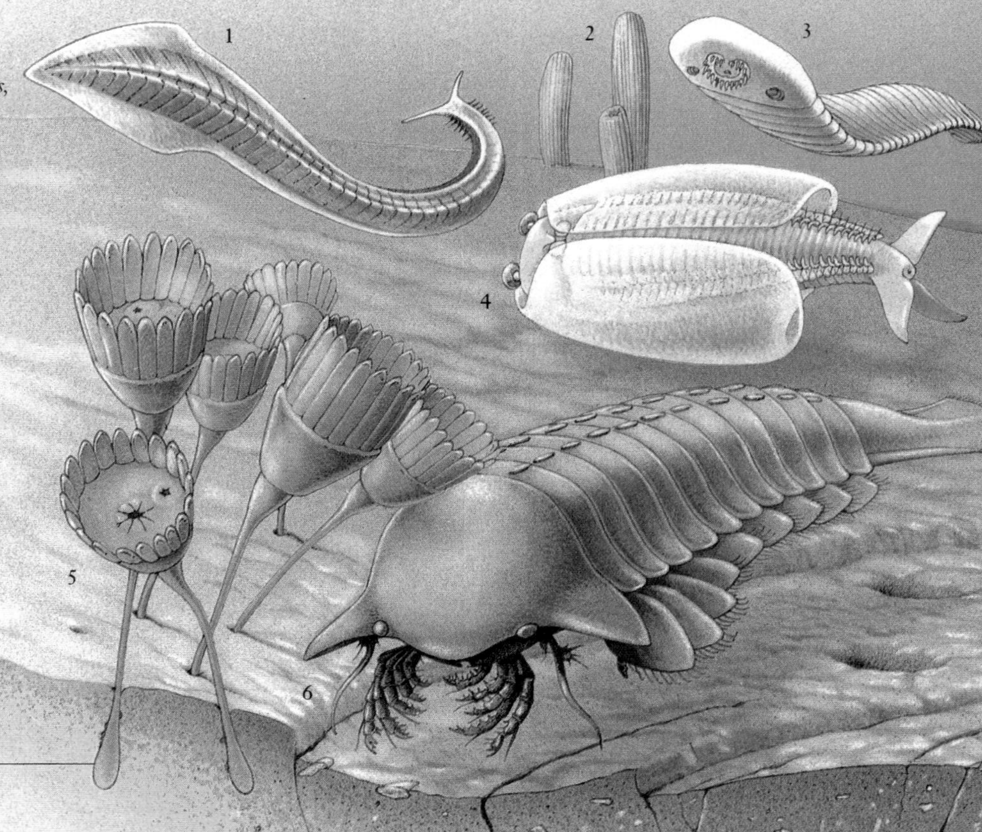

▷ The Burgess shale, in the Canadian Rockies, has the finest collection of fossils from the early Cambrian period, about 550 million years ago, shortly after the great burst of evolution called "the Cambrian explosion". These animals (not drawn to scale) lived on mudbanks in shallow water flanking a reef. Many modern groups are recognizable: sea anemones (*Mackenzia*); sponges such as *Vauxia* and *Chancelloria*; the wormlike *Odontogriphus*, whose mouth was surrounded by tentacles; *Ottoia*, a worm living in a burrow; a velvet worm, *Aysheaia*; many arthropods, including *Marrella*, *Odoraia* (which was enclosed by two valvelike shells and had a three-pronged tail), and the huge predatory *Sanctacaris*; and *Pikaia*, a small fishlike chordate, perhaps the earliest known ancestor of the vertebrates. *Dinomischus*, *Nectocaris*, *Opabinia* and *Hallucigenia* were all unlike anything still alive today.

1 *Pikaia*
2 *Mackenzia*
3 *Odontogriphus*
4 *Odoraia*
5 *Dinomischus*
6 *Sanctacaris*
7 *Chancelloria*
8 *Opabinia*
9 *Vauxia*
10 *Nectocaris*
11 *Wiwaxia*
12 *Aysheaia*
13 *Hallucigenia*
14 *Marrella*
15 *Ottoia*

or plant, the more complex is the coordination of its genetic activity.

Because soft tissues do not fossilize easily, there is very little record of the early multicellular creatures. Traces of wormlike creatures and the imprints and scratch marks of others have been found in rocks over 700 million years old. In rocks from the Ediacara Hills in Australia, some 640 million years old, many soft-bodied fossils have been found. They include at least 30 genera of fossil remains – including worms, sea pens, primitive echinoderms, jellyfish and various other creatures – as well as scratch marks perhaps made by primitive arthropods.

Most of the many phyla of modern animals began to appear 100 million years later, at the start of the Cambrian period. These new forms of life included animals with shells, mainly of calcium carbonate (chalk). With the evolution of hard skeletons, jointed limbs were possible, allowing new methods of movement which, together with jointed mouthparts, enabled animals to tackle prey in different ways. The shells could not be formed in earlier marine life forms, because the deposition of calcium carbonate from calcium salts and carbon dioxide dissolved in the oceans requires the presence of oxygen. Perhaps this was the first time there was sufficient oxygen in the atmosphere for shell formation to be possible. There were also considerable quantities of calcium in the oceans as new predators began to attack ancient reefs.

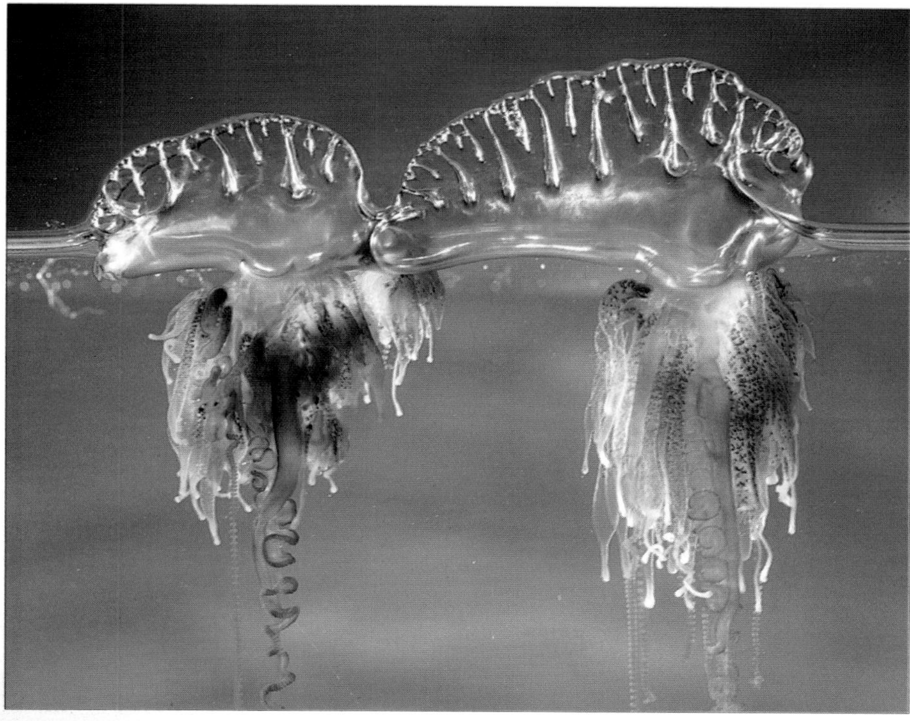

▲ The Portuguese man-o'-war is made up of a number of individual hydra-like polyps which are specialized for different functions – capturing prey, digestion, reproduction, and so on. The large float is a single individual. Yet these polyps are never found separately; the man-o'-war exists either as a colony or as a single multicellular animal.

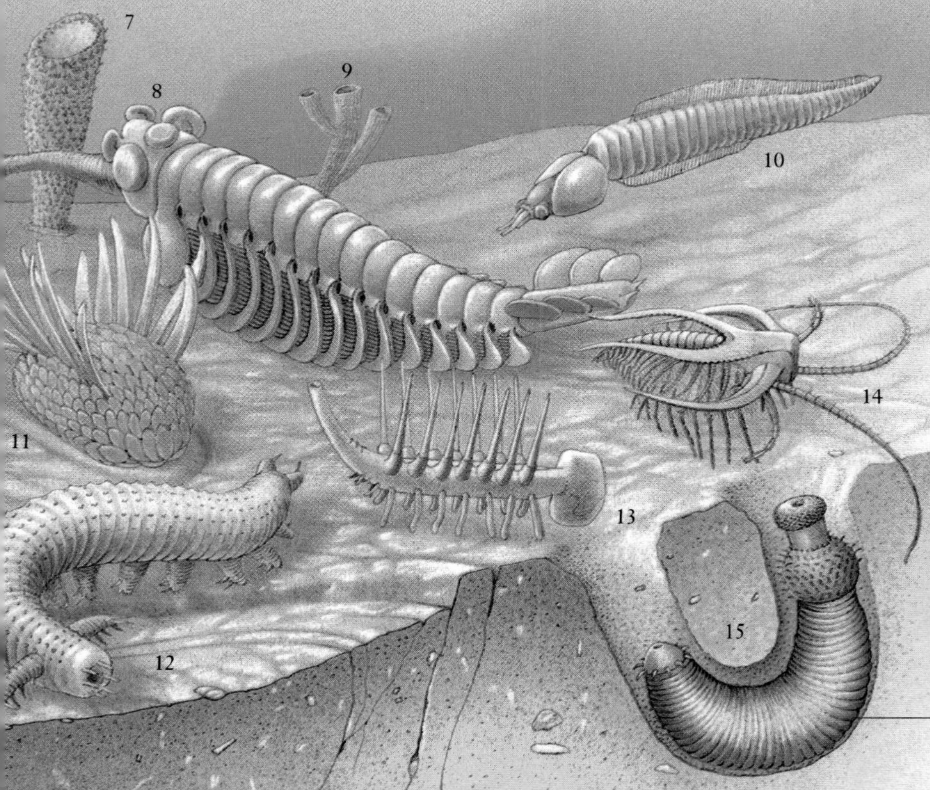

This great burst of evolution, sometimes called the Cambrian explosion, was perhaps in part the result of fluctuating selection pressures. Throughout the Cambrian period, sea levels rose and fell, destroying habitats and creating new ones. The presence of many new forms of animal life created new selection pressures. What is particularly astonishing is the wide range of basic body plans found in Cambrian animals, far greater than is found today. It is as if genetic systems have become more complex and more fixed, with less potential for radical change. Or perhaps modern animals are more specialized and therefore contain less variation upon which natural selection can work. This is one of the great debates of paleontology.

As in the evolution of the eukaryotic cell, symbiosis has played a part in the evolution of multicelled life forms. Large animal bodies can be formed by the fusion or cooperation of smaller ones. Reef-building corals, for instance, are actually soft-bodied animals rather like sea anemones, which secrete a cuplike skeleton of calcium carbonate. New individuals are produced by budding, but remain attached to the parent by a cytoplasmic connection. Over time, vast colonies are built up: the Great Barrier Reef is so large that it is visible from the Moon. The reef owes its existence partly to microscopic algae in the tissues of the corals. Their presence greatly accelerates the deposition of limestone skeletons by the corals. The photosynthesizing algae release oxygen, which is used by the host animals for respiration; metabolites are also exchanged. Such relationships are widespread: the bright colors of many corals and hydras, and the mantles of giant clams, are due to their algal partners.

Life Moves Onto Land

UNTIL about 360 million years ago, the surface of the dry land was barren: there were no plants, and no soil. However, red, brown and green algae had thrived for millions of years in the shallow water fringing the land. The first colonizers of the land were probably algae, fungi and bacteria on the wet mud around springs and swamps. Their dead remains mingled with the mud particles to form the first soil. Without the screen of water, harmful radiation was a problem on land, but by now a protective layer of ozone had formed.

KEYWORDS

ALTERNATION OF GENERATIONS
AMNIOTIC EGG
DIFFERENTIATION
SPERM

Terrestrial life poses a number of problems for aquatic creatures. The first land plants, which probably evolved from the green algae, developed a waxy covering, the cuticle, to prevent water loss. Gas was exchanged with the atmosphere (instead of with water) through small pores, or stomata, in this cuticle. Simple thread-like roots anchored in the mud became organs for absorbing water and minerals. With the evolution of networks of tubes to carry water from root to shoot and products of photosynthesis in the opposite direction, the vascular plants led the way to the final takeover of the land. The same network was reinforced to form the basis of the supporting structure – wood – which made possible great increases in size.

Despite these adaptations, the early land plants were limited in their distribution by their methods of reproduction: even though they had evolved spores which could drift on the wind, they still needed water for their sperm to swim in. It was not until the evolution of pollen that they became truly independent of water. Pollen-producing seed plants could also produce seeds containing substantial food stores, enabling them to wait for suitable conditions for germination.

At first plant life was limited to wet, muddy areas. Following close behind the plants came the terrestrial animals: worms crept out onto the mud, arthropods came to scavenge – and later to hunt – in the newly forming soil or to feed on the plants or on the plant debris. Before long, the arthropods took to the air: the insects had arrived. The evolution of insect pollination led to a swift spread and rapid diversification of both flowering plants and insects.

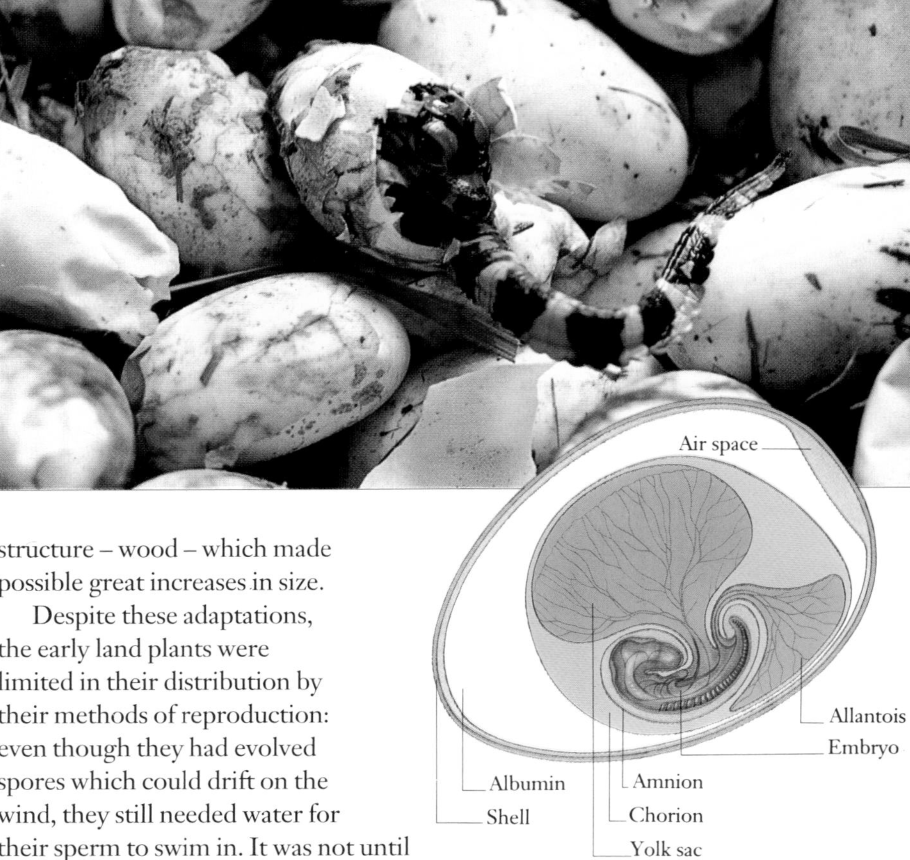

△ The key to vertebrates moving successfully onto the land was the evolution of the so-called amniotic egg. It was developed by reptiles, and is still found in modern reptiles (such as the crocodile TOP) and birds. Unlike eggs of fish and amphibians, this egg has a leathery shell to prevent it from drying out. A fluid-filled sac, the amnion, cushions the developing embryo against knocks. Another sac contains yolk to feed the embryo, while a third sac (the allantois) is used to dispose of waste. An air-filled gap at one end of the egg allows oxygen to diffuse through for respiration. Inside this private pond, the embryo is able to grow to a reasonable size before hatching, giving it a better chance of survival.

▽ The living coelacanth BELOW is a lobe-finned fish, very similar to lobe-fins that lived 400 million years ago RIGHT. Its fleshy fins are supported by bones and muscles. It uses its fleshy fins rather like paddles, moving them in the same order as newts, lizards and dogs move their legs. The coelacanth was discovered living off the coast of southern Africa in 1938.

The arthropods had a hard outer skeleton for support out of water, but another group of animals – the vertebrates – had evolved a strong supporting structure – a segmented backbone of cartilage, used as a brace for muscle action. By the late Cambrian the first fish were found. Eventually new forms of fish arose with bony skeletons. One group of bony fish, the lobe-fins, were probably related to the ancestors of the first land vertebrates. Their fins were used like paddles, but the limbs were moved in the same manner as those of amphibians and reptiles. Many lobe-fins lived in shallow, oxygen-poor water and evolved a lung which they used to breath air at the water surface. The first land vertebrates spent most of the time in water, emerging occasionally onto land. True terrestrial, four-legged forms followed, and gradually the legs "moved" under the body to lift it clear of the ground.

The moist skins of the amphibians made them vulnerable to drying out. The reptiles, which evolved later, had a covering of bony scales which allowed little moisture to escape. The early reptiles and amphibians were cold-blooded: their body temperature fluctuated with that of their surroundings. These animals therefore had long periods of inactivity when their metabolism was slowed by the cold. Three groups of reptiles – warm-blooded dinosaurs, mammal-like reptiles and bird-like reptiles – overcame this problem, developing internal temperature control to become warm-blooded. Their descendants, the mammals and birds, have fur or feathers to help maintain body temperature.

Animals, like plants, had to adapt their reproduction to the land. Many insects evolved internal fertilization, and other invertebrates enclosed their sperm in packets for transfer. Reptiles, birds and mammals also evolved internal fertilization. This permitted (in reptiles and birds) the development of eggs with waterproof shells, which were deposited around the egg after fertilization. Some reptiles and most of the mammals evolved the means of allowing the young to develop in the secure, stable environment of their mother's body.

▫ The earliest known land vertebrate, *Ichthyostega*, spent most of its life under water hunting fish. On land, it propped its heavy body up on its front legs. It also laid eggs in water. The Carboniferous swamps were luxuriant with ferns, horsetails and tree ferns. The leafless fern *Psilotum triquetrum* INSET is the only example of a living plant fossil. Like the amphibians, early ferns depended on water for reproduction. Recently evolved seed ferns use air-borne pollen instead of swimming sperm.

WINNERS AND LOSERS

ABOUT 65 million years ago, at the end of the Cretaceous period, the dinosaurs that had ruled the Earth for millions of years mysteriously disappeared, together with all other land animals weighing more than about 25 kilograms, the pterosaurs, large marine reptiles, birds, marsupials, fish, ammonites, corals, mollusks and about half of all microscopic marine organisms. Whole families became extinct. There has been much debate as to the cause of this mass extinction. There were considerable climatic changes at this time, triggered by continental drift. As Australia moved away from Antarctica, cold water from the Southern Ocean penetrated tropical seas, cooling both land and sea. But these changes would have been slow enough for many species to adapt to them.

KEYWORDS

ADAPTATION
ADAPTIVE RADIATION
EVOLUTION
EXTINCTION
PHOTOSYNTHESIS

A more catastrophic cause has been proposed. In many parts of the world there is a thin layer of rocks of that age that rich in the element iridium, which is rare in the Earth's crust, but more common in rocks from outer space. If a large asteroid had hit the Earth, a vast dust cloud would have blotted out the Sun. The cold and the darkness would have reduced photosynthesis, killing plants and affecting the food chain. Acid rain would have killed organisms near the ocean surface. On the Yucatán Peninsula of Mexico is a crater formed at this time by the impact of an asteroid measuring some 10 kilmeters across.

An alternative explanation lies in plate tectonics. In India there is evidence of vast outpourings of lava, forming the Deccan Traps, which cover an area half the size of Europe. The volcanoes producing this lava would have sent up clouds of dust enriched in iridium, as well as causing acid rain.

Whatever the cause, the loss of plant life and the low temperatures would have affected large animals such as dinosaurs. Small animals could shelter and perhaps store food underground.

Major mass extinctions have occurred at intervals throughout geological time, interspersed with more localized extinctions. At the end of the Permian period, about 240 million years ago, up to 95 percent of all species became extinct. As the continents coalesced into a single giant supercontinent, extremes of temperature may have occurred in the continental interior and the sea level fell, exposing the land to rapid erosion. Coal deposits would have been exposed to the atmosphere, and reacted with oxygen to form carbon dioxide, perhaps halving the oxygen content of the air, so many animals probably died of suffocation. Perhaps the greatest extinction of all is occurring today, as humans hunt animals to extinction, destroy or pollute their habitats, subject them to competition from introduced animals or break down natural barriers (the Panama Canal is an example), removing the isolation that has allowed many species to survive.

Extinction is a powerful stimulus to evolution: surviving life forms diversify to occupy newly vacated niches. At each extinction, the gene pool is drastically reduced, then expands as evolution corrects the loss. The demise of dinosaurs, for example, allowed mammals to embark on one of the swiftest adaptive radiations recorded. The few birds that survived the Cretaceous extinction were no longer threatened by pterosaurs, and rapidly evolved and diversified.

1 *Deinosuchus*, a giant crocodile, 15 m long

2 *Triceratops*, 9m

3 *Tyrannosaurus rex*, 15 m

4 *Ornithomimus*, 3.5 m

5 *Corythosaurus*, 9 m

6 *Alamosaurus*, 21 m

7 *Pteranodon*, a flying reptile, 7 m wingspan

8 *Alphadon*, a tree-dwelling marsupial mammal, 30 cm long

9 *Purgatorius*, a tree-dwelling primate, 10 cm long

■ The last of the great "ruling reptiles" dominate this late Cretaceous landscape of North America. *T. rex* was probably carnivorous and may have preyed on the smaller *Ornithomimus*. Medium-sized dinosaurs such as *Triceratops* were browsers, and *Corythosaurus* and *Alamosaurus* were also herbivores. Some modern life forms are present: coniferous trees, flowering shrubs and herbs, and many types of birds. Mammals such as *Alphadon* and *Purgatorius* were small and probably nocturnal.

THE EVOLUTION OF HUMANKIND

THE evolution of the human "race" illustrates the problems of reconstructing evolutionary history from fragmented fossil evidence: there are more paleoanthropologists than there are human fossils for them to work on.

Humans are primates – they belong to the group of mammals that includes the monkeys and apes. They are most closely related to the apes (gorillas, chimpanzees, and orang utans). The larger primates tend to live in complex societies, a feature that also favors a larger brain for communication and learning. Other human features, such as a long gestation (pregnancy), small litter size and long interval between births, are associtaed with our relatively large size. A social life and varied diet all require a long period of learning in the young, so social primates have an extended period of dependency on their mother, and a relatively high age of sexual maturity.

KEYWORDS

ADAPTIVE RADIATION
EVE HYPOTHESIS
MITOCHONDRIAL DNA
MORPHOLOGY
MUTATION

Many human features are related to the habitat and lifestyle of the early primates, small insect-eating tree-dwellers which evolved grasping limbs, with an opposable thumb, for gripping branches and manipulating insects and (later) fruit. In treetops, smell is less useful than sight: the snout was reduced in size, giving a flatter face; the eyes faced forward, giving good stereoscopic vision for catching prey.

The primates evolved about 60 million years ago. By 35 million years ago, the tree-dwelling ancestors of the apes had evolved. Like most living primates, they were animals of tropical forests. The first hominoids (human-like primates) appeared by 23 to 20 million years ago, when the climate was cooling and becoming drier, and forests were giving way to grasslands. The environment, and perhaps the isolation of groups of primates in islands of forest, favored the evolution of new forms.

The relationships between humans and their closest relatives – chimpanzees, gorillas and orangutan – are controversial. Evidence from comparative morphology and anatomy suggests that gorillas and chimpanzees are more similar to each other than to humans. However, DNA differences tell a slightly differet story. Comparisons of DNA sequences of humans and apes indicate that humans share 98.4 percent of our DNA with chimpanzees, and 97.7 percent with gorillas: there is a greater "genetic distance" between humans and gorillas than there is between humans and chimpanzees.

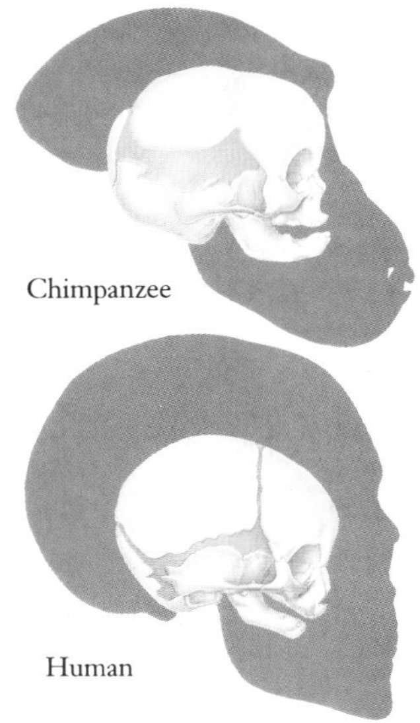

◁ **Some of the physical differences between humans and their closest relatives, the chimpanzees, have evolved by the retention of juvenile characters. Chimpanzees and humans are more similar as babies than as adults. The adult human has the head shape, almost hairless soft skin, short jaw, small teeth, thin skull and relatively large brain of the chimpanzee baby. The sutures joining the bones of the skull close up later in humans than in chimps, allowing for a longer period of brain growth.**

The oldest hominoid fossil, *Proconsul hamiltoni*, from northern Kenya, is 25–26 million years old. At about this time, there was a great diversification of hominoid forms, ranging from the size of a monkey to that of a gorilla. *Proconsul* had quite a large brain, and its tooth structure indicates a fruit-based diet. It looked more like a monkey than an ape.

The next important groups of hominoids to arise were the afropithecines and, later, the dryopithecines. These hominoids were more like the modern large apes. About 18–25 million years ago, a land-bridge developed between Africa and Eurasia, and hominoids began to spread around the world. Then came a great gap in the fossil record until about 5 million years ago, when hominoids much more like modern humans appeared. The australopithecines lived in Africa 5 to 2.5 milion years ago. Early australopithecines were probably tree-dwellers, but some later species lived on

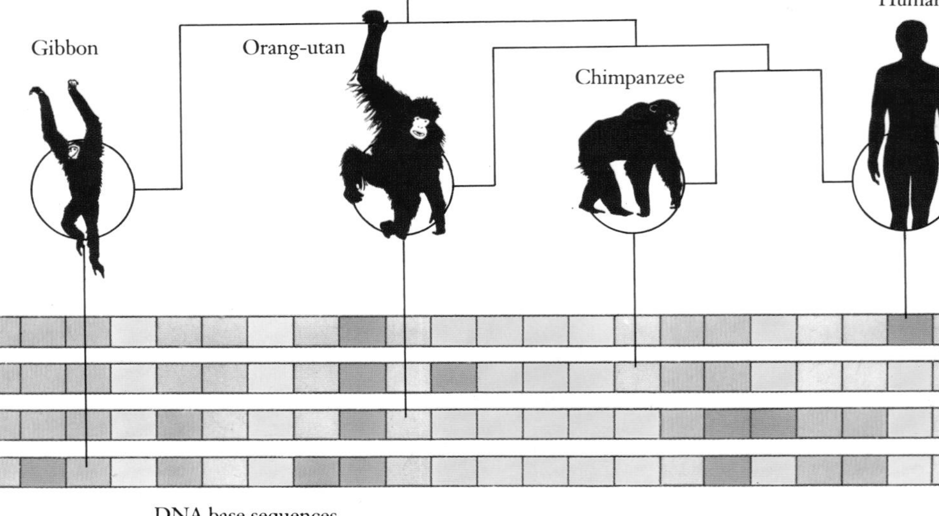

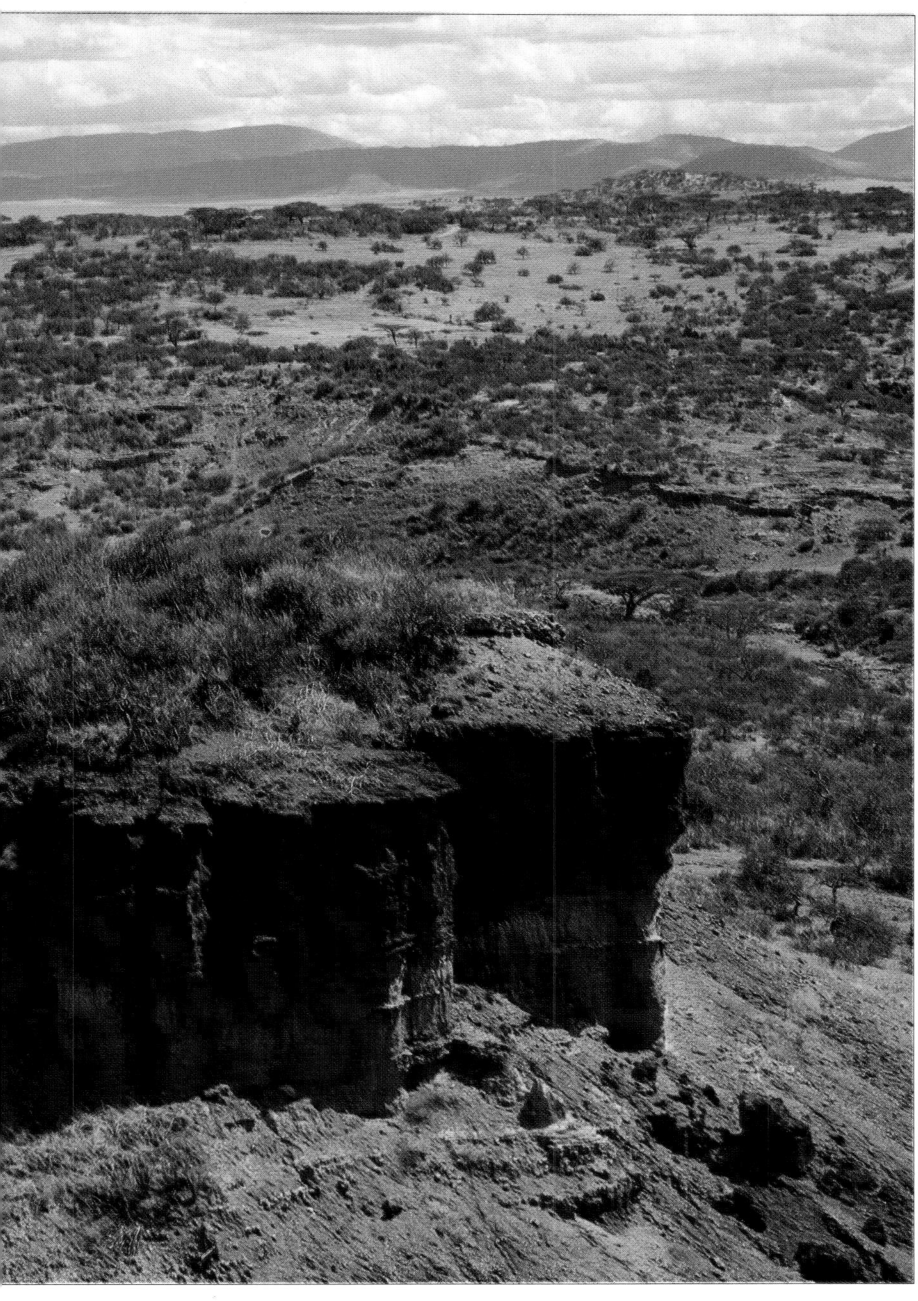

◁ **Olduvai Gorge, in northern Tanzania, has proved a rich source of fossil remains of early ancestors of modern humans, ranging between 15,000 and more than 2 million years old. Fossils are studied for inferential evidence of musculature, build, gait, diet and brain capacity. However, the fragmentary nature of many early finds mean that the relationships between the species are debatable.**

the ground. An increasingly upright stance conferred an advantage in the spreading grassland habitat. The most complete skeleton found is "Lucy", from the the Awash area in Ethiopia. Lucy was an apelike female with projecting jaws and teeth about halfway between those of humans and apes. The shape of her hip and limb bones indicate that she walked upright – the first fossil hominoid to do so. The next major step was making tools, rather than simply using objects as tools. This dates to about 2.5 million years ago.

Shortly after came the first hominids – hominoids belonging to the same family as modern humans. Their brains were larger, perhaps about 700 ml (as opposed to modern humans' 1300 ml). The remains of *Homo habilis* ("handy man") are associated with primitive stone tools. Indentations of the skull indicate the presence of tracts of the brain that in modern humans are associated with speech production.

Around 2 million years ago another hominid, *Homo erectus*, began to move out of Africa into Europe and Asia (the so-called "Beijing man" and "Java man"). *Homo erectus* had a brain of about 900 ml, prominent brow ridges, a prominent nose and very little chin. It made hand axes, and probably also used wooden tools. In most parts of the world, *Homo erectus* was succeeded by *Homo sapiens* (modern man). The first evidence of truly modern *Homo sapiens* is from Africa and the Middle East, some 100,000–50,000 years ago. By about 30,000 years ago *H. sapiens* had spread to (or possibly developed independently in) China and Australia. But modern toolmaking began only about 40,000–10,000 years ago. In time, the range of tools increased, and ceremonial burial of the dead may have occurred. Language was growing slowly. By now humans produced paintings, sculptures, clay models and ornaments of bone and ivory, and primitive flutes.

For the last 30,000 years, human evolution has been mainly cultural, involving civilizations, artistic expression (including the development of written language), and the development of science and technology. Humans are no longer at the whim of natural selection. They can modify their environment and create new niches. Science and technology allow them to dominate the natural world, but not always in a way that enhances the survival of the species.

■ **Recent evidence from immunology, protein analysis, DNA sequencing and genetic mapping indicate that humans are more closely related to African apes than to orang utans, and are closer to chimpanzees RIGHT than to gorillas. The sequence of bases in one part of the mitochondrial DNA is shown LEFT. Mitochondrial DNA accumulates mutations much faster than does nuclear DNA, and so is more useful in revealing evolutionary relationships between species.**

6

ENGINEERING *New Life*

LIKE ALL BLUEPRINTS, DNA can be altered to suit the needs of the user. Scientists have learned not only to decipher DNA, but also to alter it and to write their own. Genes can be removed from or added to organisms – even transferred to a different species. Synthesized genes can be incorporated into the DNA of rapidly reproducing bacteria and multiplied (cloned) to produce identical copies, or they can be used to synthesize many copies of the protein product of the gene. In this way hormones, vitamins, antibiotics and other medical products can be produced faster and at lower cost than by chemical process. The techniques are called genetic engineering.

Many processes involved in genetic engineering are natural. Most of the substances (enzymes) used are found in cells, where they are used to repair DNA. Transfer of DNA from one organism to another occurs naturally by viruses called bacteriophages and smaller agents called plasmids, which are commonly found in bacterial cells. These carriers are widely used in genetic engineering. But genetic engineering goes beyond natural techniques. It produces artificial DNA and modified enzymes, and directly manipulates cells, creating hybrids with nuclei from two different species, or cells with altered numbers of chromosomes.

The future of the Earth's great diversity of life may eventually depend on genetic engineering, which has made it possible to extract and store the DNA of whole organisms indefinitely. The test tube contains DNA – taken from plasmids in a sample of oral bacteria – stained with a dye that fluoresces under ultraviolet light. When scientists learned to cut DNA at particular points and to splice in genes from other species, and then reinsert the modified DNA into the original organism, they had developed a powerful technique for growing proteins at will. A new form of technology – biotechnology – was born.

REARRANGING DNA

GENETIC engineering requires large quantities of DNA. The techniques used to clone DNA – to make numerous identical copies of its segments – can also be used to store it, rearrange it and transfer it between organisms. They are collectively called recombinant DNA technology. Essential tools of this are restriction endonucleases, enzymes that cut DNA between specific base sequences. There are two types of restriction enzyme. Some cut the DNA at the same point on both strands, leaving blunt ends. The other type makes a staggered cut which leaves unpaired DNA ("sticky ends") on the resulting fragments, helping to bring pieces of DNA together. To bond fragments of DNA permanently, a DNA enzyme ligase is used.

KEYWORDS

PLASMID
POLYMERASE CHAIN REACTION
RECOMBINANT DNA
STICKY ENDS

To transfer DNA from one organism to another, a vector (carrier) is needed. Plasmids are commonly used vectors in this role. These are small circular loops of DNA found in bacterial cells but distinct from the main bacterial "chromosome". Bacteria replicate their plasmids so that a single cell may contain hundreds of identical copies. Furthermore, the bacterial cells themselves replicate about once every 20 minutes. Plasmids enter bacterial cells by transformation: the DNA adheres to the cell surface and penetrates it. Eukaryotic cells can also be transformed with the aid of chemical or electrical treatment of their cell membranes. If a selected DNA segment is incorporated into a plasmid and introduced into a bacterial cell, hundreds of copies can be made. The

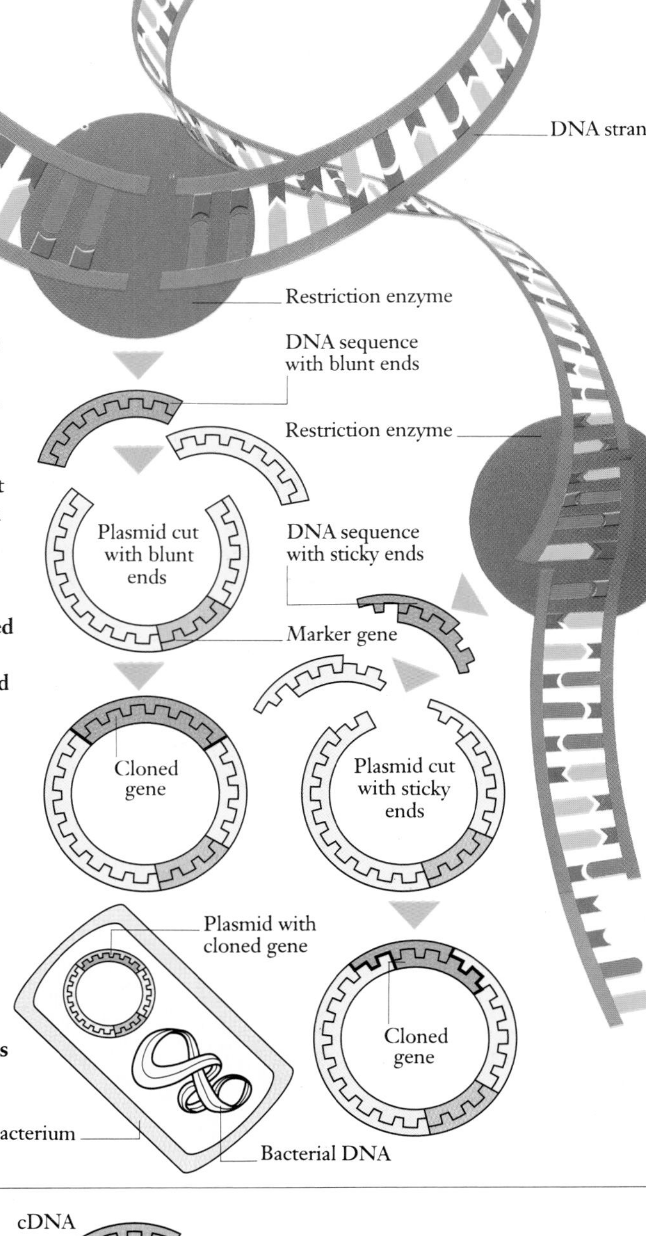

▷ DNA can be stored as fragments incorporated into plasmids kept in bacterial cultures. The DNA is first cut into fragments by restriction enzymes which recognize specific sequences of nucleotide bases. This produces blunt or "sticky" ends which can pair with matching ends on DNA fragments (for example those from a bacterial plasmid) produced by the same restriction enzyme. When the plasmid and DNA fragments are mixed in the presence of a DNA ligase enzyme, the sticky ends join and some of the plasmid genomes now contain the DNA fragments. The plasmids are incorporated into bacterial cell cultures. Though only a little DNA can be stored in this way, the fragments can be multiplied by means of the polymerase chain reaction.

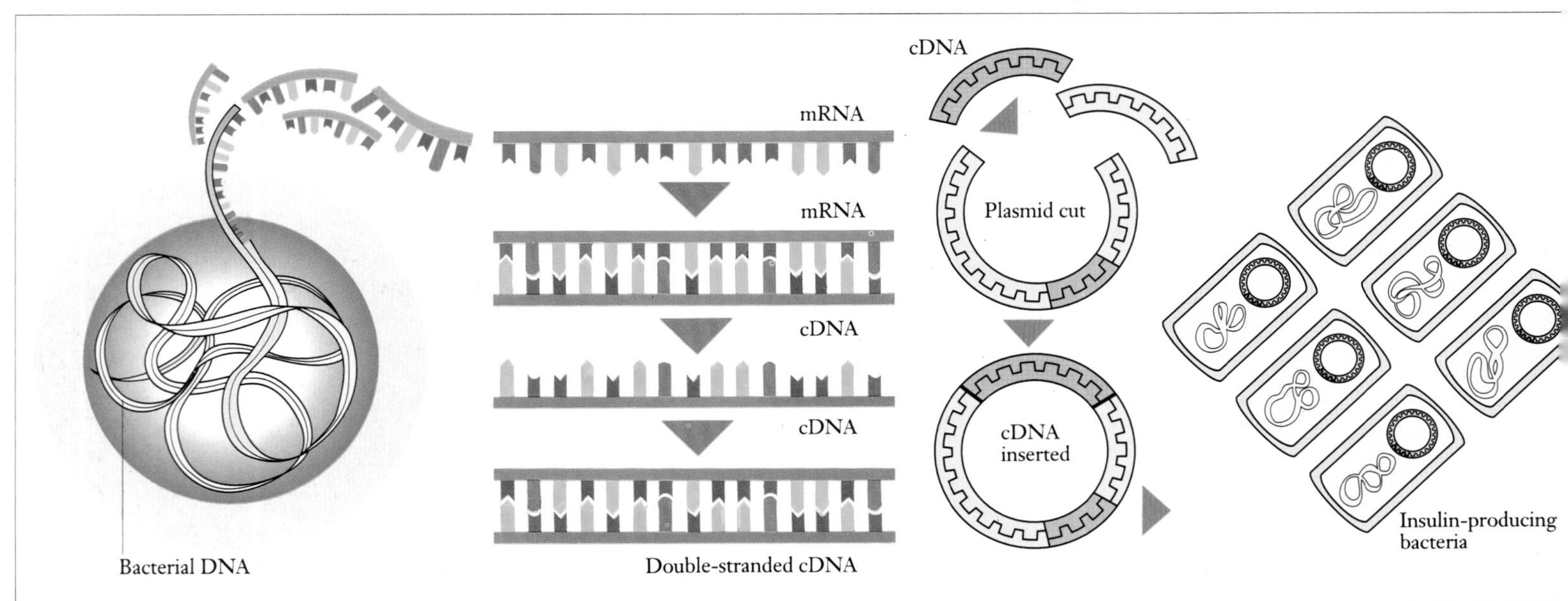

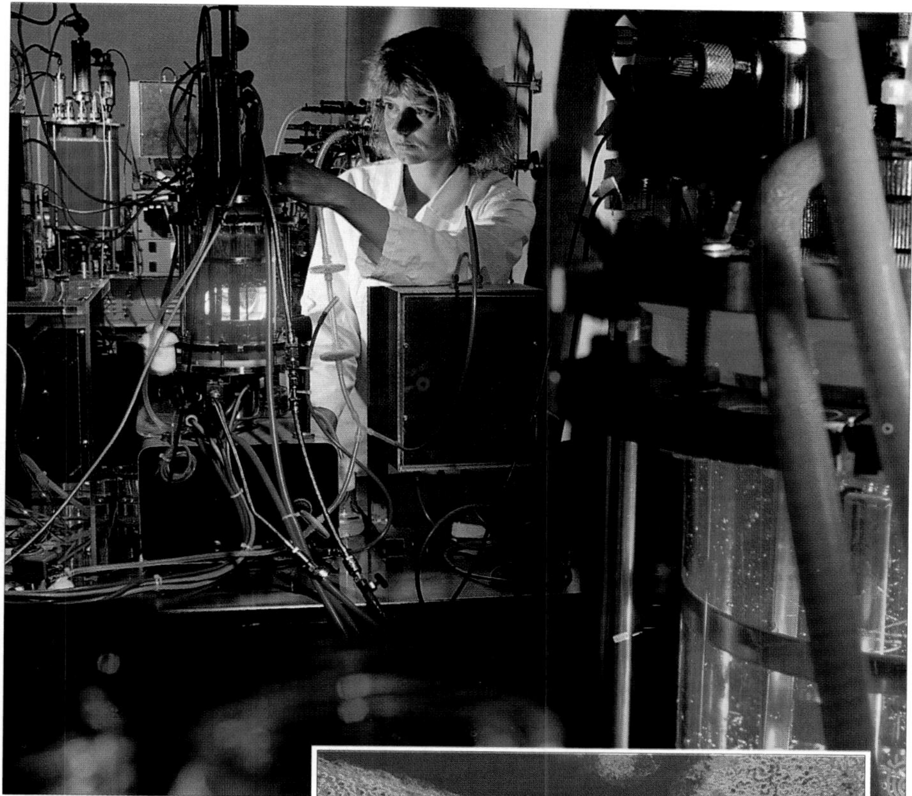

△ **In recombinant protein research, a scientist takes a sample in which genetically engineered mammalian cells are being cultured. Such cells may be used to produce human products such as hormones or blood proteins for use in therapy or medical research.**

plasmids can then be extracted from the cells and the DNA removed by restriction enzymes. Populations of bacteria can therefore be used as DNA libraries.

Efficient plasmid transfer works only for very small segments of DNA (up to 10,000 base pairs), but segments up to 24,000 base pairs long can be inserted into bacteriophages. Even longer pieces can be carried by cosmids – phages whose own DNA has been removed, except for the *cos* segments which code for packing the DNA in the phage head. For storing large segments of eukaryote DNA, yeast artificial chromosomes (YACs) are often used. These are large pieces of DNA combined with a selective marker and the regulatory elements needed to function as independent chromosomes in yeast cells. YACs can be inserted into yeast spheroplasts (cells with much of the cell wall removed) and cloned. To detect which cells are successfully transformed, a marker gene for antibiotic resistance is inserted into the recombinant DNA segment. The cells are cultured on a medium containing the antibiotic; only recombinant cells survive.

DNA can be derived from the mRNA it produces. Cells that are actively producing proteins contain large quantities of the mRNAs for those proteins. These can be extracted, then the enzyme reverse transcriptase used to synthesize complementary single-stranded DNA using the mRNAs as templates. This is then separated from the RNA by treatment with alkali, and DNA polymerase used to make a DNA double helix, copy DNA (cDNA). This can be incorporated into plasmids and into a gene library.

To clone DNA rapidly, the polymerase chain reaction is used. The DNA is split into single strands, which are used as templates for the synthesis of a complementary strand using the DNA polymerase. The enzyme used comes from the bacterium *Thermus aquaticus*, which tolerates high temperatures, and requires a double-stranded section of DNA as starting point. To achieve this, primers are used: short nucleotide sequences, complementary to those flanking the desired segment of DNA, are synthesized and added to the DNA fragment and the polymerase. The mixture is subjected to near-boiling temperatures to denature the DNA; then the temperature is lowered to stimulate base-pairing with the primer; and finally raised to 72°C, which promotes the action of the DNA polymerase. The cycle is repeated, with the newly synthesized DNA denatured to form the template for the next round of replication. Because the reaction can work with tiny amounts of DNA, it is an important forensic tool, able to clone the DNA from a single hair or scrap of skin, or a speck of blood; it can also be used in the analysis of the DNA in early embryos.

Recombinant DNA Technology

A gene for a protein such as insulin may be synthesized artificially, or extracted from mRNA from human pancreatic cells that are producing the protein. The mRNA molecules are identified by a marker chemical that binds with a sequence of bases within the gene. The mRNA is converted to complementary single-stranded DNA and then to double-stranded cDNA, by the use of the enzymes reverse transcriptase and DNA polymerase. A bacterial plasmid is cut with restriction enzymes and the cDNA segment inserted into the plasmid, using a DNA ligase enzyme to seal the cut ends. The bacterial cell is treated with chemicals to help it take up the engineered plasmid, and the plasmid is replicated and produces mRNA which instructs the bacterial cell to produce insulin.

△ **The bacterium *Escherichia coli*, commonly present in the human gut, is being widely used in biotechnology and genetic research to produce useful substances. These cells are producing human interleukin 2 (shown in red), a naturally-occurring cancer therapeutic chemical which stimulates killer white blood cells to attack certain types of tumors.**

Finding the Genes

Genetic engineering depends on locating and analyzing genes on chromosomes, and ultimately sequencing the DNA. Early gene mapping used Mendel's principles of inheritance. Alleles that are usually inherited together are assumed to be close together on the same chromosome: they are said to be linked. Such genes form a linkage group: they pass into the same gametes and are usually inherited together, so they do not show independent assortment. Cross-overs during meiosis mean these alleles may sometimes be swapped between the chromosomes of a homologous pair. Cross-overs are more likely to occur between alleles that are widely separated than between those that are close together; the frequency of cross-overs is a measure of the relative linear distance between the alleles (and their genes) on the chromosome.

KEYWORDS

CHROMOSOME MAP
CLEAVAGE
CLONE
DNA POLYMERASE
ELECTROPHORESIS
GENE LIBRARY
GENOME
NUCLEOTIDE
PHENOTYPE
PROTEIN SYNTHESIS
SOMATIC CELL HYBRIDIZATION

By analyzing cross-over frequencies for many different alleles, a linear chromosome map can be drawn up. However, this relies on phenotype characters that are readily analyzed. A linkage map shows only the relative positions of genes, not absolute distances (cross-overs may not occur with the same frequency at every point along the chromosome) and it does it not indicate the chromosome the genes are on.

Modern techniques map the DNA itself rather than the genes: the positions of short "marker" sequences are used as landmarks along the chromosomes. Once a gene has been found, its base sequence needs to be worked out before its function is studied. Sequencing has been made easier with the development of methods of cloning DNA – producing large quantities of identical fragments.

In the most commonly used DNA sequencing method the DNA chain is denatured into single strands. These are then used as templates for DNA synthesis, but in such a way that replication stops when the growing double-helix reaches a particular base on the template. In addition to supplying DNA polymerase and the four bases, A, C, G and T, small amounts of dideoxynucleotides of these bases are used. These become incorporated into the growing double helix just like ordinary bases, but they terminate the chain. The fragments are then separated by electrophoresis, and the sequence of bases on the original DNA segment can be worked out.

If the DNA fragments are labeled with a radioactive marker, the bands representing fragments of different lengths can be detected by placing the electrophoresis gel on a photographic film. Alternatively, fluorescent markers can be used. Each gel can separate only a few hundred nucleotides, so large lengths of DNA, such as that in a chromosome, are first cleaved into fragments, then overlapping nucleotide sequences are used to determine the original order of the fragments in the DNA.

This technique is being used to sequence the human genome, which contains hundreds of thousands of nucleotide pairs. It is much faster than protein analysis, and the structures of many proteins are studied by analyzing the DNA segments that code for them, then working out the amino acid sequences. The genomes of several "model" organisms are being mapped to provide the starting material for deriving the function of genes.

Bacteria have only one chromosome, but for eukaryotes, other techniques must be used to determine which chromosome a particular segment of DNA (such as a gene) belongs to. Special "somatic hybrid" cells are prepared, usually from human and mouse cells. As these cells divide, some of the human

▷ DNA fragments can be made visible by staining them with ethidium bromide, which fluoresces under UV light. Despite the huge number of bases to be sequenced, it is far quicker to study a protein by analyzing the bases that make up its gene, and to derive the amino acids that it will produce, than to analyze the complex protein molecule directly.

■ The commonest method for determining the base sequence of DNA was pioneered by the American Frederick Sanger. The DNA is first broken by specific enzymes into segments of a few hundred nucleotides.

DNA fragm
Chromosom DNA
Restriction enzyme

▷ The DNA is separated into single strands, which are incubated with the enzyme DNA polymerase (which joins together complementary nucleotides to make a second strand of DNA), radioactively labeled primers which activate the DNA polymerase enzyme to start working, and a pool of nucleotide bases. This mixture is divided into four batches, and to each a different modified base is added. When these modified bases are added to the new DNA strand, they block the action of the DNA polymerase and prevent it from adding further nucleotides. As a result new, radioactively-labeled, double-stranded segments of DNA of varying lengths are produced, each terminated with the modified base. Eventually fragments will have been created corresponding to every possible position of the base in that DNA strand. The fragments are then separated by gel electrophoresis.

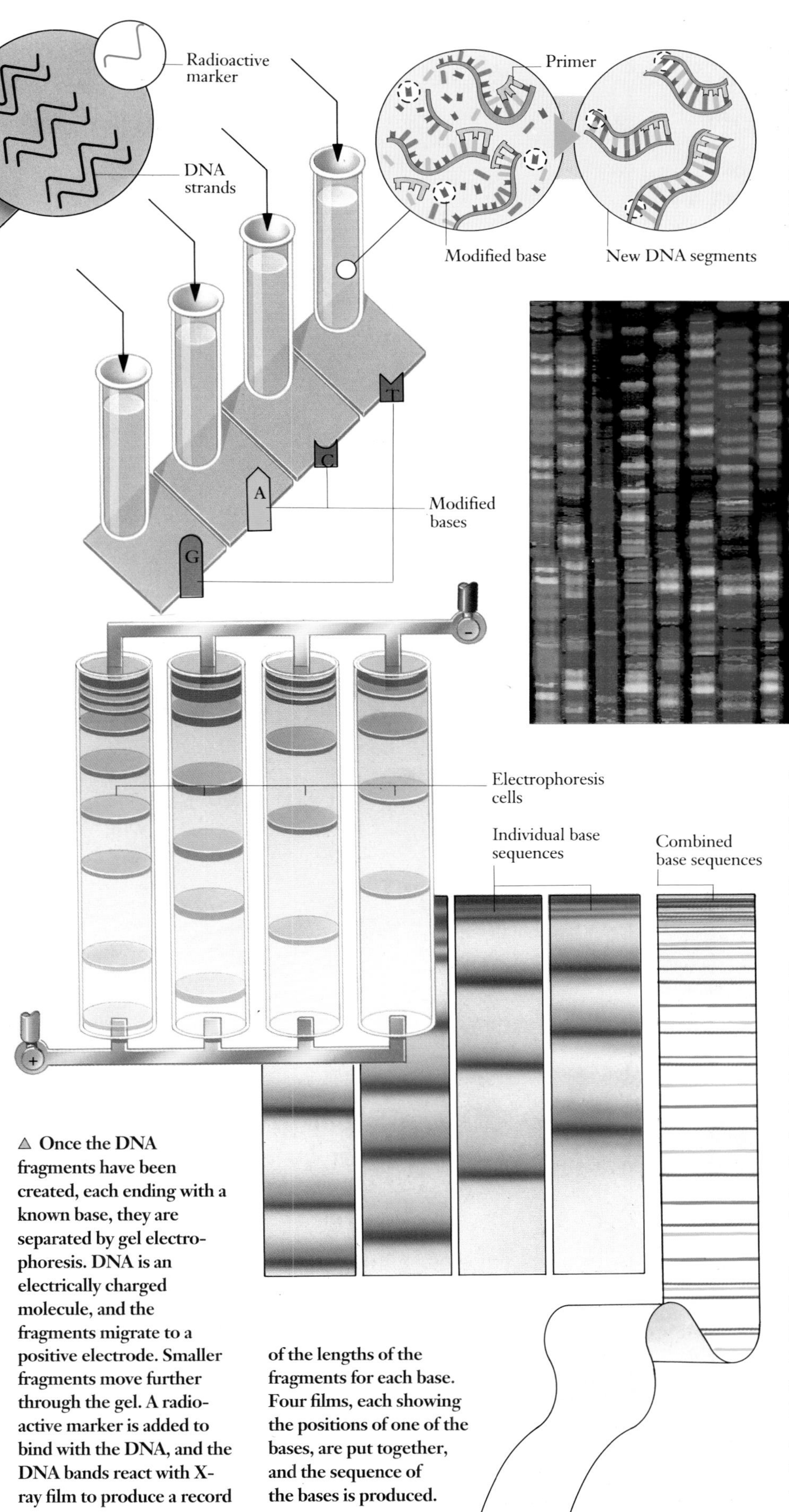

△ **Once the DNA fragments have been created, each ending with a known base, they are separated by gel electrophoresis. DNA is an electrically charged molecule, and the fragments migrate to a positive electrode. Smaller fragments move further through the gel. A radioactive marker is added to bind with the DNA, and the DNA bands react with X-ray film to produce a record of the lengths of the fragments for each base. Four films, each showing the positions of one of the bases, are put together, and the sequence of the bases is produced.**

▽ **An autoradiogram is used to decode the base sequence after electrophoresis. This technique is used to identify particular genes to be extracted from gene libraries. These normally contain a vast quantity of genetic information within colonies of microorganisms growing on a filter paper the size of a computer floppy disk. The density of genetic information on the paper has been estimated as 1000 times higher than the densest floppy disk.**

chromosomes are lost, until some cells have only one or two chromosomes. Alternatively, chromosomes can be injected into cells with no original chromosomes. The cells are then cloned. By looking for their protein products, it is possible to decide which genes are on which chromosome.

A different technique is needed to locate a particular gene on a piece of DNA, such as a DNA fragment from a gene library. Probes must be used to find which colonies of microorganisms contain the desired segments of DNA. A probe is a piece of mRNA, cDNA or ordinary DNA labeled with a radioactive marker. Copies are made of the master clones. Then the DNA is extracted and denatured into single strands, and the probe added. Only strands complementary to the probe segments will hybridize with them. These can be detected by autoradiography.

To determine the gene for a particular protein, mRNA is extracted from cells actively producing that protein; some of the mRNA molecules have been produced by the required gene. cDNA can be formed from the RNA and cloned. From the sequence of amino acids in the protein, a suitable DNA probe can be designed to find the appropriate piece of DNA. Alternatively, the different cDNAs can be separated and allowed to synthesize proteins, which are detected using specific antibodies.

Living Factories

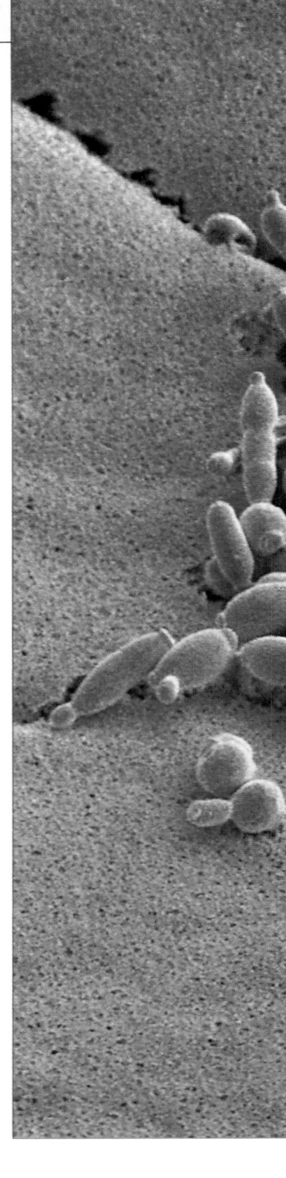

If the genetic code for a particular protein is known, in theory it should be possible to manufacture the protein from its basic amino acids in the laboratory. In practice, this is very expensive, and it is much more efficient, and cheaper, to use the existing machinery of living cells to carry out the program. Microorganisms such as bacteria and yeasts reproduce very rapidly and are easy to grow on an industrial scale under controlled conditions in large vats (fermenters). Such commercial culture may contain 10 billion identical cells per liter of nutrient fluid. The microorganisms can often be fed on cheap food such as agricultural, domestic or industrial waste. Batches of microorganisms are removed, their cell membranes broken down and the protein extracted.

KEYWORDS

BIOTECHNOLOGY
GENETIC ENGINEERING
PLASMID
PROTEIN
VECTOR

Computerized chemical analysis machines – gene machines – can decipher pieces of DNA or RNA extracted from living organisms at a great speed – up to 15,000 base pairs a day. They can also produce DNA of a required sequence. Large amounts of a specific DNA sequence can be produced using the polymerase chain reaction.

Plasmids are used to transfer the desired piece of DNA (artificially synthesized, or extracted from another organism) into the microorganism. For the "foreign" DNA to be processed into protein, it must become incorporated into the DNA of the microorganism. This does not always happen. To detect which microorganisms have taken it up, a gene for resistance to a specific antibiotic is added to the foreign DNA. By growing the microorganism in cultures containing the antibiotic, only the reprogrammed organisms survive.

By such techniques a wide range of proteins can be produced commercially, including human blood factor VIII (needed by hemophiliacs) and a modified form of hepatitis B virus for use as a vaccine. Insulin produced in this way is in widespread use for treating diabetics. A synthetic gene similar to the human gene is inserted into the bacteria. This codes for a molecule called proinsulin. Proinsulin can be purified and converted to insulin by digesting away part of the molecule. Bacteria can also produce proteins for the food-processing industry, such as lactic acid, used to adjust acidity in many foods, and to improve the flavor and texture of cheese and yoghurt, and temperature-resistant enzymes used in washing powders. Bacteria containing spider genes can produce strong, light silk fibers. Microorganisms may shortly be programmed to produce ethanol or other substitutes for gas in cars.

Microbe factories can also be used to produce food for humans and animals. A great deal of the energy taken in from sunlight by plants is lost before meat from plant-eating animals such as cows and sheep reaches the dinner table – lost as undigested food (droppings), heat, energy of movement, nervous energy, and excreta. Bacteria can produce protein much more efficiently, and can be grown on cheap sources such as oil. Molds produce mycoprotein, which can be adapted to have the texture of meat. Bacteria such as *Methylophilus* are sold in powder form as a protein-rich animal feed supplement.

Microorganisms can produce only relatively simple proteins. To obtain more complex proteins requires the more complex machinery of mammal cells. Newly fertilized eggs or the first few cells of the embryo are extracted, and the new genetic material inserted. Mammal cells are not infected by plasmids, so virus vectors or other methods have to be used. High voltage electric shocks can make cell membranes "leaky", or

◁ Genetically engineered animals can be used to produce human proteins such as certain hormones , and other proteins which may be deficient in certain genetic diseases. Since these proteins are derived from human genes, they produce fewer side effects than synthetic chemicals or those produced by other animals. A human gene has been inserted into these sheep so that it produces a blood clotting factor.

△ The pink periwinkle from Madagascar produces the substances vinblastine and vinchristine, which are effective in the treatment of certain types of leukemia. The periwinkle is a slow-growing plant, but its cells multiply rapidly when cultured, while retaining their capacity to produce drugs. Cell cultures from other plants are used to produce many drugs.

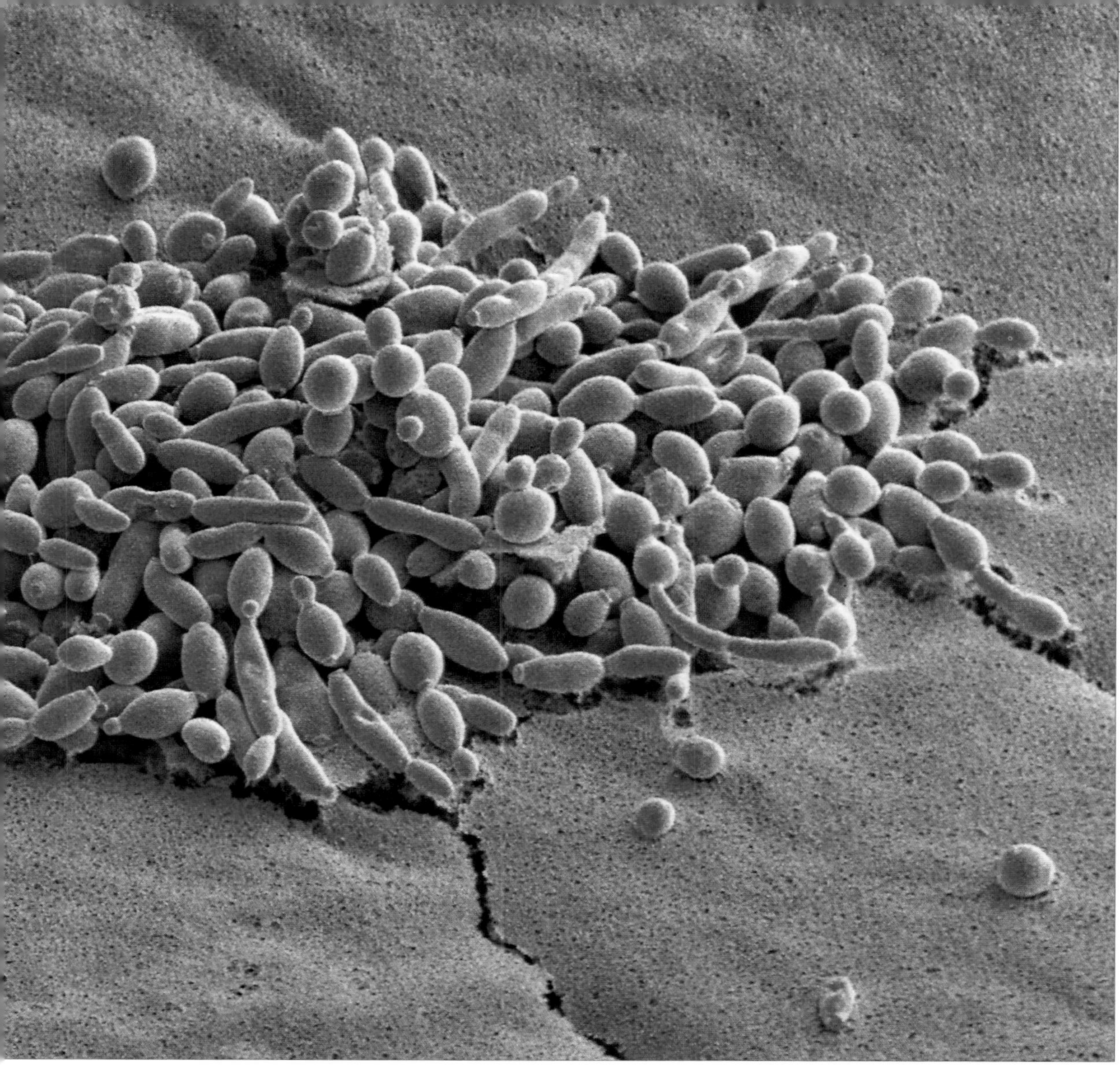

◁ Cells of the common yeast *Saccharomyces cerevisiae* multiply rapidly by budding, producing vast clones of genetically identical cells. Yeast cultures are widely used in genetic engineering, and have many commercial uses, fermenting sugar to produce carbon dioxide and make bread rise, and in alcoholic drink production.

▽ Large fermenters such as this are used to culture cells for the diagnosis or treatment of disease. Cell cultures on this scale are important in producing monoclonal antibodies, which may be used to treat disease or to attach markers to the cells of internal tumors. White blood cells producing a specific antibody are fused with tumor cells capable of indefinite cell division; the resulting hybridoma cells multiply in the fermenter, secreting large amounts of antibody.

the DNA can be inserted directly into the nucleus using a very fine glass micropipette. If sheep, for example, can be engineered to produce drugs in their milk, this will be much cheaper than producing these proteins by fermentation. Experiments are under way to insert human milk genes into cows, so that they will produce milk that is better for feeding human babies. Some mammal cells can be cultured in the laboratory, creating production lines rather like those of microbes. Others work only in their correct place in the body.

With improvements in ways of cloning mammal embryos, it is becoming easier to produce large numbers of genetically engineered animals. Embryos are split while still at the stage of only a few cells, and the split embryos are implanted into surrogate mothers. It is possible to create new breeds of cattle without bulls having to go into action, by employing test-tube fertilization followed by embryo splitting to produce several offspring with the desired genetic material. Already farmers purchase frozen embryos from test-tube fertilization and implant them into their own cows. This can easily be done with genetically engineered embryos.

THE NEW FARMING REVOLUTION

THE ability to "reprogram" plants and animals has made possible fast-growing, lean pigs, sheep and cows; cows producing lowfat milk; and crops with built-in pest resistance or antifreeze. Some of these involve reprogramming the animal or plant itself, while others use genetically engineered microorganisms to produce substances for injection.

Genetically-engineered growth hormones are now used to stimulate growth of livestock. Bovine growth hormone or somatotropin (BST) can increase milk yields by 25 percent. Epidermal growth factor can make sheep grow wool very quickly; the wool is very fine and can be brushed off, avoiding the need for shearing. But there are drawbacks. Cows injected with BST may develop diseases such as mastitis (udder infection). They may also miscarry more often. And their milk appears to contain small amounts of an insulin-like substance, raising doubts about its suitability for human consumption. For these reasons, the use of BST has been banned in Europe.

KEYWORDS

BACTERIUM
CLONE
GENETIC ENGINEERING
GENOME
IMMUNITY
TISSUE CULTURE
TRANSGENIC
VECTOR
VIRUS

Genetically engineered vaccines, produced by genetically engineered microorganisms, have more obvious benefits, and can help counter such diseases as hoof-and-mouth disease. Instead of injecting a mild form of the disease to stimulate immunity, as in the old vaccines, it is now possible to separate the part of the genome of the pathogen (disease-causing organism) which stimulates the immune response, and create a much safer vaccine from this.

▷ This beet plant has been genetically engineered to be resistant to herbicides: spraying kills any weeds but leaves the crop unharmed. Tissue cultures of the beet were disrupted to obtain single cells, which were then subjected to electric fields to make their membranes "leaky", allowing segments of DNA containing the herbicide-resistant gene to enter the cells. In a small proportion of cells, this DNA became incorporated into the beet cell genome. These cells were identified by culturing them on a herbicide-containing medium. The successful cultures were then grown to maturity; here they are shown being harvested.

▽ Using tissue culture to breed plants such as oil palms (shown here awaiting transport from a laboratory to a plantation) is much quicker than waiting for seed production to occur, and the plants are genetically identical.

An alternative approach is to alter the livestock itself, to produce its own modified hormones and generate its own resistance. This is already being done on quite a large scale. Sperm or fertilized eggs can be injected with fragments of DNA or RNA with the instructions for producing the desired product, such as a hormone. The resulting embryo is returned to the womb where, if the "foreign" DNA becomes incorporated into the embryo's own genome, it will develop into a "transgenic" animal. In practice, fewer than 10 percent of the embryos are transformed. Successfully transformed animals can then be cloned.

Plant viruses provide a convenient way of transferring new genetic code to plants. Another commonly used vector is the soil bacterium *Agrobacterium tumefasciens*, which causes cankerous growths on infected plants. It invades plant cells and releases a plasmid, which can be genetically engineered. Alternatively, isolated plant cells can be divested of their cell walls, mixed with "foreign" DNA, and subjected to a pulsating electric field to make their membranes more permeable, allowing the DNA to invade the cells. The cells can be cultured in a laboratory to provide new plantlets, a quick and effective method of cloning plants.

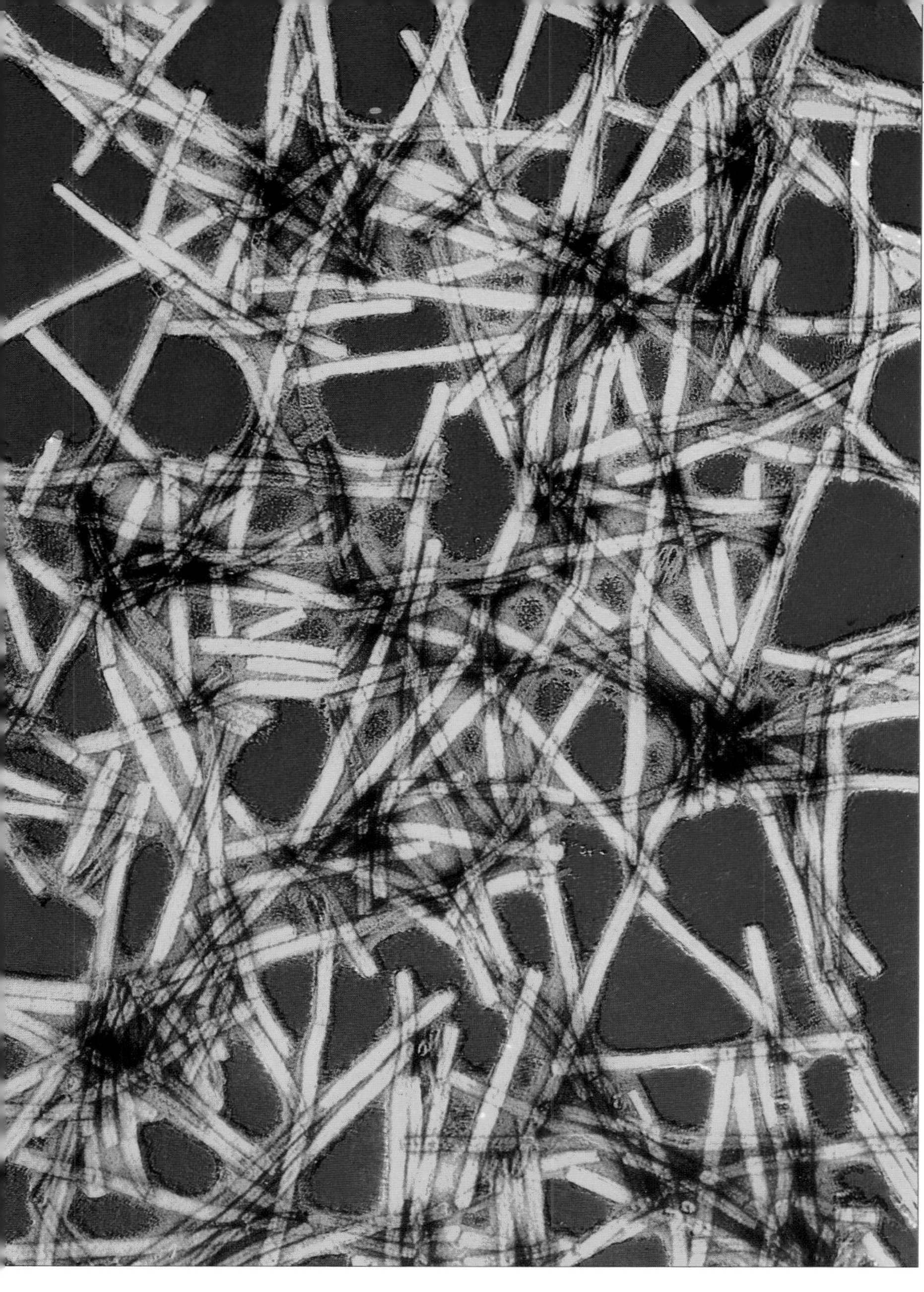

◁ Tobacco mosaic virus is a highly damaging disease of crops for which, once infection has occurred, no chemical cure is available. However, plants may be protected by genetic engineering. The virus consists of a spiral of RNA surrounded by a protein coat. If the gene coding for this protein is inserted into the DNA of the tobacco plant cells, the plants become immune to infection by the virus. Tomato plants can also be protected in this way.

Pest control has been even more successful. Many herbicides, used to control weeds, are indiscriminate, affecting all plants. They can be spread only before the crop germinates, but if the crop can be made herbicide resistant, spraying can continue almost until harvesting. Plants can also be given insecticidal properties. For example, potatoes have been produced with a gene from a soil-dwelling bacterium that produces a toxin lethal to Colorado beetles. A simpler method is to spray the plants with insect viruses that cause the insects to produce their own insecticide. Other engineered viruses cause the insects to produce excessive amounts of hormones, which prove fatal.

But there are risks. It is not yet known whether the substances produced by the introduced genes persist in the crop or fruit, or whether they affect humans who eat the produce; or how easy it is for other plant or insect viruses to pick up the engineered genes and transfer them to other hosts, perhaps proving fatal to beneficial insects or rendering weeds resistant to herbicides. There is increasing evidence that transfer of genetic material by various vectors is more common in higher plants than previously thought.

▷ Root nodules are found only in a few plant families (such as these broad bean plants) and enable them to grow in nitrogen-poor soils. They "fix" nitrogen and make organic compounds, which are then available to the host plant. Attempts to genetically engineer other crops to produce root nodules, or to introduce bacterial nitrogen-fixing genes into crop genomes, have so far been unsuccessful.

Fruits that do not bruise during transport and long-lasting mushrooms are being engineered. Genetic engineering offers scope for increasing growth rates, improving uptake and use of nutrients, tolerating drought and cold, and adapting to saline soils or other local conditions. One important field for research, not yet successful, is the attempt to improve nitrogen intake by crops, reducing the need for fertilizers. Legumes (plants of the pea family) have special nodules on their roots housing bacteria which can "fix" nitrogen from the soil into soluble nitrates and other nitrogenous compounds that the host plants can use.

▽ Lammas shoots of oak, produced late in summer, contain large amounts of toxins to deter caterpillars from eating them. Spring leaves (when few insects are around) produce few such toxic compounds.

7

HUMAN *Genetics*

THE HUMAN GENOME – the complete set of genetic information carried by each individual – is one of the largest in the animal kingdom, containing some three billion nucleotides. Scientists are attempting to sequence the entire genome to provide an international databank for genetic research. On a less ambitious scale, the analysis of segments of human DNA to provide a "genetic fingerprint" is providing an invaluable forensic tool.

Genetic knowledge and engineering have great medical benefits. Many human diseases are due to inherited genetic defects, and recombinant DNA techniques offer improved diagnostic procedures. They can help determine which genes are responsible for the defects and perhaps eventually correct them. Genetically engineered microorganisms and transgenic animals are being used to produce metabolic proteins that are deficient in people with genetic diseases; examples are insulin, Factor VIII (involved in blood clotting) and human growth hormone. Monoclonal antibodies can be used to carry drugs to specific cells such as cancer cells. New techniques will also make possible nonmedical applications, such as the selection of the gender of a child, or of characteristics such as intelligence or athletic physique, and even the cloning of human embryos. These possibilities have provoked worldwide debate on the ethical issues raised.

The study of genetics has contributed a great deal to our modern understanding of what it means to be an individual, and what we share with other members of our family, and the rest of the human race. Many difficult issues are raised, such as the discovery that an individual may be carrying a gene that seems to correlate with a propensity for a certain disease, or social attribute. The significance of this correlation remains very controversial, and, although no one doubts the medical benefits of much genetic research, the advantages of knowing that, for example, you carry the gene that may be responsible for Alzheimer's disease or a criminal propensity are far less clear.

Sickness in the Genes

Some 60 percent of people probably suffer from a genetic or partly genetic disease during their lifetime. Almost half of all stillbirths are due to genetic defects. Many genetic disorders are inherited from parents who may be sufferers or carriers of the disease, but they can also arise spontaneously from errors during meiosis and gamete production, or during cell divisions following fertilization. Some may arise in ordinary cells later in life – most cancers start in this way. Inherited genes may cause predisposition to certain genetic diseases. An example is the gene that predisposes women to breast cancer. Only if these mutations affect the sex cells do they pass to the next generation.

KEYWORDS

ALLELE
MUTATION
ONCOGENE
RETROVIRUS
SEX LINKAGE

More than 5000 diseases are known to be due to a change in a single gene, often in a single base on the DNA. Sickle-cell anemia, for instance, is due to the substitution of a single base, which results in the replacement of the amino acid glutamate by valine at a particular point in the hemoglobin molecule. Sickle-cell anemia is caused by a recessive mutant allele: heterozygotes show no symptoms, but act as carriers of the disease. Other common recessive mutations cause albinism, galactosemia and phenylketonuria. Many disorders are due to dominant mutant alleles. Achondroplasia, one of the major causes of dwarfism, is dominant, as is Huntington's chorea. Heterozygous and homozygous individuals both display symptoms.

When the faulty allele is on a sex chromosome, the pattern of inheritance is different. No known human diseases are linked to the Y chromosome, but many, such as hemophilia, are related to the X chromosome. If a woman carries the gene, half of her sons, on average, inherit a defective X chromosome. These sons suffer from the disorder, as there is be no second allele to mask the gene. Female sufferers must inherit the faulty gene from both parents.

Genetic diseases can also be caused by changes in the chromosomes themselves. Duplications, inversions and translocations may alter genes if the break occurs within genes rather than between them. Rearrangements may also separate genes from the DNA sequences that control them, with serious results. Duplication or multiple repeating of nucleotide sequences is implicated in several diseases, including Huntington's chorea, fragile X, and myotonic dystrophy. Deletion of part of a chromosome is usually disastrous.

■ Some of the most common inherited diseases among humans can be linked to specific chromosome sets BELOW. The genes implicated in some of these diseases, such as muscular dystrophy and Huntington's chorea, are dominant: a child has to inherit only one gene from one parent to be at risk. Susceptibility to other diseases, such as sickle-cell anemia, is controlled by recessive genes: the disease only appears if both parents contribute defective genes. A person who has the genes but does not develop the disease itself is called a carrier.

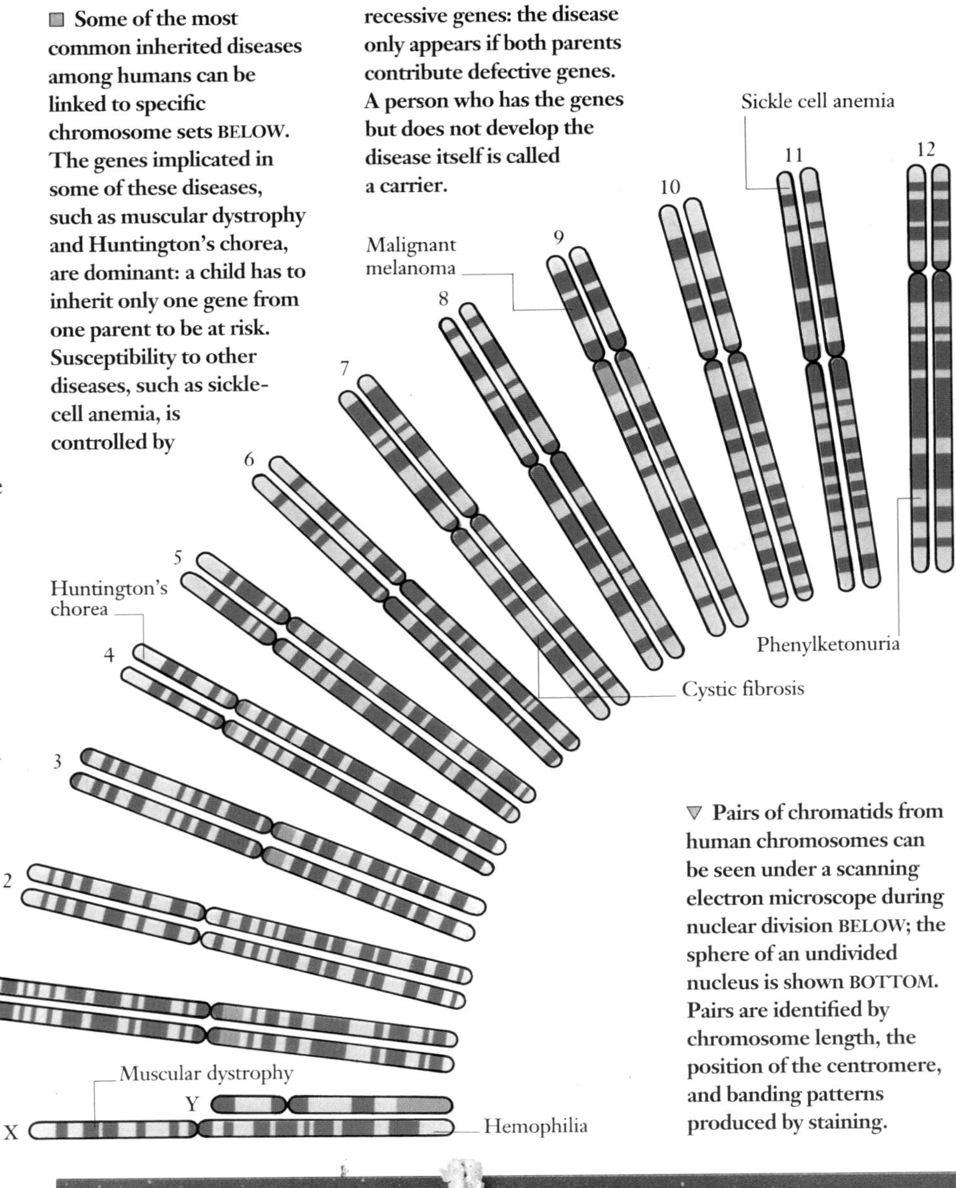

▽ Pairs of chromatids from human chromosomes can be seen under a scanning electron microscope during nuclear division BELOW; the sphere of an undivided nucleus is shown BOTTOM. Pairs are identified by chromosome length, the position of the centromere, and banding patterns produced by staining.

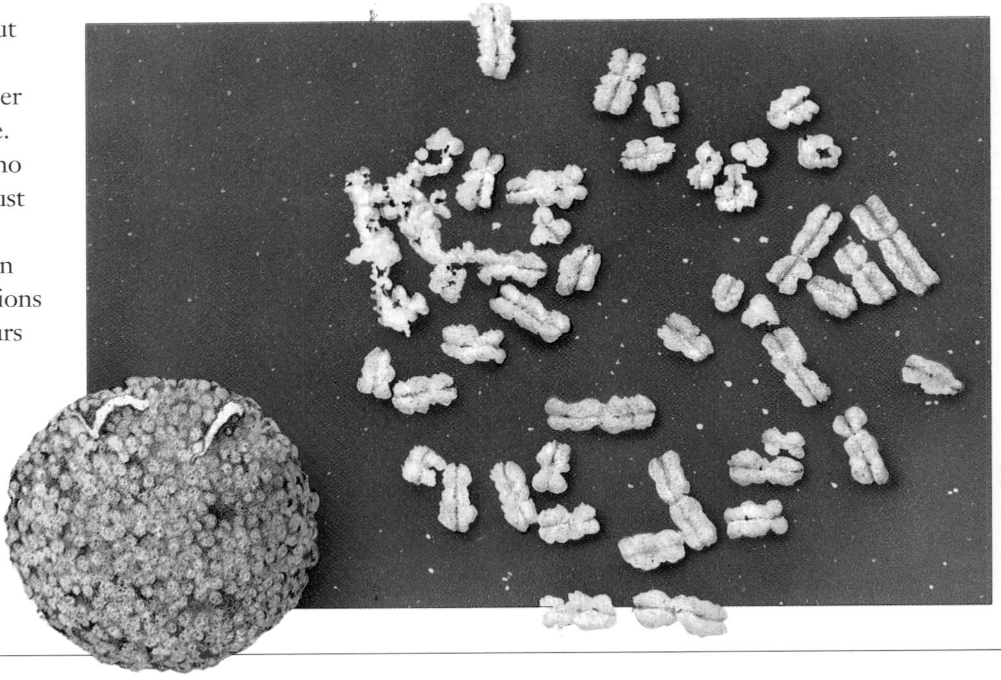

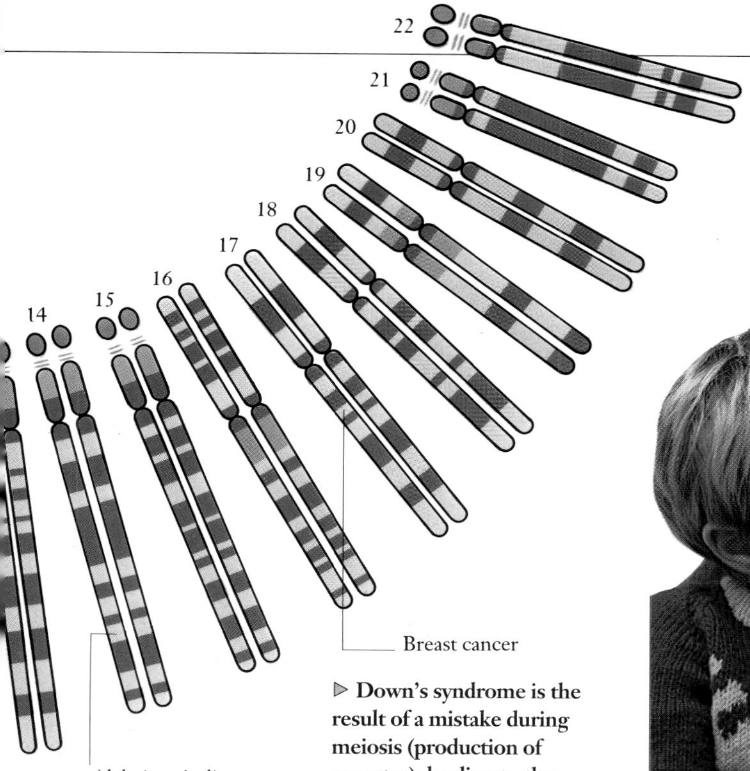

Breast cancer

Alzheimer's disease

▷ Down's syndrome is the result of a mistake during meiosis (production of gametes), leading to the cells having three copies of chromosome 21. The embryos are often miscarried, but about one child born in a thousand has Down's syndrome.

Other diseases are due to changes in chromosome number. These happen when chromosomes fail to separate properly during meiosis or when a chromosome is left behind when the new nuclear membrane forms. Mutations can be induced in a fetus if the pregnant mother is exposed to conditions, such as ionizing radiation, that can damage DNA. Serious chromosomal abnormalities cause spontaneous abortion.

Some changes affect the number of and balance between X and Y chromosomes. Turner's syndrome, which causes symptoms that include infertility and a shortened life expectancy, is due to lack of a second sex chromosome: such patients are XO. Sufferers of Klinefelter's syndrome (all male) are XXY, or even XXXY or XXXXY. At puberty, they develop feminine traits; they are sterile and may have some mental retardation. XYY individuals are more or less normal.

Some diseases – many cancers, diabetes mellitus, epilepsy, rheumatoid arthritis and multiple sclerosis – are the result of many different defective genes, and may also involve environmental factors. Consequently, the effects of the disease range from mild to severe.

Diseases such as cancer are frequently caused by mutations that arise late in life, in the ordinary body cells, often as a result of exposure to toxic chemicals or radiation. Cancers are caused by defects in the genes which control the cycle of cell division. Cell death is a normal part of the cell cycle for many cell types: after a certain number of divisions, the cell is programmed to die. Tumor cells do not usually divide more rapidly than normal cells, but they just keep dividing. One of the key factors in cancer may be the loss of signals, or the inability to respond to the signals, that cause cells to die when they should. For example, when the gene c-myc, which is involved in the choice between cell proliferation and "suicide", is switched on, the cell can divide; when it is turned off, the cell kills itself. c-myc is under the control of growth factors (hormones). Mutations in c-myc can make it fail to respond to signals that would turn it off, so division goes on unchecked and cell suicide is suppressed. One-third to one-half of all cancers involve mutation of the gene p53, which actually prevents cancers by ordering damaged or potentially malignant cells to stop dividing and repair the damage, or commit suicide.

Genes that transform normal cells into tumor cells are called oncogenes. Proto-oncogenes, the normal versions of these mutated cellular genes, regulate fundamental processes in cell division or growth. The cancer-causing retroviruses had "hijacked" proto-oncogenes from their host's genome, mutating them in the process to make malfunctioning versions that caused cancer when the virus reinfected the animal's cells. Only 15 percent of human cancers are caused by genes introduced by viruses. More often, chemicals or ionizing radiation convert the cell's proto-oncogenes into oncogenes. Cancer usually requires the mutation of more than one proto-oncogene to trigger it.

△ A patient is undergoing radiotherapy to treat Hodgkin's disease, a cancer of the lymphatic system caused by gene mutation. Radiotherapy provides only crude targeting of tumors; modern drugs can be targeted very accurately by attaching them to monoclonal antibodies that specifically seek out and bind to tumor cells.

CLINICAL AND FORENSIC GENETICS

THE sophisticated techniques of medicine and forensics allow the increasing understanding of DNA to be put to practical use. For example, DNA tests have become widespread to identify and predict inherited genetic diseases. By studying family trees of affected families, it is possible to construct a chart of genetic relationships to predict at-risk individuals, who can then be screened for genetic defects. Dominant inherited defects show up in more of the offspring than recessive defects. Some largescale chromosome abnormalities, such as deletions, additions or translocations of blocks of genes, may be seen under a microscope if the chromosomes are treated with stains which produce a characteristic banding pattern, but most require DNA analysis. A common technique uses certain enzymes, called restriction endonucleases, to chop up the DNA at specific points. The fragments are then separated by electrophoresis and identified by DNA probes. Small genetic differences between members of a family produce different-sized fragments, and hence different patterns of banding on electrophoresis. This is called RFLP (restriction fragment length polymorphism) analysis.

Several methods of screening may be used to check a developing fetus for inherited disorders such as Down's syndrome. Ultrasound scans can detect serious malformations, sometimes as early as 10 weeks into pregnancy, and are relatively harmless. Amniocentesis, chorionic villus sampling and cordocentesis are techniques by which fetal cells or fetal proteins can be obtained, cultured and used for genetic diagnosis.

Another screening technique, currently being developed, is to sample the small few fetal cells that escape into the mother's own blood

KEYWORDS

AMNIOCENTESIS
CONGENITAL
DNA FINGERPRINTING
ELECTROPHORESIS
GENETIC ENGINEERING
RESTRICTION ENZYME

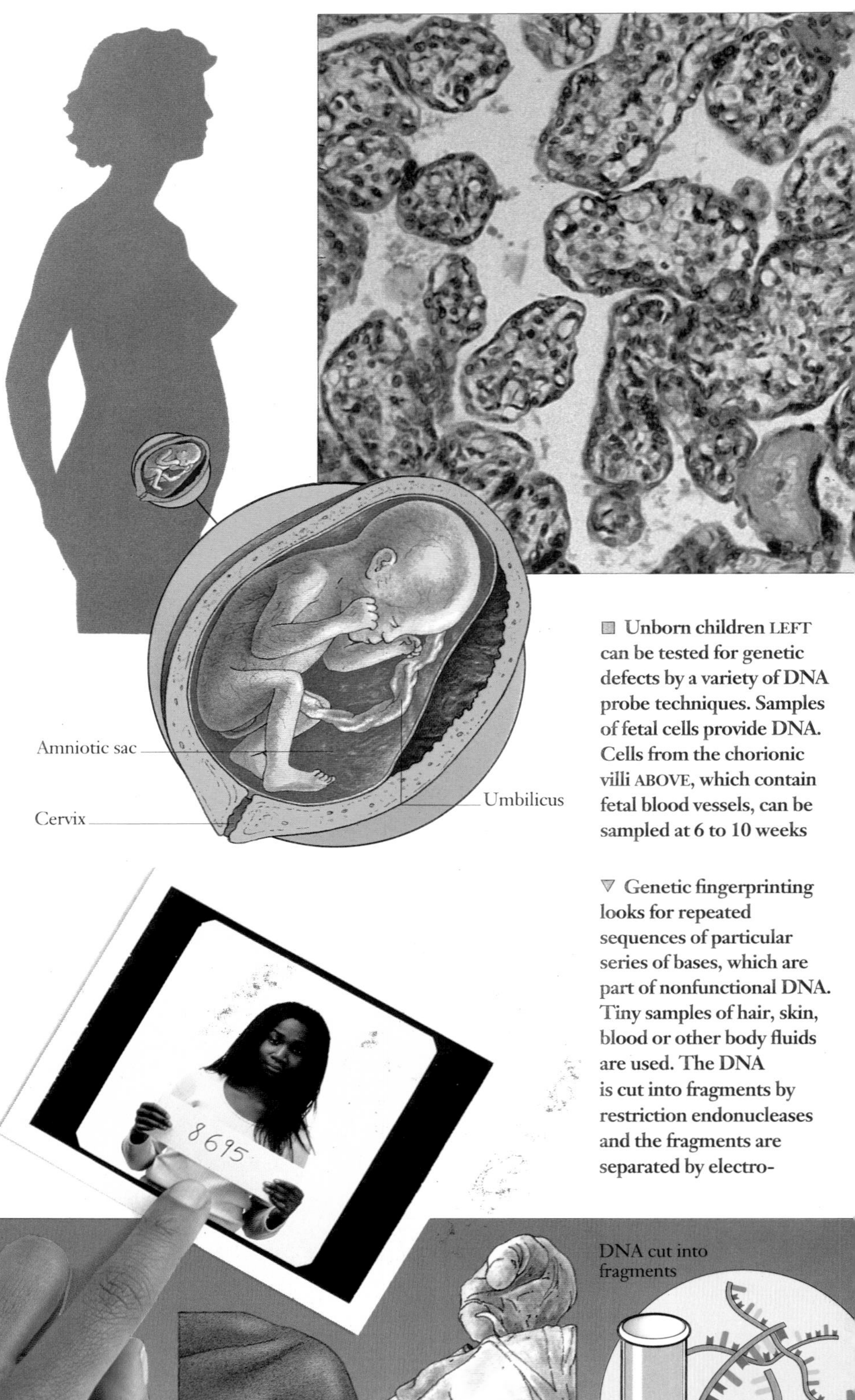

Unborn children LEFT can be tested for genetic defects by a variety of DNA probe techniques. Samples of fetal cells provide DNA. Cells from the chorionic villi ABOVE, which contain fetal blood vessels, can be sampled at 6 to 10 weeks

▽ Genetic fingerprinting looks for repeated sequences of particular series of bases, which are part of nonfunctional DNA. Tiny samples of hair, skin, blood or other body fluids are used. The DNA is cut into fragments by restriction endonucleases and the fragments are separated by electro-

▷ Some sequences of human DNA vary so greatly that the chances of two people (except identical twins) having the same pattern is one in several million. Genetic or molecular "fingerprinting" provides almost infallible proof of identity, and is used as evidence in cases of missing persons, rape, murder and paternity suits.

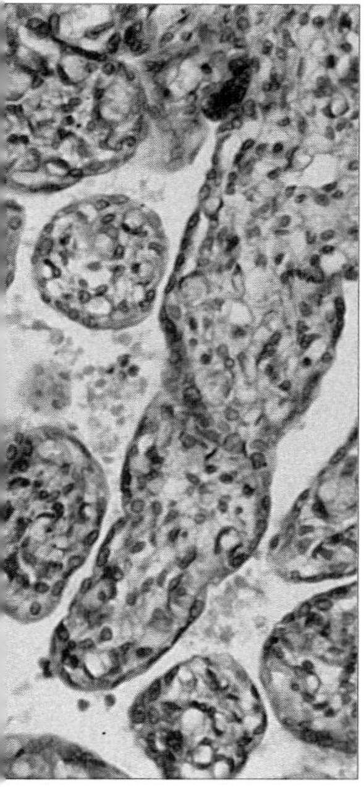

(earlier than amniocentesis). The villi are found in the chorionic membrane, which surrounds the fetus. The genes in the chorionic membrane are from the fetus, and the procedures are similar to those of amniocentesis.

phoresis. Then radioactive DNA probes are applied, which bind only to these sequences of bases. The excess unattached probe is washed away and X-ray film placed behind the column. This produces a pattern of dark bands where the radioactive probe is concentrated – this is the unique DNA profile.

circulation. These can be distinguished from the mother's cells by using fluorescent antibodies that bind only to certain fetal proteins. This form of testing is even safer than amniocentesis.

Some genetic diseases may be treated after they have developed, by adding the particular protein or hormone which is deficient, or by reprogramming the cells – a technique still in its infancy but improving all the time. Proteins, hormones and other biochemicals, as well as antibiotics and vaccines may themselves be produced by genetic engineering, using microorganisms or cultures of mammalian cells as living factories. Attempts to permanently reprogram genetically defective human cells have not yet been successful. However, when mice with Duchenne muscular dystrophy (caused by a failure to make the protein dystrophin) have the normal gene injected directly into the muscle tissue, there is a temporary improvement in their condition. Five out of 100 cells become reprogrammed, but the effect lasts for only a few months. Using viruses, it may eventually be possible to introduce corrective DNA into human cells of particular tissues, but the virus must be made to self-destruct afterward, otherwise it could pass out with the feces, and possibly infect normal members of the human population. Attempts are underway to produce an aerosol spray of live genetically engineered viruses to prevent cystic fibrosis.

Genetic engineering also has a role to play in preventing nonheritable diseases. Vaccines may be modified nonharmful viruses, such as the *Vaccinia* virus, which is being modified to provide vaccines against rabies, herpes and influenza. Up to 25 extra genes can be inserted into the viral genome to provide multiple immunity. Other vaccines, such as that for hepatitis B, may be simple surface proteins of the relevant virus coat. The virus gene is inserted into a microorganism, which then produces the vaccine. Sometimes just a few critical amino acids are enough to stimulate the body's immune system. For viruses like influenza, which constantly change their surface proteins, this is not so easy, but scientists are searching for nonchanging parts of the surface proteins.

Genetic engineering has other uses. DNA fingerprinting is an invaluable tool for forensic scientists. Like an ordinary fingerprint, the DNA fingerprint is unique to the individual (except twins). It involves looking at specific sequences of DNA, which may be obtained from extremely small samples of tissues, hair or blood, perhaps left at the scene of a crime. Just 50 microliters of blood, 5 microliters of semen or 10 hair roots will suffice, as well as mouth swabs and fetal material. Besides its use in catching criminals, especially rapists, DNA fingerprinting can be used to establish family relationships, as, for example, in paternity suits. Conservationists use it to make sure captive breeding takes place between unrelated individuals.

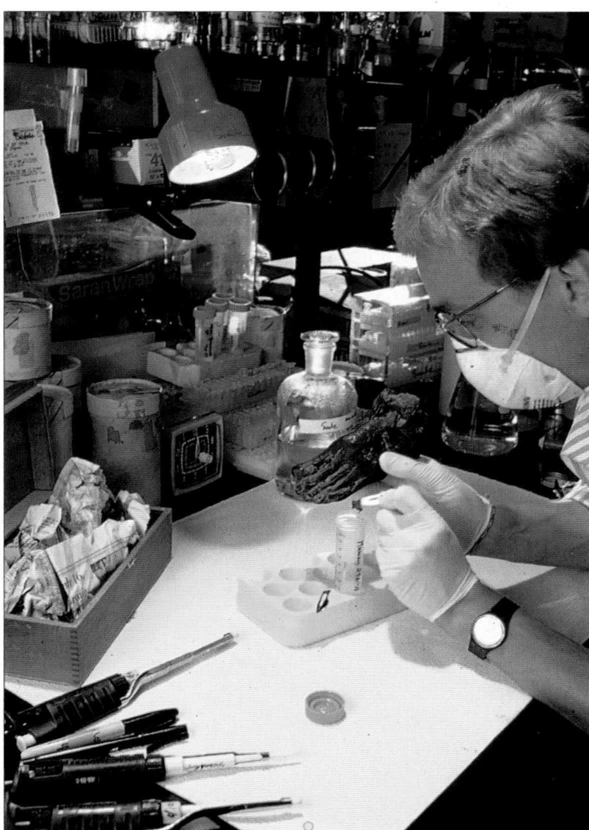

▲ DNA provides clues to the past beyond the wildest dreams of earlier generations of historians and archaeologists. Here, a researcher at the University of California at Berkeley is taking a sample of DNA from the foot of a 2000-year-old Egyptian mummy. It will be compared with DNA from modern Egyptians and other people from the region to see how the local gene pool has changed.

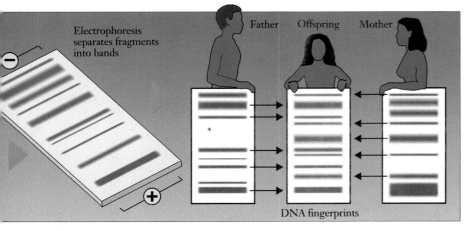

THE IMMUNE SYSTEM

THE human immune system is a masterpiece of genetic variability and adaptability. It is based on a series of specialized white blood cells (lymphocytes) that respond to the presence of foreign organisms and foreign substances (antigens). The response involves different types of lymphocytes. T cells have receptors that recognize specific antigens and destroy any cells bearing them, including infected cells whose surfaces bear foreign antigens such as the discarded protein coats of invading viruses. Other T cells – T suppressor cells – help to regulate the response; helper cells stimulate other T cells to attack. For the T cell to recognize an antigen, the antigen must be "presented" by major histocompatibility complex (MHC) proteins that distinguish "self" from "non-self". These proteins are involved in the reactions that cause tissue rejection after organ transplants.

KEYWORDS

AIDS
ANTIBODY
ANTIGEN
BACTERIOPHAGE
B CELL
CLONE
HYBRIDOMA
IMMUNITY
IMMUNOGLOBULIN
LYMPHOCYTE
PROTEIN
RETROVIRUS
T CELL
VIRUS

Another set of lymphocytes, the B cells, detect foreign antigens and produce antibodies (proteins called immunoglobulins), each specific to a particular antigen, which bind to the antigen and mark it so that macrophages (large white cells that engulf pathogens) and complement (a series of proteins that destroy antigens by protein-digesting enzyme reactions) can recognize it.

There are millions of antigens, calling for millions of different antibodies and T-cell receptors; mammals have fewer then one million genes, so there cannot be a gene for each. Antibodies, T-cell receptors and the MHC proteins are each coded for by a large family of genes. Diversity is further increased in antibodies and T cells by a process of DNA rearrangement called somatic recombination that takes place as the lymphocytes mature. The result is a large population of varied lymphocytes (10^6 to 10^8 immature cells and about 10^{12} mature ones); each B cell produces only one kind of antibody, capable of recognizing only one antigen, and each T cell produces only one specific T-cell receptor.

When a B cell or T cell is exposed to an antigen that its antibody or receptor can recognize and bind to, the lymphocyte enlarges and divides repeatedly, producing a clone of the antibodies or receptors. This is the primary immune response. After the infection has been dealt with, some of these specific B cells and

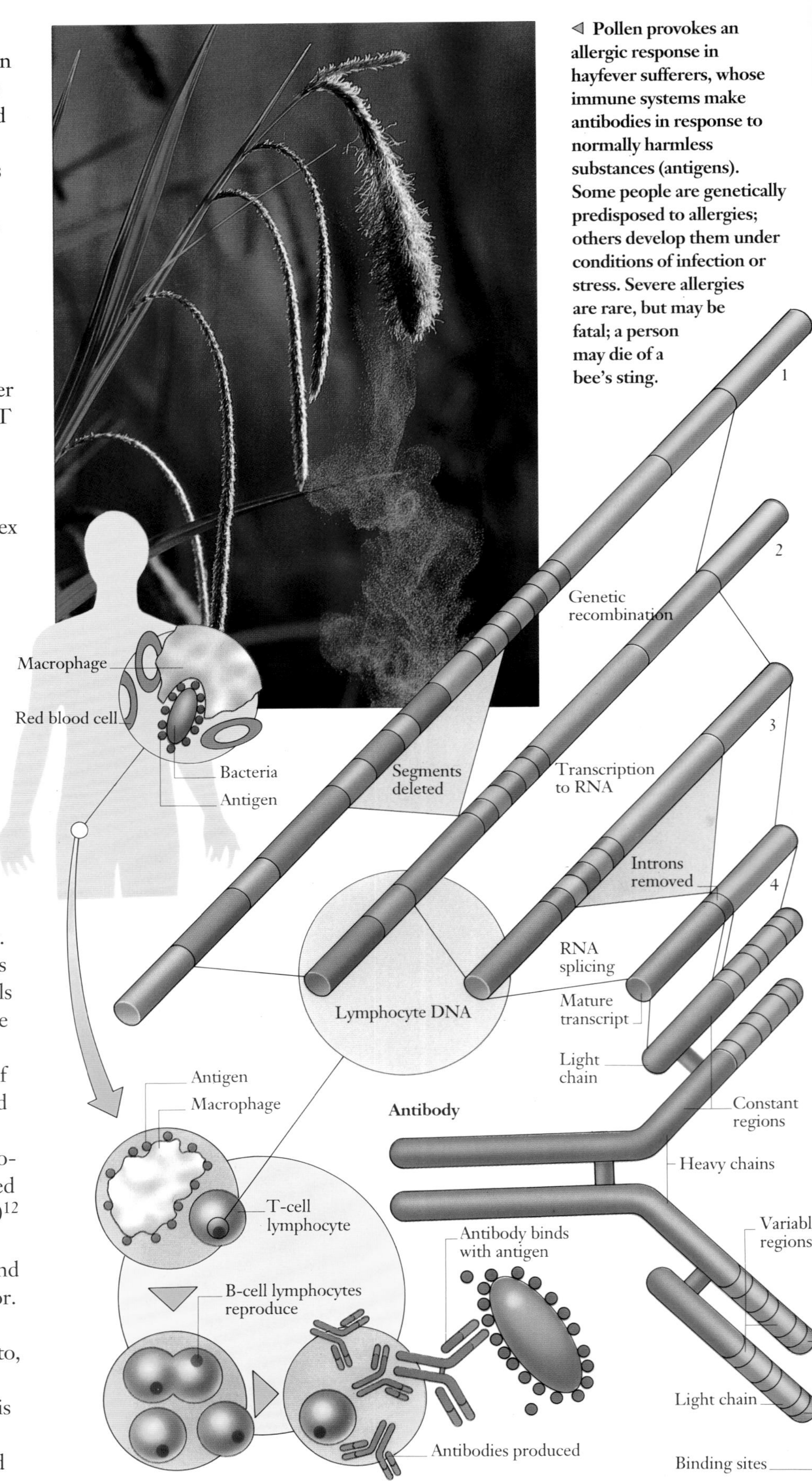

◁ **Pollen provokes an allergic response in hayfever sufferers, whose immune systems make antibodies in response to normally harmless substances (antigens). Some people are genetically predisposed to allergies; others develop them under conditions of infection or stress. Severe allergies are rare, but may be fatal; a person may die of a bee's sting.**

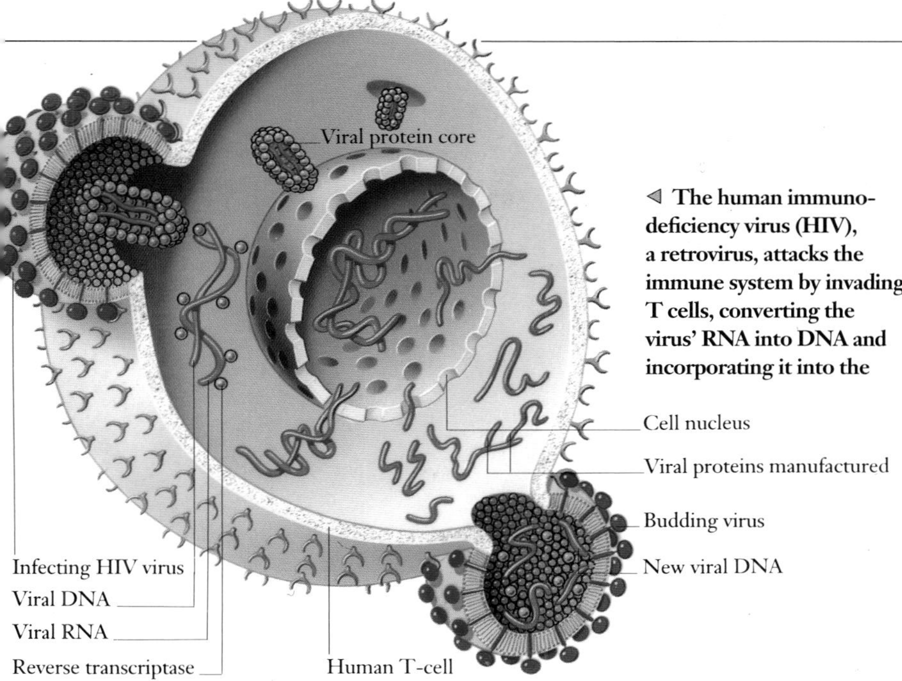

◁ **The human immunodeficiency virus (HIV), a retrovirus, attacks the immune system by invading T cells, converting the virus' RNA into DNA and incorporating it into the host DNA. When the T cell responds to an infection, it transcribes part of its DNA, including the HIV. This produces copies of viral RNA which produce new viruses that bud off from the T cell; with each new infection, more T cells are destroyed. HIV's extraordinarily high mutation rate makes it difficult to develop an effective vaccine for it.**

◁ **A human antibody is made up of heavy and light polypeptide chains, composed of constant and variable regions (found on the ends, to bind to antigens). Antibodies are produced by B cells in the blood in response to the invasion of a foreign substance. Each B cell produces only one kind of antibody, which binds to only one kind of antigen, such as chemicals on the surface of a bacterium that invades a wound. As the B cell matures, the gene segments that code for the antibody are rearranged, although there is no chromosome pairing. Recombination enzymes recognize and cut specific nucleotide sequences, snipping out gene segments and reinserting them in other places. There are three "pools" of segments to be reshuffled. More "editing" occurs on the initial messenger RNA before it leaves the nucleus. Millions of combinations of DNA segments code for each antibody chain, to create millions of different kinds of antigen-binding sites.**

T cells remain in a semi-mature state. These long-lived cells remain ready to produce a more rapid response if the body encounters the same antigen – the secondary immune response.

The body is capable of producing 10^6 to 10^8 different antibodies. An antibody is a Y-shaped molecule made up of 4 linked polypeptide chains. There are two identical light (L) chains of about 200 amino acids, and two identical heavy (H) chains 300 to 400 amino acids long. Both chains contain variable (V) regions and constant (C) regions. Receptors for the antigens are found in the variable regions. Different DNA segments code for particular parts of the immunoglobulin molecule. V segments code for V regions and C segments for C regions. Heavy chains have a third set of variable segments, D (diversity) segments; they are even more variable than light chains. To make one chain, a V segment is joined to a C (and D) segment, so that 2 (3) gene segments form an "active" gene coding for one polypeptide. This results in more than 10,000 possible arrangements of DNA for the heavy chain alone. Genes in immunoglobulin-producing cells mutate at rates far higher than normal.

Antibodies have many uses in biotechnology. Normal B cells cultured outside the body either die or soon stop producing antibodies. But if B cells are fused with certain cancer cells to form hybridoma cells, the cancer cell enables the new cell to multiply and grow in fermenters for a long time, while the B cell enables it to produce antibodies. These are identical to those produced by the original B cells and are called monoclonal antibodies. Antibodies from the blood of a person or animal infected with a disease can be cloned to make a vaccine.

Monoclonal antibodies are used to extract specific protein products, such as interferon, from cultures of genetically engineered organisms. They can also be used for diagnostic tests, and can be engineered to carry radioactive, fluorescent or other markers. The antibodies bind to antigens on the surface of disease-causing organisms. The material can be examined under a microscope for markers. Certain disorders release a particular protein into the bloodstream or the urine; this is recognized by the appropriate monoclonal antibody. Antibodies labeled with metallic or radioactive compounds and injected into patients can target specific antigens (as in cancer cells) so doctors can use X rays to detect and measure tumors. They can be used to guide drugs too toxic to be released into the blood. Antibodies also bind to other antibodies. The test for the HIV virus uses antibodies to detect HIV antibodies or proteins produced by the virus.

△ **Autoimmune diseases are caused by attacks on the body by its own immune system. People with rheumatoid arthritis have high levels of an antibody that binds to the body's own antibodies as to foreign antigens and deposits them on joint membranes, causing inflammation and fluid seepage, eventually destroying the joint.**

Interference and Ethics

NOT since the publication of Charles Darwin's *The Origin of Species* in 1859 has science generated such widespread public controversy as with the rise of genetic engineering. Like the theory of evolution, genetic engineering is the culmination of patient research and documentation, the "ultimate" prize for the scientist; like the theory of evolution, this provokes both excitement and fear. Genetic engineering tampers with the blueprint of life itself. Even among scientists there are strong misgivings about the possibility of reprogramming human beings. The risks are not merely medical but social, political and moral.

KEYWORDS

BIOTECHNOLOGY
CLONE
EMBRYO
GENE THERAPY
GENETIC COUNSELLING
GENETIC ENGINEERING
GERM CELL
IN VITRO FERTILIZATION
TRANSGENIC

Already it is possible to determine the sex of a human embryo, giving parents the chance of aborting a fetus of unwanted gender. This is causing highly unbalanced ratios of male and females in new generations in some parts of China, India and other countries. More positively, it may soon be possible to correct genetic defects in embryos, so that they do not develop certain diseases, such as cystic fibrosis. It is also possible to correct some of these defects later in life by genetically altering the tissues involved.

Most countries have refused to pass laws to permit the genetic alteration of the germ cells – the sperm, the eggs and the cells that give rise to them. The public justifiably fears a progression from correcting disease-causing defects to correcting socially undesirable traits such as low intelligence, short stature or large noses, or to programming such features as an athletic physique. In the mid-1990s, this was still not possible. Genes could be inserted into chromosomes, but without sufficient accuracy to be sure they go in exactly the right place and do not interfere with the activity of neighboring genes. Also, the correction of genetic defects could be achieved by reprogramming embryos produced by *in vitro* fertilization.

The only advantage in reprogramming germ cells themselves is that potential parents carrying defective genes would no longer need special procedures for conception. In 1994 a patent was requested for a technique to correct defective sperm. It was rejected initially, but demand from animal breeders could eventually lead to such a patent, allowing ordinary stallions, for instance, to be reprogrammed with sperm-producing cells from stud animals. To develop such techniques for humans requires research on human embryos, often those produced in surplus by *in vitro* fertilization. This leads to serious ethical questions, because the mortality rate of embryos during research is high.

There are certainly enormous advantages to be gained from genetic engineering. New strains of plants can be developed to increase food production. High-performance animals enable more meat or milk to be produced from a given amount of fodder. Plants that produce their own insecticides can reduce the need for spraying, and herbicide-resistant crop plants make it easier to remove weeds by chemical means. But there are risks. Insecticide-containing plants may increase the rate at which pests become resistant to insecticides. And the metabolic activities of these introduced genes may cause other changes in the plant, perhaps increasing the toxins in its tissues and making it harmful to humans who consume it. The herbicide-resistant genes may "jump" to other plant species, creating superweeds resistant to herbicides.

The problem of "jumping genes" is a serious one. Until recently, transmission of genetic material between different species was thought to be restricted to microorganisms such as bacteria. But there is some evidence that genes can be transmitted between different plant species by viruses. Many of the bacteria and plasmids used to transfer genetic material into engineered organisms are common in the soil, or even in the human intestine. It is possible that bacteria might escape and invade the soil or infect humans, or mutate to even more harmful forms. Other transgenic organisms could be carried by sprays, or on the feet of animals and humans, or on the wind. Small transgenic organisms that escape may be impossible to retrieve, and may upset ecological balance or harm native species. Such releases must be strictly controlled.

Most countries are attempting to develop responsible legislation, but the immense potential for profit (by the year 2000 the US biotechnology industry is expected to be worth $80 billion a year) places constraints on the legislators: if legislation is too stringent, biotechnology companies will simply move to countries with lax rules. The biological weapons industry is of particular concern, as it might lead to an arms race between genetically engineered pathogens and antidotes, or to the escape of a virulent engineered pathogen to which there is no known antidote. The populations of entire continents could be at risk.

Biotechnology and genetic engineering are not inherently dangerous or immoral: it is the uses to which humans put them that determine whether they are beneficial or deadly – to humans and to the planet.

▶ **Human life balanced against scientific progress – the debate over genetic engineering is often defined in these terms, which provoke a strong emotional response. This is especially true when the life in question is that of a baby (whether born or unborn). The ability to reprogram life – based on an ever more detailed understanding of DNA (an autoradiogram of human DNA sequencing is shown) – is still relatively crude, but it has been a much-publicized issue since the first DNA molecules were spliced in 1972. Fears about its misuse for social and political purposes have some justification; notorious medical experiments were performed not only on concentration camp inmates by Adolf Hitler's Nazi regime during World War II, but also in the United States, sponsored by the national government, on poor black Americans. Yet more than 80 percent of respondents in an American survey in the late 1980s replied that they approved of gene therapy to save children from fatal genetic-based diseases.**

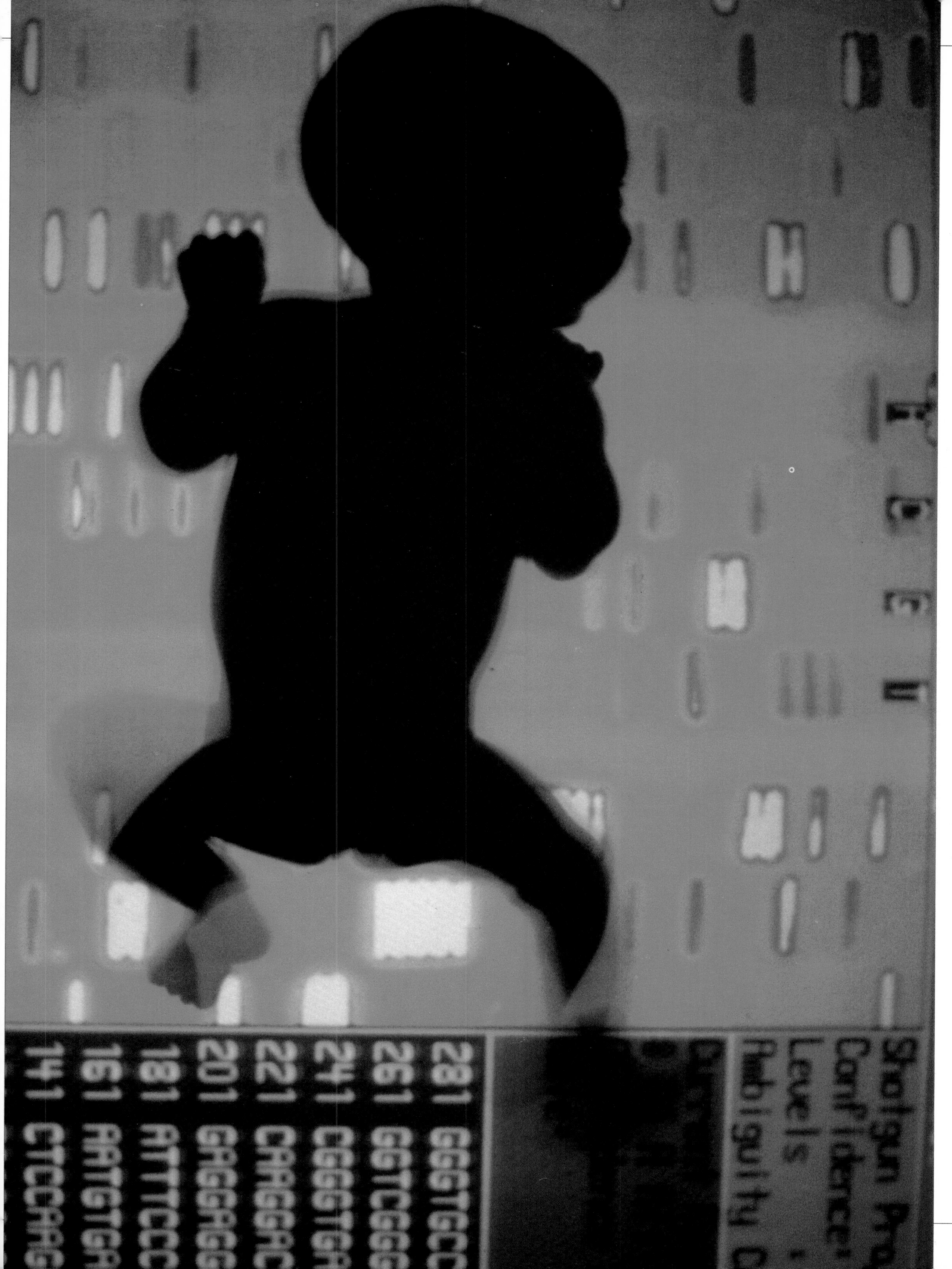

FACTFILE

PRECISE MEASUREMENT is at the heart of all science, and the several standard systems have been in use in the present century in different societies. Today, the SI system of units is universally used by scientists, but other units are used in some parts of the world. The metric system, which was developed in France in the late 18th century, is in everyday use in many countries, as well as being used by scientists; but imperial units (based on the traditional British measurement standard, also known as the foot–pound–second system), and standard units (based on commonly used American standards) are still in common use.

Whereas the basic units of length, mass and time were originally defined arbitrarily, scientists have sought to establish definitions of these which can be related to measurable physical constants; thus length is now defined in terms of the speed of light, and time in terms of the vibrations of a crystal of a particular atom. Mass, however, still eludes such definition, and is based on a piece of platinum-iridium metal kept in Sèvres, near Paris.

METRIC PREFIXES

Very large and very small units are often written using powers of ten; in addition the following prefixes are also used with SI units. Examples include: milligram (mg), meaning one thousandth of a gram, kilogram (kg), meaning one thousand grams.

Name	Number	Factor	Prefix	Symbol
trillionth	0.000000000001	10^{-12}	pico-	p
billionth	0.000000001	10^{-9}	nano-	n
millionth	0.000001	10^{-6}	micro-	µ
thousandth	0.001	10^{-3}	milli-	m
hundredth	0.01	10^{-2}	centi-	c
tenth	0.1	10^{-1}	deci-	d
one	1.0	10^{0}	–	–
ten	10	10^{1}	deca-	da
hundred	100	10^{2}	hecto-	h
thousand	1000	10^{3}	kilo-	k
million	1,000,000	10^{6}	mega-	M
billion	1,000,000,000	10^{9}	giga-	G
trillion	1,000,000,000,000	10^{12}	tera-	T
quadrillion	1,000,000,000,000,000	10^{15}	exa-	E

CONVERSION FACTORS

Conversion of METRIC units to imperial (or standard) units

To convert:	to:	multiply by:
LENGTH		
millimeters	inches	0.03937
centimeters	inches	0.3937
meters	inches	39.37
meters	feet	3.2808
meters	yards	1.0936
kilometers	miles	0.6214
AREA		
square centimeters	square inches	0.1552
square meters	square feet	10.7636
square meters	square yards	1.196
square kilometers	square miles	0.3861
square kilometers	acres	247.1
hectares	acres	2.471
VOLUME		
cubic centimeters	cubic inches	0.061
cubic meters	cubic feet	35.315
cubic meters	cubic yards	1.308
cubic kilometers	cubic miles	0.2399
CAPACITY		
milliliters	fluid ounces	0.0351
milliliters	pints	0.00176 (0.002114 for US pints)
liters	pints	1.760 (2.114 for US pints)
liters	gallons	0.2193 (0.2643 for US gallons)
WEIGHT		
grams	ounces	0.0352
grams	pounds	0.0022
kilograms	pounds	2.2046
tonnes	tons	0.9842 (1.1023 for US, or short, tons)
TEMPERATURE		
Celsius	fahrenheit	1.8, then add 32

Conversion of STANDARD (or imperial) units to metric units

To convert:	to:	multiply by:
LENGTH		
inches	millimeters	25.4
inches	centimeters	2.54
inches	meters	0.245
feet	meters	0.3048
yards	meters	0.9144
miles	kilometers	1.6094
AREA		
square inches	square centimeters	6.4516
square feet	square meters	0.0929
square yards	square meters	0.8316
square miles	square kilometers	2.5898
acres	hectares	0.4047
acres	square kilometers	0.00405
VOLUME		
cubic inches	cubic centimeters	16.3871
cubic feet	cubic meters	0.0283
cubic yards	cubic meters	0.7646
cubic miles	cubic kilometers	4.1678
CAPACITY		
fluid ounces	milliliters	28.5
pints	milliliters	568.0 (473.32 for US pints)
pints	liters	0.568 (0.4733 for US pints)
gallons	liters	4.55 (3.785 for US gallons)
WEIGHT		
ounces	grams	28.3495
pounds	grams	453.592
pounds	kilograms	0.4536
tons	tonnes	1.0161
TEMPERATURE		
fahrenheit	Celsius	subtract 32, then × 0.55556

SI UNITS

Now universally employed throughout the world of science and the legal standard in many countries, SI units (short for *Système International d'Unités*) were adopted by the General Conference on Weights and Measures in 1960. There are seven base units and two supplementary ones, which replaced those of the MKS (meter–kilogram–second) and CGS (centimeter–gram–second) systems that were used previously. There are also 18 derived units, and all SI units have an internationally agreed symbol.

None of the unit terms, even if named for a notable scientist, begins with a capital letter: thus, for example, the units of temperature and force are the kelvin and the newton (the abbreviations of some units are capitalized, however). Apart from the kilogram, which is an arbitrary standard based on a carefully preserved piece of metal, all the basic units are now defined in a manner that permits them to be measured conveniently in a laboratory.

Name	Symbol	Quantity	Standard
BASIC UNITS			
meter	m	length	The distance light travels in a vacuum in 1/299,792,458 of a second
kilogram	kg	mass	The mass of the international prototype kilogram, a cylinder of platinum-iridium alloy, kept at Sèvres, France
second	s	time	The time taken for 9,192,631,770 resonance vibrations of an atom of cesium-133
kelvin	K	temperature	1/273.16 of the thermodynamic temperature of the triple point of water
ampere	A	electric current	The current that produces a force of 2×10^{-7} newtons per meter between two parallel conductors of infinite length and negligible cross section, placed one meter apart in a vacuum
mole	mol	amount of substance	The amount of a substance that contains as many atoms, molecules, ions or subatomic particles as 12 grams of carbon-12 has atoms
candela	cd	luminous intensity	The luminous intensity of a source that emits monochromatic light of a frequency 540×10^{-12} hertz and whose radiant intensity is 1/683 watt per steradian in a given direction
SUPPLEMENTARY UNITS			
radian	rad	plane angle	The angle subtended at the center of a circle by an arc whose length is the radius of the circle
steradian	sr	solid angle	The solid angle subtended at the center of a sphere by a part of the surface whose area is equal to the square of the radius of the sphere

Name	Symbol	Quantity	Standard
DERIVED UNITS			
becquerel	Bq	radioactivity	The activity of a quantity of a radio-isotope in which 1 nucleus decays (on average) every second
coulomb	C	electric current	The quantity of electricity carried by a charge of 1 ampere flowing for 1 second
farad	F	electric capacitance	The capacitance that holds charge of 1 coulomb when it is charged by a potential difference of 1 volt
gray	Gy	absorbed dose	The dosage of ionizing radiation equal to 1 joule of energy per kilogram
henry	H	inductance	The mutual inductance in a closed circuit in which an electromotive force of 1 volt is produced by a current that varies at 1 ampere per second
hertz	Hz	frequency	The frequency of 1 cycle per second
joule	J	energy	The work done when a force of 1 newton moves its point of application 1 meter in its direction of application
lumen	lm	luminous flux	The amount of light emitted per unit solid angle by a source of 1 candela intensity
lux	lx	illuminance	The amount of light that illuminates 1 square meter with a flux of 1 lumen
newton	N	force	The force that gives a mass of 1 kilogram an acceleration of 1 meter per second per second
ohm	Ω	electric resistance	The resistance of a conductor across which a potential of 1 volt produces a current of 1 ampere
pascal	Pa	pressure	The pressure exerted when a force of 1 newton acts on an area of 1 square meter
siemens	S	electric conductance	The conductance of a material or circuit component that has a resistance of 1 ohm
sievert	Sv	dose	The radiation dosage equal to 1 joule equivalent of radiant energy per kilogram
tesla	T	magnetic flux density	The flux density (or density induction) of 1 weber of magnetic flux per square meter
volt	V	electric potential	The potential difference across a conductor in which a constant current of 1 ampere dissipates 1 watt of power
watt	W	power	The amount of power equal to a rate of energy transfer of (or rate of doing work at) 1 joule per second
weber	Wb	magnetic flux	The amount of magnetic flux that, decaying to zero in 1 second, induces an electromotive force of 1 volt in a circuit of one turn

☐ THE EVOLUTION OF LIFE

In the 19th century, the geological timescale – defining the history of the Earth's physical development – was fully established, with the major divisions over millions of years identified from major breaks in types of rock and other factors. One of the features that enabled geologists to date rocks was the presence of different types of fossil. Changes from one period to another were often marked by abrupt changes in the fossil record.

The most common fossils of the Paleozoic era are ammonites, trilobites, and brachiopods. By careful taxonomy of the fossils, supported by radiometric dating techniques, scientists were able to establish an evolutionary history for these species and others associated with them, and also for the rocks in which they are found.

Most animals are invertebrates and the study of fossil invertebrates has thrown important light on the process of evolution; however, vertebrate paleontology has traditionally provided more to evolutionary biology. Other important fields are paleobotany and micropaleontology, including the study of fossil bacteria and blue-green algae, which date back 3.5 billion years.

The fossil record shows several periods at which huge numbers of species became extinct. They probably relate to drastic climatic change. The most important of these was at the end of the Permian, 248 million years ago.

The positions of the continents have changed considerably throughout geological time, and the discipline of paleobiogeography studies the distribution of life forms on the Earth as it was in the past.

Epoch	Period	Date (years ago)	Geological events	Record of life	Mass extinctions
CENOZOIC ERA					
Quaternary	Holocene	10,000 – present		Modern humankind	Humankind threatens mass extinction in modern times
	Pleistocene	2.5 million – 10,000	Major glaciations	Early humankind	
Tertiary	Pliocene	5–2.5 million	Continental plates split, drift and collide creating mountain ranges	Large carnivores Upright posture for hominids	
	Miocene	25–5 million		Grazing mammals	
	Oligocene	38–25 million		Large browsing mammals	
	Eocene	55–38 million		Rise of modern plants	
	Paleocene	65–55 million		First placental mammals, including horses, cattle and elephants	
MESOZOIC ERA					
Cretaceous		144–65 million	Pangea breaks up, forming inland seas	Early flowering plants, origin of birds	76 percent of species, 47 percent of genera
Jurassic		213–144 million		Flying reptiles, first mammals Dinosaurs dominant	
Triassic		248–213 million		Spread of dinosaurs, ammonites and cycads	Extinction of many marine species
PALEOZOIC ERA					
Permian		286–248 million	The supercontinent of Pangea forms	Primitive reptiles and paramammals Appearance of beetles and conifers	96 percent of all species 84 percent of genera
Carboniferous (Pennsylvanian)		320–286 million	Repeated glaciations and the central Tethys Sea forms	Spread of amphibians, great coal forests	
Carboniferous (Mississippian)		360–320 million		Origins of reptiles and insects; tree-like ferns	
Devonian		408–360 million		Rise of mosses and ferns Ammonites and spiders	82 percent of species 55 percent of genera
Silurian		438–408 million	Gondwana drifts north Laurasia forms	Corals; sporebearing vascular plants Jawed fish appear	
Ordovician		505–438 million	Gondwanaland drifts to South Pole	Appearance of primitive fishes, trilobites, mollusks and crustacea abundant	85 percent of species 60 percent of genera
Cambrian		590–505 million	Land is concentrated near Equator		
PRECAMBRIAN ERA					
		1.2 billion–590 million	Oxygen is found in atmosphere	Jellyfish, worm burrows, flatworms	
Proterozoic		2.1–1.2 billion	Widespread glaciation and super-continent of Laurentia splits apart	Marine algae	
		2.98–2.1 billion		Abundant carbon of organic origin	
		3.2–2.98 billion		Oldest stromatolites	
		3.49–3.2 billion		Earliest known record of life Anaerobic respiration	
Archean		4.5–3.49 billion	Formation of crust oxygen-free atmosphere	Oldest rock about 4 billion years ago	

EVOLUTION OF THE HORSE

The evolution of the modern horse, *Equus*, from the probable ancestor of horses, *Hyracotherium*, or *Eohippus*, involved an increase in size and significant changes in anatomy which have allowed scientists to determine the changing environment in which the animals lived. *Hyracotherium* was not much larger than a modern cat, with padded feet. The toes gradually became fewer, leading eventually to the modern hoof, which is effectively a single enlarged toe. At the same time the brain became larger and acquired a more complex structure. The molar teeth became more complex as well, reflecting a change in diet from young leaves, berries and branches in swampy forests to grass on the open savannah.

Historically there have been many genera of horses or equids, but today there is only one; the others died out as they failed to adapt to changing environmental conditions.

Many of the ancestral species of horse lived in what is now North America, though several moved to Eurasia and some, in more recent times, to South America. However, *Equus*, the modern horse, became extinct in North America about 10,000 years ago and flourished only in Eurasia, where it was domesticated about 6000 years ago. The horse was reintroduced to North America by the European conquerors some 500 years ago.

Genus	Location	Comment
Holocene 10,000 ya –		
Equus (ass)	Eurasia	
Equus (zebra)	Africa	
Pleistocene 2.5 mya–10,000 ya		
Equus (horse)	North America	Modern horse; becomes extinct in New World and is reintroduced in modern times
Hippidion	South America	
Pliocene 5–2.5 mya		
Hipparion	Africa, N. America	Three-toed, savannah-dwelling, ancestor of the zebra
Pliohippus	North America	Genuinely single-toed. 120 cm (47 in) high at shoulder
Miocene 25–5 mya		
Dinohippus	North America	
Anchitherium	Eurasia	
Merychippus	North America	Grass-eating; only one toe reaches the ground; 100 cm (39 in) high at shoulder. First of the family of modern horses
Hypohippus	North America	Forest dwelling, three-toed
Archeohippus	North America	Forest-dwelling
Oligocene 38–25 mya		
Parahippus	North America	
Miohippus	North America	
Mesohippus	North America	Three toes; lives in open country; 65 cm (25 in) high at shoulder; lower crowned teeth than *Hyracotherium*
Orohippus	North America	
Hyracotherium *(Eohippus)*	North America	Browses on leaves; four toes at front, three at rear; 40 cm (16 in) high at shoulder

EVOLUTION OF HUMANITY

Homo sapiens is one of 185 primate species found in the world today. There are four major divisions of primate: prosimians, such as lemurs; tarsoids (such as tarsiers), ceboids or New World monkeys such as spider monkeys; cercopithecoids or Old World monkeys such as baboons; and hominoids such as apes and humans. All these groupings were established by 30 million years ago, derived from shrewlike ancestors in the late Cretaceous, about 70 million years ago, in what is now Europe and North America. The hominoids are further broken down into pongids (orangutan, gorillas and chimpanzees), hylobatoids (gibbons) and hominids, which are humans and their recent ancestors, such as *Homo erectus* and *habilis*, *Paranthropus* and the australopithecines.

It remains very controversial to draw evolutionary family trees of the hominoid primates, and particularly so of the relationship between the earliest hominids, such as the australopithecines, and other apes. The interpretation of the scanty fossil evidence for the hominids themselves is equally controversial. Some researchers argue that modern humanity emerged separately from *Homo erectus* communities in several parts of the world, whereas others argue for a distinctively African origin, followed by a migration around the world, usurping the *erectus* survivors as it did so.

Years ago	Development
Holocene 10,000 ya –	
9000 ya	First agricultural communities
Pleistocene 2.5 mya–10,000 ya	
20,000 ya	*Homo sapiens* reaches the Americas
30,000 ya	Cro-Magnon Man flourishes in Europe, producing sophisticated art, and takes over from *Homo neanderthalis*
30,000 ya	*Homo sapiens* spreads to East Asia and Australasia
100,000 ya	*Homo sapiens* spreads into Eurasia
150,000–30,000 ya	*Homo neanderthalis* flourishes in Eurasia
150,000 ya	*Homo sapiens sapiens* in Africa
200,000 ya	"Mitochondrial Eve" in Africa, source of mitochondrial DNA in modern humans
200,000 ya	"Chromosomal Adam", source of DNA variability on Y chromosome of modern humans
400,000 ya	Archaic *Homo sapiens* emerges
1.8 mya	*Homo erectus* spreads into Eurasia
2 mya	*Homo erectus* in Africa
2.25 mya	*Homo habilis* in Africa, manufacturing stone tools
2.5 mya	Stone tools are used
Pliocene 5–2.5mya	
3 mya	*Australopithecus afarensis* ("Lucy") flourishes in Africa
4.5 mya	First hominids, *Australopithecus ramidus*
Miocene 25–5 mya	
12 mya	Split between colobine and cercopithicine monkeys
20 mya	African hominoids spread into Eurasia
25 mya	The earliest hominoids (*Proconsul*)
Oligocene 38–25 mya	
25 mya	New World monkeys in South America
34 mya	First known tarsiers
35 mya	*Plesiadapis*, a tree-dwelling primate, flourishes widely
Eocene 55–38 mya	
50 mya	First known simians
Paleocene 65–55 mya	
60 mya	First modern-looking primates (60 mya)
Cretaceous 144–65 mya	
70 mya	First known archaic primate (*Purgatorius*) lives in the New World

AMINO ACIDS

Amino acids are the building blocks of proteins, the vital organic compounds that form the basis of living tissues and are coded for by DNA and RNA. More than 170 amino acids are known to occur in living organisms, of which 26 are found in proteins. There are 20 commonly occurring amino acids. Plants are able to make all their amino acids by modifying compounds produced by photosynthesis, but animals must derive some of their amino acids – essential amino acids – from plants. These comprise cysteine (or methionine), isoleucine, threonine, tryptophan and valine. The remainder are made by modifying these essential acids.

Amino acids are polar molecules: at one end is the amino (–NH_2) group, which tends to attract hydrogen ions and is therefore slightly electropositive; at the other is the carboxylic acid (–COOH) group which readily dissociates in solution, liberating H+ ions and acquiring a small negative charge. Amino acids contain another organic group, the "R" group, which differs in each amino acid. The R groups give amino acids their distinctive characteristics. Some consist mainly of hydrocarbon chains, others are ring structures.

Amino acids can form bonds with other amino acids or with groups such as the heme of hemoglobin. They are linked in proteins by peptide bonds, relatively strong bonds between the carboxyl group of one amino acid and the amino group of another, with the elimination of a molecule of water. Ionic bonds result from the attractions between oppositely charged groups at certain acidities. They are easily broken. Hydrogen bonds form where hydrogen atoms attached to the oxygen or nitrogen of a slightly positive group share electrons with the oxygen atoms of a neighboring electro-negative group. These are also weak bonds, but there are so many of them that they help to stabilize protein molecules. Disulfide bonds form between the sulfhydryl (–SH) groups of sulfur-containing amino acids, linking the two sulfur atoms. These bonds hold folded chains of amino acids in place.

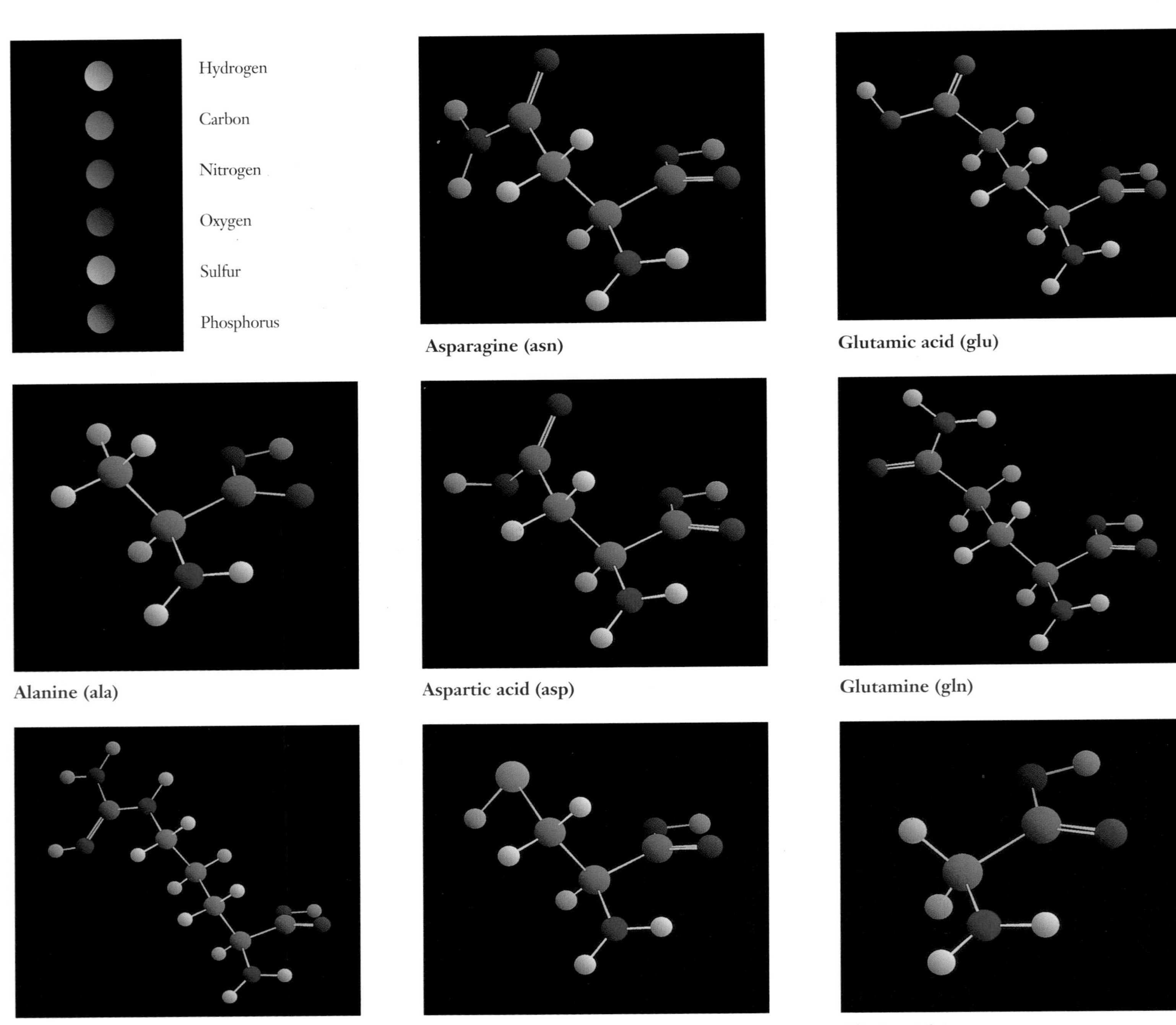

Asparagine (asn)

Glutamic acid (glu)

Alanine (ala)

Aspartic acid (asp)

Glutamine (gln)

Arginine (arg)

Cysteine (cys)

Glycine (gly)

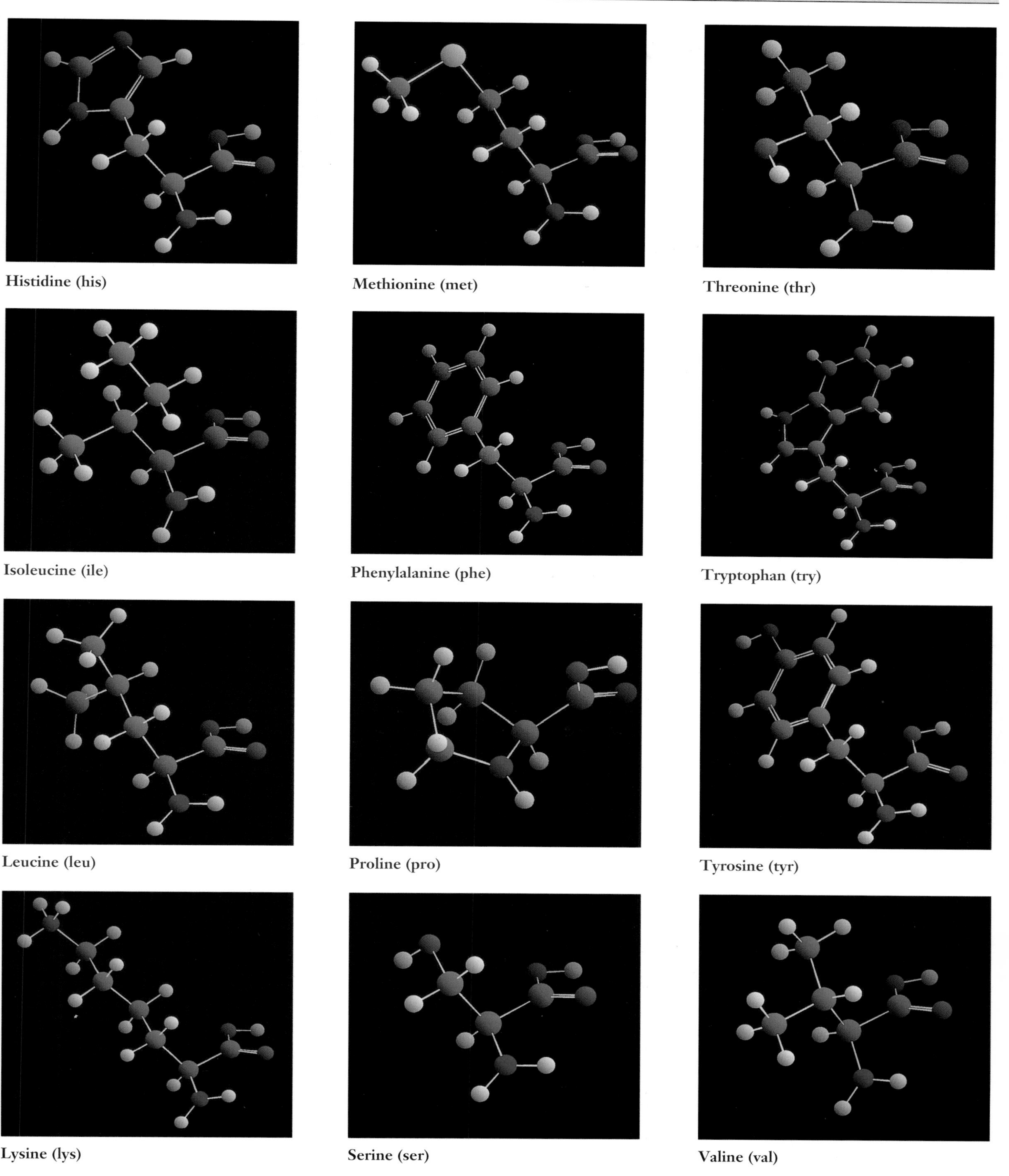

Histidine (his)

Methionine (met)

Threonine (thr)

Isoleucine (ile)

Phenylalanine (phe)

Tryptophan (try)

Leucine (leu)

Proline (pro)

Tyrosine (tyr)

Lysine (lys)

Serine (ser)

Valine (val)

☐ PROTEIN STRUCTURES

Some proteins have a structural role while others, such as enzymes and hormones, are involved in the control of metabolic activity, including the synthesis of other cell components such as carbohydrates and fats. They are also used for oxygen transport, movement, storage, protection and much else.

Proteins are composed of chains of amino acids held together by peptide bonds (the primary structure). The sequence of amino acids determines the biological function of a protein. These chains are then twisted into a helix or folded into pleated sheets held together by hydrogen bonds (the secondary structure). These helices and sheets can be further folded by interactions between amino acids, including more hydrogen bonds, ionic bonds and disulfide bridges. This tertiary folding is influenced by the positions of water-loving (hydrophilic) and water-hating (hydrophobic) groups, the latter being repelled by the aqueous medium of the cell. More complex proteins consist of several polypeptide chains held together (quaternary structure), sometimes incorporating other "prosthetic" groups.

Type	Function or occurence	Example
Contractile	Stationary and moving filament in muscle tissue	Actin, myosin
Enzyme	Essential catalyst for most biochemical reactions	Glutamine synthetase
Hormone	Regulator of growth, glucose metabolism, and functions of adrenal glands	Somatotrophin, insulin, ACTH
Protective	Combine with foreign proteins, precursor of fibrinogen (in wound healing)	Antibodies, fibrinogen
Storage	Proteins in albumen (egg white) and milk	Casein, ovalbumin
Structural	Bone, cartilage, connective tissue, feathers, hair, horn, insect exoskeleton, ligaments, mucous secretions, nail, skin, tendons	Collagen, sclerotin, keratin,
Toxin	Cause of diphtheria, some enzymes	Diphtheria toxin, venom
Transport	In blood, carrying fatty acids, lipids (fats), oxygen	Hemoglobin, myoglobin

AMINO ACID SEQUENCE – CYTOCHROME C

(Amino end) NH_2

1 5 10 15
Gly–Asp–Val–Glu–Lys–Gly–Lys–Lys–Ile–Phe–Val–Gln–Lys–Cys–Ala–

16 20 25 30
Gln–Cys–His–Thr–Val–Glu–Lys–Gly–Gly–Lys–His–Lys–Thr–Gly–Pro–

31 35 40 45
Asn–Leu–His–Gly–Leu–Phe–Gly–Arg–Lys–Thr–Gly–Gln–Ala–Pro–Gly–

46 50 55 60
Phe–Thr–Tyr–Thr–Asp–Ala–Asn–Lys–Asn–Lys–Gly–Ile–Thr–Trp–Lys–

61 65 70 75
Glu–Glu–Thr–Leu–Met–Glu–Tyr–Leu–Glu–Asn–Pro–Lys–Lys–Tyr–Ile–

76 80 85 90
Pro–Gly–Thr–Lys–Met–Ile–Phe–Ala–Gly–Ile–Lys–Lys–Lys–Thr–Glu–

91 95 100
Arg–Glu–Asp–Leu–Ile–Ala–Tyr–Leu–Lys–Lys–Ala–Gly–Asn–Glu–COOH
(carboxyl end)

☐ ENZYMES

Enzymes are biological catalysts: molecules that assist the progress of a chemical reaction by acting on one or more of the reactants (the substrate). The shape of the enzyme molecule plays an important part in this process, as the substrate commonly fits into a particular site (the active site) to enable the catalysis to begin; this is known as the "lock-and-key" mechanism. Some enzymes can be inhibited by other molecules that obstruct the active site, either by distorting the overall shape of the enzyme (allosteric inhibition) or by binding to the active site (competitive inhibition).

Enzymes fulfill a wide range of functions within the cell, and they are categorized and named for the type of reaction that they catalyze. Enzyme names conventionally carry the suffix "-ase". With the development of techniques in biotechnology, it has become simpler to grow enzymes by fermentation in microorganisms than to synthesize them, and the use of enzymes in industry and a wide range of commercial products has grown significantly in the last two decades.

Group type	Examples	Catalyzed reactions
Hydrolases	Lipase, peptidase, phosphatase	Hydrolysis reaction
Isomerases	Isomerase, mutase	Rearrangement of intramolecular groups
Ligases	Synthetase	Bonding two molecules together (using ATP-derived energy)
Lyases	Decarboxylase	Adding or removing a chemical group (other than by hydrolysis)
Oxidoreductases	Dehydrogenases, oxygenases	All oxidation–reduction reactions
Transferases	Phosphorylases, transaminases	Transfer of a chemical group from one compound to another

INDUSTRIAL USES OF ENZYMES

Application	Enzymes used	Uses
Baby foods	Trypsin	Predigesting food
Baking	Amylases	Break down starch to sugar (yeast acts on sugar to make CO_2)
	Proteases	Lower protein level in flour used to make cookies
Brewing	Enzymes in barley and synthetic enzymes (amylases, glucanases)	Degrade starch and protein to sugars and amino acids for use by yeast
	Amyloglucosidase	Low-calorie beer production
	Proteases	Clarify beers
Dairy foods	Rennin	Splits protein in cheese manufacture
	Lipases	Ripen blue-mold cheeses
	Lactases	Break down lactose to glucose and galactose
Detergents	Bacterial proteases	Presoak stage of fabric washing
	Amylases	Break down starch residues during dishwashing
Fruit juices	Cellulases, pectinases	Clarify juices
Paper	Amylases	Degrade starch for sizing and coating paper
Photography	Protease	Dissolving gelatin from film

CHROMOSOMES, GENES AND ALLELES

The genetic information of an organism is carried in nucleic acids (DNA or RNA) in its cell or cells. Segments of DNA (genes) code for particular polypeptides, which in turn make up proteins. The gene that codes for a particular characteristic may occur in more than one form, producing different versions of that characteristic, such as eye color.

In relatively simple organisms, such as algae, bacteria and mosses, each cell contains only one copy of the code – that is, the cells are haploid. In most other organisms, there are two copies: so two versions (alleles) of a gene may occur within a single cell. Only one version (the dominant allele) will be expressed, unless both alleles have equal dominance (they are codominant), in which case the expressed characteristic (the phenotype) is a blend of the two. The particular alleles contained in the genes of an individual organism comprise its genotype.

A situation similar to the haploid condition occurs where genes are located on the sex chromosomes. In many organisms, including humans, there are two different kinds of sex chromosome, X and Y. In humans, females are XX and males are XY. In males, therefore, alleles occurring on the X chromosome are unpaired and must be expressed in the phenotype.

The pattern of inheritance of alleles – Mendelian inheritance – can be expressed by genetic diagrams, showing the genotypes of the parents, the gametes they produce, the possible combinations of those alleles in the offspring, and the ratio of the various phenotypes in the next generation. These ratios assume that the genes are unlinked – that the alleles segregate at random into daughter cells when the gametes are produced.

However, the ratios may be different if the genes under consideration are on the same chromosome, as there is less chance that they will become separated by crossing over. (The farther apart they are, the more frequent the crossing over.) The result is an unexpected ratio of recombinants (new combinations of alleles) in the offspring. The proportion of recombinants is an indication of the distance apart of the two genes on the chromosome.

MONOHYBRID INHERITANCE

A cross involving a single pair of alleles:
R (dominant) for round seeds
r (recessive) for wrinkled

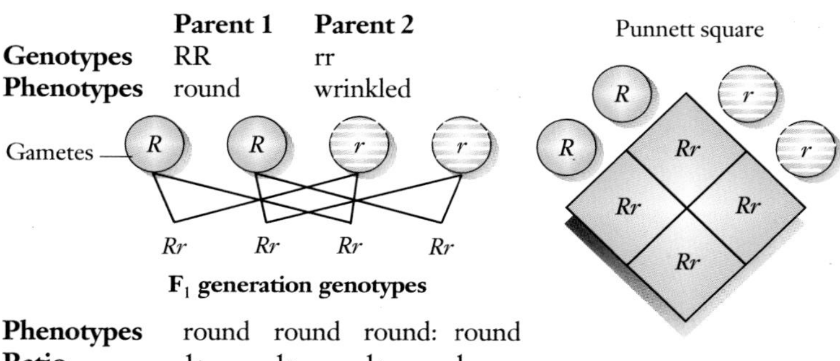

If the F_1 offspring are crossed among themselves:

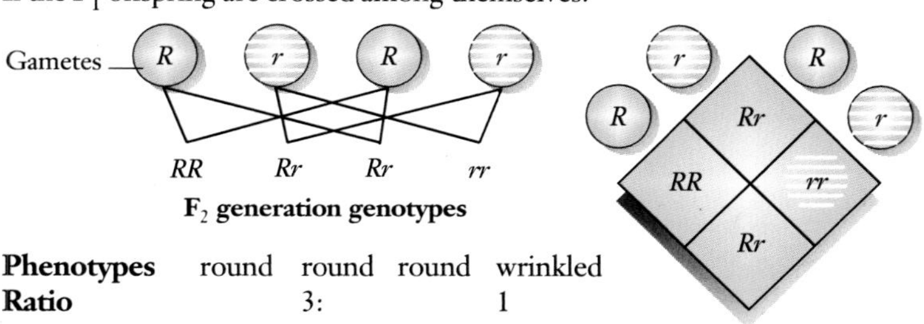

SEX-LINKED INHERITANCE

In species with specific sex chromosomes, the expression of alleles located on those chromosomes depends upon which sex chromosomes are present in the offspring. In humans, males are XY whereas females are XX. Any recessive allele present on the X chromosome is expressed in the male, where it is unpaired. Color blindness (c) is an example:

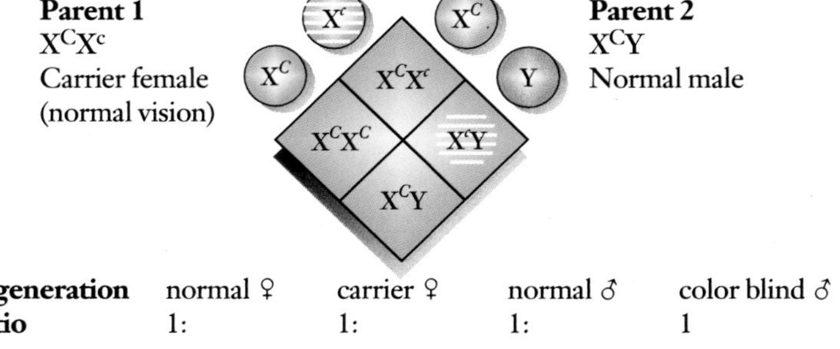

DIHYBRID INHERITANCE

A cross involving two pairs of alleles:
R (dominant) for round seeds
r (recessive) for wrinkled seeds
Y (dominant) for yellow seeds
y (recessive) for green seeds

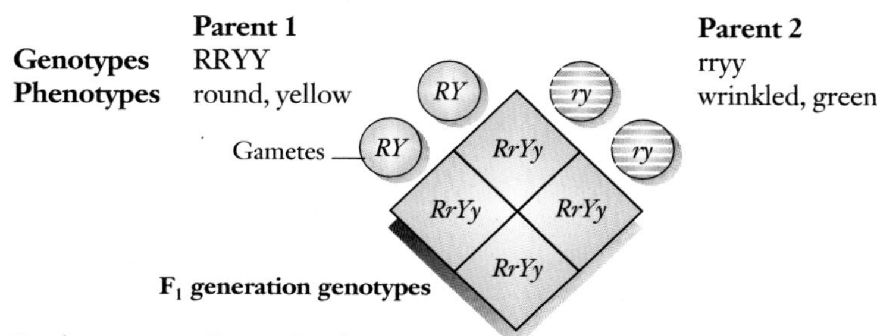

F_1 phenotypes all round, yellow

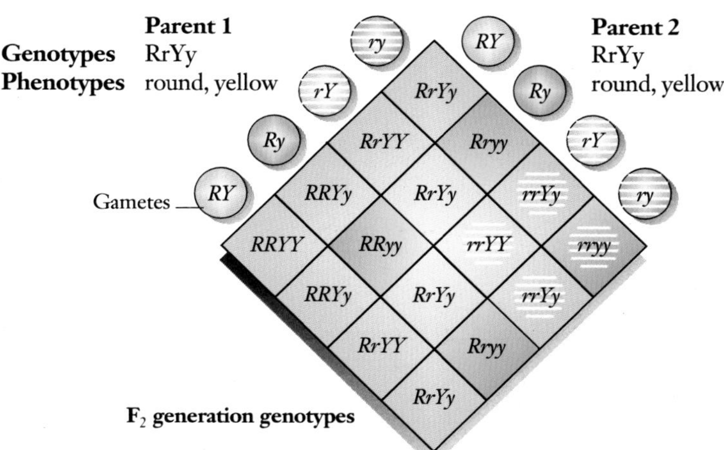

Phenotypes	round, yellow	round, green	wrinkled, yellow	wrinkled, green
Ratio	9:	3:	3:	1

TESTCROSS

The F_1 hybrid (RrYy) is crossed with a homozygous recessive (rryy). R and Y are on different chromosomes and inherited independently, producing four possible genotypes. This shows that the parent hybrid is heterozygous. If they were on the same chromosome they would be inherited together (unless crossing over occurred), and the offspring could be only two possible genotypes, RrYy and rryy.

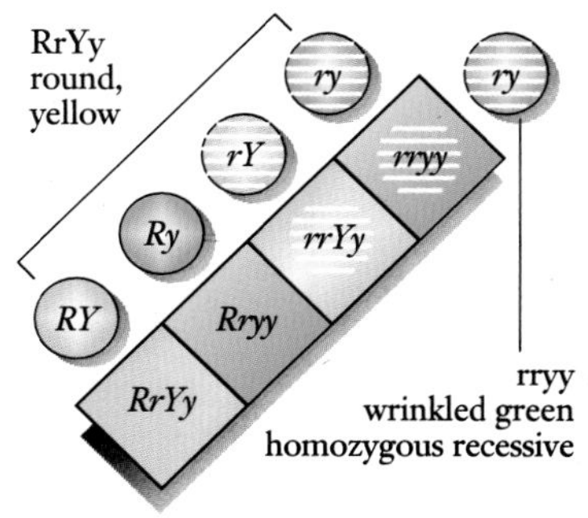

GENES AND CHROMOSOMES

The particular makeup of an individual organism – the alleles (or different versions of the genes) it possesses – is called its genome. These alleles comprise segments of nucleic acid (DNA or RNA) which occur in each of the organism's cells. However, the actual amount of nucleic acid that an organism possesses is no indication of its total genetic content, nor is the number of chromosomes it possesses. Sometimes closely related species may have widely differing DNA contents. In eukaryotes (cells in which the nucleic acid is housed in a discrete nucleus) in particular, there may be substantial quantities of redundant or "junk" DNA. This often takes the form of repeated sequences of nucleotide bases. When the DNA is transcribed to form messenger RNA (for transport out of the nucleus to the ribosomes to code for the assembly of amino acids into proteins), this redundant material is edited out of the initial transcript by certain enzymes, so that only the functional code leaves the nucleus. The reason for the presence of this excess DNA is unknown, but there is speculation that it may play a small role in evolution by accumulating mutations that may eventually produce a new protein.

The table here compares the numbers of chromosomes and the total size of the genome in a wide range of organism. Some typical examples of different types of eukaryote are included.

Organism	Host	Genome (kb)	No. of genes
Bacteriophages			
MS2	E.coli	3.6	3
M13	E.coli	5.4	10
T4	E.coli	166	150+
Eukaryotic viruses			
Parvovirus	Mammals	1.6	5
Hepatitis B	Mammals	3.2	4
Tobacco mosaic	Plants	6.4	6
Influenza	Mammals	22	12
Retroviruses	Mammals	6–9	3
Adenovirus	Mammals	36	30
Vaccinia	Mammals	240	240

Prokaryotes	Genome (kb)	No. of chromosomes
E. coli	2800	1 chromosome

(1 kb = 1000 base pairs)

Organism	Genome (kb)	Chromosomes	Genes
Eukaryotes			
Yeast	20,000	16 chromosomes	
Fungi	9400–175,000		
Nematodes	75,000–620,000		
Coelenterates	280,000–685,000		
Mollusks	375,000–5,100,000		
Insects	47,000–12,000,000		
(Fruit fly)	165,000	4 chromosomes	1000
Crustaceans	660,000–21,250,000		
Fish	2,650,000–6,950,000		
Amphibians	950,000–10,150,000		
Reptiles	1,600,000–90,100,000		
(Salamander)	90,000,000	12 chromosomes	
Birds	1,125,000–1,975,000		
Mammals	2,235,000–5,550,000		
(Humankind)	3,000,000	23 chromosomes	80,000
Fern	600,000–4,050,000		
Flowering plants	95,000–120,000,000		
(Corn)	15,000,000	10 chromosomes	

HUMAN GENES AND CHROMOSOMES

Most humans – other than those suffering certain diseases, such as Down's syndrome, which mean that the individual has extra chromosomes – have a total of 23 chromosomes pairs, one of which is the pair of sex chromosomes, X and Y. The remaining chromosomes are paired, with one of each pair inherited from each parent. The chromosomes are not equal in size, and are conventionally numbered in order of their size.

Chromosome	DNA content kb (1000 base pairs)	Chromosome	DNA content kb (1000 base pairs)
1	250,000	13	110,000
2	240,000	14	105,000
3	190,000	15	100,000
4	180,000	16	85,000
5	175,000	17	80,000
6	165,000	18	75,000
7	155,000	19	70,000
8	135,000	20	65,000
9	130,000	21	55,000
10	130,000	22	60,000
11	130,000	X	140,000
12	120,000	Y	60,000

FURTHER READING

Attenborough, David *The Living Planet* (Collins, London 1984; Little, Brown, New York, 1986)

Attenborough, David *The Private Lives of Plants: A Natural History of Plant Behaviour* (BBC Publications, London 1995)

Bailey, Jill and Seddon, Tony *The Young Oxford Book of the Prehistoric World* (Oxford University Press, Oxford and New York 1994)

Berry, R.J. and Hallam, A. *The Collins Encyclopedia of Animal Evolution* (Collins, London 1986; Facts on File, New York 1987)

Brown, Terence A. *Genetics, a Molecular Approach* (Chapman and Hall, New York and London 2nd ed. 1992)

Connor, James M. and Ferguson-Smith, M.A. *Essential Medical Genetics* (Blackwells, Oxford, 4th ed. 1993)

Cook, William *The Gene Hunters: Adventures in the Genome Jungle* (Aurum Press, London 1994)

Crick, Francis *Life Itself: Its Origin and Diversity* (Simon & Shuster, New York and Macdonald, London 1982)

Darwin, Charles *The Origin of Species* (illustrated edition, Faber and Faber, London 1989)

Dawkins, Richard *The Blind Watchmaker* (Longmans, London 1986, W.W. Norton, New York 1987)

Dawkins, Richard *The Extended Phenotype* (Oxford University Press, Oxford 1982)

Dawkins, Richard *The Selfish Gene* (Oxford University Press, London 1978)

CHROMOSOME MUTATIONS

Genetic variation is the result of mutations – changes in the genetic material. These may occur as errors during replication or transcription, or by interference, such as from radiation or "foreign" chemicals. Only mutations in the germ line, which comprises the gametes (sex cells) or the cells which give rise to them, are passed on to the next generation. Mutations in other cells (somatic cells) affect only that cell, unless they produce malignant growths.

The effect of a mutation depends on where it occurs. Much of the DNA in cells is not used; mutations have little effect on it, though they may give rise to new proteins over generations. But a mutation in the DNA coding for the active site of an enzyme has a much greater effect than in another part.

The genetic code is read in triplets of three bases. If one or two are added or deleted, the rest of the sequence is read in the wrong triplets. If three consecutive bases are affected, this may have little effect unless they code for an amino acid; then the shape of the protein may be altered at a critical point.

Breakage of whole chromosomes is more serious and is usually lethal, especially if it occurs in the middle of a gene. This is most likely to happen during meiosis (gamete production), when pairs of chromosomes exchange segments. Changes in the chromosome number may occur if the chromosomes fail to segregate properly during nuclear division, so that one daughter cell gains an extra chromosome and the other is short.

DNA MUTATION

DNA base sequence	mRNA sequence	Amino acids	Comment
CAA TTC CGA CGA	GUU AAG GCU GCU	val lys ala ala	Normal
CAA TT**T** CGA CGA	GUU AAA GCU GCU	val lys ala ala	Point mutation, unchanged amino acid sequence
CAA **C**TC CGA CGA	GUU GAG GCU GCU	val glu ala ala	Point mutation with amino acid substitution
CAA **A**TC CGA CGA	GUU UAG GCU GCU	val STOP	Point mutation with premature termination
CAA T←CC GAC GA	GUU AGG CUG CU	val arg leu	Base deletion with frame shift
CAA TTT C→CG ACG	GUU AAA GGC UGC	val lys gly cys	Base insertion with frame shift

CHROMOSOME NUMBERS

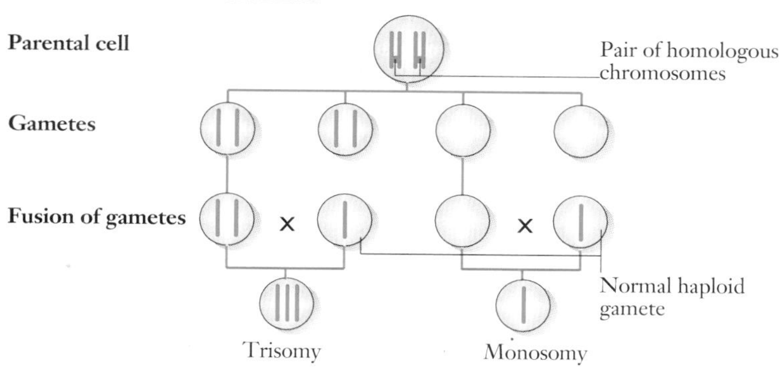

CHROMOSOME MUTATION

Original gene sequence		Final gene sequence
A–B–**C–D–E**–F–G	Deletion	A–B–F–G
A–B–**C–D–E**–F–G	Inversion	A–B–E–D–C–F–G
A–B–**C–D–E**–F–G **X–Y–Z**	Translocation	A–B–F–G E–D–C–X–Y–Z
A–B–C–D–E–**F–G**	Duplication	A–B–C–D–E–F–G–F–G

◁ **In nondisjunction, the chromosomes fail to separate in meiosis. If one chromosome is missing (monosomy) the gamete may not develop at all, but it often develops if there is one extra (trisomy), producing severe mutations such as Down's syndrome.**

Dixon, Dr Patrick *The Genetic Revolution* (Kingsway Pubs, London 1993)
Gamlin, Linda and Vines, Gail (eds.) *The Evolution of Life* (Collins, London and Oxford University Press, New York 1987)
Gould, Stephen J. *The Book of Life* (W.W. Norton, New York 1989 and Ebury Hutchinson, London 1993)
Gould, Stephen J. *Eight Little Piggies: Reflections in Natural History* (Jonathan Cape, London 1993, and W.W. Norton, New York 1994)
Gould, Stephen J. *This Wonderful Life* (W.W. Norton, New York 1989, and Penguin Books, Harmondsworth 1991)
Green, N.P.O., Stout, G.W. and Taylor D.J. *Biological Science* (Cambridge University Press, Cambridge 1990)
Hodgson, John *Biotechnology: Changing the Way Nature Works* (Cassell, London 1989)
Lambert, David *The Ultimate Dinosaur Book* (Dorling Kindersley, London and New York 1993)
Jones, Steve *The Language of the Genes: Biology, History and the Evolutionary Future* (Anchor, New York 1994)
Jones, Steve (ed.) *The Cambridge Encyclopedia of Human Evolution* (Cambridge University Press 1992)
Leakey, Richard E. *The Origin of Humankind* (Weidenfeld &Nicolson, London 1994)
Leakey, Richard, and Lewin, Roger *Origins Reconsidered: In Search of What Makes Us Human* (Little, Brown, London and Doubleday, New York 1992)
Lewin, Benjamin *Genes V* (Oxford University Press, Oxford 1994)
Macdonald, Dr David *An Encyclopedia of Mammals* (Oxford University Press, New York and Andromeda Books, Oxford, UK 1995)
Maynard Smith, John and Szathmáry, Eörs *The Major Transitions in Evolution* (W.H. Freeman, New York 1995)
Maynard Smith, John *The Theory of Evolution* (Cambridge Univeristy Press, Cambridge and New York 1993)
Norman, David B. *Dinosaur!* (Boxtree Publications, London 1991)
Shapiro, Robert *The Human Blueprint: The Race to Unlock the Secrets of Our Genetic Code* (Cassell, London and St Martin's Press, New York 1991)
Starr, Cecie and Taggart, Ralph T. *Biology: The Unity and Diversity of Life* (Wadsworth Publishing Co. Inc. 6th ed 1992)
Ward, Peter Douglas *On Methusaleh's Trail: Living Fossils and the Great Extinctions* (W.H. Freeman & Co., New York 1992)
Watson, J.D. *The Double Helix: a Personal Account of the Discovery of DNA* (Macmillan Publishing, New York, 2nd ed 1981)
Whitfield, Philip *The Natural History of Evolution* (Transworld Publications, London 1993)
Wilson, Edward O. *The Diversity of Life* (Penguin Books, London 1992 and Harvard University Press, 1993)

☐ THE STRUCTURE OF DNA

Nucleic acids, the blueprints of life, are composed of chains of nucleotide bases linked together in a helical structure by a chain of alternating sugar and phosphate groups. Each turn of the helix contains some 700 atoms. There are two important forms: RNA (ribonucleic acid), which contains the sugar ribose, and DNA (deoxyribonucleic acid), which contains the sugar deoxyribose. The sugar-phosphate chains form a parallel twisting backbone to the molecule, from which the bases protrude at regular intervals. The two chains, which run in opposite directions (antiparallel), are linked together by hydrogen bonds between the bases.

There are four nucleotide bases in each acid: cytosine (C), guanine (G), adenine (A) and thymine (T) in DNA, and cytosine, guanine, adenine and uracil (U) in RNA. Adenine and guanine are purines, with a double ring structure, whereas thymine, cytosine and uracil are pyrimidines, with a single ring structure. Base pairing is highly specific: cytosine with guanine, and adenine with thymine or uracil. Pairing always is between a purine and a pyrimidine, ensuring a constant diameter for the helix, and the specific pairing means that when the molecule is duplicated, the sequence of bases is preserved. The sequence of the nucleotide bases comprises the genetic code. Bases are "read" in groups of three (triplets or codons), each codon specifying a particular amino acid.

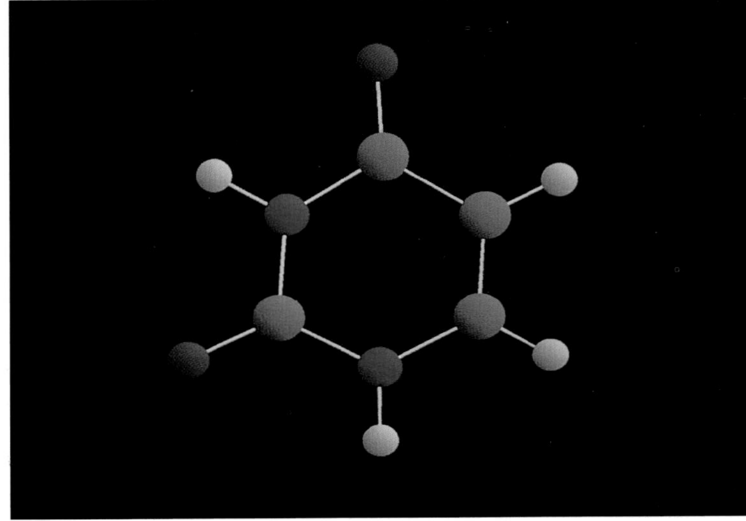

Uracil

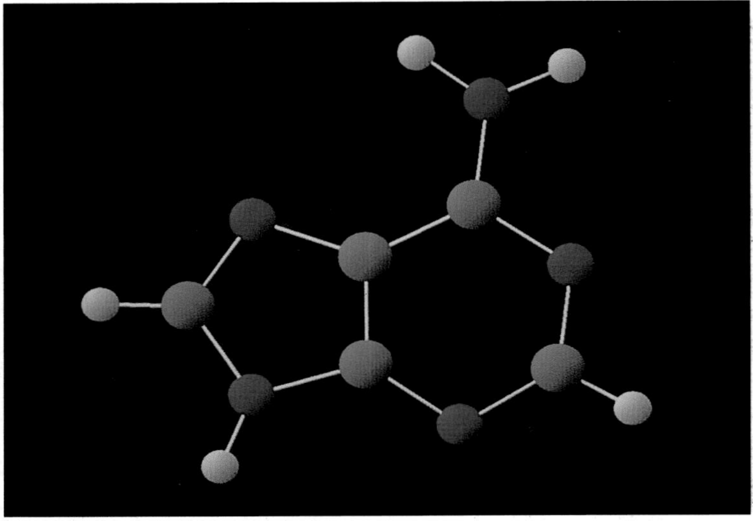

Adenine

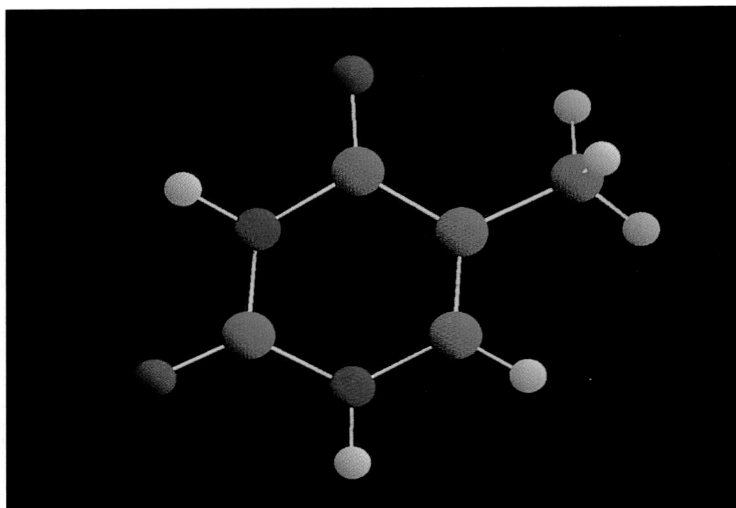

Thymine

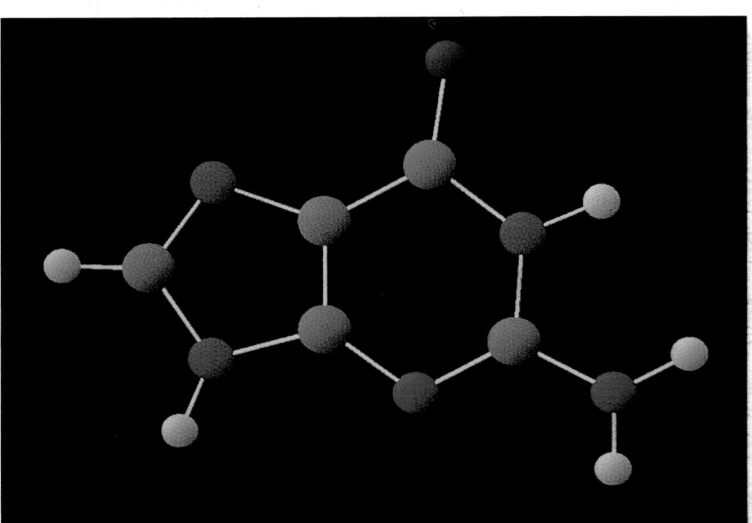

Guanine

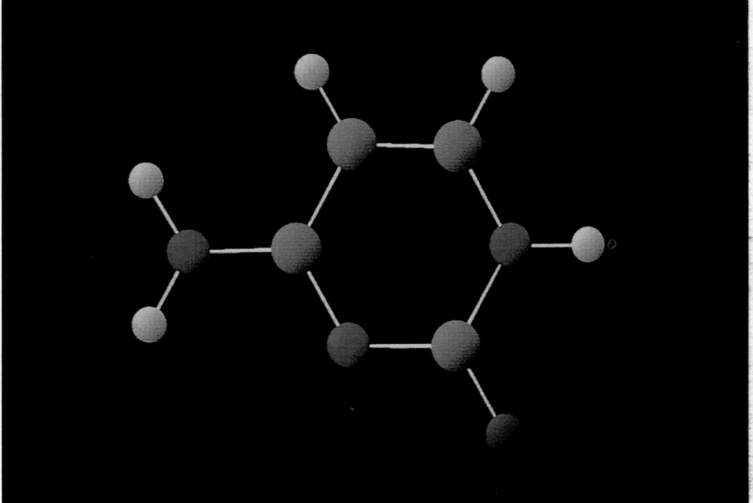

Cytosine

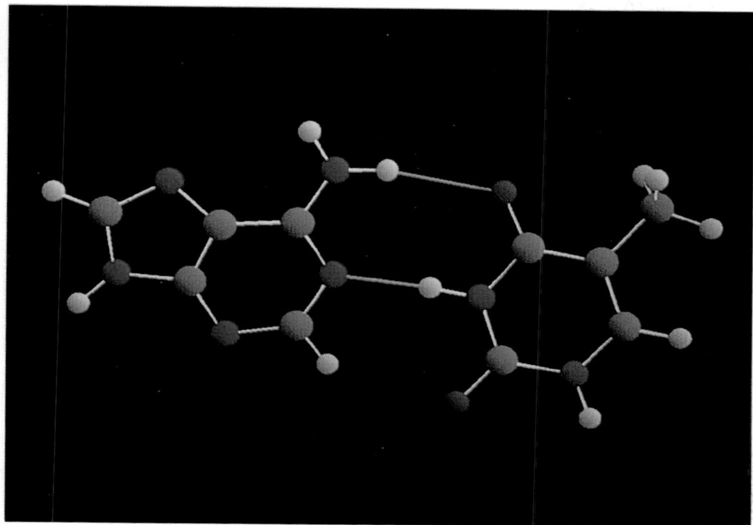

A–T base pair

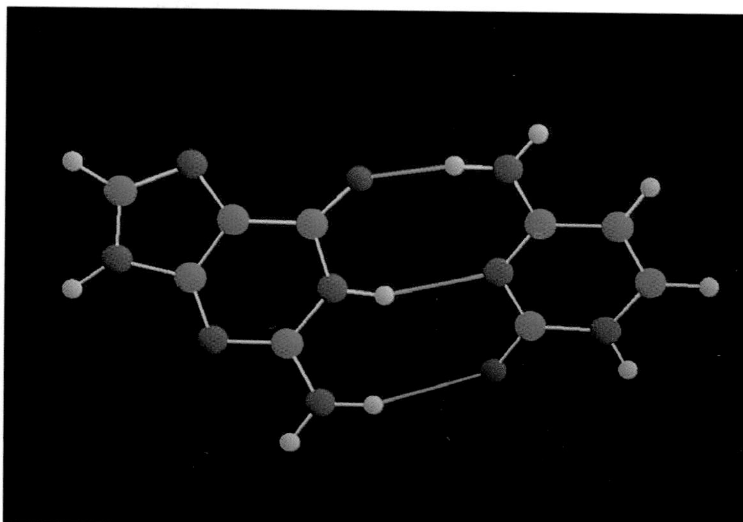

G–C base pair

Deoxyribonucleic acid

INDEX

Figures in *italic type* refer to the captions to the illustrations, and to Timechart entries; figures in **bold type** refer to the Keywords and Factfile articles.

ACKNOWLEDGMENTS

Picture credits

1 SPL/Uni. la Sapienza Department of Anatomy/Prof. P Motta **2-3** Z/Xinhua-News **5t** SPL/Geoff Tompkinson **5b** OSF/Kathie Atkinson **6** OSF/Michael Fogden **7t** SPL/Stammers/Simon **7bl** SPL/Eurelios/Philippe Plailly **7br** BCL/Jane Burton **48-49** SPL/CNRI **50-51** SPL/M I Walker **52-53** SPL/CNRI **55l** SPL/Science Source **55r** SPL/A Barrington Brown **58-59** SPL/Uni. la Sapienza Department of Anatomy/Prof. P Motta **59** SPL/Manfred Kage **60** SPL/CNRI **61** SPL/Stammers/Simon **62-63** SPL/Will and Den McIntyre **64** RHPL/Jane Legate **66-67** SPL/Philippe Plailly **69** SPL/Prof. Oscar Miller **70-71** RHPL/Carol Jopp **71t** PEP/Robert Arnold **71c** NHPA/Bill Wood **72** Tom Kaufman/Department of Zoology **73bl** FLPA/M Rose **73bc, br** University of Liege/Dr A Haverlange and G Belurer **74** BCL/Frieder Sauer **74-75** RHPL/Andy Williams **75** HL **76-77** OSF/David McDonald **79** SPL/Dr L Caro **81t** Harry Smith Collection **81b** SPL/Jacki Lewin, Royal Free Hospital **83t** Spectrum/Mrs Cumbers **83b** RHPL **84t** FLPA/A J Roberts **84b** HL **85b** Holt Studios/Ingo Spence **86-87** OSF/Michael Leach **88** NHPA/Michael Tweedie **90-91** OSF/Derek Bromhall **91c** OSF/Michael Fogden **91b** OSF/Animals Animals/Breck P Kent **93b** OSF/Michael Fogden **95** OSF/J A L Cooke **96-97** BCL/Jane Burton **97r** SPL/ Jeremy Burgess **98-99** BCL/Johnny Johnson **99t** SPL/D Phillips **99b** OSF/Rudie Kuiter **100c** BCL/Hans Reinhard **100b** Natural Science Photos/D Yendell **101t** OSF/John Cheverton **101b** OSF/Animals Animals/Richard Kolar **102** OSF/Richard Packwood **102-103** NHPA/Kevin Schafer **103t** PEP/Peter David **103b** OSF/Animals Animals/David C Fritts **104-105** OSF/Photo Researchers/Jeff Lepore **105c** OSF/Okapia/K G Vock **105b** OSF/David Fleetham **106** Ardea **108c** Nature Photographers Ltd/Andrew Cleave **108inset** NHPA/Andy Rouse **108-109** OSF/Owen Newman **110t** BCL/Jane Burton **110bl** PEP/Peter David **110r** M & P Fogden **111t** OSF/Michael Fogden **111b** Biofotos/Paul Simons **112-113** OSF/Kathie Atkinson **114-115** Natural Science Photos/Steve Pridgeon **115cr** OSF/Kathie Atkinson **115br** SPL/Dr Jeremy Burgess **116tl** SPL/Vaughan Fleming **116tr** SPL/David Scharf **117** OSF/Kathie Atkinson **118t** Z/Xinhua-News **118b** PEP/Peter Scoones **119** OSF/Wains Cheng **122-123** Z/Bond **123** BCL/Peter Davey **124-125** SPL/National Institute of Health **127t** SPL/Geoff Tompkinson **127b** SPL/J C Revy **128** SPL/Geoff Tompkinson **129** SPL/Philippe Plailly **130bl** SPL/Eurelios/Philippe Plailly **130br** Heather Angel/Biofotos **130-131** SPL/David Sharf **131** SPL/Celltech Ltd/James Holmes **132t** SPL/Philippe Plailly **132b** Unilever **133t** SPL/Dr Jeremy Burgess **133b** SPL/Adam Hart-Davis **134-135** HL/C Hughes **137t** SPL/Gary Parker **137b** SPL/Martin Dohrn **138** AOL **138-139** SPL/Astrid and Hans Frieder Michler **139** SPL/Peter Menzel **140** NHPA/Stephen Dalton **141** HL **143** SPL/Peter Menzel **148-9 all pictures** AOL/OCD **154-5 all pictures** AOL/OCD

Abbreviations
b = bottom, **t** = top
l = left, **c** = center, **r** = right

AOL	Andromeda Oxford Limited, Abingdon, UK
BCL	Bruce Coleman Ltd, London, UK
FLPA	Frank Lane Picture Agency, Suffolk, UK
HL	Hutchison Library, London, UK
NHPA	Natural History Picture Agency, Sussex, UK
OCD	Oxford Chemical Design, Oxford, UK
OSF	Oxford Scientific Films, Oxford, UK
PEP	Planet Earth Pictures, London, UK
RHPL	Robert Harding Picture Library, London, UK
SPL	Science Photo Library, London, UK
Z	Zefa Picture Library, London, UK

Origination by
J Film, Bangkok, ASA Litho, UK

Printed in Spain by
Graficromo SA

Editorial assistance
Michael Allaby, Peter Lafferty, Ray Loughlin, Andrew Sugden, Alison Stewart, Lin Thomas, Claire Turner

Artists
Rob and Rhoda Burns, Bill Donohoe, Loraine Fergusson, Trevor Hill, Ron Hayward, Ruth Lindsey, David Russell, Ed Stuart, Del Tolton, Peter Visscher

Studio photography
Richard Clark

Index
Ann Barrett